Bauman and contempo

MANCHESTER
1824

Manchester University Press

Ali Rattansi

Bauman and contemporary sociology

A critical analysis

Manchester University Press

Published by Manchester University Press
Altrincham Street, Manchester M1 7JA

www.manchesteruniversitypress.co.uk

British Library Cataloguing-in-Publication Data
A catalogue record for this book is available from the British Library

ISBN 978 1 5261 0587 5 paperback

First published 2017

The publisher has no responsibility for the persistence or accuracy of URLs for
any external or third-party internet websites referred to in this book, and does
not guarantee that any content on such websites is, or will remain, accurate or
appropriate.

Typeset by
Servis Filmsetting Ltd, Stockport, Cheshire
Printed in Great Britain by
CPI Group (UK) Ltd, Croydon CR0 4YY

For Shobhna and Parin, and in memory of Aziz and Zubeida

Contents

Acknowledgements

In writing this book, I have incurred a large number of debts and it is a pleasure to acknowledge the great many people who have helped make the book a reality.

A huge and probably irredeemable debt is owed to Peter Walsh of Cambridge University. He put my text through a forensic and invaluable examination. His innumerable suggestions have made the text far more readable, while also saving me from some errors. A continuous dialogue with him helped to clarify many ideas; I am deeply grateful to him.

Several other people have read all or part of the text and have also offered generous and very helpful responses. If I have not always taken their advice, this is partly due to my obduracy or, mostly, limitations of space. Of course, I take full responsibility for the text. Chief among those who have read and commented on my manuscript have been Barry Smart and Nicholas Gane, the reviewers appointed by Manchester University Press, who have kindly waived their anonymity: their comments have been a huge source of encouragement as well as offering much food for further thought, although I have had to be parsimonious in incorporating their very helpful suggestions.

Mike Rustin offered a stimulating view on parts of the manuscript, and I am deeply grateful to him for his generosity and continuing dialogue. My discussions with Keith Tester have been an object lesson in the joys of collegiality and amicable disagreement; I thank him for giving so generously of his time and for his thoughts on Bauman's project.

Many others discussed the work of Zygmunt Bauman with me. Anthony Giddens met me several times and provided me with sumptuous tea and scones at the House of Lords and kindly gave me the benefit of his formidable intellect by addressing sharp questions to my own views. This is also a good opportunity to publicly acknowledge my gratitude to him for his encouragement and support throughout the time I have known him from the early 1970s, when he supervised my PhD thesis at Cambridge University.

I have also benefited more than they probably realise from

discussions with Shaun Best, Chris Rojek, Gregor McLellan, Mark Davis, Richard Kilminster, Dennis Smith, David Slater, Bhavesh Doshi, Gurminder Bhambra, my brother Aziz and my uncle Professor Piyo Rattansi. I would also like to thank Steve Seidman for his kind support.

Maxine Molyneux, David Held, Phil Cohen, Jagdish Gundara, Avtar Brah, Jean McNeil and Graham Murdock have been constant sources of encouragement through many years of warm friendship, and it is a particular pleasure to thank them publicly for their support through some dark times. It has been comforting to know that they have always been there for me.

Caroline Wintersgill has been a wonderful editor to work with. Fiona Little did an outstanding job of the copy-editing and it has been my very good fortune to have had her hawk-eyed and patient assistance. She has saved me from innumerable errors and omissions. Of course, I take full responsibility for any remaining errors and omissions.

Without Shobhna this book either would have never got off the ground or would possibly never have got to the point of publication. Her constant love and care and her profound contribution to my well-being will not need mentioning to all those who know the two of us. I have also constantly discussed the thought of Zygmunt Bauman with her, and she has borne my obsession with patience, good humour and excellent advice on difficult dilemmas.

I have dedicated this book to Shobhna, my sister Parin and my brother Aziz and in memory of my dear departed sister Zubeida. All of them have made this book possible in ways that are impossible to put into words.

Introduction

The likes of Zygmunt Bauman will never be found in the world of academia again. He is one of that generation of Central and European intellectuals who literally lived through the disasters of the twentieth century. He experienced what others only write about ... By the time he was twenty, Bauman had confronted anti-Semitism, Stalinism, Nazism and warfare. (Keith Tester, *The Social Thought of Zygmunt Bauman*, 2004)

Bauman's recent writings travel light, burdened neither by research nor theoretical analytics, but borne up by an unusual life wisdom, a trained observer's eye and a fluent pen. (Goran Therborn, *From Marxism to Post-Marxism?*, 2008)

A day without scribbling feels like a day wasted or criminally aborted, a duty neglected, a calling betrayed. (Bauman, *This is Not a Diary*, 2012)

If you are not failing now and again, it's a sign you're not doing anything very innovative. (Woody Allen (timeless))

My book was already in press when the sad news of Zygmunt Bauman's passing was announced in January 2017. My tribute to him, together with those of Tony Blackshaw, David Owen and Caroline Wintersgill, is available at www.manchesteruniversity press.co.uk/remembering-bauman/.[1]

This project did not start its life as a book on the voluminous writings of Zygmunt Bauman, who has been described as perhaps 'the greatest living sociologist' (Fearn 2006) and who has been such a prolific writer that a complete bibliography of his publications is not available, although he has probably written over seventy books and numerous articles, and by his own (ac)count (Bauman, Jacobsen and Tester 2013: 68) has had his work translated into thirty-five languages. To those who will decide to read this book, it might truly be said that he needs no introduction in the formal sense of that term.

Bauman was going to be part of a wider project that I had conceived after finishing a two-book project that resulted in *Racism* (2007) and *Multiculturalism* (2011). These two texts bore fruit as part of my attempt to bring research from the social sciences and humanities, and the *re*thinking I had been pursuing in the fields of racism and multiculturalism, to a wider readership than the academic one which I had so far addressed, in a number of books and papers (see, for example, Donald and Rattansi 1992; Rattansi 1994; Rattansi 2002; Rattansi 2005).

My initial idea was to write about the rise and very sudden demise of the 'postmodern turn' in the social sciences and humanities. I had embraced and reworked *some* aspects of this new wave, especially its poststructuralist elements as found in the work of Foucault, Derrida, Hall, Laclau and Mouffe and the 'postcolonialist' holy trinity of Said, Bhabha and Spivak. Feminism had also had a profound effect on my thinking, and my work on racism made a determined attempt to confront and reveal how issues of sexuality and gender were deeply, although in a complex manner, entangled with racism. Here I had found the work of Frantz Fanon, Stuart Hall, Phil Cohen, Sander Gilman, Michele Barret, Nancy Stepan, Ann McClintock, Catherine Hall, Avtar Brah, Floya Anthias, Nira Yuval-Davis, Ann Phoenix and Patricia Hill Collins and others of great help in thinking through these difficult issues. Most – though not all – of them had deployed poststructuralist insights in a variety of ways that I had found helpful. A reading of three works by Bauman, *Legislators and Interpreters* (1987), *Modernity and the Holocaust* (1989b) and *Modernity and Ambivalence* (1991), had been part of my wider exploration of the postmodern turn (Boyne and Rattansi 1990; Rattansi 1994; Rattansi 1995; Rattansi 2002) that had convulsed the social sciences and humanities, especially after the English translation of Lyotard's *The Postmodern Condition* (1979, English translation 1984) had been published.

In trying to understand the rise and especially the rapid decline of postmodernism I decided to start my project by way of a reading of Bauman's own explanations for what seemed to be an emphatic rejection of his postmodern turn (Bauman and Tester 2001; Bauman and Gane 2004). I noted, too, that two of the better-informed commentators on Bauman, Tester (2004) and more especially Blackshaw (2005), had not seen Bauman's move from viewing the present as 'postmodernity' to what he had now called 'liquid modernity' as marking a radical departure. When I read Bauman's first post-postmodern work, *Liquid Modernity* (2000b), I understood why Tester and Blackshaw had not made very much of the liquid modern phase. Even a cursory reading of *Liquid Modernity* explains this, for it was clear that Bauman had not changed his perspective very much. He had only distanced himself from what he regarded as unsuitable but unnamed 'bedfellows' with whom he had found himself lumped under the wide umbrella of postmodernism (Bauman and Gane 2004), and said that he also wanted to provide something more positive than the blank space left by the 'post', which only indicated what was passing away without any guidelines on that which was emerging in the wake of modernity. But most of the themes from his postmodern phase had survived the transition to liquid modernity intact. His critical remarks in this interview with Gane on the alternative idea of 'reflexive modernity', a term preferred by Beck, are very revealing, and I discuss their significance later in the book.

By this stage I was intrigued by Bauman's whole intellectual trajectory and the idea for a book on Bauman took shape, one which would address the original question, especially of the demise of postmodernism, but as only one aspect of a closer inquiry into the evolution of Bauman's thinking. An initial impulse was provided by my reading of the other single-authored English-language books on Bauman by Smith (1999), Beilharz (2000), Tester (2004) and Blackshaw (2005), all of which are merely exegetical; my close reading of Bauman's output convinced me that what was now required was a single-authored *critical* engagement with Bauman's work.

The initial intention was to comment on all of Bauman's English-language writings, but given the extraordinary number of his publications, the necessary limitations of space, and the fact that there seemed little of contemporary interest in his earlier works such as *Between Class and Elite* (1972), a study of the British labour movement, or *Culture and Praxis* (1973) or even *Socialism: The Active Utopia* (1976a), I decided to focus on the postmodern and the liquid modern phases of his work. However, as I will argue in this book, there were important continuities in Bauman's work throughout his intellectual career, and these require some understanding of his earlier English-language writing, especially as manifested in *Towards a Critical Sociology* (1976b), *Hermeneutics and Social Science* (1978) and *Memories of Class* (1982). Works written while he was still in Poland, and especially the intellectual influences that shaped his thinking then, are important in understanding the nature of his mature sociological thinking, and I will address some of the relevant issues briefly here before writing about his postmodern and liquid modern phases.

I should make clear that this is not a biography of Bauman nor, strictly speaking, an intellectual biography. It is primarily a critical engagement with Bauman's ideas and arguments as found in key selected texts and interviews of his postmodern and liquid modern phases which form part of his formidable oeuvre. I need to emphasise that I have made no systematic attempt at concerning myself with the minutiae of intellectual influences on Bauman during different phases of his intellectual career, although in a more general sense I have of course referred to obvious important influences, for example those of Simmel, Adorno, Foucault, Bourdieu, or Rorty, where necessary. However, I do need to point out that having studied Bauman's English-language works relatively thoroughly, I take the view that despite his eclecticism, which has been much remarked upon, and despite the influence of intellectual figures such as Simmel, Foucault, Rorty and, latterly, Bourdieu, Bauman is best understood as a latter-day representative of the German Critical Theory tradition and its humanistic, somewhat tangential version of Marxism much influenced by Weber, inaugurated by the Frankfurt School (Held 1980; Bronner 2011; Wiggerhaus 2010). Thus, as we shall see, some of the main influences on Bauman's thinking were Adorno, Horkheimer and Marcuse. He was briefly but strongly influenced by another latter-day representative of the Frankfurt School, Habermas, but Habermas's influence on Bauman waned when he embarked on a massive systematisation of his own eclectic views and incorporated forms of sociology which Bauman found particularly distasteful; Bauman and Habermas also parted company on the question of postmodernism. I will discuss these issues as and when they are relevant.

Bauman himself cited the Italian Marxist Antonio Gramsci as a strong formative influence, but apart from absorbing from him the importance of 'culture', and in principle a non-deterministic

Marxism, in my reading of Bauman he failed to do justice to the nuanced and complex manner in which Gramsci saw cultural hegemony as a legitimating but always unstable process that shored up the power of the elites and upper classes in the Western European social order. For Gramsci, the 'common sense' of citizens was a contradictory phenomenon, containing both conservative and oppositional elements. At one level Bauman grasped this, but Bauman's is a more totalising interpretation of the manner in which popular cultural forms dominate the understanding of the world of ordinary citizens that is more in keeping with the critique of the 'culture industry' that Horkheimer and Adorno, in particular, formulated after the fall of Nazism and which reappeared in Marcuse's *One-Dimensional Man* (1964). Hence, too, the attractions of Christopher Lasch's *The Culture of Narcissism* (1979) and Neil Postman's critique of popular culture, *Amusing Ourselves to Death* (1987) for Bauman. Bauman's critique of positivism and scientism in sociology was also heavily influenced by Adorno and Horkheimer's equally dismissive perspective, although like them, he was not averse to deploying positivist research, in Bauman's case the work of experimental psychologists such as Milgram, in the case of Adorno and Horkheimer the extraordinary positivism of their involvement in the project of *The Authoritarian Personality.*

My book should be judged by its success or otherwise in actually engaging critically with the substance of Bauman's changing postmodernist and liquid modernist arguments. I have written it as a commentary on the coherence, usefulness and evidential basis of Bauman's major works in his postmodern and liquid modern phases. This introduction draws out themes from some key earlier works, but briefly and only in so far as they assist in an understanding of what I see as important continuities as well as departures in his postmodern and liquid modern periods. I will also be parsimonious in providing biographical details about Bauman, except when these are deemed especially relevant to understanding his analyses.

This is a critical study, not an attempt at a comprehensive appreciation of Bauman's many achievements and insights. My book is thus primarily a critique of Bauman. It is, to reiterate, an attempt to redress the balance in single-authored English-language books on Bauman, especially those of Smith, Tester, Blackshaw and

Beilharz. Mark Davis (2008) and Best (2013) are more critical in their different ways, but Davis's text is limited in focus and now out of date, while Best's concerns are also different from mine, especially in his attempt to explain, as his sub-title says, 'Why Good People do Bad Things'.

It is important to provide an outline of key events in Bauman's life, for as my epigraph from Tester implies, Bauman's singularly unique biography was an important stimulus to his thinking. Tester (2001: 3), though, warns against autobiographical reductionism, although he seems to have changed his mind by the time he came to write his excellent exegesis of Bauman's social thought (Tester 2004). Jay (2010) has suggested that there is something 'mercurial' about Bauman, and that this may have something to do with his Jewishness. Certainly, displacement and dislocation, as well as racism, were experiences that loomed large in his life. However, as will become clear later, Bauman was oblivious to the racism suffered by Britain's Asian and black ethnic minorities.

Bauman was born to relatively poor Jewish parents in Poznań, Poland, in 1925. With his family he fled from the Nazis to Russia, where he had ambitions to study physics but ended up joining the army, fighting against the Nazi armies in Russia and Poland. Bauman was by now a committed communist and stayed in the army, but was driven out by a nasty anti-Semitic purge in 1953 (see, especially, Tester 2004 and Best 2013 for valuable, more detailed biographical narratives). Bauman went on to study sociology and philosophy and became an academic. He was particularly influenced by two of his teachers, Hochfeld and Ossowski. He absorbed from them a profoundly anti-positivist, that is to say, anti-scientistic version of sociology (Bauman and Tester 2001: 20–1; Tester 2004: 34–43; Satterwhite 1992: especially 61–6), one which eschewed the notion of a value-free social science. Their passionately held view that any sociology worth practising had to take a moral stance, focus on the eradication of social evils and relentlessly stand up to the powerful, was one that obviously left a life-long mark on Bauman's thinking. Bauman became active as a dissident against Stalinism in the Polish Communist party, especially influenced by a workers' uprising in Poznań in 1956 and the Hungarian uprising of the same year, together with a number of other 'revisionists' such as Kolakowski, Brus, Hirszowicz, and

Kuron and Modzelewski (Kolakowski 2005: 1153–62; Satterwhite 1992).

Bauman's essay 'Modern Times, Modern Marxism', first published in 1967 and then made available in 1969 in Peter Berger's *Marxism and Sociology: Views from Eastern Europe* (Berger 1969: 1–17), gives an important insight into his thinking at this time, for he emphatically rejects economic determinism ('Modern Times': 2, 15), dismisses a natural science-derived positivism for its 'Quantification' and 'atomization' ('Modern Times': 3), cannot imagine 'Marxian thought made to the measure of the managerial type of social problems' ('Modern Times': 7), and affirms, in a profoundly humanist and anti-deterministic manner, that the 'predictions' of social science are intertwined with praxis, for 'conscious human beings are the only actors' who can make predictions become reality ('Modern Times': 16– 17). In the social sciences such as Marxism, truth itself is 'a process', rather than a timeless, reified, stable set of verified propositions. These ideas reappear in his *Towards a Critical Sociology* (1976b) – which he recommends to readers in *What Use is Sociology?* (Bauman, Jacobsen and Tester 2013: 74–5) – and *Hermeneutics and Social Science* (1978), written in exile in Leeds, where he and his wife Janina had finally settled, via Israel, after Bauman's expulsion from his academic position in Poland in yet another anti-Semitic and anti-revisionist purge. His relatively late interviews, published as *What Use is Sociology?* (Bauman, Jacobsen and Tester 2013), rehearsed many of these themes, including the one that marked his formal departure from Marxism, *Memories of Class* (1982). This latter text is notable for its strongly argued view that Marxism had been mistaken in seeing the now declining industrial working class as the agent of a new type of society and that consumerism was becoming the dominant ideology of the Western world; and it prefigures a persistent strain of pessimism in Bauman's thinking.

My book is both an introduction to Bauman's later work and a critical appreciation of it, although in effect I have ended up shining an unwavering critical light on Bauman's postmodern and liquid modern phases. However, the idea of a critique of Bauman's thinking and writing runs into a number of cautionary warnings by many commentators, particularly his ardent admirers. Especially, one has to contend with assertions regarding the special and unique quality of his form of sociological analysis. Bauman, his admirers argue, was no 'ordinary sociologist'. Indeed, one such admirer (Blackshaw 2006) has suggested that Bauman, in not being 'respectable' in British sociology, is actually 'too good for sociology'. The suggestion is that most sociologists, especially in Britain, fail to appreciate the special qualities of Bauman's sociology, qualities that indeed made him not only unique but also particularly insightful. Thus, the same author, in expounding the virtues of Bauman, says that the reader should be made aware that Bauman is a 'poet-intellectual', and that Bauman does not work under the illusion that 'fantasy', 'magic' and 'reality' are 'something apart' (Blackshaw 2006: 295).

This 'poetic' and 'literary' character of his sociology is particularly what sets him apart and creates supposedly irrelevant criticisms that he is not a proper sociologist. Bauman's analyses proceeded by way of metaphors and analogies as much as, indeed more than, by recourse to empirical research and the 'facts of the matter'; and Bauman was not 'concerned with methodological issues in sociology as such' (Jacobsen and Marshman 2008: 20). But lest it be thought that this makes him a non-sociologist, the argument is made that it is sociologists who misunderstand what their enterprise is about. They tend to see a strict distinction between sociology and the arts, but are simply mistaken in this assumption. Mark Davis, Director of the Bauman Institute at the University of Leeds, is only one among many who refer anyone reading Bauman to Nisbet's pioneering essay 'Sociology as an Art Form' (1962) in which it is argued that sociological theories should be 'tested as much by their reach as their grasp, their importance as their validity, and their elegance as their congruence with such facts as may be at hand' (Nisbet 1962: 67; M. Davis 2013: 4). Thus, as Tester and Jacobsen (2005) suggest, if Bauman is judged by conventional standards he is probably a 'very poor sociologist', but it is precisely his liberal use of metaphors that gives his sociology its strengths.

When Jacobsen and Marshman encapsulate Bauman's sociology with the label 'Humanistic, Hybrid Sociology', they are suggesting that it has the unusual merits, according to them, of 'humanising sociology', of recalling for us our 'common humanity', for Bauman is concerned with the intricate connections

between 'social structure and lived experience'; he develops a
sociology that 'poetically and poignantly' mirrors 'lived experience from the point of view of those human beings being described'
(Jacobsen and Marshman 2008: 20–1), something that Bauman
confirms as the main purpose of his sociology in an interview with
Jacobsen and Tester (Bauman, Jacobsen and Tester 2013: 105).
In Bauman's act of concerning himself with 'lived experience', his
metaphors are 'inherently *moral*, they give voice to the voiceless,
they recall to us our inescapable human and moral responsibility for the Other' (Jacobsen and Marshman 2008: 22, emphasis
in original). Simultaneously, they function to point to alternative
possibilities that remain hidden 'behind the immediate observable
reality' which is obscured in more conventional social science by
'mechanical models, mathematical reasoning or *rational argument*'
(Jacobsen and Marshman 2008: 22–3, my emphasis). Metaphors
'defamiliarize' the ordinary world, thus opening eyes to the reality
that the actually existing world is not the only one possible, and
that it is not immutable but amenable to human intervention and
change precisely because it is a human-made world, not a natural
given that has to be accepted with all its suffering and injustice.
Thus Bauman's is a 'sociology of hope'. His 'awe-inspiring body of
work' is particularly concerned to address 'the plight of those "cast
out" from society, those who have been marginalized, forgotten
and ultimately "wiped out"' (Jacobsen and Marshman 2008: 23).

This common refrain from many interpreters of his work is
undoubtedly true to Bauman's intentions, but is often belied by
the actual style of his work, or so I shall argue in this book. Asked
by Jacobsen, Marshman and Tester (2007: 29), 'For whom do you
write?', Bauman turned to Adorno for help with his answer, arguing that the disappearance of the working class as a historical agent
does not mean that all hope for emancipation should be abandoned.
Even *disengagement* from political activity, Bauman avers, following Adorno in *Minima Moralia*, is a way of 'showing some measure of solidarity with those down and out' (Bauman in Jacobsen,
Marshman and Tester 2007: 34–5; reprinted in Bauman, Jacobsen
and Tester 2013: 47). An abiding concern with the 'down and out'
means that emancipation should never be 'taken off the agenda';
'the noxious persistence of social ills is one more and admittedly
powerful reason to try harder' to conceive of alternatives. Much

like C. Wright Mills in *The Sociological Imagination*, Bauman took the view that the job of a sociology 'up to the task' is the 'laying bare [of] the complex network of causal links between pains suffered individually and conditions collectively produced'. Bauman says that Adorno's recommendation to keep producing the 'message in the bottle' describes what he himself is following. The bottles have no named, 'preselected addressees', but there will always be 'sailors in our liquid modern world' who will be seeking guidance for the problems of our times, and these are the ones on whom Bauman pinned his hopes, for these sailors 'will be eager to open the bottles and absorb the messages inside them' (Bauman in Jacobsen, Marshman and Tester 2007: 35). Elsewhere (Bauman, Jacobsen and Tester 2013: 105) Bauman implied that it is only individuals *as individuals* who will open these bottles, because 'in our increasingly individualized society ... the resolution of socially created problems is relentlessly shifted from social powers onto the shoulders of individual men and women'.

One might think that the 'down and out', even as individuals, upon whom 'social ills' weigh most heavily, might be the very ones who will be tempted to open the bottles; by so doing they will not only understand how their suffering is collectively produced, but will find hope for emancipation in Bauman's scribblings put to sea in books-as-bottles. Thus we come back to the thinking behind Bauman's metaphors: when he speaks of 'vagabonds', 'tourists', 'nomads' and those suffering 'wasted lives', those who are callously dismissed as 'collateral damage', those sailing in 'liquid' modernity, all, one might think, will read and find illumination in Bauman's writings.

But I shall argue in this book that however laudable Bauman's intentions, his prose style as well as his general 'method' of doing sociology militated against his admirable intentions. His style is often highly abstract, and neither his way of delineating his main concepts nor his metaphors will necessarily help the 'down and out' or the sympathetic sociologist, or at least not in any straightforward manner. For example, for all Bauman's interest in inspiring hope in emancipation, he often speaks in highly depersonalised terms whereby all human agency is 'wiped out', to use his own phrase. Thus, as we shall see, he often speaks in highly reified terms of 'modernity' and 'postmodernity' setting

themselves 'tasks', or of having a 'mind'; despite Bauman's severe
objections to the 'systemic' sociology of Talcott Parsons he nevertheless speaks of 'postmodernity' as a separate, almost self-sustaining 'system'; and as even Mark Davis, Director of the Bauman
Institute, admits (2008: 107), it is often not clear to whom the
metaphors of 'vagabond' or 'tourist' actually apply, so these figures are not likely to recognise that it is for them that Bauman's
bell tolls. Bauman at one point – as I shall demonstrate – even
argued that those 'seduced' by contemporary consumerism were
so *totally* seduced that they were not likely to be at all convinced
by a critique of consumerism when it was presented to them by
intellectuals who *knew* better, and had somehow escaped (it is not
clear how anyone failed to be seduced, including Bauman himself) the lures of consumerism. The messages in Bauman's bottles
were simply likely to baffle them according to some of the nostrums of his own sociology. Moreover, Bauman provides few hints
concerning what alternative social arrangements might look like,
thus severely blunting his intention to challenge the notion of
'TINA' (taken from the political slogan, 'there is no alternative'),
although he not only claimed to be a socialist but argued that 'this
world of ours needs socialists more than at any other time, and ...
this need has become much more poignant and urgent yet after
the fall of the Berlin Wall' (Bauman and Tester 2001: 153). And
Bauman certainly had more than a streak of utopianism in his
thinking (Jacobsen 2008).

There is also what Mark Davis (2008: 107) has called Bauman's
'will to dualism', which results in abstract and unhelpful dualities
such as 'modernity' and 'postmodernity', 'solid' and 'liquid' modernity, 'vagabonds' and 'tourists', the 'seduced' and the 'repressed'.
I shall argue that often the abstract dualities result in entities that
are more than just 'ideal types' which selectively shine their light
on important aspects of the social world that Bauman wants to
highlight: they actually end up as caricatures, 'solid modernity'
and 'liquid modernity' being entities of this sort, as I shall argue.
Also, there are various degrees to which his work collapses into
reductionisms, especially economic reductionism, partly as a
result of over-extending sketchy generalisations about modernity
and, especially, consumerism, but also 'liquidity' and globalisation. Moreover, his views on the complete hold that consumerism

supposedly had on individuals also typified his habit of producing unsupportable totalisations in social analysis.

This is connected to another problematic aspect of Bauman's writings. Although Mark Davis argues, as I have shown above, that Bauman is interested in revealing how it *feels* to be living particularly oppressed lives, and he and others have suggested that Bauman's is a sociology of 'lived experience' and the everyday or 'quotidien' (Blackshaw 2005; Jacobsen and Marshman 2008; Bauman, Jacobsen and Tester 2013: 105), it is noteworthy that Bauman rarely if ever quotes from the people living these lives. His aversion to conventional, empirical sociology extends to ethnographic accounts produced by non-empiricist sociologists as well as journalists and other rapporteurs who study the 'down and out'. Thus what the anthropologist Geertz has called 'thick description' is rarely to be found in Bauman's work. But this is precisely what the reader who wants to learn about 'how it feels' to be poor and oppressed, or what the lived reality of the vagabond might be like, might justifiably expect from Bauman's voluminous output on issues of exclusion that Jacobsen and Marshman argue is his abiding concern (Jacobsen and Marshman 2008: 25–7). It is difficult to accept their claim that what Bauman provides is a 'voice for the voiceless', for these voices are conspicuous by their absence in Bauman's work.

To put it in somewhat stark terms, Bauman's poetic (Blackshaw 2005), genre-blurring (Jacobsen 2013b), story-telling (Smith 1999) form of sociology, which is full of metaphors and literary examples, often failed to meet the standards of adequacy that his admirers and even he himself seemed to set for his writings. Although Bauman's sociology is regarded as having a deep affinity with the literary and especially the novel as a form (Jacobsen 2013b: 194) this claim is misleading, for novels show us the internal world of their characters, while Bauman eschews this kind of 'thick description', dwelling upon archetypes such as 'vagabonds' and 'tourists' whose actual inner life is neglected by Bauman. I shall have more to say about the role of metaphors in Bauman's sociology in the section of the book – Part III – devoted to a discussion of liquid modernity. There I also discuss how one might judge the metaphors that abound in Bauman's work, that is, the extent to which sociological metaphors might be judged by the methodology of sociology, mainstream or otherwise. It is worth pointing out here, meanwhile, that although Bauman readily admitted that his metaphors were meant to be selective (Jacobsen 2013a: 17–18), he had a tendency to totalise what was meant to be selective, as I have said about his analysis of consumerism: thus, in his writings on liquid modernity, almost all aspects of social life are seen as dominated by liquidity, something reflected in the titles of his books: *Liquid Love, Liquid Fear, Liquid Surveillance, Liquid Evil*; one book is simply titled *Liquid Life*, which exemplifies my point.

It is worth emphasising that Bauman did not wish to abandon or transcend sociology, and indeed in 2011 he accepted the British Sociological Association's 'Lifetime Achievement Award'. Jacobsen and Poder (2008: 2–3) have rightly stressed that Bauman sees an important role for sociology as a form of critical analysis (see also Bauman and Tester 2001: 33–4, 40); it is simply that he wants to push sociology to its 'furthest outer limits' and, as Mark Davis (2013) and Jacobsen and Poder (2008) emphasise, Bauman wants to do this in his own unconventional way: he was eclectic and made decisions to employ metaphors not necessarily on empirical grounds but on 'literary and artistic' grounds (M. Davis 2013: 6). It is precisely the aesthetic quality of his sociology, Davis suggests, that has allowed it to 'travel' globally, to speak to so many throughout the world, despite being viewed with some scepticism in Britain (M. Davis 2013: 4). Bauman confessed to being 'monumentally bored' of professional sociology journal articles (Bauman and Dawes 2011: 147–8).

When asked which books he might like to take with him on a desert island, Bauman chooses literary texts by Perec, Calvino, Musil and Borges rather than any sociology tomes (Bauman and Tester 2001). Citing Bauman's answer to the 'desert island discs' question, Mark Davis, founder of the Bauman Institute and therefore a privileged spokesperson for Bauman's project, repeats his assertion (M. Davis 2013: 5) that Bauman's work 'appears to be much closer to Nisbet's "sociology as art" than to "sociology as science"', and should be judged by its 'analytical reach' rather than 'empirical grasp' (M. Davis 2013: 5), although in his *Freedom and Consumerism* Davis criticises Bauman's analysis for lacking 'any supporting empirical evidence' (M. Davis 2008: 109).

Mark Davis's later (2013: 5) assertion about the need to understand and judge Bauman on other than conventional sociological grounds is very much in line with recommendations by Jacobsen, Tester, Blackshaw and other interpreters of Bauman's work that he should not be judged in conventional sociological terms. But the distinction between 'analytical reach' and 'empirical grasp' proposed by Davis (2013: 5) is not only unhelpfully vague, but potentially misleading in its implication that analytic reach and empirical grasp are two entirely separate realms of judgement. By contrast, it is my view that the former must inevitably rely to a greater or lesser degree on the latter. Thus in this book I shall refuse a complete bifurcation between analytic reach and empirical grounding: I shall judge Bauman's project by way of both, and by also by interrogating the claims of Jacobsen, Blackshaw, Davis and others that Bauman tells it 'like it feels', gives 'voice to the voiceless', uses metaphors in a manner that humanises sociology as against forms of sociology which by using systematic and overarching theory and statistical and other empirical write human beings out of sociology, and that his sociology genuinely 'travels' because it transcends the bounds of his location in Europe; on the last, as we shall see, Bauman's Eurocentrism in fact was a crippling weakness which considerably limited the analytical reach and empirical grounding of his sociology. His imprisonment in his own gender and ethnicity, I will show, is also a source of considerable weakness in his work.

It might be argued, too, that he is mainly an essayist (Tester 2001: 6), and that his books should be treated as essays for a variety of audiences and therefore should not be judged on grounds of scholarship, academic rigour and so forth. But he only really became an essayist and populariser in the late 1990s, and especially in the early 2000s, so it is difficult to treat this defence of some of his weaker work as plausible. *Modernity and the Holocaust* (1989b), for example, can hardly be regarded as merely an essay.

Arguably, his is a particular form of the sociological imagination; and, later, a strategy of 'messages in a bottle'. But it makes for repetition and verbatim reproduction without warning or acknowledgement (Walsh and Lehmann 2015). His prose, though, is exceptional: it is luminous, sparkling and sometimes simply dazzling. No sociologist that I have read writes as well as Bauman does, in what is probably his third language (of at least five, also including Polish, Russian, French and German).

But Bauman's writing is given to huge generalisations, whether about modernity, postmodernity, consumerism or globalisation. There is a typical lack of nuance, caveats, qualified or tentative judgements, reference to relevant research even when it is readily available, for example on the effects of television. There is rarely any serious or elaborate justification for his adopted standpoints, for example his use of relativism from the work of Rorty.[2] In his economic deterministic moments – of which there are many, as I will show – he comes across as an old-fashioned Marxist, despite his early and perfectly justified criticism of deterministic perspectives.

These criticisms of Bauman's postmodern and liquid modern phases are spelled out in some detail in the book. However, this should not be taken to imply that there is little of value in his thinking. He would hardly have attained such a high degree of influence if his writings were worthless. It is my view that there are several significant merits to his work: his relentless – if sometimes flawed – critique of consumerism; his metaphors, though also flawed, nonetheless have proved to be highly productive and stimulating for many who read him; his focus on those who suffer the worst forms of exclusion in contemporary Western societies. His eclecticism is something I take delight in; and his refusal to treat the ethical and the sociological as separate realms, thus making his sociology not only an analytical exercise, but also a series of ethical demands on the readers of his works, is admirable. This ethical demand, intrinsic to so much of his work, will perhaps be his greatest legacy.

Notes

1 Accessed February 2017.
2 Rorty's influence on Bauman was particularly pronounced in *Legislators and Interpreters* (1987) and throughout the 1990s. There are some useful collections debating various aspects of Rorty's work, including his alleged relativism and his flirtation with postmodernism: see Brandom 2000; Malachowski 1990; Festenstein and Thompson 2001. An excellent overview of Rorty's work can be found in Gascoigne 2008. See also Geras 1995.

Part I

The dark side of modernity

The early years of the 1980s were a period of hope for Bauman. The flame of Solidarity was still burning bright in Poland, while Western societies looked as though they were entering a period of crisis that could yet see a renewal of radical impulses pushing towards a more progressive future. Socialism, then, was still an 'active utopia', its fires by no means completely extinguished and perhaps even heading for a period of 'maturation'.

But in the course of Bauman's writing *Memories of Class* there was a distinct change of mood. Class conflict of the old type was indeed becoming a memory, an idea etched in the very title of the book. Talk of capitalism in Bauman's work was beginning to be displaced by a conceptual vocabulary of industrialism and post-industrialism. A discussion of the importance of consumerism had now begun (*Memories of Class*, 1982: 124).

Very significantly, *Memories* includes a quote from the Cambridge political philosopher John Dunn which, in hindsight, can be seen as presaging a wholesale shift in Bauman's perspective: 'Who now, except an imbecile, can still expect a *guaranteed* progress?' (*Memories*: 125, emphasis in Dunn's original).

The question of modernity

A radical new answer to Dunn's question emerges in *Legislators and Interpreters* (1987), on the very issue of 'progress'. The startling new conceptual centrepiece of this book is 'modernity', and that, too, from an explicitly 'postmodernist' viewpoint. This was at a time when most of British and American sociology had not yet registered the fervent debate about 'modernity' and 'postmodernity', and 'modernism' and 'postmodernism', that had engulfed Continental Europe and the English and philosophy departments of American universities.

This was not surprising. Little in the preceding years had prepared Anglo-American sociology for what was about to hit them. Marx, Weber and Durkheim, the revered greats of classical sociology, had not used the concept of modernity, although of course they were acutely aware of the novelty of the times they were living in (Ray 1999). Only George Simmel (1858–1918), a relatively little-known figure in mainstream sociology, had discussed 'modernity', but in a limited manner, reflecting on the fragmented experience of the modern city or 'metropolis' as he called it (Frisby 1986, 2002; Berman 1982: 131–71).

In the 1950s and early 1960s, American sociology, especially that part of it which focused on the newly emerging postcolonial nations, had had much to say about the need for 'modernization' in these societies. But the patently ideological character of much of this analysis had led to an early demise of the concept, for 'modernization' was a thinly veiled celebration of American society. Modernisation meant progress, and this too towards the good society, but as defined in idealised American terms: individualism, the declining significance of class and the growth of an ever larger middle class, meritocracy, liberal democracy and a benign capitalism. So strongly had this form of what Woodiwiss has called 'social modernism' (1993) become the world view of American sociology, and so uncritically had it been embraced by its major representatives, that Daniel Bell, one of the most pre-eminent of these sociologists, was able to proclaim 'the end of ideology' in a book of that title in 1960, for there seemed to be no doubt that the main features of the good society were already present in contemporary America and no more serious debate remained (prefiguring the much later 'end of history' thesis of Francis Fukuyama in the aftermath of the collapse of the Soviet Union). Unprecedented prosperity as well as a conscious attempt to counter the threat of Soviet communism were part of the heady mixture that produced an ideology of American narcissism (Woodiwiss 1993: 5). As Offe points out, as a temper of the times, this viewpoint was prompted by the question of how it was that the US had become so successful; and the answer was 'modernisation', more broadly identified with Westernisation (1996:3; see also Habermas, 1984: 2–3). 'Modernisation' became, for American sociologists, simply a synonym for 'progress'.

However, the struggle for the basic civil rights of African Americans, protests against America's war in Vietnam, student uprisings, the development of the counter-culture among the post-1960s youth, the discovery of poverty in the midst of plenty and growing awareness of the biting observations of Galbraith about the 'private affluence but public squalor' of American cities (Galbraith 1958) soon undermined the complacency with which the 1960s had started. Sociologists re-read their Marx and Weber and soon questions of class conflict and the future of capitalism became centre stage in the discipline, especially in Britain.

Bauman was thus well ahead of his time. While debates raged in the 1980s between Marxist and neo-Weberian sociologists about class and capitalism, Bauman had begun to go beyond what seemed to him a narrow family quarrel among broadly left sociologists who were united more than they were divided. Although Bell had moved on to discuss post-industrialism (1973), and had begun to worry about what he called 'the cultural contradictions of capitalism' in a book of that title (1978, first published 1976), Bauman, captivated by developments in Continental Europe, began to paint on an even broader canvas. Like Lyotard, who had published his ground-breaking *The Postmodern Condition* in French in 1979 (with an English translation in 1984), which I shall discuss in Part II of this book, Bauman had 'modernity' in his sights. And this from a firmly 'postmodernist' perspective, a notion, as I have pointed out, foreign to most British and American sociologists.

Modernity and the Enlightenment

It is arguable – and indeed Woodiwiss (1997) has advanced a plausible case for just such an interpretation – that the supposedly new concept of 'modernity' that became the subject of heated debate in the 1980s and 1990s had more than a passing resemblance to the notion of modernisation, with its underlying conception of modernity, than is often realised. But there is one fundamental difference that prevents any assimilation of the 'modernity' at play in the two discourses: while modernisation *celebrated* modernity, the new perspectives *problematised* modernity. Far from seeing in modernity the basic contours of the good society, postmodernists sought to debunk its claims. And in this critique, the Enlightenment movement that flourished in eighteenth-century Europe became a key focus of contention.

The Enlightenment is of paramount importance in Bauman's self-proclaimed postmodernist critique of modernity in *Legislators and Interpreters*. I will discuss Bauman's views on postmodernity in Part II. Here I shall focus on Bauman's analysis of modernity and, to begin with, his interpretation of the relationship between modernity and the Enlightenment as presented in *Legislators*. Both *Legislators* and *Modernity and Ambivalence* (1991) contain much on Bauman's perspective on postmodernity too, but I shall postpone an exposition and critique of Bauman's interpretation of postmodernity and postmodernism until Part II, where I will be able to give them the attention they merit.

Bauman on the Enlightenment and modernity

It is highly improbable that by the time he came to compose *Legislators and Interpreters* Bauman had not read Lyotard's *The Postmodern Condition*, which had, after all, kick-started the debate about modernity in the social sciences. However, although there is no mention of Lyotard in the book, Bauman was pursuing a parallel project: a wholesale critique of the universalist pretensions of the European Enlightenment of the eighteenth century.

Intellectuals and the Enlightenment

The originality of Bauman's approach is not in doubt, for he analysed the Enlightenment and indeed the whole of Western modernity and postmodernity from a perspective that focused on the changing status of intellectuals in relation to the state. Indeed, the very emergence of intellectuals as a separate and special social category is said by Bauman – although he is not alone in this view – to be inextricably tied to the Enlightenment. The book is sub-titled 'On Modernity, Postmodernity and Intellectuals'.

The emergence of general intellectuals in the eighteenth century, Bauman argues, was a specific product of what he called the new 'power/knowledge syndrome' of modernity, with more than a nod to the writings of the French historian and social philosopher Michel Foucault (Gordon 1972, 1980). Modernity and intellectuals were part and parcel of two major new phenomena that began to flourish during the eighteenth century: the simultaneous emergence of a form of state power with the will and resources to mould society according to a pre-conceived plan; and the development of relatively autonomous groups of people, collectively called *les philosophes* in France, able to articulate sets of discourses and plans which in turn enabled the creation of blueprints for the state to follow. At its inauguration, modernity for Bauman was a period in which intellectuals and the state had a common project and

co-operated to implement it. 'Postmodernity', as we shall see, signifies a period when the marriage of intellectuals with the state is
dissolved and both undergo major transformations.

While Bauman does provide the outlines of what he takes to be
the modern condition, he does not delve into the origins of the term
itself; so it is worth adding some brief remarks to Bauman's account,
as otherwise the impression remains that the term originates with
the Enlightenment itself. While it is not possible to be certain about
this, a variety of scholars have suggested that 'modern' derives
from the fifteenth-century Latin usage *modernus*, from the adverb
modo, meaning 'recently' or 'just now', which was used to define
the emergence and establishment of the Christian era, differentiating it from the pagan, Roman epoch. It marks a new approach
to the notion of time, away from, especially, a cyclical view
(Calinescu 1987: 13; see also Habermas 1983: 3–4; Smart 1990:
17). Modernity as seen through the eyes of the Enlightenment proclaimed the period beginning in the seventeenth century and flow-
ering in the eighteenth as distinctive by virtue of its opposition to
religion and superstition, enthroning, instead, the reign of reason
over human affairs. Not surprisingly, the Enlightenment period
is often dubbed the 'Age of Reason' by historians, and Bauman
retains this interpretation of the Enlightenment.

At this stage it is also worth noting that the idea of 'the
Enlightenment' as some sort of unified social era is of more recent
provenance, emerging in the late nineteenth century, although
contemporaries had used versions of the 'enlighten' metaphor, as
in Kant's *Was ist Aufklärung?* (What is Enlightenment?), and the
notion of *les lumières* was also used by contemporaries in relation
to the intellectuals of the period.

The term 'intellectual', Bauman points out, is a twentieth-
century French invention. So in what sense did the Enlightenment
exist and how can the *philosophes* be considered to have some
unity? For Bauman, both were to be explained by unique historical circumstances, and for him *it was only in France, and that too for
only a brief period*, that a unique coincidence between knowledge
and power existed, which made it possible for us now to talk of
'the Enlightenment', although he is not consistent in restricting
the implications of his analysis to France. In a superb exercise in
the sociology of intellectual development, Bauman cites six con-

ditions which in France 'short-circuited knowledge and power' (*Legislators:* 25). First was the emergence of absolutist power in the hands of the French monarchy; second, the demotion of the nobility from its previous dominant status; third, the vacuum left by the demise of aristocratic power; fourth, unlike what happened in Germany, where intellectuals held positions in universities or the civil service, in France a group emerged that was unhampered by such commitments, and so could develop as 'freelance' commentators who could imagine that they had a commitment to the whole of society; and fifth, there existed a network of clubs and salons in which they could meet. Finally, with the collapse of the old order, the emergence of a huge number of social problems required rapid and determined solution by the new centralised power-the perfect setting 'in which power needed, and sought knowledge' (*Legislators*: 25–6).

One among many major problems that confronted the monarchy in the new post-aristocratic society was that of the 'poor', who had previously been offered some relief by noble landowners. To keep an eye on landless vagrants and others, the state began forms of surveillance that soon began to expand into an apparatus that took on more and more administrative functions. A whole host of new laws were promulgated, colonising what was seen as 'an empty land'. But this was a novel task which no one had attempted before, requiring a new skilled elite not tied by patronage to the older aristocratic elites (*Legislators*: 29). The despot needed enlightening, and a new breed of intellectuals was there to provide this; so was born the age of Enlightened Despotism. The state might lay claim to absolute power, but in many senses it was also relatively powerless against growing uncertainty, especially that posed by the new marginal groups of beggars, vagabonds and others (*Legislators*: 38, 41). A new sort of centralised state was coming into being, and with it a new form of power that could regain control.

The old system of power did not penetrate into the lives of those on whose labour the nobility depended for its sustenance and wealth; the peasants organised their own work routines, only being required periodically to hand over a 'surplus' to those who owned the land. This system of oversight was not equal to the task of overseeing a population that was rapidly freeing itself from the feudal system and crowding into ever-growing towns.

At this point Bauman's narrative relies even more heavily on Foucault's analysis, this time in *Discipline and Punish* (1984), of the new disciplinary power embodied in the design of Jeremy Bentham's 'Panopticon' in which a single watchman could survey below him all of the inmates of a building, but who themselves could never be sure when and how they were being watched. Moreover, now the whole of the life of the inmates could be subject to a rhythm and regimentation devised by those in power, penetrating into the very bodies of the inmates as they were forced to internalise new habits of conduct. And, equally significant, those occupying the new positions of surveillance over the majority required a novel expertise, they had to be skilled practitioners of a new art.

A new system of power/knowledge was emerging, and expertise was crucial to it. Bauman points out, as Foucault had emphasised, that the social sciences were born of this moment, later providing the scientific 'objectivization' of 'human objects into categories amenable to statistical processing' (a theme prefigured in his earlier work, especially *Towards a Critical Sociology*).

The meaning of modernity: the gardening metaphor

Bauman, following the lead of Ernest Gellner, now draws upon a metaphor that was to be a defining feature of his conception of modernity in this period of his intellectual development. Modernity, he argues, can be seen as a garden as opposed to wild land. Gardens need cultivation; they require constant vigilance and swift action to keeps weeds at bay. If in pre-modernity a 'gamekeeper'-type figure was all that was required to keep 'wild' lands in order, now a gardener, a quite different kind of order-maker, constantly on the lookout, always active, was needed.

In this 'modernity', reason was married to the state to create a 'legislator or design-drawing despot', who recognised the essential brittleness of post-feudal social life and relied on experts, who deployed reason to devise the means to rational rule (*Legislators*: 54–5).

And so the opposition between 'reason' and the 'passions' was born, haunting the thinkers of the eighteenth century. As against the historian of ideas Albert Hirschman, who had written (1977) with great insight about the debates provoked by this opposition between the wildness in humans and the need for man-made order, Bauman insisted that this was not just a debate about 'the nature of man' but about the 'pragmatics of power', and thus about what sort of new state power was needed. And an important function of the new form of state was to control emotions and 'passions', especially of the lower orders. It is no wonder, then, that folk festivals and other manifestations of popular culture were subject to such cruel repression, a 'cultural crusade', from the seventeenth century onwards; in this lay the social roots of the 'age of reason' (*Legislators*: 59–67, 74).

The new group of intellectuals, Voltaire for example, had nothing but contempt for the lower classes. The destruction of popular culture, the new zeal of the state for reconstructing the social order and the emergence of Panopticon-style surveillance and power meant that 'the people' would now be remade individually, each person sharing only the attribute of 'the infinite capacity to be acted upon, shaped, perfected' (*Legislators*: 68). And the transformation was to be 'guided by those who converse with Reason' and hence 'know what the common interest demands'. 'This', Bauman argues, 'was the view shared by the elites of the early modern era.' *Note that what began as an analysis of the French case has now been extended by Bauman to the whole of north-western Europe*; I will clarify the significance of this broadening soon.

Crucial to the reconstruction of the social order was the 'education' of the public, with the creation of new schools. Not the transmission of knowledge, but the 'total predictability of behaviour' was the goal, an aim advocated by no less a figure than Robespierre, who was in favour of a Panopticon model with 'austere discipline' and 'detailed rules of conduct'. Thus would be achieved a two-fold goal: rational policies emanating from the state and the rendering harmless of those who would later be called *les classes dangereuses*.

For Bauman, the emergence of the concept of culture in the eighteenth century was no surprise: it was a thoroughly modern discovery that human beings were eminently capable of being moulded. It was in modernity, too, that 'culture', 'civilisation' and 'policing' acquired their affinities, positing the need for civility and refinement to be allied with self-control. Bauman chides Elias, author of the justly famous *The Civilizing Process*, for overlooking the fact that what emerged in the later feudal and early modern period was a concern not just with good manners, but with centralised control, and the destruction of the 'wild cultures' of local, popular traditions.

Interrogating Bauman's Enlightenment

Bauman self-consciously presents an 'ideal-typical' version of the Enlightenment, but soon slips into a mode of argument which ignores the internal diversity of viewpoints and begins to treat his deliberately selective portrayal of the Enlightenment as synonymous with the Enlightenment *tout court*. It is this slippage in his analysis which enables him to treat the symbiotic relation between intellectuals and the state as a central defining feature of the *whole* of Western modernity and also allows him to elevate the pronouncements of a small number of *philosophes* to *the* philosophy of the Enlightenment. It is remarkable how few actual *philosophes* he mentions; the number of works written during the period cited by him is even smaller.[1] This is what enables a conflation between modernity, a totalising belief in the power of Reason, and the 'legislator' role of intellectuals, and also therefore permits him, later in the text, to identify the postmodern period as one in which the legislator-intellectuals lose their power.[2] That is, we get an argument in which the role of intellectuals widens to become *the* defining characteristic of modernity and postmodernity. We therefore end up with the clichéd viewpoint which sees the Enlightenment as the 'Age of Reason'.

This view of 'the Enlightenment Project' (Schmidt 1996), as it came to be called in debates over postmodernism (see Bauman's usage, *Legislators*: 75), sees the Enlightenment as pinning all its hopes on what Bauman calls 'the Kingdom of Reason' (*Legislators*: 111). This interpretation of the Enlightenment as being a period which believed in reason and the powers of the scientific method to deliver unending Progress can be sustained only by treating some key French *philosophes* as typical of the Enlightenment.

Rasmussen's compelling depiction in *The Pragmatic Enlightenment* (2014) shows that far from being out-and-out rationalists and universalists, several key Enlightenment intellectuals – Montesquieu, Voltaire, Hume and Smith, and others – favoured empirical and historical methods as against *a priori* deduction from first principles in Cartesian fashion; constantly emphasised the limitations of Reason; regarded sentiments and the 'passions' as having a powerful and constructive role to play in human affairs; argued that there was no guarantee that scientific method would deliver anything more than fallible, probabilistic knowledge; were against the creation of totalising systems of knowledge or blueprints for social reorganisation; believed that morality could not be rationally grounded, whether by appeal to 'human nature' or abstract principles in the manner of Kant; and based their pleas for tolerance partly on the frailty of human reason and therefore the difficulty of arriving at indubitable truths. In short, they opposed all forms of dogmatic thought and argument and had great doubts about the possibility of any overriding role for rationality in human affairs. Indeed, some historians (for example Himmelfarb 2008) have suggested that the British Enlightenment, in particular, was quite different from the French rationalist version in being more empiricist (see also Gordon 2001).

Ironically, what emerges from Rasmussen's corrective picture is a portrayal of central Enlightenment motifs in epistemology and ethics that are much closer to the Rorty-like Pragmatism favoured by Bauman in his espousal of a postmodern perspective in the latter part of *Legislators*. Some of the most powerful intellectual figures of the Enlightenment can be seen to be attempting to provide a non-foundationalist stance in epistemology and ethics, contrary to the sort of conventional view found even in more sophisticated accounts (see, for example, Gray 1995).

Even Condorcet, one of the few *philosophes* actually mentioned by Bauman (*Legislators*: 102, 112) as representative of his version of the Enlightenment, turns out on closer inspection – and by a reading that extends beyond his posthumously published essay on the history of the *Sketch of a Historical Picture of the Human Mind* – to be a figure whose views seemed to be in a constant state of flux on many of the key issues and opinions that Bauman treats as emblematic of the Enlightenment. As Rothschild points out in a study of Smith and Condorcet (2002), more often than not Condorcet's views are at odds with Bauman's portrayal of him as a 'legislator' wanting to draw up systematic blueprints, recommending the methods of geometry in ordering human affairs and wanting the creation of a rigid disciplinarian educational system for the lower orders. He

sometimes enunciated such views, but also displayed scepticism as
to the 'application to societies and individuals of the deterministic
ideas of the mechanical sciences' (Rothschild 2002: 198). He also
regarded the imposition of universal and eternal principles as 'the
most sinister of despotisms' (Rothschild 2002: 196), argued that
overall human beings would have to be 'content with more or less
great probabilities' (quoted in Rothschild 2002: 198) and, far from
wanting a uniform code of education, as suggested by Bauman,
came to the view in his main last published work, on principles of
education, that the inculcation of 'the diversity of opinions' was
a 'preeminent good' and that no opinion should be presented as
'received truth' or 'universal belief'. Moreover, much like Hume
and the others, he recognised the important role of emotions and
sentiments in human conduct. In the light of the importance that
Bauman was later to give to the reading of literature and novels,
it is ironic that Condorcet, this supposed über-rationalist, recom-
mended novels as giving the best insight into 'the people who sur-
round us' (quoted in Rothschild 2002: 200).

What should be clear by now is that the architecture of
Bauman's interpretation of the Enlightenment and modernity is
built on shaky foundations. Too many of the supposed 'legislators'
were not simply rationalists and universalists. Nor did they believe
in the inevitability of continuing progress or the unlimited applicability of the scientific method to any and all matters. In fact, they
doubted that society could be ordered simply on rational principles
and unbending discipline, revealed by indubitable truths valid for
all time.

What Bauman also fails to notice or mention is that the
Enlightenment was a 'wider ferment, inaugurated, sustained and
spread by a vastly larger number of relatively obscure thinkers,
writers, readers and contact loops'. And, Porter adds, 'Nor could it
ever have flourished without extensive support networks of friends,
sympathisers and fellow-travellers-comrades who gave refuge to
exiles, or passed on letters and books to those living underground,
in hiding' (Porter 2000: 40–1). Publishers also played a vital role,
often risking prosecution and ruin by publishing banned or sub-
versive pamphlets and books. Of course, it suits Bauman's thesis
to foreground only a select few intellectuals; giving importance to
a wider range of intellectuals as well as ordinary people and taking

account of the fact that those who read the publications were primarily a small middle class of 'lawyers, administrators, the higher clergy, landowners and provincial dignitaries' (Porter 2000: 43) would have dented his (overly) neat thesis of a symbiotic and all-important relationship between intellectuals and the absolutist state, or between power and knowledge.

Women, too, get only an occasional mention in *Legislators*, usually being lumped in with other Others such as the lower orders, racialised colonial subjects and savages. Note, for the time being, that although Bauman devotes a whole chapter to the emergence of the concept of culture in the eighteenth century, he fails to emphasise that women were defined as *nature* to *men's* culture. It was to (middle- and upper-class) men that the ability to self-cultivate, self-actualize and exercise freedom and rationality was ascribed. Women were to be confined to the domestic, private sphere, for they were by and large seen as 'emotional, credulous, and incapable of objective reasoning' (Outram 1995: 83). However, they were simultaneously regarded as crucial to the creation of a new morality, which would be more 'natural' by being more polite and modern (Tomaselli 1985). The new medical discourses, especially those which 'proved' that women had smaller brains than men, meaning that their rationality could be 'scientifically' doubted, were particularly drawn upon. It took Mary Wollstonecraft in her ground-breaking *Vindication of the Rights of Woman* (1792) to deconstruct the binaries of nature–culture and rationality–irrationality and expose the contradictions at the heart of mainstream Enlightenment assumptions about the status of women. Like Voltaire, Wollstonecraft pointed out that to confine women to an inferior, domestic realm was to replicate the arbitrary system that privileged the monarchs, aristocrats and slave owners. The male–female division was overlain by class differences, for it was difficult to doubt the strength of peasant and working-class women engaged in heavy manual labour, and thus as Wollstonecraft argued, the legitimation of the subordination of feminine middle- and upper-class woman was that much easier.

But the whole male–female, masculine–feminine dichotomy was also being undermined by the fact that more and more women were able to earn an independent living as journalists and writers. Meanwhile, upper-class women played a key role as organisers of the salons in which 'periwigged' intellectuals could 'prattle', to borrow again from Roy Porter's acerbic account (2001). Many of these women were intellectuals in their own right, for example the Marquise du Châtelet, who translated Newton's *Principia Mathematica* into French and was Condorcet's companion (Israel 2014: 122–3). Condorcet, as Israel (2014: 123–5) and a host of others point out, together with figures such as Diderot, Montesquieu and Voltaire, dissented strongly from Rousseau's misogynistic attempts to argue for women's confinement to domesticity and motherhood (Knott and Taylor: 2005).

The publication of *Vindication of the Rights of Woman* in 1792 was of special significance. For we should acknowledge, as Israel (2010) has urged us to, that the Enlightenment took a distinctly more radical turn in the last two decades of the eighteenth century. Israel goes so far as to distinguish between two Enlightenments, a 'moderate' one (labelled 'pragmatic' by Rasmussen) that was dominated by Voltaire, Montesquieu, Hume, Smith and others of the same ilk, and a 'radical' and subsequently revolutionary version that was more associated in a variety of ways with the French Revolution (Israel 2014); it was far more egalitarian, wanted grander, more widespread root and branch institutional reform, and in its later incarnation was associated with Thomas Paine, Mary Wollstonecraft, William Godwin, Joseph Priestley, Diderot, Helvetius, d'Holbach and a host of other writers from all over Western Europe. It was this more egalitarian and democratic strand that fed into the American and French revolutions as well as the Dutch ferment of 1780–87. However, even Diderot, one of Israel's radical heroes, turns out on closer inspection to have had a more pessimistic side, as Sharon Stanley (2012) has shown in her excellent study of 'cynicism' in the French Enlightenment.

What we are left with is a much more complex picture of the Enlightenment than the one that Bauman presents us with, this latter one being particularly difficult to square with his equation of the Enlightenment with elitism. Whether we now have two or three Enlightenments, or whether we should drop the very idea of the Enlightenment as any kind of unity, is a subject of much debate among historians of the eighteenth century (Schmidt 2000, 2001; Delacampagne 2001). This need not detain us, for my purpose has merely been to show that Bauman's thesis as presented

in *Legislators* simply cannot withstand informed historical interrogation. *Ipso facto*, his whole conception of modernity (and postmodernity) as presented in *Legislators* is open to serious question,
an argument which, in a variety of forms, I intend to pursue later.

There is one final set of issues that demand consideration before
I take leave of *Legislators* for the time being. The architecture of the
book is hugely indebted to the framework of the power/knowledge
constellation in modernity as set out by Michel Foucault. It is
hardly surprising then that Bauman's discussion is marred by an
omission that is also a characteristic feature of Foucault's work:
the neglect of the analysis of discourses and practices of racism,
imperialism and colonialism in the Enlightenment. Just as wom-
en's Otherness is neglected by both authors, so is the Otherness of
the non-Western world, although Enlightenment thinkers – just
like some of their Renaissance predecessors, Montaigne especially
– were much excited, and troubled too, by the discovery and tales
of peoples in the new worlds that Columbus and his successors
encountered and who posed acute questions about the unity of
humankind and the specificity of contemporary European culture.

The neglect of questions of racial difference until very late in
his life, and its implications for how we judge Foucault's work,
has been discussed in a superb piece of scholarship by Ann Stoler
(1995). Bauman's failure to understand the significance of these
issues is only partly due to the influence of Foucault, because it is a
feature of his earlier works too. But there is a peculiarity about its
absence in *Legislators* that must be also be remarked upon. Edward
Said's *Orientalism*, published in 1979, had used Foucault's power/
knowledge framework to throw new light on how the West had
governed and to some degree even created an Other, by colonisation and the production of myriad discourses, including travel
writing, early forms of ethnography, translations of texts, novels
and fantasies of all kinds, censuses and so forth. *Orientalism* had an
immediate and profound effect on a wide range of disciplines and
indeed spawned one of its own in the form of postcolonial studies.
Said's argument was soon subjected to important criticisms, but its
crucial galvanising contribution was equally and just as quickly
recognised, and served to disseminate Foucault's insights over
an astonishing range of disciplines. It is remarkable that in using
Foucault so productively in his analysis of the Enlightenment,

Bauman appears to have remained unaware of Said's work and its significance for his own understanding of the Enlightenment, for discussions of the non-Western world played a constitutive role in the formation of the Enlightenment.

For obvious reasons, I cannot make up for this lacuna in any depth in my own discussion of Bauman. I can provide only a brief outline of the diverse ways in which the non-Western world animated discussions among European intellectuals in the Enlightenment period. Perhaps the most important point to make in this context is that the new cultures that were 'discovered' in ever greater numbers and in much more detail than ever before provoked a profound ambivalence in Enlightenment attitudes towards the 'new' peoples; and the growing knowledge of non-Western worlds came to be deployed in a wide range of discourse, debates and reflections, with the ambivalences producing acute dilemmas which led prominent thinkers to change their views in the course of their lives. Kant is an important example. He moved from a blatantly racist position towards black people (Eze 1997: 38) to a more serious interest in anthropology in which his cosmopolitanism marginalised his racism; it is possible that in fact he changed his mind completely on the inferiority of blacks. It is certainly the case that he became an anti-imperialist (Muthu 2003: 172–209). Most of the French *philosophes* too were against imperialism and colonisation, as Muthu (2003) has comprehensively and convincingly documented. Moreover, idealisations of American aboriginal peoples and especially the inhabitants of Tahiti, in the form of the 'noble savage', were used to criticise contemporary manners and what was thought to be excessive artificiality and materialism, as opposed to the 'natural' condition of these 'rude' peoples, as they were also called (Meek 1976; Whelan 2009: 48–77; Carey and Trakulhun 2013). Diderot especially used this to great effect, although he was wise enough also to question the authenticity of the accounts of Tahitian culture that had so excited many of his contemporaries (Vogel 2000; Muthu 2003). Nor should we forget the great veneration during the Enlightenment of Chinese civilisation, the elevation of Confucius to a sort of cult figure and the impact of Chinese art and porcelain manufacture, leading to the emergence in France of what has been called *chinoiserie*, with Voltaire being a leading light in this wave of Sinophilia (Clarke

1997: 37–53; Pieterse 1994). Changing attitudes to China exemplify the Enlightenment's ambivalence to non-Western cultures, with the same thinkers sometimes praising the Chinese system of rule and at other times denouncing what they took to be an unacceptable form of 'Oriental Despotism', one of the regimes of governance included in Montesquieu's highly influential typology of forms of government.

Despite the anti-slavery views of key Enlightenment figures and also the abolitionist beliefs of revolutionaries such as Robespierre, the French Revolution of 1789 did not lead to a swift end to slavery. This happened in only 1794 and was confined to Saint-Domingue (later to be called Haiti) because of pressure from a slave revolt eventually led by Toussaint L'Ouverture. The rebellion became more widely discussed only in the wake of C. L. R. James's pioneering *The Black Jacobins* of 1938. Bauman, of course, does not mention slavery, nor the heroic rebellion of the slaves of Saint-Domingue; the revolution led by L'Ouverture was in fact the first to proclaim universal emancipation, widening the freedoms hitherto given only to white, propertied males in both the French and American revolutions (Nesbitt 2008).

Although my judgement on the many limitations of Bauman's interpretation of the Enlightenment has obviously benefited from scholarship produced after his book was published, the basic thrust of my critique could and should have been articulated at the time the book was published, for the internal diversity of the Enlightenment and the constitutive role of women and racialised Others in forming the Enlightenment's discourses was already a subject of considerable debate, as is evident in Bauman's own admittedly occasional references to these issues. Bauman's marginal references, when brought to the centre, allow a Derridean deconstruction which exposes a white, male, Eurocentric framing which systematically distorts the entire text.

Notes

1   Porter (2000) points out that those who present a stereotyped version of the Enlightenment often fail to refer to many actual *philosophes* or publications from the period, and Bauman is a good example of this tendency.

2 Cassirer's *The Philosophy of the Enlightenment*, first published in 1934
   and translated into English in 1951 (Cassirer 1951), was highly influential in disseminating a view of the Enlightenment as putting all its
   faith in reason; a more sophisticated view was propounded by Gay
   (1973). For an illuminating discussion of the changing interpretations
   of the politics of the Enlightenment since Gay, see de Dijn (2012).

The Holocaust's modernity

Hannah Arendt was one of the first intellectuals to confront, in 1945, the enormity of what had happened to six million Jews and millions of Roma, Poles and others in what came to be called the Holocaust. In its immediate aftermath she pronounced, with conviction, that 'The problem of evil will be the fundamental question of postwar intellectual life' (quoted in Bernstein 1996: 137). And indeed it did occupy her, in one form or another, for the rest of her life. But as Bernstein also points out, 'most postwar intellectuals avoided any direct confrontation with the problem of evil'.

Bauman also admits, in his famous *Modernity and the Holocaust*, published in 1989, that he too was guilty of simply ignoring the myriad questions thrown up by the massacre of Jews and others. By the time he came to write the book a great many historians, especially, had produced insightful and deeply researched works on which he was able to draw. So how was it that he too had failed to confront the evil of the Holocaust?

He says in the preface that it was his wife Janina's moving memoir of her life in the Polish Warsaw ghetto, published as *Winter in the Morning* (1986), that jolted him, awakening in him the desire to confront and understand the Holocaust. In the process of researching the book Bauman also reflected on how and why it had taken him so long. His answers are fascinating, providing as they do an incisive analysis of the vagaries of scholarship on the Holocaust and, especially, the continuing failure of sociologists to deal with what he now realised should have been an urgent and vital set of questions.

Interestingly enough, his brief stay in Israel had obviously also failed to prompt him into delving deeper into the Holocaust, and he does not mention his and Janina's stay in Israel anywhere in the book. It was her memoir that set him off on the quest to understand what had happened. He read the historians, and realised that what they provided was not a picture but a window; and what he saw was not 'at all pleasing', as he put it in a deliberate understatement (*Modernity and the Holocaust*: viii). But the more depressing the view, the more he realised that he simply had to step through the window and search the landscape. He realised that, in part, what had blinded him was what had also prevented other sociologists from confronting the Holocaust: it seemed to hold no lessons for the present, for it had simply been an aberration, 'a momentary madness among sanity' (*Modernity and the Holocaust*: viii).

Bauman's main thesis is boldly set out in the preface, and it is very different from what had become the received view. For Bauman, the Holocaust may have been a Jewish tragedy, but Jews were six million among the twenty or so million who lost their lives because of Hitler. It was true that the Jews alone had been marked out for total obliteration. Nevertheless, this was not only an event solely in Jewish history. Bauman emphasises that '*The Holocaust was born and executed in our modern rational society, at the high stage of our civilization and at the peak of human cultural achievement, and for this reason it is a problem of that society, civilization and culture*' (*Modernity and the Holocaust*: x, emphasis in original).

This truth could not, for Bauman, be denied by viewing the Holocaust as only a peculiarity of German history or Hitler's evil personality and the cruelty, the moral decrepitude and sometimes the sheer indifference of those who in one way or another were implicated in such vile deeds. The effect of any such interpretation is to see the Holocaust as only something to do with Germany or Germanness, thereby absolving everyone else of responsibility, and, in particular, of shifting the blame away from the typical characteristics of modernity so widely taken for granted. For Bauman the factors involved were indeed 'quite ordinary and common'; but they had come together in a historically unique encounter. The taken for granted civilisational framework which in fact harboured the seeds of the Holocaust consisted of the modern nation-state, the concentration and centralisation of the means of violence in its apparatuses and the adoption of a bold and sweeping project of social engineering by those in command of this immensely powerful state. The capacity of the leaders was enhanced by the dismantling of all sources of opposition and the possession of a particular modern apparatus of administration: a state bureaucracy. Science and modern technology had their own crucial role to play in the terrible sequence of events. It is in the combination of these common features of modern civilisation within a particular historical period that Bauman finds the basic causes of the Holocaust.

Sociology and the Holocaust

As a sociologist, Bauman was especially keen to explore why, when compared with historians and theologians, sociologists had had so little to say about the Holocaust and, when they did tackle it, why it was seen as a specialist area of interest with little to say to the central concerns of sociology (*Modernity and the Holocaust*: 11).[1] For Bauman the deepest reason for sociology's failure to deal adequately with the Holocaust is to be found in sociology's being too much a *part of modernity* to be able to understand how modernity itself was responsible for the Holocaust. What Bauman finds problematic is, especially, sociology's typical *modus operandi*, to be found in its scientism, its empiricism, its ties to a positivist methodology for producing explanations by a systematic setting out of variables and correlations, statistical compilations and calculations, as for example in Fein (1979). These were criticisms that had first been articulated in *Towards a Critical Sociology* (1976b), and were heavily influenced by the Frankfurt School (although surprisingly enough Bauman does not refer either to his earlier book or to the similar criticisms made by Adorno, Horkheimer and others of positivist sociology).

The nub of his critique of sociology in the face of the Holocaust is that *in effect, the Holocaust comes to be seen, in orthodox sociology, as a failure, not a product of modernity* (*Modernity and the Holocaust*: 5). Bauman's own thesis of the Holocaust's modernity, Bauman argues, is impossible to formulate within conventional sociological frameworks. It is the normality of the Holocaust that Bauman of course seeks to elucidate: that is, that it is entirely in keeping with the key features of modern civilisation (*Modernity and the Holocaust*: 8). Bauman, though, is aware that this is not entirely an original insight on his part. As early as 1964, Stillman and Pfaff had made this point by underlining the similarity between modern mass production and the method of mass killing in concentration camps. Raul Hilberg, the great historian of the Holocaust, in his magisterial *The Destruction of the European Jews* (1985), had also made the connection between the normal 'machinery' of German society and the 'machinery' of destruction that was the Holocaust. And even more strongly, Rubenstein (1978) had drawn what Bauman calls the 'ultimate lesson of the Holocaust', that it bore witness to *'the advance of civilization'* (*Modernity and the Holocaust*: 9, quoting Rubenstein). The Holocaust had revealed, Rubenstein averred, one of the hitherto hidden potentials of our admiration for technical efficiency and good design. In particular, Bauman cites Rubenstein's observation that civilisation and savagery, creativity and destruction are inseparable, for the same civilisation that has given us exquisite works of art and music had also been accompanied by slavery, wars and exploitation.

But Bauman's point is that none of these acute commentators are sociologists. Hilberg was a historian and Rubenstein a theologian. Thus emerges Bauman's project, to treat the Holocaust as a 'sociological laboratory', as a *'rare, yet significant and reliable, test of the hidden possibilities of modern society'* (*Modernity and the Holocaust*: 12, emphasis in original). In citing Rubenstein as someone who had grasped the Holocaust as the other, often hidden, dark side of modernity, Bauman reproduces a passage where Rubenstein refers to modern civilisation and also included in its perpetration of horrors 'slavery, wars, exploitation, death camps'. Here it is Bauman who is guilty of not noticing something important: a history of imperial racism and slavery, and pre-Holocaust death camps, which Rubenstein mentions perhaps only in passing but with powerful intent. I shall have more to say about the great significance of this omission on Bauman's part.

Bauman of course was too well read not to have noticed that sociologists such as Mann and Giddens had commented on the centrality of the concentration of means of military and other violence in the hands of the state, but in his view this alternative perspective had not displaced the sociological myth of (modern Western) civilisation (Bauman takes it for granted that 'civilisation' in sociology refers mostly to the modern Western type).

Bauman also shows an understanding, brought home to us by every serious historian of the Holocaust, that the process of mass extermination was not there from the start of the Nazi project and not even when the Nazis first acquired untrammelled power

(*Modernity and the Holocaust*: 15). This 'final solution', as it came to be called, only took shape after the infamous Wannsee conference of 20 January 1942 in the aftermath of the stalling of the initial plan to deport Jews further east in Europe and even to Madagascar. But what Bauman wants us to grasp is the fragility of the human response when confronted by 'a factory-produced vehicle' for the destruction of humans, a project that came into being after the fateful decision made at Wannsee, designed by scientists and engineers, and above all executed at the top by an ultra-modern, scientifically informed organisation, operating with 'matter of fact' efficiency: a 'civil service', a *bureaucracy*, informed by the latest thinking in 'scientific management'.

Then emerges Bauman's *explanatory* claim, the one that goes beyond orthodox sociology and is worth reproducing because of its particular, presumably well thought through wording: 'Modern civilization was not the Holocaust's *sufficient* condition; it was, however, most certainly its *necessary* condition. Without it, the Holocaust would be unthinkable. It was the rational world of modern civilization that made the Holocaust thinkable' (*Modernity and the Holocaust*: 13, emphasis in original). Commentators on, and critics of Bauman's thesis have missed a crucial ambiguity in this formulation. I shall remark on it later when I come to assess Bauman's claims with regard to the Holocaust and modernity.

The initial 'solution', the forced mass emigration of Jews, had been designed with the same meticulous planning and expert knowledge that was then transferred to the Final Solution; both, for Bauman, were text-book cases of Weber's analysis of bureaucratic functioning and its dynamics. 'Goal displacement' was one typical and endemic feature of this mode of organisation, with more and more initiatives and functionaries, and thus a constant 'expansion of the original purposes'. What this meant was a proliferation of measures of discrimination against Jews which had not been spelled out in the original decisions; once the aim had been set, bureaucratic rationality saw to it that the process carried and gained momentum, with knowledge being supplied by experts. Modern engineering technology, bureaucracy and, underlying both, an ethos of 'instrumental rationality', devoid of ethical concerns, were enough to create a project that could not be regarded as unreasonable or irrational; the idea of making Germany *Judenrein*, or free of Jews, became a matter of problem-solving, social engineering, a form of ridding the 'garden' completely of 'weeds'.

In effect, the process was one of 'the social production of moral indifference', whereby a modern bureaucracy could organise and co-ordinate the actions of individuals who might have morals, but who became enmeshed, without scruples, in ends that were totally immoral (*Modernity and the Holocaust*: 18).

Eichmann and others involved were not, and did not have to be, sadists or psychopaths, and indeed most were pronounced perfectly 'normal' when examined by psychiatrists after the war. Had the Nazis won, as Eichmann's defence counsel argued, Eichmann would have been decorated; he was facing death by hanging because his side lost the war, for no one on the victors' side was to stand trial for crimes against humanity. In fact, as we now know, the Nazis were careful in trying to keep out anyone they thought abnormal, in terms of sadism or having selfish motives like looting from joining the *Einsatzgruppen* and others who would be at close quarters with the actual killings. We now know from various accounts that the Nazis were not always scrupulous or successful in this form of weeding. Nazis wanted unemotional types for this dirty work, as Arendt had noted, with Bauman citing her in this context (*Modernity and the Holocaust*: 20); discipline, organisational loyalty and commitment to routine were the qualities that were sought after. Arendt had pointed out, in her famous observations from the trial of Eichmann, that these were the ways round what she regarded as the 'animal pity' that all normal people would feel when confronted with such terrible suffering.

Bauman borrows from the scholarly literature the view that the three conditions under which violent atrocities can be committed, in other words the processes that overcome inhibitions and 'animal pity', involve the *authorisation* of the acts, from those with legal entitlement to issue orders; the *routinisation* of such acts by making them strictly procedural and a matter of following rules; and the *dehumanisation* of the victims by ideological indoctrination. All three were met, Bauman argues, in the manner in which the Nazi bureaucratic machine operated. Moral qualms were quelled by the responsibility's being borne by superiors, and in this case the final responsibility lay with the Führer, Hitler, on whose orders the whole process of making Germany *Judenrein* had commenced. As part of his evidence, Bauman cites the testimony of Ohlendorf, in charge of a unit of the murderous *Einsatzgruppe*, whose actions were distasteful to Ohlendorf. When asked why he had not resigned, Ohlendorf replied that to do so would have been to shift the blame, wrongly, onto the men under his command. This piece of evidence is important to bear in mind when the time comes to evaluate Bauman's thesis, but for the present let us note that Bauman cites verbatim Ohlendorf's statement that 'I surrender my moral conscience to the fact that I was a soldier, and therefore a cog in a relatively low position of a great machine' (*Modernity and the Holocaust*: 22).

Bauman also underlines what he calls the mediation of action. Using Hilberg as a source, he points out that the 'moral blindness' of those involved at an administrative level was considerably reinforced by the fact that by and large they were not actually shooting Jews nor turning on the gas in the gas chambers. Indeed, there was a sanitisation of the language describing these processes, especially the gassing. The chambers were described as 'bathrooms' to the victims, who were lured willingly by the promise of a pleasant shower after an arduous, filth-ridden and over-crowded journey in trains from ghettos where a great deal of suffering and isolation had been inflicted on Jewish people. Meanwhile, the bureaucrats in their clean offices were involved in routine, rational, administrative activities such as drawing up plans, attending conferences and planning meetings, giving orders by telephone or writing memos. They had no need to explore the process as a whole and no need to worry except about the consequences of not being efficient enough as decided upon by superiors whose orders were being carried out. Thus, even if some moral doubts arose, these were easily quelled by thinking about immediate concerns rather than large questions about morality and evil-doing. This stratagem was made even easier by the victims' being by and large invisible to the bureaucrats engaged in paperwork. Bauman also refers to the sort of psychological distancing that allowed pilots to drop the horrific bomb on Hiroshima, or the way workers in an armaments factory might react when redundancy is avoided by another huge order for armaments; in the latter case the workers are more likely to rejoice at the 'stay of execution' than worry about the end use of their products in far-away wars and massacres (*Modernity and the Holocaust*: 22–4).

Of course, there were the battalions, the *Einsatzgruppen*, who were called upon to fire upon groups of helpless Jewish men, women and children before gassing became the method of choice for mass murder. *Bauman has surprisingly little to say about this initial method of killing and its psychological consequences*, which is a matter of some importance and will be discussed later.

Moreover, a dehumanising process was also set in motion which removed Jews from the 'universe of obligation', that is, made them into beings to whom no moral qualms could apply. With Jews being stripped of their German citizenship and described as lice and other vermin, the task of mass murder was made that much easier; it enabled a re-description of the killings as a process of racial self-defence and political hygiene.

It is only with a recognition of the extent to which the various elements of modern rationality, science and modern methods of dehumanisation came together in the Holocaust that it is possible, Bauman argues, to see it as just another side of modern civilisation, a side that enables instrumental reasoning to displace questions of morality to another universe: this is the 'major lesson' of the Holocaust (*Modernity and the Holocaust*: 28).

For Bauman this involves not only a revision in our understanding of modern civilisation, but one of its offspring, modern sociology. For in espousing the idea of a value-free, scientific activity, sociology becomes a form of discourse and practice from which moral concerns are expelled. It is no wonder then, that notions such as 'the sanctity of human life' or 'moral duty' '*sound as alien in a sociology seminar as they do in the smoke-free, sanitized rooms of a bureaucratic office*' (*Modernity and the Holocaust*: 29, emphasis in original).

This is as powerful an indictment of modernity and sociology as has ever been made. Surprisingly, though, Bauman omits to acknowledge that from the 1960s onwards, and especially with the involvement of US social scientists in legitimating the war in Vietnam, the idea of value-free sociology as a cover for atrocity had come under constant scrutiny and criticism, and that there had always been varieties of sociology that had never fully subscribed to what Gouldner (1973) had called 'the myth of value-free sociology'.

Modernity and anti-Semitism

Without anti-Semitism – a term that was coined only in the second half of the nineteenth century –the Holocaust, aimed first and foremost at Jews, would obviously not have been possible. Anti-Jewish sentiment was clearly a necessary condition for the Holocaust. But as a causal explanation for the Holocaust it faces several problems according to Bauman. To begin with, German anti-Semitism was, if anything, less strong than anti-Semitism in other European countries, particularly France. Moreover, there is little evidence that 'the Jewish question' was uppermost in the minds of ordinary Germans in the inter-war period, when the severe economic depression, unemployment and raging inflation were much more of a preoccupation. And while festering anti-Jewish sentiment had been a feature of German society, and more widely European society, for millennia, the Holocaust was quite unprecedented. Periodic pogroms suffered by Jews during earlier periods were of a small scale and usually instigated by elites for a variety of reasons (often because they owed large sums to Jewish moneylenders, usury being banned by the Church; Jews were the only group allowed to engage in it, although Bauman does not mention this as one of the explanations for pogroms: see Rattansi 2007: 15–16). Even so, Bauman concludes that 'Alone, antisemitism offers no explanation of the Holocaust' and adds that in his view that sort of resentment cannot offer an adequate explanation of any genocide (*Modernity and the Holocaust*: 33). While the Jewish diaspora was, together with the Roma, perhaps the only minority in Europe to share an endemic homelessness, and therefore blurred the boundary between those who belonged and those who did not – Jews were 'psychologically unnerving' for they had the status of foreigners who were nevertheless also insiders – the intensity of hostility to them depended upon the strength of boundary-drawing pressures in the communities in which they lived. For the greater part of the European Middle Ages, Jews were able to become one of the many self-enclosed estates and castes of medieval society, living in separate quarters of towns and wearing distinctive dress. In societies which practised endemic legalised inequality, Jews were only one group that had to accept an unequal status that was externally defined. Of course, Jews had a peculiar history and position within

Christian societies as simultaneously the begetters of the founder of the Christian religion and the rejecters of his message despite every opportunity of conversion. One peculiarity of this status of the Jews was that their presence could be felt, and hostility to them could be engendered, even among Christians who had never actually encountered any Jews. The Jew was an abstraction, and Jewish separation could thus be inserted into the modern secular period as well. The 'conceptual Jew' was a signifier that could function to condense a variety of meanings precisely because of this abstraction, although always aided and abetted by the way the Jew upset the self-certainty of Christianity and the individual Christian believer. The conceptual Jew, Bauman says, was 'slimy', borrowing the term from the anthropologist Mary Douglas; the Jew served to signify the limits of the community, the cultural boundary beyond which lay *'not another order, but chaos and devastation'* (*Modernity and the Holocaust*: 39, emphasis in original). Just as the collapse of the certainties of the old medieval order was accompanied by a period of intense witch persecution, so in the same manner the Jew too could become a threat and a victim as new boundaries began to be drawn; indeed the abstract or conceptual Jew could be made to straddle a whole range of boundaries and 'barricades', for the Jew was a multi-dimensional incongruence (*Modernity and the Holocaust*: 41).

The Jew could thus be represented as everything that might be feared and despised. He or she could be a Bolshevik, a revolutionary communist or a greedy capitalist; the liberal who signified the rottenness of democracy; the cowardly pacifist as well as the instigator of wars. While other out-groups could be made fearsome as elites *or* masses, Jews, uniquely, could be stigmatised as both, depending on the circumstances.

The advent of modernity meant that the 'sliminess' and prismatic qualities of the Jew could be put to new uses, but also demanded new solutions. Jews could fall foul of the necessity for uniformity and the centralisation involved in the modern state's particular 'civilising' mission and boundary-creating project. Also, modernity was experienced as a disturbing phenomenon by all sectors of society, as old boundaries and statuses collapsed. While it created a new social order, the process of modernisation was one of profound dislocation, tension and destruction, and the Jew could be made to symbolise all that was fearsome; the Jew could be made to epitomise the new uncertainty. As Bauman puts it in his inimitable prose, '*the fate of the Jews epitomized the awesome scope of social upheaval and served as a vivid, obtrusive reminder of the erosion of old certainties*' (*Modernity and the Holocaust*: 45, emphasis in original). With the victory of modernity assured, its anti-modern phobias, Bauman argues, were repressed but found a form of exorcism through the use of thoroughly modern achievements: the concentrated power of the state, sophisticated technology and scientific management.

It is in this context that Bauman acknowledges the role of usury in the Jewish predicament. The Jews were rich but contemptible. Hence their suitability to be the 'lightning rod' for anti-modernist sentiment and anxiety, with the first form of modern anti-Semitism being promulgated by fierce anti-modernists such as Proudhon and Fourier, who fused anti-Semitism with a critique of finance, capitalism and the industrial system. Money and power could be identified with the Jew. Marx was not immune to this type of conflation, and nor were the socialist movements that sprang up in the latter part of the nineteenth century.

The Jew, then, epitomised Simmel's *stranger*, 'always on the outside even when on the inside', questioning established conventions, especially in the name of universalism and humanism, and against parochialism. How could such a figure be admitted to full membership of the nation? On the other hand, the Jews were useful to modernising elites: they could be made to do the dirty work of tearing up old parochialisms, but were made to take the blame when the lower orders opposed the modernisers.

The Jews were caught up in a long list of incongruities as the modern 'gardening' state began its centralising process and its programme of imposing cultural uniformity: '*They were the opacity of the world fighting for clarity, the ambiguity of the world lusting for certainty*' (*Modernity and the Holocaust*: 56, emphasis in original).

Modern racism, modern anti-Semitism

Racism properly so-called, Bauman points out, is thoroughly modern, unthinkable without modern science and the modern state. Modernity, Bauman argues in curiously functionalist vein, 'created a demand for racism', for in a world where traditional, hereditary distinctions were vanishing, there was a need for a new form of ascriptive boundary drawing and maintenance (*Modernity and the Holocaust*: 61–2). But Bauman rightly points out that it is unhelpful to conflate modern racism with the always universally present prejudice or 'heterophobia'; racism is not simply inter-group resentment or 'prejudice', a mistaken premise in an influential work by the French commentator on racism, Pierre-André Taguieff (2001). For Bauman, 'heterophobia', a fear of the different, is simply a manifestation of a much wider phenomenon in which anxiety is aroused by a situation of uncertainty, a state of affairs potentially out of control. And in such circumstances fears can easily find anchor in one object or another, including cultural groups seen as different, something particularly common in fast-moving modernity where uncertainties multiply.

It should be pointed out that Bauman's own argument is not immune to criticism, for he provides no evidence or elaborate justification for the view that fear of the Other should be seen as simply part of a general fear of uncertainty. Bauman in effect conflates racism and eugenics, something evident in his claim that 'racism manifests the conviction that a certain category of human beings cannot be incorporated into the rational order' despite the best efforts of modern science, technology and 'cultural manipulation' (*Modernity and the Holocaust*: 65). And Bauman's characterisation of racism is too closely tied to a Nazi-type project, for he asserts that if conditions allow, racism demands that the offending category ought to be removed beyond the territory occupied by the group it offends, and that if such conditions do not exist then 'racism requires that the offending category is physically exterminated'. The problem with this definition becomes obvious if one considers the issue of the white enslavement of blacks, where the primary purpose is exploitation of labourers who cannot escape rather than expulsion from territory; indeed, proximity is important in this context so as to maintain physical control. Bauman's definition of racism seems to have been formulated to fit perfectly Nazi racism against Jews, but is inadequate when other kinds of cases of racial classification, discrimination and oppression are brought into consideration. Not only slavery, but more generally modern imperialist projects underwritten by racial ideologies, such as those of

British, French and other European imperial projects, are not easy to fit into Bauman's rather narrow definition of racism, although he is right to make a distinction between generalised prejudice and modern racism.

Bauman's reflections on racism are marked by constant attempts to tie racism to social engineering and modernity, rather than seeing it as a broader phenomenon. He is thus able also to make connections with a conception of modernity as the Enlightenment Project (as defined by him) writ large, and the notion of scientific racism (*Modernity and the Holocaust*: 68–9). Social engineering and the gardening state, as already pointed out, remain central to Bauman's conception of racism. Thus he remarks that Hitler's own language was replete 'with images of disease, infection, putrefaction, pestilence', allying gardening and medicine in his project of 'cleansing' Germany of Jews, a project that constantly invoked notions of racial health and hygiene, while the gardening metaphor of 'cultivation' was also explicitly deployed.

Of course, the accomplishment of the Holocaust also required that the German population at large, not just a few Nazi functionaries and leaders, should imbibe a murderous anti-Semitism. But Bauman concludes that the historical evidence shows that the Nazi propaganda machine by and large failed in its ideological and 'brainwashing' crusade (although many historians such as Herf (2006), have challenged this). *Kristallnacht*, the notorious mob violence against Jews, provoked widespread revulsion. This convinced the Nazi high command that they needed a different strategy to rid Germany of Jews, a new policy that involved not the arousal of emotions but a silent aversion of their gaze, an indifference to their fate. Administrative measures of discrimination, segregation and disempowerment against the Jews met with a more positive response among ordinary Germans, especially when Jews could be made scapegoats for a wider anxiety and insecurity.

Thus, mob violence came to be replaced by the quiet efficiency of the modern state bureaucracy. The Führer may have expressed a romantic *vision* of a racially cleansed society, but the *means* required a 'coolly rational bureaucratic process', staffed by experts, and the splitting up of the overall task into a large number of skilled but partial and specialised functions. Thus Bauman's concludes, drawing heavily from the work of Gordon: '*The murderous compound was made of a typically modern ambition of social design and engineering, mixed with the typically modern concentration of power, resources and managerial skills'* (*Modernity and the Holocaust*: 77, emphasis in original).

Post-Holocaust anti-Semitisms, for Bauman, are of a different type, more the result of cultural diffusion than a response to the actual presence of Jews; no wonder that a country like Japan has spawned a version of anti-Semitism, which is blamed by some Japanese for the impact of supposedly Jewish-inspired global economic trends on the tribulations of the Japanese economy (*Modernity and the Holocaust*: 78–9). In Western countries vestiges of anti-Semitism are being replaced by stronger forms of racism against newer post-Second World War immigrants. But the chances of the Holocaust being repeated in the West, for Bauman, are remote, in part because of the diminishing role of the state, which is abandoning larger and larger social spaces to market forces.

Thus, Bauman argues, although the Holocaust was most certainly a product of modernity-and modernity is after all still with us even if, seemingly paradoxically, in a postmodern form-its implementation was the product of a historically unique combination of factors that appeared in a specific period of German and global history, not necessarily ever to be repeated again. But there remain in Bauman's narrative, as I shall argue, important areas of ambiguity about the relationship between modernity, German history and the Holocaust.

The question of the uniqueness of the Holocaust

Both Stalin and Hitler were involved in murdering people in their millions, in a form of genocide unprecedented in history and not repeated since, although post-Stalin and post-Holocaust genocides have been a constant though not common feature of the world since the world war that brought Nazism to an end. What makes these types of genocides unlikely in Western democracies is that pluralism is now an entrenched, strongly institutionalised feature of this world. Absolute power of the sort required to carry out another Holocaust simply does not exist, for there are now too many countervailing spaces of power in modern societies (*Modernity and the Holocaust*: 93).

The unique conditions which led to the Holocaust, Bauman argues, included the adoption of this exterminatory anti-Semitism by a powerful, centralised state; emergency conditions produced by a period of war; and a largely accepting public that turned a blind eye to the horrors being perpetrated. However, while exterminatory anti-Semitism and a period of war were unique conditions, the rest may be regarded as 'normal' features of modernity, for centralised state power and generally quiescent populations are common in modern Western societies (*Modernity and the Holocaust*: 95). *But that this does not resolve the issue of the historical uniqueness of Germany bears repeating and will be discussed at greater length later.*

One defining aspect of modern civilisation, according to Bauman, is that a form of disciplined self-control of the body is now an institutionalised feature of everyday behaviour. While they are obviously not totally effective, there are cultural prohibitions against violence in normal interactions that were not present in non-modern times, and these are enforced by the fact of centralised power in the hands of the state.

Moreover, and here Bauman reinforces his already stated interpretation of the role of bureaucracy, in modernity violence has become a form of 'technique', freed from emotional investment; it has become coldly rational, something evident in the way in which B-52 bombers can be deployed by the USA and justified in instrumentally rational terms against an 'object' regarded as obviously 'undesirable': the communist Vietcong (*Modernity and the Holocaust*: 98).

This instrumental rationality, dissociated from questions of ends, that is, distanced from ethical and moral considerations, is a key feature of modern bureaucracy and is first and foremost an effect of the hierarchical division of labour that is so distinctive of modern bureaucracies. Two processes are involved here, Bauman argues. First, there is a functional division of labour in which the larger task is separated out into smaller, more specialised tasks; this has the effect of distancing any particular individual from concern with the larger project towards which the bureaucracy is working, to the extent that individual functionaries do not come into contact with the final outcomes and indeed may have difficulty in even visualising the final outcome. Commands can be given without full knowledge of their consequences. The real human beings who are being processed are reduced to abstract numbers and graphs in bureaucratic files. Any particular task becomes by itself meaningless, whether it is the issuing of a command to load bombs onto a plane or involvement in the production of deadly chemical weapons. Why would workers in a factory producing napalm accept responsibility for the burning of babies in Vietnam?

Second, the individual functionary in such a form of organised labour is more likely to worry about whether he or she is doing the job to the satisfaction of superiors than to fret about the overall objective of the organisation. *Technical* rather than *moral* responsibility comes to the forefront of concern; moral standards become irrelevant, eclipsed by standards of technical success (*Modernity and the Holocaust*: 101). And Bauman reiterates that bureaucratic procedures result in dehumanisation, for quantitative measures can reduce human beings to the status of objects.

This was not unique to Germany, Bauman argues, for it is an outcome of bureaucracy in general. In contemporary Western societies, for example, soldiers are told to hit targets, not kill people, employees are required to destroy competition, and officers of welfare agencies have supplementary benefit recipients as objects of their activities. The moral indifference that is engendered by such linguistic objectification, Bauman argues, means that resistance by human 'objects' is treated not as a moral issue but an inconvenience that is obstructing the smooth flow of bureaucratic practice.

'The overall conclusion', Bauman says, 'is that the bureaucratic mode of action, as it has been developed in the course of the modernization process, contains all the elements which proved necessary in the execution of genocidal tasks' (*Modernity and the Holocaust*: 104).

'Intentionalist' and 'functionalist' interpretations and the question of the uniqueness of Germany

Interpreters of the Holocaust have long been divided over what have come to be called 'intentionalist' and 'functionalist' explanations. The former emphasise that Hitler had decided from the start on the extermination of Jews, waiting only for a suitable opportunity, while the latter argue that while Hitler had a vision of Germany as free of Jews, this was not clearly articulated at the start and remained muddled even after the start of the war, and that the decision to actually exterminate the entire Jewish population emerged piecemeal, when attempts to simply 'export' them into other, non-German territories ran into intractable problems. Historical scholarship decisively favours the functionalists, Bauman suggests (*Modernity and the Holocaust*: 105), although as we shall see this is something of an exaggeration; but it serves to pinpoint Bauman's own position, for he is without doubt in the functionalist camp. Both schools of interpretation accept, of course, that whatever Hitler's intentions, without the involvement of a vast bureaucratic apparatus in problem-solving, his vision would not have progressed very far.

In implementing the tasks undertaken by the bureaucracy, the path had already been cleared by a variety of features of modern societies. The first was that violence had been removed, to a much greater extent than in the pre-modern past, away from everyday life to the state and its armed forces and police. This left the ordinary citizens literally disarmed in the face of organised state violence of the type involved in the genocide of the Jews.

Science played a crucial role in the Holocaust, Bauman points out. In general, it had marginalised questions of morality and ethics as merely subjective, leaving the field open for a form of instrumental, amoral rationality to dominate the cultural sphere. Science became 'morally blind and speechless', and thus without any resources with which to prevent co-operation or engender resistance against a morally monstrous project. Modern science also requires huge funds, so when the Nazi government came forth with generous grants for the equipment, laboratories and staff required for tasks which it set, but which were also of interest to scientists – for example those interested in eugenics – there was little questioning of the morality involved in the projects, for scientists had immunised themselves to moral qualms. They were even prepared to lose some colleagues with the 'wrong' (Jewish) type of ancestry in the pursuance of a greater goal: scientific progress. 'With relish', Bauman says, 'German scientists boarded the train drawn by the Nazi locomotive towards the brave, new racially purified and German-dominated world. Research projects grew more ambitious by the day and research institutes grew more populous and resourceful by the hour. Little else mattered' (*Modernity and the Holocaust*: 109; see also 126–7).

The Church, another institution that citizens would have regarded as a bastion of morality against evil-doing, also remained silent. Hitler, a Catholic by birth, was never excommunicated, which would at least have been a token gesture of Church disapproval. And whatever reservations ordinary citizens may have had, they became by and large silent 'bystanders' as a grisly, highly uncivilised project of mass murder unfolded against their fellow citizens (*Modernity and the Holocaust*: 111; Hilberg 1993).

Above all, the failure of political democracy to take root, its ignominious failure to withstand the Nazi onslaught in inter-war Germany, left Hitler and his colleagues free to act in a genocidal manner with scant opposition. Not only old elites, but autonomous labour organisations were swept aside as the 'gardening state' engaged in a murderous weeding-out of Jews. No vestige of cultural and political pluralism could stand in the way. Without a strongly institutionalised political democracy, Bauman avers, the genocidal potential of modernity can express itself unchecked.

But even in democracies, the dominance of instrumental rationality allows genocidal projects room to flourish. Only twenty years after the defeat of Nazism, scientists were involved in designing the 'electronic battlefield' to enable American generals to plan murderous attacks against the Vietnamese. In a prescient analysis, Bauman points out that information technology, allowing the use of force at a considerable distance, is even more effective as a dehumanising shield, the human objects who will feel the full force of deadly, explosive violence being too remote to engender moral uneasiness.

The issue of the uniqueness of the cultural and political history of Germany becomes for Bauman a marginal question; it is 'modernity' that takes centre stage. As we shall see, though, this creates serious problems for Bauman's interpretation of the Holocaust.

Why did victims co-operate with the Nazi project?

Hannah Arendt's *Eichmann in Jerusalem* has become famous for coining the phrase 'the banality of evil'; this was her way of dismissing Eichmann as a thoughtless, not particularly intelligent cog in the bureaucratic machine that attempted the annihilation of European Jewry, an interpretation that chimes well with Bauman's own representation of the role of the bureaucracy as a sort of machine, staffed by amoral technocrats and administrators, which had been received with disbelief by Jews and others who had attended the Eichmann trial. Arendt's criticisms of Jewish co-operation in the Holocaust had provoked even more outrage.

Arendt cites an estimation that suggests that if the Jewish leaders had withheld co-operation and instead tried to organise some sort of escape plan or had developed a strategy of going underground, perhaps half of those who were exterminated might have been able to save themselves (Arendt 1994: 125). Janina Bauman (1986), in her memoir of experiences as a young girl in Nazi-occupied Warsaw, often refers to the role of Jewish Councils (*Judenrate*) and the Jewish police who helped the Nazis create order and organise the shipping-out of Jews. Arendt's view was that Jewish co-operation was an integral and successful part of the Nazi plan of extermination (Arendt 1994: 124), something Bauman himself accepts as being the case (*Modernity and the Holocaust*: 121–2).

Bauman, though, expresses some reservations about Arendt's claims about the extent of Jewish co-operation (*Modernity and the Holocaust*: 117–18). Nevertheless, he feels compelled to ask: how can one explain even this degree of Jewish co-operation? How was it that Jewish elders and other Jewish elites, especially, complied with Nazi demands, thus making the Nazi task so much easier? Bauman argues that the answer lies in the way modern bureaucracies are able to induce required actions even among those for whom the actions are '*jarringly at odds with the vital interests of the actors*' (*Modernity and the Holocaust*: 122, emphasis in original). What a modern bureaucracy is able to do is to 'enlist the victims' own rational motives among the resources it can deploy in the pursuit of its task' (*Modernity and the Holocaust*: 123).

Bauman labels the bureaucratic mode of eliciting co-operation as 'The "save what you can" game' (*Modernity and the Holocaust*: 129). This involved, among other things pleading by particular Jews for special treatment, a strategy pursued by members of the Jewish Councils and the Jewish police forces, and by members of the Councils on behalf of other Jews. One sinister Nazi strategy was the creation of the so-called *Mischlinge*, Jews of mixed Jewish and German or other non-Jewish ancestry who could plead for leniency. But of course, any game in which special pleading was involved meant that the overall rules of the game, the destruction of most Jews, were thereby accepted and reinforced. The Church argued for the saving of converted Jews, while other Jews tried desperately to find ways of making out a special case for themselves; this only served to confirm that only a special kind of Jew deserved to be saved, an invidious strategy of exceptionalism in which divisions between Eastern and Western Jewry played into the gruesome Nazi 'game' of 'save what you can' which the Jews found themselves forced to play. Western Jews had long held prejudices that the Eastern, Yiddish-speaking Jews were uncouth and posed a threat to their own hard-earned respectability. This led to a false belief among the Western Jews that the fate of annihilation that they saw clearly awaiting Eastern Jews as they were bundled daily into trains, would somehow not be their fate as well. The fate of Polish Jews, it was thought, was surely not that which awaited Dutch, French and German Jews; this sort of complacency, Bauman argues, militated against the emergence of a unified Jewish response to Nazi policy. And of course, it was only an inter-communal version of the special pleading that went on within the Western Jewish communities suffering immense hardships in a struggle for survival in cruel conditions in the ghettos. The quiescence of Western Jews and their leaders enabled the Nazis to engage in a staggered but relatively smooth process of annihilation of all the Jews, Western and Eastern, the urban bourgeoisie as well as the 'immigrant' Jews from the *shtetl*.

Every time one trainload of Jews was seen speeding off to the camps, the rest reasoned that 'it was necessary to sacrifice the few in order to save the many' (*Modernity and the Holocaust*: 133, quoting Hilberg). At each stage of the ghastly process, it was in one sense 'rational' for groups and individuals to save what and whom they could, desperately aiming for exemption, but thereby, even if 'obliquely', co-operating. But this individual and group rationality served Nazi purposes very well, Bauman argues. It saved them the difficulties that would have arisen if they had had to organise and supervise the day-to-day existence and welfare of Jews in the ghettos and to maintain law and order, tasks that were undertaken by the Jewish Councils. At the same time, it enabled Jews to retain a semblance of their own way of life and some degree of self-government. However, the end result was that only a handful of Nazi officers were required to exercise control over thousands of Jews.

The terrible irony was that the Jews and their leaders were left to find rational solutions to problems created by a bureaucratic and ideological project that lacked all but instrumental rationality. Like 'K' in Kafka's *The Castle*, Jews kept responding rationally – for example by trying to be economically useful and productive for the Germans – but were doomed to fail because the Nazi project was not based on any normal form of rationality. As Bauman puts it, 'Before the twisted road wound up in Auschwitz, many bridges on the River Kwai were built by skilful and keen Jewish hands' (*Modernity and the Holocaust*: 138). The strategy nearly succeeded for a while when military commanders found that the only skilled labourers they had were Jewish; but this was a rational response, soon overwhelmed by Nazi orders to continue with the liquidation of Jews, something which made no economic sense. The Nazi project had never met the requirements of economic rationality, something that Arendt had emphasised very early in her reflections on the Holocaust, for an enormous amount of industrial infrastructure which could otherwise have been used in the war was instead used in the project to rid Germany, and then Europe, of its Jews.

Many members of the Councils did refuse to follow Nazi orders. A number committed suicide; for example, the whole of the Jewish Council of Bereza Kartuska committed suicide at their meeting of 1 September 1942 (*Modernity and the Holocaust*: 140–1). However, most succumbed to the rules of the game, which then dictated that it was reasonable to sacrifice the few in order to save the many. They rationalised their actions in a variety of ways, for example by claiming that they did not decide who died but only who lived, or that it was necessary to 'cut off a limb in order save the body', or that their place might be taken by councillors who were even more cruel.

The rationality of 'saving the many by sacrificing the few' made sense only in a situation where some indeed would be spared, a lie that the Nazis managed to create and perpetuate. But this also created moral corruption in the victims, as they desperately sought to save themselves or their families and friends. Bauman insists – and one can only agree – that it would be unfair to judge those who succumbed to this desire, given the grotesque situation in which they found themselves (*Modernity and the Holocaust*: 144). The rich tried to bribe their way out of this nightmare by offering fortunes, hoping in vain to escape the fate of the poorer members of the community. Life in the ghetto was a zero-sum game, with self-preservation the only form of success.

For Bauman the nightmare and the desperation of the ghetto in the end reflected nothing more than 'modern bureaucratic rationality', for the false choices offered to the victims served the purpose of achieving 'maximum results with minimum costs and efforts' (*Modernity and the Holocaust*: 149).

Bauman's dissection of the morality of the ghetto appears to be a powerful indictment of an uncritical admiration for bureaucratic rationality while at the same time throwing light on what Arendt had described as the darkest chapter in a dark history.

The perpetrators and the 'agentic state': the normality of cruelty in special social settings

If it can be shown that there was some form of rationality in the manner in which victims were able to co-operate with their oppressors, and Bauman succeeds in showing how this might be the case, we still need to understand how apparently ordinary people, the foot soldiers of the Nazis who carried out abominable acts, were able to act as they did. Apart from some who were sadistic, it appears to have been established beyond reasonable doubt that the agents of mass murders were, in other ways, normal individuals who loved their families, cared for their friends and so forth. What enabled them to shoot and gas people in their hundreds of thousands in acts of brutality and mass murder that seem unimaginable to us?

It would be more comforting to believe that the police battalions and sections of the armed forces that engaged in these actions were in some or other way not normal, but carried in their personalities a pathology that enabled them to carry out mass murder, that made them act in evil ways. One such interpretation had been attempted by Adorno and his colleagues in a widely read but equally criticised study entitled *The Authoritarian Personality* (1950) where they had argued that those inclined to participate, in one form or another, in Nazi genocide were indeed pathological. That is, they were particularly prone to obedience to authority and cruelty towards the weak, and the assumption was that Nazi Germany had had a particularly large number of such individuals. In the final analysis, this study, instead of providing an adequate explanation, had ended up in unhelpful tautologies: 'Nazism was cruel because Nazis were cruel; the Nazis were cruel because cruel people tended to become Nazis' (*Modernity and the Holocaust*: 153).

Instead, Bauman turns for an explanation of how ordinary Germans (neither more nor less ordinary than the citizens of other modern societies) had committed mass murder to a series of controversial experiments conducted by the American psychologist Stanley Milgram (1974). Milgram had concluded that, in particular social settings, perfectly normal people were capable of otherwise incomprehensible cruelty.

In his experiments, participants, who were paid to take part, were told that the purpose was to test and improve learning outcomes. Individuals were told to administer electric shocks to other individuals when they appeared to give incorrect answers. Before he began his experiments Milgram had asked colleagues and others what they thought would occur; there was a strong consensus that as the intensity of the shocks grew, more and more of those administering the shocks would drop out, unwilling to inflict cruelty on those who were supposedly being experimented upon. However, only some 30 per cent withdrew consent when asked to administer high levels of electric shock, while the intensity of the shock they were prepared to inflict was up to three times as much as expected by professional psychologists and members of the public. In fact, those to whom shocks were being applied were actors and no actual surges of electricity were inflicted.

Although the experiments have been the subject of considerable criticism (the criticisms are discussed later), Bauman concludes that Milgram had '*proved*' that inhumanity is a matter of social relationships. As the latter are technically perfected, so is the 'capacity and the efficiency of the social production of inhumanity' (*Modernity and the Holocaust*: 154, emphasis in original). Bauman thus agrees with the conclusion that because the experimenter had scientific authority as the expert in charge, and took responsibility for the actions, ordinary people were willing to put aside their feelings of compassion or revulsion and continued to apply ever more dangerous levels of electric surges. Another aspect of Milgram's experiments that Bauman emphasises is that the greater the visibility of the subjects of the experiments and the proximity of the subjects to those taking part, the greater the reluctance to administer shocks. In other words, there is an 'inverse ratio of readiness to cruelty and proximity to its victims' (*Modernity and the Holocaust*: 155).

Other aspects of the experiment are also regarded by Bauman as important, firstly the fact that the experimenting scientist and the (unknowing) perpetrator were united, while the subject was in effect treated as an object. The collective nature of the action enabled acts to be committed which might have been less likely if the actor were alone. Moreover, there was a sequential increase in the severity of the actions, which created a moral dilemma: at what point was it appropriate to stop? And if the action was stopped, this served only to underline that previous acts of commission were morally reprehensible. That the moral dilemma is felt by a group means that sequential, collective action binds the perpetrators together in sustaining immoral or criminal action. This type of momentum is reinforced also by the fact that it is easier to rationalise cruel actions if they are underwritten by the authority of science, which is precisely what happened here. What happened in Milgram's experiments, for Bauman, shows how technology can be given moral licence, as the 'needs' of science and the experiment can neutralise moral misgivings. Bauman's previous analysis of bureaucracy becomes relevant here, for the whole process is even more effective when there is a chain of command, as in a bureaucracy, where it becomes easy for intermediaries in the ladder to see themselves as engaged only in technical tasks devoid of responsibility for the overall project. And the whole series of cruel acts is underwritten by an authority that takes ultimate responsibility, enabling a shifting or responsibility. In situations of this type, Milgram argues, and Bauman agrees, that actors seem to exist in an 'agentic' state, where they forgo any autonomy; they accept the definition of the situation as defined by those in authority. In bureaucratic organisations, Bauman extrapolates, there occurs a situation of 'free floating responsibility', for responsibility becomes essentially 'unpinnable' (*Modernity and the Holocaust*: 163), and moral responsibility is incapacitated.

Milgram introduced into his experiments a further element which Bauman also regards as pertinent to the Holocaust. In some experiments subjects found themselves under the authority of more than just the one experimenter, and the experimenters were made to disagree openly and argue over the instructions. In this new, more plural situation, as soon as disagreements broke out among the experts, a substantial majority of the subjects refused to co-operate. Not surprisingly, Bauman draws two conclusions from these additional investigations: first, that '*pluralism is the best preventative medicine against morally normal people engaging in morally abnormal actions*'; and secondly, that the Nazis 'must have first destroyed the vestiges of political pluralism to set off on projects like the Holocaust'. '*The voice of the individual moral conscience is best heard in the tumult of political and social discord*' (*Modernity and the Holocaust*: 165–6, all emphases in original).

Bauman also refers to experiments conducted by Zimbardo (Zimbardo, Hanley and Banks 1973), where students were divided into two groups, with one given sole authority, in the role of prison guards, over the other group, who were given the role of prisoners and suitably clothed and deprived of their previous identities as much as possible. Humiliating rules and regulations were devised that served to dehumanise the 'prisoners'. Very soon, the 'prison guards' heaped even more humiliation upon the hapless 'prisoners', for example by making them clean toilets with their bare hands. In effect, these normal and to all purposes decent American young men began to behave in a manner not unlike the 'monsters' who had humiliated prisoners in the Auschwitz and Treblinka concentration camps. Bauman, though, disagrees with any interpretation which seems to suggest that hidden inside every normal human being is a 'latent Eichmann'. Rather, the viciousness, he argues, stems from a vicious social arrangement, not from the latent viciousness of the participants. What was important was that some people were given total, untrammelled power over others; what the experiments demonstrated was the ease with which 'most people slip into the role requiring cruelty or at least moral blindness', as long as this has been sanctioned by an authority regarded as legitimate by the perpetrators (*Modernity and the Holocaust*: 168).

There is of course a curiosity about Bauman's use of Milgram and Zimbardo: they confirm sociological accounts that privilege social conditions in the production of immoral behaviour, something that early in *Modernity and the Holocaust* Bauman had rejected as too reductionist, although he had done so by denying that society, or society alone (Bauman is ambiguous about this), produces morality. I will come back to this issue at various points in this book.

Evaluating Bauman's Holocaust thesis, 1: questions of racism, functionalist and intentionalist interpretations, and necessary and sufficient conditions

It would not be unfair to say that before the publication of *Modernity and the Holocaust* in 1989, Bauman was a relatively minor figure even in British sociology, and certainly lacked a serious international profile. *Legislators and Interpreters* did have some impact, but the real transformation in his reputation began with his book on the Holocaust. It was awarded the European Amalfi Prize for Sociology in 1989, and by the very nature of its subject matter had a particularly large impact in Germany (Varcoe 1998). But it was also widely read elsewhere in Europe and the USA because debates about modernity and postmodernity were in full swing, and following on from Bauman's espousal of a postmodern stance in *Legislators*, his stark indictment of modernity and its complicity in the Holocaust guaranteed the book a wide readership.

Bauman's lucid prose and the stark simplicity of its main theses also played a part; the book has a clarity and readability that were to become a hallmark of Bauman's work. All these traits had been well to the fore in *Legislators* too, and had helped gain that book a wide readership and may well have created a sense of anticipation about where his sharp intellect was going to be deployed next, especially with regard to debates around modernity.

In assessing the merits of *Legislators* I have pointed out that for me a key problem of Bauman's argument lay in the curious manner in which he marginalised the issue of historical specificity as opposed to abstract argument around modernity and postmodernity. With regard to the Enlightenment, Bauman had displayed a tendency to over-generalise from the French experience to modernity in general, while wanting to maintain at the same time that his argument was particularly applicable *only* to *some* aspects of the French Enlightenment. In the case of the Holocaust, the issue of the historical specificity of the German case is central to how one assesses Bauman's argument.

However, before addressing that issue let me direct attention to two others, which are related to the question of historical specificity but which I will treat separately for ease of exposition. One of these I have already alluded to, regarding Bauman's definition of racism: I have pointed out in relation to his definition that although he is right in rejecting a conflation between 'prejudice' and modern racism, he provides a definition that generalises from the specificity of Nazi anti-Semitism and its racial state in such a way that his definition of racism fails to encompass the forms of racism that were embedded in and legitimised European imperialist and colonialist projects, an issue to which I will return.

There is a second problem with the way in which Bauman frames his overall argument. As I have highlighted earlier, he claims that 'modern civilization' was a *necessary* but not a *sufficient* condition for the Holocaust. But there is a crucial ambiguity here; it may have been a necessary condition, but that does not necessarily mean that it was the *overriding*, or *the most important* necessary condition, which is the conclusion that Bauman comes to in his book. Another way into this issue is to consider what Bauman says about anti-Semitism as a causal factor: anti-Semitism, he says, was also a *necessary* but not a *sufficient* condition in explaining the Holocaust. But this too does not resolve the issue of *how important* anti-Semitism was in explaining the Holocaust, especially in comparison with 'modern civilization' or 'modernity'. Was it *only a minor necessary condition?* That certainly seems to be Bauman's argument, for he is adamant that Germany was no more anti-Semitic, and possibly less anti-Semitic, than many other European countries, especially France. But his bald argument can easily be interpreted differently, indeed turned around completely. Bauman's is a 'functionalist' rather than 'intentionalist' account of the Holocaust, emphasising that the Final Solution was not intended from the start but only emerged piecemeal during the Third Reich; and it also forms part of his argument foregrounding the role of bureaucracy, the concentration of the means of violence in the state and the role of science and technology in explaining the Holocaust, and thus treating anti-Semitism as important only in setting the process in motion without being a central motivating force. In a remarkable afterthought ('The Holocaust's Life as a Ghost', 2000a: 16–17), Bauman has even said that 'the presence of a quantity of Jew-haters' is not even a *necessary* condition of a Holocaust-type genocide, but this is so implausible an argument that it may be set it aside as a momentary aberration on Bauman's part, although it might also be regarded as a slippage that says something about how little causal efficacy Bauman gives to anti-Semitism.

But even Bauman's less extreme argument in Holocaust does not stand up to scrutiny. Arguably, anti-Semitism was not just a minor necessary condition, one that merely set the process in motion, but a hugely important condition of the Holocaust throughout its occurrence, an issue that is simply elided in Bauman's abstract formulation of necessary and sufficient conditions. Although many others were murdered during Hitler's period in power, the major defining feature of the Holocaust was its desire to rid Germany of all Jews, simply on the basis of their Jewishness, and it succeeded in killing something like a third of all European Jews and practically all Eastern European Jews (Ray 2011: 170). The Roma population – 'Gypsies' – were the only other people systematically targeted, but they were not as central to the project as Jews. Bauman's general arguments about necessary and sufficient conditions obscure the question of the weight to be assigned to the two necessary but not sufficient conditions, that is, modernity and anti-Semitism. Indeed, within the terms of his formulation, they both could be equally important necessary conditions and could together be the sufficient conditions for the perpetration of the Holocaust. The statements Bauman makes about necessary and sufficient conditions clarify very little if anything at all about the relative importance of anti-Semitism and modernity. They thus obscure as much as they illuminate.

This is an issue that also becomes salient in considering the role of Hitler in the Holocaust, which is given importance in more 'intentionalist' accounts. It hardly bears repeating that Hitler became early in his life a rabid anti-Semite, and for him the idea of a *Judenfrei* Germany was an overriding goal. So how important (or necessary) was he as an individual in explaining the Holocaust?

Despite Bauman's attempts to downplay the role of Hitler, it is important to note that Bauman *approvingly* quotes the following passage from Ruth Gordon's historical work: 'when the millions of Jewish and other victims pondered their own imminent deaths and wondered "why must I die ...?" probably the simplest answer would have been that power was totally concentrated in one man, and that man happened to hate their race' (*Modernity and the Holocaust*: 77). As Kershaw has argued, and this is an interpretation generally accepted by historians, 'Without Hitler's fanatical will to destroy Jewry, which crystallized only by 1941 into a realizable aim to exterminate physically the Jews of Europe, the Holocaust would almost certainly not have come about' (Kershaw 1985: 106; see also Kershaw 1997, 1998). Moreover, as Kershaw has also pointed out, the debate between functionalist and intentionalist schools over-simplifies a complex issue of historical explanation: the role of the civil service bureaucracy was also crucial, as was the active co-operation of the leaders of German industry who manufactured the 'death machinery' and 'set up their factories at the concentration camps' (Kershaw: 1985: 106; see also Oxaal 1991: 164–5). Hitler's role should not be exaggerated – a 'Hitlerist' account of the Holocaust is implausible – but it certainly does not merit the perfunctory treatment it receives in Bauman's analysis, especially when it is combined with a narrative in which anti-Semitism has a relatively minor role.

Thus more needs to be said about Bauman's interpretation of anti-Semitism. In wanting to reinforce his thesis regarding the modernity of the Holocaust, Bauman also ends up over-emphasising the modernity of the type of anti-Semitism that was involved in Nazism. Bauman argues that gradual Jewish emancipation and the assimilation of more and more Jews led to their occupying a particular role as 'strangers' in German society. They were 'slimy'. They were not as visible in modern Germany as they had been in pre-modern times, being ghettoised both geographically and socially. This, Bauman argues, led to a specific form of anti-Semitism, in which the Jew became visualised as a hidden saboteur, able to play a destructive role in the process of capitalist transformation which had adverse effects on a range of strata in German society. Bauman cites Arendt in this context: 'Jews had been able to escape from Judaism into conversion; from Jewishness there was no escape'

(*Modernity and the Holocaust*: 59). Hence the significance of the scientific racism, of which modern anti-Semitism became a part, which relied on pseudo-scientific concepts of racial hygiene and created fears of the degeneration of the Aryan race. But as Oxaal argues, it is unconvincing to make too rigid a distinction between previous and modern forms of anti-Semitism; the two were intimately interlinked, with large periods of pre-modern and Christian anti-Semitisms providing a necessary breeding ground for modern Jew-hatred (see also Bauer 2002: 72–3; Pulzer 2010: 118; Stone 2010: 160–202). Jew-hatred is difficult to conceive of without the nourishment it found in Christianity and deeply embedded pre-modern anti-Semitism. Moreover, the same modernity that produced scientific racism also gave rise to notions of individual freedom and equality that enabled Jewish assimilation in the first place, and had led to resistance to anti-Semitism in cities such as Vienna and Paris (Oxaal 1991: 159). Bauman is too ready to dismiss the peculiarities of Western and central European culture as opposed to universal features of 'modernity', which is not surprising given his overall thesis about the centrality of 'modernity' to the Holocaust. It is worth mentioning in this context that Nazi anti-modernism is also neglected by Bauman.[2] The Nazis were not only repulsed by the modernist avant-garde in art, but were also hostile to Enlightenment ideals of liberalism and equality, which is why the most important Enlightenment-derived element in their work was the science of race and the doctrines of racial *inequality* which had their origins in the eighteenth century.

And here the imperialist legacy becomes important.[3] Scientific racism was strongly linked with historically specific European imperialist and colonialist projects which also became bound up with class and sexuality in the fast-changing Europe of the nineteenth century (Rattansi 2007: 33).

In this context it is crucial to remember that there were important continuities between Nazi genocide and what Olusoga and Erichsen (2010) have called 'Germany's forgotten genocide' in the territory that is now Namibia. Indeed, Hermann Göring, in his defence at the Nuremberg trials, pointed to the irony that the prosecuting powers, in the process of building up their colonial empires, had used tactics of mass killing and forms of racist ideology not far removed from the crimes for which they were trying German Nazis

(Olusoga and Erichsen 2010: 5). The Germans, in pursuit of their own imperial ambitions, had committed genocide in May 1883 against the Herero and Nama peoples of South-West Africa who had tried to resist German occupation of their lands. Concentration camps had been set up where African prisoners were worked and starved to death, and many of the same German soldiers and bureaucrats involved had, during the Nazi period, used the ideologies of racial superiority and the technologies of the concentration camp which they had developed in their African conquest (see also Stone 2010: 232–9). Note, too, Hitler's admiration for the British Empire, his project of colonising Eastern Europe and his notion of Ukrainians and Russians as the 'negroes' of Europe (Stone 2010: 213–22; Baranowski 2010; Shaw 2007: 37–47; see Jones 2006 for a comprehensive discussion of the Holocaust as part of genocide studies).

The overall marginalisation of the historical specificity of German and European history in Bauman's *Modernity and the Holocaust* remains one of its most glaring weaknesses, and as we shall see also haunts his analysis of the role of bureaucracy and instrumental rationality. The problem of the absence of any reference to the imperial and colonial projects of the European powers in an understanding of Nazism and the Holocaust, though, is not Bauman's alone; it is part and parcel of the Eurocentrism of much of the historiography of the Holocaust, including that which emphasises the uniqueness of Germany and its bureaucracy.

Evaluating Bauman's Holocaust thesis, 2: the role of bureaucracy and the uniqueness of Germany

The intrinsic nature of the bureaucratic organisation of tasks, the instrumental rationality underpinning it, the resulting tendency to a form of dehumanisation of those subject to bureaucratic action, the ability of bureaucrats to distance themselves from the overall project of the bureaucracy and the state by simply following orders and focusing on technical issues – all of these of course play an absolutely pivotal role in Bauman's thesis that it was the modernity of these features that enabled the Holocaust to take place.

Bauman's inspiration for his understanding of the nature and role of bureaucracy was Max Weber, who had analysed bureaucratic authority as one ideal typical form of rule, which contrasted with traditional, charismatic and value-laden forms of authority. However, scholars with a deep understanding of Weber have thrown doubt on the form of appropriation of his work by Bauman. Most importantly, they have argued that Bauman ignores the fact that Weber's analysis was heavily influenced by the particular historical context of bureaucracy, elite power and state formation that confronted Germany at the time when Weber wrote.

Du Gay (1999) has pointed out, for instance, that some of Weber's critical remarks on bureaucracy cannot be understood without taking into account that Weber was concerned about the appointment by the Kaiser of bureaucrats to leading political positions for which they were unsuited, for what Wilhelmine Germany needed according to Weber were good politicians, accountable to elected assemblies, who could take bold initiatives and genuinely lead (see also O'Kane 1997: 51–2). Du Gay also argues that Bauman misinterprets Weber as fearing the domination of bureaucratic rationality, when, first, Weber had not seen rationalisation as a monolithic linear process, and second, he had praised bureaucracy for its depersonalisation of recruitment procedures by setting strict qualification requirements which ensured not only a degree of expertise but ensured the independence of the bureaucracy from domination by traditional elites and other political appointees. Bureaucracy, with its own ethos, was a bulwark against patronage and corruption. Moreover, Weber had seen it as important to the functioning of democracy, for it involved, as part of its ethos, equality of treatment within and by the bureaucracy; bureaucracy, for Weber, was part of a process of democratisation. By ripping Weber's analysis from its historical context as well as by reading him tendentiously, Bauman emphasises bureaucracy as allowing a distancing from morality (Waxman 2009: 99; Stone 2010: 122–5), rather than seeing state bureaucracies as having their own ethical imperatives, which formed one element in a plural, democratic order where other organisations and practices had other moral foundations and goals and where political democracy could act as a check on bureaucratic power. Fine rightly points to Weber's acute understanding that bureaucrats could not be seen as cogs in a machine, thoughtless pen-pushers, for even the act of 'following a rule' – assuming for an unrealistic moment that that is all a real bureaucrat does – requires a degree of interpretation and moral evaluation (2000: 29). Bauman's reading of Weber yields a poor sociological harvest very far from the riches to be obtained from a rigorous grasp of Weber's analysis and thinking.

What Weber had feared was the domination of bureaucracies by external, 'substantive' doctrinaire ideologies and religious zeal. And as Michael Mann points out, this is precisely what happened in Nazi Germany: the bureaucracy became subject to Nazi politicisation and in this sense, in addition to exercising instrumental rationality, it functioned more like an apparatus that was dominated by what Weber had called 'value rationality', this being, in this case, the overriding evil goal of the annihilation of Jews (Mann 2005: 188). Mann in turn, however, fails to see that the notion of charisma has applicability to the role of Hitler (Noakes 2004: 35–6, although Noakes does not explicitly refer to Weber, drawing more upon Kershaw; see also Stone 2010: 124, who does refer to Weber and provides a re-interpretation of Weber's rationalisation thesis). As Vetlesen (2005) expresses it, under the Nazis, the state bureaucracy was 'de-bureaucratized', for in fact it was not allowed to function as a bureaucracy in Bauman's sense of following due process and procedure. More often than not it was by-passed, with a blatant disregard for the rule of law, and in the process the bureaucracy that was inherited by the Nazis from the Weimar era was radically transformed and 'revolutionized'. Du Gay has gone so far as to argue that Nazi leaders 'sought to turn bureaucrats into something else entirely: a cross between pre-modern serfs and political activists' (2000: 50), and in complete contrast to Bauman, Vetlesen suggests that in the 1930s and 1940s the bureaucracy under the Nazis increasingly 'assumed *premodern* features' (2005: 45, my emphasis).

Moreover, it has been argued by many historians that the state bureaucracy had a power, authority and legitimacy in Germany that it did not possess elsewhere, for Germany had to some degree a more authoritarian culture in which the population had become habituated to taking orders from officials and in which bureaucratic practices had permeated all spheres of social life (Varcoe 1998: 59). *German bureaucracy was, in many ways, unique in the position it occupied and this singularity needs to be recognised rather than assimilated to a more generalised interpretation of bureaucracy within modernity.* However, this is not to take on board all of the *Sonderweg* ('special path') interpretation, which sees too direct a connection between nineteenth-century German history and the rise of Hitler, a view decisively undermined since the publication of Blackbourn and Ely's *The Peculiarities of German History* (1984). They point out that the *Sonderweg* thesis relies too heavily on discredited views that see Germany as 'peculiar' in not having undergone a 'proper' bourgeois revolution of the French and British type, when in fact each country, including Germany, had diverse patterns of 'bourgeois' development. They point out that neither the French Revolution of 1789 nor the English Civil War of the mid-seventeenth century – both assumed by the *Sonderweg* thesis to be bourgeois revolutions – can be seen as 'bourgeois' revolutions in which the bourgeoisie acceded to power (see also Varcoe 1998: 61; Noakes 2004: 123–5).

Bauman, of course, is aware that the rise to power of Hitler and the Nazis occurred in the context of unique historical circumstances, but he dismisses the significance of this too easily, and the effect is to completely misunderstand the singularity and unique functioning of the Nazi bureaucracy. The question of the historical uniqueness of German history is highly complex and has several other interrelated strands that are worth teasing out and deployed in an evaluation of Bauman's interpretation of the Holocaust.

To begin with, one of the broader issues which weakens Bauman's thesis, and to which he gives little consideration, is why the Holocaust did not happen in France or Britain or the USA. After all, these were no less modern than Germany, and possibly even more so. *And why was it that Italian fascism did not take an anti-Semitic form* (see Mann 2004: 93–138)? If modernity is to be given such causal primacy in explaining the Holocaust, then the question of these historical specificities looms large and cannot be ducked. It is difficult to avoid the conclusion that there were indeed unique aspects of the course of German history which led to the Holocaust, thus severely weakening Bauman's thesis (Bauer 2002: 75; Oxaal 1991: 160). In this context, it is worth mentioning Best's argument (2013) that Bauman has a tendency to conflate the *process* of the Holocaust, which did involve specifically modern elements such as the bureaucracy, industrial technology and so forth, with the causal explanation of *why* the Holocaust happened, which enables him to marginalise issues of historical specificity. Another way of putting it is by way of Stone's argument that Bauman's argument vacillates between a strong version which attributes primacy to bureaucracy in the genesis of the Holocaust and a weaker one in which bureaucracy and other modern features were merely conduits for anti-Semitic goals set elsewhere, by the Nazi leadership (Stone 2010: 122). Stone goes so far as to argue that Bauman's emphasis on modernity ends up by 'telling us nothing more than the *reductio ad absurdum* that the Holocaust occurred in the modern age' (Stone 2010: 144). Modernity in any case is a highly abstract conceptual construction and does not in itself have the qualities of an actor or agent, something also emphasised by Ray; as we have seen with *Legislators and Interpreters*, Bauman has an unfortunate tendency to reification, giving agent-like or actor-like properties to abstractions, especially 'modernity'.

With regard to the exceptional path of German history, Bauman underplays to an unwarranted degree the specific permutations and vicissitudes of anti-Semitism in the Germany of the 1880s, in the years immediately preceding the First World War and in the crisis-ridden period after the war. These were specific to Germany. In the 1880s several populist movements and uprisings had taken a distinctly anti-Semitic turn; in the period before the war, in the twentieth century, historians have identified the period from 1916 to 1923 as one in which anti-Semitism gained considerable ground and emerged from its more marginal position in German political culture to an increasingly dominant one; and the severe economic crises of depression, inflation and political instability, exacerbated by violent street battles between left-wing and right-wing groups, fed the growth of more radical anti-Semitic mass parties which pre-dated but prepared the ground for Nazi anti-Semitic ideologies. Heilbronner, in whose excellent historiographical survey are highlighted many of these issues regarding the specificities of German history, concludes that these factors, in the context of the regular and demoralising crises of the Weimar Republic, 'contributed more than anything else to the dehumanization of German society and its elites' (2004: 11) and their subsequent embrace of Hitler and the Nazi party. Similar factors eventually led masses of ordinary Germans to vote for the Nazi party, in the hope of acquiring 'bread, jobs and hopes for the future' (Heilbronner 2004: 9). Moreover, populist anti-Semitism and that of the upper echelons of the Nazi party also had a specific history. The disastrous hyper-inflation of the years of 1922–23, together with a sense of national humiliation, anger at the excessive reparations demanded by the victors and massive unemployment, combined with hostility to the more Orthodox and less assimilated Jews who fled from Eastern Europe to Germany (Mann 2005: 182) and created particularly fertile ground for anti-Semitism among students and the intelligentsia (Heilbronner 2004: 13; Stone 2010: 125). The anti-Semitism of the Nazi leadership was tactically underplayed by it in the period after 1929 in an attempt to garner support from a wider range of Germans (Mann 2005: 190), and virulent anti-Semitic propaganda was unleashed by the Nazis only after 1933. Anti-Semitism also had regional variations in Germany. The specific character of German nationalism also needs to be taken into account (Mann 2005: 181–3). There is thus a complex relationship between German nationalism, popular anti-Semitism, that of the elites, the anti-Semitism of the Nazi leadership and the complex variety of reasons, other than anti-Semitism, why Germans voted in large numbers for the Nazi party. All of this serves only to underline the specificity of German history, most especially in the aftermath of the First World War, which eventually led to the Holocaust. The idea of 'modernity' as a causal factor simply fails to do justice to these peculiarities of German economic, political and cultural history and the complex evolution of the murderous version of Nazi anti-Semitism which was ultimately to play a decisive role in the Final Solution.[4]

Moreover, as Mann has stressed, a group that, like the Nazi party, promised to end the quasi-civil war between rightists and leftists and 'bang their heads together' again involved particular German circumstances that led to the rise of the Nazis (Mann 2005: 183, 233). The fear of socialism and Bolshevism thus had much to do with the vote for Hitler, more so than a hatred of Jews, although the Nazis had already planted the seeds of an ideology which combined Bolshevism with anti-Semitism; and the Nazis offered, too, an alluring vision of national rebirth (Noakes 2004: 29).

Bauman also under-emphasises the fact that Nazi bureaucracy

was operating under totalitarian conditions, in a terror state. For one thing, this means that he simply ignores the fact that it was dangerous for officials to express dissenting views. Indeed, it is particularly evident that Bauman fails to examine historical evidence on the actual beliefs of the bureaucrats involved in the Holocaust. On the one hand, he takes their behaviour as an indication that they had abdicated from all moral judgement, but he cites no evidence that bureaucrats had no moral qualms (O'Kane 1997: 47). At the same time, it is arguable that in emphasising the routine, amoral attitude of bureaucrats Bauman also ignores the fact that many were highly committed anti-Semites who relished the tasks they were undertaking (Lozowick 2002). In this sense, Bauman appears to have been too much influenced by Arendt's view of Eichmann as a thoughtless bureaucrat (Arendt 1994).

After a thorough study of Eichmann and other key bureaucrats, Lozowick's verdict on the bureaucrats, Arendt's judgement and by implication Bauman's interpretation could not be more damning:

> this was a group of people completely aware of what they were doing, people with high ideological motivation, people of initiative and dexterity who contributed far beyond what was necessary ... They hated Jews and thought getting rid of them would be to Germany's good. They knew that not everybody thought this way, and they deliberately hid information that might have deterred others from cooperating. While most of them sat behind desks rather than behind machine guns, from time to time some were called to face flesh and blood Jews and decide their fate, and this they did, ferociously, without batting an eyelid ... The facts that stare us in the face ... indicate the opposite of Arendt's thesis: there was nothing banal about the evil of Eichmann and his comrades. (Lozowick 2002: 8)[5]

As far as Eichmann is concerned, and especially in so far as he serves to typify the task-oriented, amoral bureaucrat, the point is that Arendt ignored evidence that was already available that Eichmann held strong anti-Semitic views and proclaimed himself – especially while in exile in Argentina but in other contexts too – extremely proud of his role in the annihilation of Jews (Cesarani 2005; Stangneth 2014). Far from simply being a cog in a machine, carrying out orders, he took many initiatives and was involved in the formulation of many exterminatory policies, as Lozowick also points out.

Bauman surprisingly also fails to mention Adorno and Horkheimer's *Dialectic of Enlightenment*, which expresses a view similar to his, although Stone thinks that Adorno and Horkheimer's interpretation was in some respects more sophisticated than Bauman's (Stone 2010: 114–15, 124). Questions thus arise about the originality of Bauman's interpretation (Bauer 2002: 71; Ray 2011: 173; Adler 2000: 71, 80, 97n),[6] although it is important to remember that Bauman is clear about the extent to which he was relying on historians, as opposed to sociologists; it appears that it is to the latter that the book may be seen to be primarily addressed.

There is more to be said about the totalitarian context, for the German bureaucracy under the Nazis was operating in exceptional circumstances of war and genocide in a system dominated by the principle of rule by Hitler (Fine 2000: 29–30). This made for distrust and an unwillingness to raise moral concerns, for betrayal could have unpleasant consequences. It is simply illegitimate to extrapolate from actions under these conditions to bureaucratic behaviour in general, or in 'modernity.

It is worth noting, too, that part of the reason why individuals like Eichmann had so much room for independent action and initiative was that the Nazi bureaucracy was very far from being the efficient, rule-bound, disciplined machine that emerges from Bauman's account. Kershaw among many others has underlined the chaotic and improvised manner of decision-taking, the proliferation of decision-making centres, the absence of coherent planning for middle-range goals, the lack of collective decision-making, all ensuring that the Nazi bureaucracy was 'a *jungle* of competing and overlapping agencies' of rule (Kershaw 1997: 96, my emphasis; Fine 2000: 30; Cesarani 2005: 76, 110, 125, 131; Noakes 2004: 34; Gruner 2010: 327).

Evaluating Bauman's Holocaust thesis, 3: understanding the perpetrators

Not only does Bauman show scant interest in examining the motives of the bureaucrats, thus missing possible ideological commitments to Nazism or moral qualms they might have felt too scared to express, but he has a tendency, as O'Kane (1997: 49) remarks in an insightful passage, to treat all perpetrators as 'bureaucrats', whether these are genuine bureaucrats like Eichmann or soldiers, 'the secret police, concentration camp guards, torturers and experimenters'. Hence my earlier alert concerning one of Bauman's few quotations from Nazi officials, who pleaded that he was only 'a cog in a relatively low position of a great machine' (*Modernity and the Holocaust*: 22). The quotation is in fact from a *soldier*, Ohlendorf, commander of the SS *Einsatzgruppe D*; as O'Kane rightly remarks, soldiers are used to following orders, but they are not bureaucrats, and nor are other groups whom Bauman implicitly subsumes under the category. Incidentally, Ohlendorf, as Mann points out (Mann 2005: 30, 263), had been a professor of sociology.

This then raises the broader question of who the perpetrators were and what motivated them. I have already noted that Bauman, oddly enough, makes no mention of Eichmann and his defence of merely following orders, nor of Arendt's dismissal of him as a thoughtless bureaucrat, all of which fit neatly into Bauman's own interpretation, although he would then have had to contend with Arendt's neglect of Eichmann's anti-Semitic views, a neglect underlined by Arendt's critics soon after her *Eichmann in Jerusalem* was published (Cesarani 2005: 346–7).

The only serious attempt by Bauman to grapple with the motives of perpetrators is an oblique one, via his exposition and interpretation of the Milgram experiments. Before turning to historians' revelations of perpetrator motives, it is worth exploring the plausibility of Bauman's use of Milgram. Bauman, of course, admits that the experiments have been controversial, but he nevertheless interprets the experiments, as I have pointed out earlier, as having 'proved' that '*inhumanity is a matter of social relationships*' (*Modernity and the Holocaust*: 154, emphasis in original).

Cesarani points out that Milgram's own references to Eichmann were an opportunistic attempt to draw attention to his experiments, for they had not originally been designed to throw light on the Holocaust (Cesarani 2005: 352). In any case, for Cesarani (2005: 355), Milgram's experiments are of 'dubious value for understanding Eichmann' and the Holocaust, for several reasons. First, it transpires that some of the subjects believed that they would not be fully paid if they withdrew too early; second, nearly half of them suspected the experiments to be a sort of 'set up' anyway and therefore not genuine; third, the actor pretended to be a mild-mannered Irish-American accountant, and the subjects had not been indoctrinated in any way to dislike him (unlike the perpetrators of the Holocaust, who in some degree or another had experienced Nazi and other propaganda and an atmosphere of anti-Semitism); moreover, if the subjects had been told that the 'learner' was black or a Jew, 'they might have been inhibited by the very history' the experiments were later used to explain. Also, Cesarani quite rightly asks whether the subjects would so readily have obeyed a man in a black uniform with SS insignia: instead, they were being directed by a man in a white coat who posed as (and was) a scientist, and thus not a figure from a government agency or political grouping that they might have been inclined to be suspicious of. An abstract experimental situation is quite different from one that is 'shot through with history, politics and cultural preconceptions' (Cesarani 2005: 355; see also Vetlesen 2005: 49; Best 2013: 73). Indeed, I would add, given Bauman's antipathy to positivist research it is remarkable that he is willing to go so far as to say that Milgram's experiments '*proved*' anything. Bauman's use of Milgram is even less convincing when it is taken into account that subsequent research has not always obtained the same result: in one follow-up study, subjects were willing to inflict mild pain, but not a level of pain that could harm the victim (Mann 2005: 27). Cesarani also argues, and this is a point I have made earlier in relation to Eichmann, that Nazi killers were not merely following orders: they often had considerable autonomy, took initiatives and showed enthusiasm.

Bauman also deploys Milgram in an analysis of the role of proximity and visibility in murderous acts, extrapolating from the experiments the view that the less visible the victim, and the further away the act in a long chain of command from the actual outcome of mass murder, the easier it was to commit the heinous murders.

But this neglects the fact that a large proportion of perpetrators of the Holocaust were physically close to the victims. Let us note that the early phase of the destruction of Jews involved individual as well as collective shootings at close quarters, documented in gruesome detail by Browning (2001), Goldhagen (1996) and many others. And the sites of the majority of the mass killings, the concentration camps, were far from clinical factories; instead, they involved gross amounts of cruelty, sadism and gratuitous humiliation, face to face, making Bauman's interpretation of the typical process of mass murder in the Holocaust quite fanciful. Power and cruelty went hand in hand in the camps, as even a cursory acquaintance with survivors' accounts makes clear (see, for example, Levi 1979; Vetlesen 2005: 36). Sofsky's study (1999) of concentration camps is important in highlighting the camps as almost theatrical arenas for the exercise of 'absolute power' and excessive, gratuitous violence against inmates.

Some German perpetrators were reluctant killers of *German* Jews, especially, for they shared a language and culture with them; this did not apply to the the *Ostjuden* of Eastern Europe, who were mostly Polish, more likely to be traditionally garbed and with long hair in curls, and whom the Germans found culturally alien. In turn, ethnic Germans from countries such as Poland, often holding lowly positions and despised by German officers for their less sophisticated German and their rough, peasant origins, had particular motivations for cruelty to both Jews, who were seen as exploitative traders, and Polish officers who had previously lorded it over them (Mann 2005: 227).

Nevertheless, the relentless killings took their toll on the psychological health of Nazi officers in the camps, and the provision of large amounts of alcohol was intended to dull their senses as well as quell moral inhibitions and qualms (Mann 2005: 246, 254–5, 267, 271, 276). Both Himmler and Eichmann found it difficult to watch killings and avoided visiting concentration camps or kept their visits as short as possible (Mann 2005: 246; Cesarani 2005: 11, 106). To some extent this bears out Bauman's thesis about the effects of proximity, but not entirely. For there were many among the killers who enjoyed murderous and other cruel acts, as many eye-witness accounts testify (Mann 2005: 262; Levi 1979: Sofsky 1999), and neither Himmler nor Eichmann flinched from pursuing the annihilation of Jews. Browning, in a superb in-depth study of Reserve Battalion 101, gives many examples of needless cruelty and humiliation (see, for example, Browning 2001: 21, 41, 82–3), and even of the pleasure experienced by many close-proximity killers, notoriously by a certain Lieutenant Hartwig Gnade (Browning

2001: 108), although there are also instances of reluctance to kill, firing in the air, requests to be excused from killing duties and moral qualms.

Bauman's lack of historical inquiry into the sheer variety of perpetrators means that he is able to give overwhelming emphasis to the role of bureaucracy, an interpretation that is simply not borne out by the evidence. Historical evidence suggests quite clearly that there were a wide range of motivations and that any particular individual may have had mixed motives. Although few members of Reserve Battalion 101 were Nazis, the higher up the hierarchy one went in the Reich, the more likely it was that functionaries were committed Nazis, while those at the top were of course fanatic anti-Semites and believers in Nazi ideology (Mann 2005: 215), including Eichmann among others. Mann, after a detailed examination of the evidence, argues that some professions were over-represented among Nazi supporters – teachers, lawyers and doctors – and that Nazi ideology appealed to them because it claimed to transcend class conflict by 'nation-statism', and of course these groups were 'closely entwined with the German state'. In relation to those involved in close-proximity killings, Browning argues that peer group pressure, careerism and obedience to superiors provided a mixture of motivations both for individual perpetrators and in explaining the functioning of the murderous battalion as a whole. Among the other factors that he mentions, male bonding and the fear of not being thought masculine enough stand out, and this is an issue that will get further attention later in my discussion.

Bauman's lack of interest in ordinary perpetrators is characteristic of his general practice of sociology, which shows little reading and citing of ethnographies. Cultural depth is not one of his strong points, as I have pointed out in earlier sections of the book, and it is a fatal flaw in his study of the Holocaust as well. It is striking that Bauman makes little use of survivor testimonies. Had he done so, he would have had to confront what a famous survivor, Primo Levi, called the 'grey zone', which I discuss below. It may well be that in so far as an argument can be mounted around modernity and the Holocaust, it was more a question of the creation of a modern mass movement and an organic, statist nationalism than of the role of bureaucracy, which was a secondary factor (Mann 2005: 278, 317).

Browning, in other work, has distinguished among three types of German perpetrators in the camps: 'dangerous', 'corrupt' and 'decent' (2005: 50–4). Mann, in a more fine-grained analysis of 'ideal types', distinguishes among 'ideological', 'bigoted', 'violent', 'fearful', 'careerist', 'materialist', 'disciplined', 'comradely' and 'bureaucratic' killers (Mann 2005: 27–9, 189). Bauman and Milgram focus only on the last category, thus missing the real complexity of the motivations and types of killers who perpetrated atrocities in the Holocaust. And they fail to deal with the question of *violence*, the sheer visceral quality of killing and its psychological pre-requisites as well as the effects on perpetrators (Ray 2011).

Evaluating Bauman's Holocaust thesis, 4: the co-operation of the victims

Arendt's claim that fewer Jews would have perished if the members of the *Judenrate* had not co-operated is rightly rejected by Bauman as highly implausible (*Modernity and the Holocaust*: 117).[7] Moreover, unlike Arendt he is careful not to impose moral judgements on actions in ghettos because the leaders and ordinary Jews were faced with conditions that were extraordinary in their cruelty and allied to impotence in the face of the Nazi project of complete subordination as a route to extermination (*Modernity and the Holocaust*: 144). Nor does he mention Hilberg's controversial suggestion of a long period of Jewish passivity (Lawson 2010: 248–9).

To have agreed with Hilberg's interpretation of alleged Jewish historical passivity would of course have undermined Bauman's own emphasis on the rationality of the behaviour of the *Judenrate* and especially their 'save what you can' strategy, a view which Hilberg seems to agree with (1993: 114–15), although without abandoning his views on the role of Jewish historical passivity.

There is little doubt that Bauman's interpretation of the behaviour of the *Judenrate* has plausibility as well as historical support. But it is by no means unproblematic. For example, for Bauman, Jewish resistance, both armed and unarmed, which was more extensive than is often recognised, is a marginal part of the narrative. But while this serves his interpretation of the rationality of compliance and co-operation, it not only grossly underestimates the willingness of thousands of Jews to fight the Nazis, but robs

Jewish history of a certain heroic quality which also ought to be part of the story and legacy of the Holocaust. Of course, there are difficult issues surrounding how 'resistance' is to be defined in this context – Hilberg for instance had initially focused only on armed resistance – but the general weakness in Bauman's narrative remains. A balanced account would have considered the motivations of both co-operators and resisters, and would have therefore also had to confront the question of the *rationality of the resisters.*

Moreover, a broader consideration of the motivations and achievements of the *Judenrate* in the context of ghetto conditions would have yielded a more sympathetic and indeed sociological interpretation. One of the first set of reflections on ghetto life had been published by the sociologist Samuel Gringauz in 1949, and even at this early stage he had criticised a contentious tendency, later to be reflected in the work of Hilberg and Bauman, both of whom interpreted the ghettos and their leadership as part of a teleological narrative that failed to understand the ghetto as part of a particular *Jewish* history rather than only part of the *Nazi* history of Jewish annihilation (Lawson 2010: 260–1).

What Gringauz, as part of a different analysis, was able to highlight was the fact that the Jewish leadership played an important role in preventing the complete moral collapse of a community in conditions so dire that survival had become the main imperative. The survival of a distinct cultural and religious life, the provision of both secular and religious education and so forth were for Gringauz a miraculous achievement.

This is what other Jewish historians have identified by the Hebrew term *Amidah*. Bauer, one of those involved in developing this idea, includes within *Amidah*, in addition to the preservation of religious and cultural life and education, 'smuggling food into ghettos, mutual self-sacrifice within the family to avoid starvation ... the work of doctors, nurses, and educators to consciously maintain health and moral fibre to enable individual and group survival' as well as armed and unarmed resistance (Bauer 2002: 120).

While Bauman scrupulously avoids moral judgements, arguably he also abdicates a responsibility to consider the moral life of the ghetto (as well as the concentration camp, which is completely ignored by Bauman, a phenomenon that I will discuss later in this section). The ghetto was not only an arena for 'rational' action of the sort Bauman focuses upon, but one in which residents were faced with extraordinarily difficult *moral* choices. And once these are brought into focus what emerge are the ambiguity, complexity and duplicity of moral life in the ghetto (Lawson 2010: 262–3).

Ignoring the moral dilemmas of the ghetto enables Bauman to sidestep some complex moral aspects and deal only with what he deems the 'rational' features of ghetto life. Even if bureaucrats, as he alleges, were able to sideline moral issues, ghetto residents and leaders could not, and any interpretation of the Holocaust that in other respects is so concerned with the ways in which moral responsibility was shunted off is deficient if it fails to deal with the moral issues that the victims simply could not avoid but had to confront in the cruellest of conditions.

Moral dilemmas and the imperative of survival were both even more desperate in their urgency in the grotesque conditions of the concentration camps. Acts of gratuitous cruelty and the prospect and fear of death were even more strongly a part of the daily life of inmates in the camps. What was the 'rational' course of action for inmates of various different ages, genders, health conditions and skills? The absence of any consideration of the culture of the concentration camp is quite remarkable in a book so suffused with moral questions involving life and mass murder. At the time when Bauman was composing his book there was already a great deal of material available which would have allowed him to examine what could count as moral action and how this related to the rational course of action in a context in which any false move could mean instant death or provoke a severe beating. Whatever the degree of credence to be given to survival testimonies as historical records of daily life in the camps, and this is an issue that I will discuss elsewhere in this book, there are some powerful and insightful accounts available, not least from Primo Levi. While it is beyond the scope of the present book to consider the issues in any depth, I feel compelled to draw attention to what Levi referred to as the 'grey zone' in his *The Drowned and the Saved* of 1988 (all references are to the edition of 2013: 31–72; see also Todorov 2000: 182).

Levi recounts in graphic detail (and other such accounts were available to Bauman) the role of what he calls the 'senior' prisoners', some of whom had managed to obtain meagre privileges, and the way they treated newcomers and others who were raking out an existence characterised by the merest semblance of physical survival and only the ragged shreds of dignity. Describing the cruelty meted out to newcomers to the camps by the seniors, Levi suggests that this was indeed a 'grey zone', a space between the Nazis and the lower or newer prisoners, in which 'the despised crowd of seniors was prone to recognize in the new arrival a target on which to vent its humiliation, to find compensation at his expense, to build for itself and at this expense a figure of lower rank on whom to discharge the burden of offences received from above' (Levi 2013: 36). The near-impossibility of survival from the miserly rations handed out to prisoners meant that extra food was the only way to survive, and 'to obtain it a large or small privilege was necessary; in other words a way, granted or conquered, astute or violent, licit or illicit, to lift oneself above the norm' (Levi 2013: 37).

The extraordinary cruelty of the 'functionary-prisoners', as Levi also refers to the seniors, was the first, shocking encounter of the newcomer with the realities of life in the camp. Levi not only recounts many instances of the extent of this sort of cruelty, but also analyses, with great insight and nuance, the motivations of various ranks of prisoner-functionaries, how crucial a role they played in enabling the Nazis to create order in the camp and also the extent to which many seniors also used their knowledge and influence in winning small but vital concessions for ordinary prisoners and thus acting as both collaborators and resisters (Levi 2013: 42–8 and passim). The parallels with the *Judenrate* are obvious, and Levi himself remarks on this by discussing the notorious Chaim Rumkowski, Jewish president of the Lodz ghetto (Levi 2013: 61–71). Levi attempts to portray the complexity of a man almost universally reviled for his tyrannical ways and his pretentious assumption of a regal role in the ghetto.

In contrast, Bauman's account errs on the side of a misleading and one-sided exercise in the abstract analysis of the role of a supposedly well-oiled, almost clinical bureaucratic process and its role in accomplishing a relatively smooth form of mass murder. It is no wonder that the really gruesome, gory aspects of the Holocaust are so seldom mentioned by Bauman, if at all. Bauman has a top-down approach, heavily influenced by Arendt and Hilberg, in contrast with Friedlander's attempt at an integrated history in which the voices of the victims, especially those available in survivors' accounts, are fully taken into account (Wildt 2010).

Evaluating Bauman's Holocaust thesis, 5: the question of gender

It must be stated at the outset that although Bauman's work is generally characterised by a neglect of issues of gender, the omission of gender in his analysis of the Holocaust must also be seen, equally, as a result of the general neglect of questions of gender in Holocaust studies until the 1970s and 1980s. These issues came under scholarly scrutiny only as a result of the general rise of women's studies that followed in the wake of 'second wave feminism'. There is yet much research that needs to be done, and is being done; thus my intention in this short section is not to be critical of Bauman as such but to highlight a set of issues that future books on the Holocaust simply cannot ignore.

The first explicitly gendered accounts of the Holocaust, from authors such as Sybil Milton and Joan Ringelheim, tended to highlight what they took to be the distinctive survival strategies used by Jewish women (Pine 2004: 364–5; Baumel 1998). There was considerable emphasis on the ways in which women had better survival skills than men, in relation to both bonding with each other and caring for each other, but also in caring for themselves by being able to cook, sew and maintain cleanliness in abominable conditions that men found more demoralising. Male survival accounts of the camps tended to portray a Hobbesian world of warring individuals hell-bent on individual survival, and Levi was by no means alone in pointing to the experience of the camps as one of overwhelming shame (Levi 2013: 72–93). However, his account is typical in not recognising that part of the shame, at least, resulted from the emasculation, the undermining of men's masculinity; and it is typical in not mentioning women at all, although Levi does refer with some disgust to women German and Polish workers in another of his accounts, *If This is a Man*, while at the same time discussing the shame of looking bedraggled and smelling foul in front of these women (Levi 1988: 148; Bergen 2013: 21). In the passages devoted to the events here the affront to his masculinity is palpable but not fully acknowledged as being just that.

Women survivors' narratives were replete with descriptions of how attempts were made to recreate a semblance of family life among inmates in the camps. And historians have pointed to the vital role played by women in the ghettos in obtaining food and other necessities – often going without food in order to feed children – and in trying to maintain the morale of their families (Lawson 2010: 296; Pine 2004: 365–6, 369; Saidel 2006; Helm 2015). Women had higher survival rates than men in the ghettos, partly because it was easier for them to pass as 'Aryan' – men could be easily found out by the 'trouser test', revealing circumcision, as well as by their beards and locks – and in Poland, women, having been educated in Polish schools while the boys had attended Jewish schools, had greater linguistic and cultural skills which enabled them to pass as non-Jewish (Pine 2004: 369). However, men were more likely to have emigrated not just out of the ghetto but out of the country: male heads of households left first, for they were considered more likely to be harassed or arrested by the Gestapo and the SS, and immigration quotas in the UK and USA favoured men over women (Stibbe 2003: 60).

More recent feminist writings on the Holocaust have questioned the extent to which women's own accounts have over-emphasised traditional stereotypes of women's roles (Lawson 2010: 298). Nevertheless, when the matter is looked at from another angle, it is quite clear that Jewish men and women were treated differently by the Nazis. Men were likely to be imprisoned earlier than women (Pine 2004: 367), and in the earlier phase of murder by shooting, men were usually the first to be shot: as Browning has shown there were many Germans who initially balked at shooting women and children (2001: 64–5; Waxman 2010a: 313). But in the camps women's survival rate was lower, for a variety of reasons: pregnant women and women with children were the first to be gassed, and often women willingly went into the chambers with their children rather than survive without them, as well as wishing to support the children; and women were less useful as labourers in camps where hard physical work was required of prisoners while they all awaited their almost inevitable death (Waxman 2010a: 313).

Women's trauma in the camps was gendered and sexualised in two specific respects. First, the usual stripping-off of clothes required of all arrivals was that much more humiliating but also frightening for women, their feelings of sexual vulnerability being heightened by their nakedness (Ringelheim 1993: 376; Waxman 2010a: 296). Some women were enslaved in brothels (Sommer 2010: 45–60; Bergen 2013: 26–7), and there was a great deal of rape and other forms of sexual violence against Jewish women in the period of the Holocaust (Ringelheim 1993: 376–7; Hedgepeth and Saidel 2010; Sinnreich 2010; Goldenberg 2013: 99–127). Of course, many women found that the only way to obtain extra food was to barter for it with sexual acts, but as Goldenberg remarks in a deliberate understatement, 'Sex in exchange for food is neither rape nor prostitution, but it is not exactly consensual sex' (Goldenberg 2013: 115).

The role of German women in the Holocaust has also come under increasing scrutiny. Firstly, they were important in maintaining family life and normality for the innumerable men involved in the mass murder of Jews, and also performed a vital function in upholding the Nazi vision of the ideal 'Aryan' family (Stephenson 2001: 23–32; Lawson 2010: 295). Moreover, as many as 4,000 women worked as guards at concentration camps and killing centres (Browning 2001: 138; Mann 2005: 220) and, although always under male supervision, exercised a considerable degree of power (Bergen 2013: 19–20). Many others worked in white-collar and professional jobs, in the former as stenographers and clerks, in the latter especially as teachers, nurses and doctors (Stephenson 2001: 61–5). Women nurses and doctors were involved in the pre-war 'T4' euthanasia project when the mentally ill and physically disabled were killed off to protect the stock of the German, 'Aryan', race, as were Roma, who, although not part of the 'T4' project, were considered genetically prone to criminality (Charlesworth 2004: 245; Hancock 2004: 387; Mann 2005: 204–5).

Women's active participation as accomplices and actual killers has been graphically documented by Wendy Lower in her remarkable study, *Hitler's Furies*, sub-titled 'German Women in the Nazi Killing Fields' (2013). As Lower puts it, 'Hitler's Furies were zealous administrators, robbers, tormentors and murderers in the bloodlands' (Lower 2013: 6, 8). They confiscated Jewish belongings and hosted parties while watching Jews being marched to their deaths (Lower 2013: 117). One specialised in killing children, luring them with sweets (Lower 2013: 127); another shot a group of children one by one with a pistol (Lower 2013: 133). 'Genocide', Lower argues, 'is also women's business' (Lower 2013: 166).

Research on masculinity and the Holocaust has hardly got off the ground. Browning's research on Reserve Battalion 101, though, is revealing, although unwittingly so, for gender is not a special preoccupation in his *Ordinary Men*. The pressure to conform to conventional standards of masculinity was mixed in with the desire to obey orders and not let the battalion down (Browning 2001: 71), and Browning also refers to the pressure to affirm 'macho' values where toughness was exhibited by the willingness to kill (Browning 2001: 184–5; Mann 2005: 254). Male bonding was part of the process by which men became killers (Mann 2005: 284). Haynes (2002) has re-read Browning, Goldhagen and other historians with an eye for what is revealed unwittingly about the role of particular forms of masculinity and gender relations in the Holocaust. Some of what he finds in Browning, for example, I have already cited from my own reading of *Ordinary Men*, but Haynes unearths more, and also from Goldhagen's research into the same battalion. Among the insights revealed by this attentive re-reading are the role of the families of the killers in supporting them, the indoctrination of notions of masculine toughness as essential to the proper execution of the murders, and the conception of killing Jews as a 'Jew-hunt' and thus as a typical male sport.

Mann also refers to the role of young working-class male forms of masculinity involved in the 'licensed thuggery' of *Kristallnacht*, when Jewish shops and individual Jews were attacked, as well as the sexual violence of German camp guards towards Jewish women inmates (Mann 2005: 198, 251).

Much, though, remains to be done in the task of understanding the various layers of entwinement between masculinity, Nazi ideology and the Holocaust (see Waxman 2010b). And any such research must explore the more general relationship between masculinity, gender relations and violence (Jones 2006: 325–42; Jones 2009; Ray 2011: 83–103).

Modernity and the Holocaust contains a profoundly significant 'Appendix' on what Bauman calls the 'Social Manipulation of Morality', sub-titled 'Moralizing Actors, Adiaphorizing Action'. This is in fact Bauman's acceptance speech for the European Amalfi Prize for the book. Among other things, it continues discussion of a theme that he had broached in the final chapter, 'Towards a Sociological Theory of Morality', which tries to explore the social production of immoral behaviour and evil, and provides a critique of the manner in which sociology has tried to deal with the question of how humans become moral beings. So the book ends with the theme with which it had started, a critique of sociology, except that this time it is on a wider front, for now Bauman is not just concerned with sociology and the Holocaust but also with sociology and how it analyses the general relation between society, morality and evil. The philosopher Emmanuel Levinas makes one of his first appearances in Bauman's writing in this final chapter, and I will discuss his huge significance for Bauman's thinking on ethics in Part II.

But the question of Bauman's interpretation of the Holocaust still confronts us. Following the myriad criticisms set out above, what now remains of Bauman's main thesis? Only a provocation survives, in my view: a provocation to a more sophisticated understanding of Western modernity and of the relation between social theory, sociological analysis and historical inquiry; arguably, Mann (Mann 2005) has provided just the type of blend of history and sociology that is required, making Bauman's critique of sociology, the key animating thread of *Modernity and the Holocaust*, redundant. The initial, searing impact of the book has now given way, among scholars of the Holocaust, Western modernity, modernity, bureaucracy and genocide to a relegation of the text to the margins of interest. Mostly, it acts as a foil to more considered, nuanced, historically deeper and sociologically more complex, more apposite reflection on these topics. If 'modernity' is still invoked, it is not Bauman's modernity, but is more likely to be Mann's, with its primary emphasis not on bureaucracy but on politicised nationalism and ethnicity, in a context where citizenship, democracy and welfare are, as he puts it, 'tied to ethnic and national forms of exclusion ... Murderous ethnic cleansing is a hazard of the age of democracy since amid multi-ethnicity the ideal of rule by the people began to entwine the *demos* with the dominant *ethnos*, generating organic conceptions of the nation and the state that encouraged the cleansing of minorities' (2005: 8).

No more stinging critique of Bauman's interpretation is available than Mann's judgement on the role of bureaucracy in the Holocaust:

all that remained bureaucratic was the continuous stream of lies told to the outside world ... The five death camps, especially their gas chambers ...were not very hi-tech ... the actual killings were not bureaucratic. In the death camps, screaming, naked, blood-ied, defecating prisoners were beaten towards the gas chambers by drunken guards with whips and rifle butts ... The perpetrators were not insulated from the horror, except by alcohol that they ... consumed in enormous quantities ... Even desk killers knew what they were doing and believed they had good reasons for doing it ... Bauman's theory is based on Weber's notion of instrumental and technical reason. This is wrong ... Nazis believed they were extermi-nating their enemies for good ideological reasons. Modernity's evil has been more ideological and blood-spattered than bureaucratic and dispassionate. Bureaucratic states do not commit murderous cleansing; radicalized ones do. (Mann 2005: 242)

Notes

1   Geras, concerned by the similar neglect of the Holocaust in political theory, has written *The Contract of Mutual Indifference* (1998) to start off a necessary discussion, with a special focus on 'bystanders'. His basic contention is that if one refuses to intervene to help in situations such as the Holocaust and other human atrocities and misfortunes, then one cannot expect to be given assistance by others when finding oneself in similar circumstances. A problematic aspect of his argument is that he interprets non-intervention by bystanders as *indifference* on their part, without considering the possibility of fear of consequences by concerned 'bystanders', especially in totalitarian conditions. He fails to probe the various reasons that might prevent bystanders from active intervention, as Waxman (2009) points out.
2   See Herf 1986; Pulzer 2010: 118–20. For a somewhat different view which stresses the provision by fascism of not anti-modernism but a different form of modernity and modernism, see Griffin 2007.
3   Arendt, in her *The Origins of Totalitarianism* (first published in 1951), had been one of the first to see a connection between colonialism and fascism (Stone 2010: 228). The Nazi project of expanding into Eastern Europe has been seen by some scholars as analogous to British and French – and earlier German – colonialisms. Hitler was an admirer of the British Empire and of the dispossession of American Indians by white settlers, while his 'table talk' reveals him comparing Russians and Ukrainians to 'negros' and other colonised peoples: Stone 2010:

223–5; see also Gilroy 2000. For Italian imperialist massacres in Libya and Ethiopia see Mann 2005: 308–10. Caroline Elkins (2005) has documented the use of torture and brutality in prison camps in Kenya by the British as their empire wound down in the period after the Second World War. For an understanding of the Holocaust in the broader context of studies of genocide, see Shaw 2007, especially 37–47. A comprehensive overview of genocide studies is provided by Adam Jones (2006; for Jones's analysis of the Holocaust see 147–84).

4 Although Goldhagen's view that a large proportion of the German population was in the grip of murderous anti-Semitism has been effectively questioned by a large number of scholars; see, for example, Browning 2001: 191–223; Finkelstein 1997. There is also a section in *Modernity and the Holocaust*: 242 where Bauman criticises Goldhagen's 'crazy' thesis (to use Finkelstein's term).

5 There has been much discussion of Arendt's phrase 'the banality of evil' as a description of and judgement on Eichmann. The phrase, it seems, was not entirely Arendt's, for it appears to have been prompted by comments by Karl Jaspers in correspondence with Arendt: see Bernstein 1996: 148. In an excellent, probing interpretation of Arendt's infamous expression, Baehr (2010) has suggested that a more apposite phrasing to convey Arendt's meaning would be 'banality *and* evil' rather than the 'banality *of* evil'.

6 Stone (2010: 121) argues that Bauman simply provides a sociological gloss on the historian Hilberg's interpretation of the role of the bureaucracy in the Holocaust.

7 Cesarani (2005: 345–7) suggests that Arendt's criticisms of Jewish co-operation betrayed prejudices, verging on racism, that were typical of the views of Eastern European Jews held by middle-class, highly educated German Jews.

The ambivalences of modernity: a preliminary interrogation of Bauman's Eurocentric, white, male gaze

Bauman published *Modernity and Ambivalence* (1991) a mere two years after *Modernity and the Holocaust*. Perhaps the rapid turnaround in the publication of this book should not surprise us, for much of the groundwork for it had already been laid in the previous book; much of *Modernity and Ambivalence* is also about 'the Jewish question'. More accurately put, this book is also about the Jewish *tragedy*, and again in the bounds of modernity, but this time more with an eye to the double-binds of modernity for a minority that wishes to assimilate, to identify itself with a larger entity, the modern nation-state, an issue already explored in *Modernity and the Holocaust*. The text, then, is about identity and difference, majorities and minorities, and the dilemmas created for certain groups of outsiders trying to become insiders by attempting to fit into pre-ordained categories, within overall classifications not of their own making, and therefore constantly at the mercy of those able to do the work of defining who does and does not fit in, who does and does not really *belong*. As such, it carries a message far beyond the confines of early twentieth-century Germany. It speaks as much *to* the early, far more globalised twenty-first century, where diasporas have multiplied, while speaking *about* the early twentieth century and the specific Jewish diaspora in Europe.

I do not intend to provide a detailed exposition of this text. In many respects it is an extended footnote to *Modernity and the Holocaust*. But there are some significant aspects of the text that are worth remarking upon. And none is more so than the fact that *Modernity and Ambivalence* is itself an illustration of one of the central theses of *Modernity and Ambivalence*. The book reveals all too clearly *Bauman's own deeply ambivalent perception of modernity*. Glimpsed one way, Bauman sees modernity as inherently pluralist; totalitarianism of the Nazi or Stalinist type is only one possibility within modernity, bursting forth in very particular circumstances. But more often than not, as in *Legislators and Interpreters*, in some aspects of his analysis in *Modernity and the Holocaust*, and in *Modernity and Ambivalence*, Bauman ends up emphasising, too one-sidedly, the 'gardening', disciplining, Panopticon-like, monolithic side of modernity. Thus in *Modernity and Ambivalence*, Bauman regards even intellectuals as totally co-opted by 'modernity', because now intellectuals are part of the state as employees in universities, government scientists, civil servants and social workers (*Modernity and Ambivalence*: 91). And as in *Legislators*, so in *Modernity and Ambivalence* and other works of the 1990s: pluralism becomes more a feature of postmodernity than modernity; indeed part of what distinguishes the postmodern for Bauman is the pluralisation of the social, political and intellectual conditions facing humanity when compared with modernity.

Modernity and Ambivalence is structured around the attempts within modernity, and especially within the confines of the nation-state, to impose order and clear-cut boundaries, neat classifications, of things, people, fauna and flora, nature in general and the constant slippages and leakages that subvert these attempts at 'gardening'. What interests Bauman is the variety of phenomena, and especially groups of people, who simply cannot be clearly one or the other. Bauman's own indecision over the monolithic and pluralist versions of modernity unwittingly reflects what he sees as an endemic feature of modernity in which there are many phenomena, including cultural groups, which are impossible to capture on one side or the other, despite the efforts of the most determined of classifiers.

The Jew is one such anomalous figure in modernity. Despite his – and I use the masculine advisedly – attempt to assimilate by conversion to Christianity, by speaking and writing the language better than the 'native', making myriad brilliant contributions to European sciences, culture and intellectual life and so forth, Bauman argues that the Jew remained for Europeans a Jew. Jewishness as defined by the European remained stubbornly a property that clung to Jews and made them, in the last instance, unassimilable.

For Bauman, the Jew in modernity typifies the 'stranger', especially as analysed by Simmel, that modern forms of classification find 'slimy' and difficult to accommodate: the stranger, Bauman argues, is 'the bane of modernity' (*Modernity and Ambivalence*: 61), for he is incongruous, the source of ambivalence, sitting astride modernity's tendency to see order and chaos as the only possibilities. He is neither friend nor enemy, neither order nor chaos, neither inside nor outside. 'He stands for the treacherousness of friends, for the cunning disguise of the enemies, for fallibility of order, vulnerability of the inside' (*Modernity and Ambivalence*: 61).

There are some profound insights in Bauman's analysis of the predicaments encountered by both modernity and the stranger in their fateful encounter. Using the example of the great novelist Franz Kafka, Bauman provides a particularly illuminating discussion of the difficulties that the Jew as 'stranger' had to face when attempting to assimilate into the nation, to become accepted as a full member – a 'native' – and be completely trusted as a citizen *Modernity and Ambivalence*: 90, 179–84). Bauman has a particularly acute understanding of the way in which the Jews who tried to assimilate were in fact only ever provisionally accepted. Not only were Jews having to constantly prove that any charges against them were false, but 'the same people who brought the charges would pronounce on the cogency of the proofs' (*Modernity and Ambivalence*: 112–13). That this is indeed the fate of all ethnic minorities in liberal democratic states is something that Bauman briefly alludes to, but he fails to translate this insight into any broader discussion from the Jews in early twentieth-century Western Europe to black and Asian ethnic minorities in the second half of the twentieth century, an omission particularly puzzling given that Bauman cites the excellent analysis of this question by Dench but draws from it only lessons for the Jewish population of the early twentieth century (*Modernity and Ambivalence*: 71).

But Bauman's framework for analysing 'modernity', ambivalence and the vicissitudes of strangerhood or strangeness is problematic on other grounds and exposes a variety of failings that typify his whole description and analysis of modernity, and my critical comments therefore apply to his analysis of modernity in *Legislators*, *Modernity and the Holocaust* and *Modernity and Ambivalence*, and indeed carry on into his conceptions of postmodernity and subsequently what he came to call 'liquid modernity', as we will see.

There is, to begin with, Bauman's reification of 'modernity', making it into an agent in its own right as being responsible, in some abstract manner, for all manner of phenomena that are within its ambit. This occurs throughout *Modernity and Ambivalence* and previous works, so here just a couple of examples may be allowed to stand in for a chronic tendency: more or less at the beginning of *Modernity and Ambivalence*, for instance, Bauman refers to the 'impossible tasks that modernity sets itself' and states, 'Modern consciousness criticizes, warns and alerts'; referring to 'culture' as 'His Majesty's Opposition', Bauman asserts that 'modernity resents its critique' (*Modernity and Ambivalence*: 4). This often combines with a form of *functionalism* in which modernity supposedly has 'needs', such as when he says, 'Modern state and modern intellect *need* chaos – if only to go on creating order' (*Modernity and Ambivalence*: 9, my emphasis).

In this form of reification of modernity, Bauman robs human actors and collectivities of agency, for modernity becomes the agent, the actor, while individuals and groups simply become the carriers and handmaidens of 'modernity'. *This makes for a totalising, deterministic framework*, while also allowing functionalism to slip into the analysis so that modernity itself has functions, needs and forms of 'dysfunctionality'. 'Dysfunctionality of modern culture', Bauman says, 'is its functionality. The modern powers' struggle for artificial order needs culture that explores the limits and the limitations of the power of artifice' (*Modernity and Ambivalence*: 9).

Apart from being unjustifiable in social analysis, this endemic abstract functionalism is deeply ironic, for Bauman's contempt for Durkheim, Parsons and the functionalist tradition in sociology has been equally long-standing.

Moreover, Bauman identifies modernity with the modern nation-state, and states that its origins lie in the period beginning with the seventeenth century, followed by the Enlightenment and the industrial revolution (*Modernity and Ambivalence*: 4). In focusing on the nation-state, Bauman ignores the fact that nation-building in Europe was *preceded* by imperialist expansion and that the twin processes of nation-building and overseas colonisation became inextricably intertwined. Indeed, as Chakrabarty (2000) has noted with great insight, writing the history of modernity largely in terms of nation-states that supposedly emerged in isolation, in Europe, without reference to the constitutive role of what was outside Europe, in the colonies, builds Eurocentrism into the heart of the narrative, for it was in Europe that the nation-state emerged, but only in a process of constant intertwining with imperialism and colonialism, as we shall see. In turn, this means that the centrality of imperialism in forming the internal identities of European nation-states, especially Britain, is completely erased by Bauman, and this sort of exclusion of the 'outside' of Europe, resulting in a treatment of European developments such as the nation-state and industrialisation as purely internal phenomena, is one of the defining features of Eurocentrism, as I show in Part III.

Bauman's analysis of modernity fails to appreciate the degree to which the very definition of what it meant to be 'modern' was not simply a development internal to the West, but as Stuart Hall has put it, was deeply influenced by a conception of the binary divide between 'the West and the Rest' (S. Hall 1992a). That is, modern Western national and supra-national identities were put in place through a process in which non-Western Others were excluded. Thus the West came to see itself as civilised, white, Christian, male, adult and so forth, by characterising non-Westerners as 'Orientals' and 'Blacks' with the opposite qualities: savage, uncivilised, pagan, effeminate, over-emotional and child-like. Bauman's blindness to the entanglements between the imperial and the national means that his understanding of 'modernity' remains profoundly unsatisfactory. I remarked upon his neglect of Said's Foucault-inspired *Orientalism* in my critique of *Legislators*, and I have also pointed out that in *Modernity and the Holocaust* Bauman remained unaware of how imperialism had been connected to the Holocaust; the analysis in *Modernity and Ambivalence* remains similarly innocent of any awareness of the centrality of imperialism and colonialism to the formation of identities in European nation-states.

There is by now a large literature on the entanglements between the coloniser and the colonised in producing the institutions and identities of the modern West, as a result of the development of a set of academic researches that have come to be called 'postcolonial studies' (for overviews see, among many others, Rattansi 1997; Gandhi 1998; Loomba 1998; Williams and Chrisman 1993; Ashcroft, Griffiths and Tiffin 1995; Quayson 2000), upon which I will draw briefly to highlight the ways in which it is necessary to move beyond the Eurocentric, white male perspective so evident in Bauman's work.

Mitchell's conclusion to his seminal analysis of Orientalism
and the colonisation of Egypt is instructive and provides a suitable
starting point:

> What Orientalism offered was not just technical knowledge of
> Oriental languages, religious beliefs ... and methods of govern-
> ment, but a series of absolute differences according to which the
> Oriental could be understood as the negative of the European ...
> The Orient was backward, irrational, disordered, and therefore in
> need of European order and authority: the domination of the West
> over the non-Western world depended on this manner of creating a
> 'West', as singular Western self-identity. Like the 'Arab' town, the
> Orient was created as the apparent exterior of the West; as with the
> colonial city, what is outside is paradoxically what makes the West
> what it is, the excluded yet integral part of its identity and power.
> (Mitchell 1988: 166)

And as his analysis of the colonisation of Egypt illustrates, and
as has been revealed by a great many studies of European colonialism, many of the modalities of governmentality that are analysed in Foucault's work and in Foucault-inspired narratives like
Bauman's, of the formation of the modern European state as being
internal to Europe, were actually pioneered in the colonies and then
imported into Europe to govern Europe's own internal populations.
Significantly, Bentham, whose Panopticon style of surveillance is
central to Foucault's and Bauman's analysis of the formation of
the European state, was in close contact with Bowring, the British
adviser in Cairo (Mitchell 1988: x), and Bentham corresponded
with rulers in India, North and South America, Russia and Egypt.
A Panopticon-style factory was in fact used in Bentham's brother's
factory in the Ottoman Empire between 1768 and 1774 (Mitchell
1988: 35 n6). And the reform of the British civil service was carried out by a group of politicians and intellectuals who had earlier
helped create the Indian civil service.

Moreover, the construction of the colonial subject – Oriental
and African – as child-like ran in parallel with the rise of the notion
of childhood in Europe, and assisted in conflating the 'primitive'
with childhood, requiring strict supervision and tutelage (Nandy
1983: 15) while at the same time consigning India and other
colonies to backwardness, a stage that Europe had long passed

through on the way to adulthood and 'civilisation'. It is important to note in this context that monitorial schooling for children was first invented by the British in early nineteenth-century Bengal (Mitchell 2000: 3) and only then imported into Britain as part of the process of disciplining the growing youth population of the rapidly expanding cities. And the study of English literature as part of the project of forming the subjectivities of a subordinate population began in India and was subsequently introduced into the educational system of Britain as part of national identity-formation (Viswanathan 1989).

Schooling has to be seen as integral to a key Foucauldian theme, that is, the idea of the 'population' as the object of governmental power, but this also first emerged as part of the colonial project of administering 'population' in India (Prakash 1999; Chatterjee 1993, 2006; Kalpagam 2014); relatedly, concerns within Britain over motherhood, infant mortality and race were profoundly entangled with empire, for the British state became involved in the expansion of the population and the production of healthy Britons who could compete against the Germans, especially, to be the 'master race' in a competition for global dominance (Davin 1978). And this process was influenced by processes of control of the body first pioneered by the practice of colonial medicine in India (Arnold 1993; Prakash 2000; Collingham 2001). The British judge William Herschel first developed and utilised finger-printing in India before it was imported into Britain (Cohn 1996: 11), where it was further developed by Francis Galton and others into a crucial weapon in the control of crime. In this context it should be remembered that forms of management of prisons owed much to governing and controlling native populations. Most crucially, the development of the factory system, and thus the efficiency of European industrialisation, was greatly influenced by the methods of the organisation of work in sugar plantations that had been developed in the Caribbean (Mintz 1986), and of course the exploitation of slaves and then colonial labour and resources generated an enormous amount of wealth which was important in the development of the industrial revolution that is taken by Bauman, in common with others, as marking the beginning of 'modernity'. *At the heart of industrial modernity lay the interconnection with and subordination and exploitation of Europe's Others.*

Note too that the concept of 'culture', which plays a central part in Bauman's work in a variety contexts and for a range of purposes, was not a development solely 'internal' to Europe, as is implicit in Bauman's narrative of the Enlightenment in eighteenth-century Europe. As a number of authors have argued, the West's encounters with the non-Western world played a significant, constitutive role in the emergence of 'culture' as a marker for the distinctiveness and identity of peoples, for it was part of the discourses and institutions involved in the process of colonisation and in the emergence of anthropology as a discipline (Dirks 1992: 3–4).

The development of a specifically European identity also had much to do with the colonial enterprise and the doctrines of race. Stoler (1997), for instance, has shown how the notion of 'European' emerged as part of the process by which settlers from the Netherlands in the East Indies and from France in Indochina attempted to differentiate themselves from those of mixed blood – the *métis* – and poorer whites and imported the idea of 'European' back into the metropole, and also how the process was a sexualised one, for mixing was of course profoundly marked by sexual attraction as well as repulsion and policing. Stoler (1995) has also revealed how parochial and Eurocentric Foucault's analysis of sexuality turns out to be once the role of colonial sexualisation is brought into the narrative of the formation of middle-class European sexuality and selfhood.

Given the centrality of the nation-state to Bauman's account of modernity, and of course he is part of a well-established tradition, it is important to note that the emergence of nationalism and that of the nation-state were profoundly interconnected with Europe's encounters and exploitation of the lands and populations of non-white, non-Europeans (Mitchell 2000: 4–5; Bhambra 2007: 119–23). As Bayly says, in a magisterial study of what he calls the 'birth of the modern world', 'Imperialism and nationalism were part of the same phenomenon' (2004: 230). Also, the importance of the Empire to the formation of British national identity has received sustained attention in recent scholarship (see, from a large literature, Colley 1992; Wilson 2004; Hall and Rose 2006), and there is now a serious acknowledgement that these identities have been profoundly gendered, with masculinity in particular playing a crucial role in the effeminisation of colonial subjects and in the formation of an imperial subjectivity and identity. Catherine Hall's *White, Male and Middle Class* (1992) and Sinha's *Colonial Masculinity* (1995) are outstanding examples of this genre of historical writing (see also Hyams 1990; Rutherford 1997; Wilson 2003).

The general point, of course, is that imperialism, colonialism and the modern nation-state emerged together; and the development of the European nation-state has to be seen as part of an interconnected history in which the colonial encounter played a seminal role in the forms of modern governmentality and state that emerged. Moreover, to reiterate Chakrabarty's argument (2000), writing the history of modernity as the (solely internal European) history of the nation-state simply reproduces a European bias, for this is where the nation-state emerged. Given the intertwining of metropole and colony, it is small wonder that Thomas claims that 'modernity itself can be understood as a colonialist project in the special sense that both the society internal to Western nations, and those they possessed, administered and reformed elsewhere, were understood as objects to be surveyed, regulated and sanitized' (1994: 4; see also Mamdani 1996).

In turn, it should now be acknowledged that Bauman's understanding of *the Jewish predicament*, which is so central to *Modernity and Ambivalence*, is also impoverished by his neglect of the role of colonial Others in the formation of European identity. Thus he is unable to grasp that part of what made 'the Jew' difficult to assimilate fully, and thus ensured that he remained a source of ambivalence within modernity, was that he was seen as *Oriental, straddling the binary opposition in Western culture between Occident and Orient, the West and the East.* This continues to haunt Jewish assimilation, for Israel is located broadly in the East, and the Jewish religion is seen as having its main fountain head in an Oriental location (Davidson and Penslar 2005).

As my critique of Bauman's analysis of modernity also highlights, Bauman ignores the extent to which 'Woman as Other' has also been constitutive of Western identity, and that *'Woman' as a category and a figure remained a profoundly ambivalent presence within modernity*, disturbing its unity and the security of its foundation in male dominance. The masculinity of the modern West, deeply ingrained within national cultures, has seen the female as closer to nature because of the capacity to give birth, but also lacking in self-control, over-emotional, lacking in the capacity for rationality, child-like and, like colonial Others, in need of supervision and government by (white) men. The second wave of feminist research, to which Bauman remains oblivious, has by now shown conclusively the degree to which female subordination and ideologies of male superiority have been central to conceptions of modernity (McMillan 1982; Ortner 1982; Lloyd 1984; Poole 1990; Seidler 1994; Marshall 1994). But it is also necessary to understand how the female and the non-Western Other have been superimposed on one another so that the colonial and imperial relationship was thoroughly racialised, gendered and sexualised (Stepan 1990; Gilman 1992; Rattansi 1997; McClintock 1995; Stoler 1995; Hyams 1990; Gill 1995; Levine 2006).

But class was also central to modern identity-formation, and class, race and gender became fused in complex chains of equivalence, such that the working class was seen in the same terms as women, Orientals and blacks, requiring upper-class domination, tutelage and civilisation (Thorne 1997). Often, the lower orders were seen as part of a separate race, as were other whites such as the Irish who were often seen as black (Gibbons 2000, Rattansi 2007).

One of the fruits of postcolonial studies has been the highlighting of the *ambivalence* provoked by the colonial Other, although not in Bauman's sense of ambivalence produced by the normal operation of language and classification, but rather as originating in the psychic economy of *desire*. The colonial Other is not simply feared, but also desired in the form of the unclothed primitive woman, the Oriental woman and the black woman, but there is also an ambivalence about some imperial males across another dimension, for the Orient and Africa were spaces enabling the freer expression of homosexual desire (Hyams 1990). As Stuart Hall (1992: 256) puts it, 'fear and desire double for one another and play across the structures of otherness, complicating its politics'. This undoubtedly has relevance also in understanding German male sexual violence against Jewish women.

The colonial Other provoked another kind of ambivalence, one that continues to play across the politics of black and Asian accommodation in the post-imperial age of immigration from former empires. Bhabha (1994) identifies this as the destabilising of coloniser–colonised relations by the ability of the colonised subject to mimic the coloniser, acquiring his language and mode of behaviour, returning the coloniser's gaze in a disconcerting manner (Thomas 1994: 15; Prakash 1999: 5).

In *Modernity and Ambivalence* Bauman argues that the uncertainty and contingency which Jewish intellectuals experienced foreshadowed an existential condition and experience that was to be the lot of large sections of the population in a later, postmodern period. However, as we can now see, this was not only the lot of Jewish intellectuals, for many sections of educated colonial subjects found themselves in a similarly ambivalent situation, and Bauman fails to understand the interconnection between the two groups provided by the category of 'Oriental', and nor does he recognise the contradictory and ambivalent play of desire in choreographing these relationships.

In the latter half of the twentieth century and now in the twenty-first century, this provokes a series of predicaments for ethnic-minority immigrants from the former colonies, as the majorities demand assimilation and yet *value* and *define* difference, making assimilation impossible; and so debates rage about forms of 'integration', 'multiculturalism' and the 'social cohesion' of the nation-state (see, inter alia, Rattansi 2011), within the overarching framework of liberalism.

It is striking and quite remarkable that Bauman has nothing to say about racism against black and Asian ethnic minorities in the UK and elsewhere in Europe, and very little on the fate of African Americans. This is in keeping with his continuing Eurocentrism; the only minority in which he evinces any sustained interest is the Jewish diaspora. As we shall see, this has repercussions for his analyses of postmodernity and liquid modernity. His male gaze, too, remains undisturbed by any acknowledgement of the issues raised by women's subordination. And what used to be called the Third World, now usually subsumed under the name 'Global South', remains absent from his understanding of the world, although there had been some reference to it in *Memories*. Africa, China, India, Latin America, south-east Asia and Japan have either no visibility or only a marginal presence in the main works on modernity, a neglect that, like the near-absence of ethnic minorities, means that Bauman presents analyses of modernity, postmodernity and, later, liquid modernity that are extraordinarily narrow and selective.

The emergence and development of liberalism also play little or no part in Bauman's account of modernity, although as I have remarked, in *Modernity and Ambivalence* he shows an awareness of the traps set within liberalism for minorities who wish to assimilate into the dominant culture. But he does not analyse liberalism and liberal democracy as central competing and constitutive ideologies within Western modernity, and as I have argued, this serves to give Western modernity, in his trilogy, a much more authoritarian cast. Discourses of liberalism are central to understanding the formation of the West and its governing institutions, as Foucault was well aware, although Bauman, despite borrowing extensively from Foucault, fails to incorporate Foucault's more acute understanding of liberalism into his own analysis (Burchell 1996; Rose 1996). However, liberalism too has its own 'dark' side, for as Losuro (2014) has argued in an illuminating study, slaves, colonial subjects and women remained ambivalent figures in liberal discourses; for very long periods they were deemed unfit to exercise the liberties granted only to white males, although as we have seen the more radical figures of the Enlightenment were principled critics of slavery and some favoured greater equality for women.

The weaknesses in Bauman's understanding of modernity continue to haunt his conception of postmodernity, to which the discussion now turns.

Part II

Living with postmodernity

It is in the 1987 *Legislators and Interpreters* that Bauman presents the first fruits of his growing engagement with the debates about postmodernity that had convulsed intellectual life in Continental Europe and, increasingly, North America. *Modernity and the Holocaust*, which followed *Legislators*, although written from a postmodern perspective, makes no mention of these debates. However, this is hardly surprising because Bauman's focus in this book is on a historically specific period and set of events in Western modernity. But in holding 'modernity' responsible for the Holocaust, Bauman was well in tune with a postmodern turn in the humanities and social sciences that was increasingly replacing capitalism with 'modernity' as the preferred conceptual framework for analysing European history from the Enlightenment onwards. Indeed, modernity was coming to be seen and criticised as emerging out of a unified 'Enlightenment Project' that culminated in both capitalism and the actually existing 'communist' world of the Soviet Union and its satellite states in Eastern Europe.

But we need to begin with what might seem an oddity, and must have seemed so to mainstream sociologists when Bauman published *Legislators* in 1987. That is, Bauman's discussion of modernity and postmodernity also includes a discussion of *modernism* and *postmodernism* in the arts, by which I mean not just painting, but literature, music, architecture, photography and cinema – human endeavours that are usually discussed within the broad ambit of the arts, humanities and aesthetics, not social science. Why should a sociological discussion of historical epochs usually seen in terms of socio-economic conditions have to include an analysis of artistic movements?

Modernism and postmodernism

'Modernism' is a term usually reserved for a set of movements in the arts that began in the latter part of the nineteenth century in Europe, gained a particular momentum in the early years of the twentieth century and continued to flourish until at least the middle of the twentieth century, the periodisation being dependent on when one believes that a new set of aesthetic strategies and products, dubbed postmodernist, began. As we will see, for many commentators postmodernism in the arts was, by and large, a continuation of modernism, hence the doubts and debates about the periodisation of modernism.

The short answer to the question of why artistic movements are significant to the debates about modernity and postmodernity in the social sciences, and sociology in particular, is that these debates first gained prominence in the arts and aesthetics, and only then, but quite rapidly, engulfed academic disciplines such as sociology, philosophy, cultural anthropology and history. Interestingly, a connection between the two had already been made in two significant contributions by the American sociologist Daniel Bell – whose work I alluded to briefly in Part I – once he had moved on from the 'end of ideology' thesis. In *The Coming of Post-Industrial Society* (1973) and *The Cultural Contradictions of Capitalism* (1978, first published 1976; all references are to the later edition) Bell had already made a connection between aesthetic and social changes, and had put both within an overarching sense of an ending of one epoch and the beginning of another.

In the first book Bell argued that Western industrial societies were undergoing a profound transformation, driven primarily by the development of computers and the mass media. In particular, the new era was characterised by the growing significance of information and theoretical knowledge and science and engineering. As a consequence, the information worker and the knowledge worker were fast displacing the industrial worker. The new information economy, in his view, was making that old order and the previous capital-labour conflicts redundant. And he was already pointing out that the new era was being heralded by the emergence of a huge new conceptual vocabulary in which everything was post-something, and he went on to list, among a host of other terms, 'post-modern' (1973: 53–4).

The change in aesthetic sensibility hinted at here is developed much more fully in the second text, and is allied to that all-important 'post-Puritan' era cited in the first. In *Cultural Contradictions* Bell discusses both modernism and postmodernism in the arts as significant markers as well as arguing that they are constitutive of the social changes underway (see also Boyne and Rattansi 1990: 6). In a now uncontroversial interpretation, Bell connects modernism with new perspectives and experiences of space and time opened up by the new modes of travel and communication and the novel speed and fragmentariness of the rapidly growing cities of the late nineteenth and early twentieth centuries.

Bell recognised that in the post-industrial era in the West something significantly transformational was happening that involved technological changes, new patterns of consumption, novel attitudes to sex, disrespect towards established political authorities and new movements in the arts, although he did not give it the name 'postmodernity'. That honour went to the French philosopher Jean-François Lyotard, whose *The Postmodern Condition* was first published in French in 1979 and was followed by an English translation in 1984 with an introduction by the American cultural critic Frederic Jameson.

As Jameson noted in his introduction (Jameson 1984: xvi), although Lyotard had previously been involved in a variety of artistic projects, in *The Postmodern Condition* he focuses on post-industrialism, the new role of knowledge in the economy and developments in science, drawing out what he regarded as their radical philosophical consequences. He had little to say about aesthetics and the arts. This is no doubt because the book was the result of a request to Lyotard from the President of the Conseil des Universités of Quebec to construct a report on the current state of knowledge in the advanced industrial societies. And almost at the beginning of the book, Lyotard mentions the work of both Bell and the French sociologist Alan Touraine on post-industrialism, announcing that

'Our working hypothesis is that the status of knowledge is altered as our societies enter what is known as the postindustrial age and cultures enter what is known as the postmodern age' (1984: 3). Thus Lyotard makes the same association between post-industrialism and postmodernism that Bell had made, though for Lyotard, in sharp contrast, the postmodern marked a radical break with the modern.

Here one immediately enters a terminological and conceptual minefield. Bell did not talk of postmodernity, only of postmodernism as a minor variant of modernism. In his title, *The Postmodern Condition*, Lyotard does not just refer to cultural movements, but implies that post-industrialism is associated with a whole new postmodern epoch. On the other hand, in an essay appended to his seminal text, entitled 'Answering the Question: What is Postmodernism?', Lyotard claims that the postmodern 'is undoubtedly part of the modern' (1984: 79), and in the context of discussing modernism in the arts we find the following enigmatic formulation: 'A work can only become modern if it is first postmodern. Postmodernism thus understood is not modernism at its end but in the nascent state, and this state is constant' (1984: 79; see also 1988: 276)). Moreover, in this essay he jousts with the German philosopher Jürgen Habermas in a discussion of the significance of the Enlightenment. Habermas, in a widely read article, 'Modernity: An Incomplete Project' (1981; all references are to the reprinted version, Habermas 1983), regarded not just the Enlightenment but the whole promise of Western modernity as threatened by the new postmodern thinkers, especially those whom he labelled the 'young conservatives', among whom he included the French thinkers Bataille, Foucault and Derrida (Habermas 1983: 14), though not Lyotard (Habermas 1983: 6–7).

For the time being, let us note that part of Lyotard's originality and influence lay in his (somewhat ambiguous) definition of postmodernity as also an *intellectual* condition: 'Simplifying in the extreme', Lyotard says, 'I define postmodern as incredulity toward metanarratives. This incredulity is undoubtedly a product of progress in the sciences: but that progress presupposes it' (Lyotard 1984: xxiv). And among the modern 'grand narratives' that are in his sights, the ones that for him have legitimised modern discourses and are discredited – or should be, for what he regards as a *fait accompli* was hardly uncontroversial – are 'the dialectics of Spirit, the hermeneutics of meaning, the emancipation of the rational or working subject, or the creation of wealth' (Lyotard 1984: xxiii).

That the Enlightenment, Kant and Habermas are key targets he makes immediately clear (Lyotard 1984: xxiii–xxiv). Much debate has ensued as to exactly which other grand narratives Lyotard has in mind, but the general tenor is clear: he is against any story that purports to see human history as uniformly tending towards progress, the good and rational social order and the general emancipation of all individuals in society. Marxism, liberalism – especially when allied to a Whiggish belief in continuing progress – science and technology, as universally liberating forces, all seem obviously to fall into the category of modern grand narratives that he regards as now exhausted beyond resurrection. No more totalising discourses, no more positing of unified goals of history (Lyotard 1984: 6).

Instead, Lyotard proposes that the postmodern is a time for local narratives, for a sensitivity to difference, for an acceptance of incommensurability between 'language games' and thus an acceptance of the impossibility of global or overarching epistemological and narrative consensus.

It did not take long for critics to point to myriad problems in Lyotard's loosely conceptualised idea of the postmodern. Chief among them was that his own distinction between the modern and postmodern was itself a grand narrative, that within the idea of grand narrative whole different levels of narrative had been shoe-horned, and the issue of why we should abandon all grand narratives simply because some were clearly implausible (Kellner 1988). Moreover, as Fraser and Nicholson argued (1988), Lyotard also had a grand narrative underlying his thesis that the whole postmodern epoch was singularly dominated by the demands of 'performativity', that is, an efficiency of outcomes.

For the time being, I will not follow the voluminous debate about modernity and postmodernity, modernism and postmodernism, as it unfolded in myriad books and journals in the 1980s; Boyne and I have presented an overview, one to which I will return (Boyne and Rattansi 1990). My purpose has been only to set the scene for a discussion of Bauman's *Legislators and Interpreters*, which positions itself in a very specific manner in relation to these debates. We will learn more about these debates from a serious exploration of Bauman's first text on the question of 'modernity', from a postmodernist perspective, which inaugurated a prolific period of publications by him on the subject.

The fall of the legislator-intellectuals

It was the *philosophe* Destutt de Tracy who coined the term 'ideology' to name the science that would lead to a science of society, given the name 'sociology' by Auguste Comte in the nineteenth century (*Legislators*: 104). However, before this fateful event, it was Napoleon who challenged the pretensions of the *philosophes* in the early nineteenth century, for he saw them as competitors and obstacles in his bid for supreme power. Bauman saw this conflict between the ambitious Napoleon and the *philosophes* as decisive, and fatal, for the Enlightenment Project of the intellectuals; henceforth a permanent gulf opened up, which was later to manifest itself as a division between the pragmatic approach of politicians and the theoretically informed, and principled but – as politicians were to see it – dogmatic attitudes of experts in rationality who thought they knew better. This was a battle that the intellectuals were bound to lose. For as the modern state grew more powerful it had less needed for overbearing intellectuals, preferring subservient technicians and bureaucrats who would devote themselves to finding solutions to problems defined by politicians and the state.

Modernity from a postmodern perspective

As we have seen, for Bauman much of modernity was given its defining contours by the Enlightenment Project; and this for him is especially brought into sharp focus from a postmodern viewpoint. Equally obvious, according to Bauman, is that from a postmodern perspective it is possible to recognise that modernity is in terminal decline and indeed is in the process of being superseded by a new postmodern era. Bauman, though, is at pains to distance himself from notions of post-industrialism, for they remain, for him, imprisoned within the limiting parameters of modernity. (*Legislators*: 117).

How then to define this new epoch if not in terms of technological and social changes? For Bauman a whole civilisation is at stake:

The postmodernist discourse ... is about the credibility of modernity
itself as a self-designation of Western civilization, whether industrial or post-industrial, capitalist or post-capitalist ... The postmodernist debate is about the self-consciousness of Western society and
the grounds (or the absence of grounds) for such consciousness.
(*Legislators*: 118)

Postmodernity, postmodernism and modernism: an initial critique of *Legislators and Interpreters*

Deciding that the origins of the new postmodernist self-
consciousness originated in the critique of rationalist modern
architecture, Bauman, unlike some commentators, is quite clear
that there is a broad unity between movements in the arts, philosophy and the social sciences, and the whole new temper of
Western culture, although he was later to claim (Bauman and
Tester 2001: 96) that he had always distanced himself from postmodern*ism* and was interested only in postmodern*ity*): the unity
between the arts and social sciences lay in a generalised lack of self-
confidence in the West's conviction of itself as offering a superior
model of life as against those that had been dismissed as 'primitive'
and 'pre-modern'. Thus he saw a similarity between the erosion
of 'objective grounds' in art, the inability now to pronounce on
the difference between good and bad art and indeed the division
between art and non-art, and the collapse of philosophical certainties, signalled by the growing popularity of 'post-Wittgensteinian
and post-Gadamerian hermeneutics in social sciences, or the vitri-
olic attacks of the '"neo-pragmatists" against the Carthesian [sic]–
Lockean–Kantian tradition in modern philosophy'. For Bauman,
postmodernist movements in the arts, philosophy and the social
sciences, supposedly disparate phenomena, were 'manifestations
of the same process' (*Legislators*: 118).

First and foremost, though, postmodernity is seen by Bauman as
a cultural and intellectual phenomenon, whose break is with modernist tenets. In particular, Bauman argues, whereas modernity
was underpinned by a belief in *certainty*, in having 'objective, absolute foundations' and a universalist belief in its superiority, this
no longer holds true. For the modern temperament 'it was evident
that the West was superior to the East, white to black, civilized to

crude, cultured to uneducated, sane to insane, healthy to sick, man to woman, normal to criminal, more to less, riches to austerity, high productivity to low productivity, high culture to low culture' (*Legislators*: 120; this is the only place in the text where the overlapping denigration of women, black people and other populations is explicitly acknowledged).

Note for the time being several other distinctive features of Bauman's definition of postmodernity. For him what began as a self-deprecating move in architecture and some of the arts has now engulfed the whole intellectual and cultural foundation of Western civilization. Moreover, his argument shifts at various points from a focus on intellectual and artistic movements to a transformation in the conditions of *global political power*. Modernity, in keeping with his earlier emphasis on the fateful conjoining of knowledge and power, was seen as inextricably bound up with the West's global dominance, and postmodernity is identified with a decline in that hold over the globe. Postmodernity thus is also a reflection of and constitutive of a new global political order.

This muddies the waters regarding a significant debate about how to define the 'postmodern', for in referring to changes in the global political order Bauman was implying that postmodernity was a new condition, distinct from modernity, and not just a transformation in intellectual self-consciousness. Simultaneously, Bauman argued, the West's self-conception as the sole repository of Reason was also being undermined. The various overlapping criteria for periodising modernity and postmodernity make for confusion in Bauman's analysis of the end of modernity/modernism and the emergence of postmodernity/postmodernism. Moreover, no reason is given as to why movements in, say, architecture or sculpture should be or came to be connected with changes in the global political order and how these are connected to an undermining of Western philosophical confidence in its version of rationality.

Bauman remains vague on several other crucial issues. At this point in his narrative, his discussion of postmodernism in the arts – which he regards as apolitical and conservative – remains cursory, as does his delineation of changes in philosophy and the social sciences; and he has nothing to say about what was, at the time of the composition of his book, the still unchallenged economic, scientific and technological superiority of the West, although he *may* have had the humiliating American withdrawal from Vietnam and the economic competition generated by Japan's rise as an industrial power in mind. Nevertheless, his failure to elaborate upon his cursory remarks is frustrating. Thus the exact meaning and causal analysis of the West's decline are nowhere properly discussed, except in throwaway casual remarks.

But Bauman is clear that now intellectuals have been decisively dethroned from the legislator role which they had assigned themselves during the Enlightenment. Thus the crisis of modernity is inseparable from the crisis of intellectuals, and both are inseparable from the decline of older disciplinary modes of centralised power. The state has now discovered new modes of social control, with narrowly qualified, specialised social workers, probation officers and administrative bureaucrats taking over from broadly educated intellectuals. The 'general intellectual' is dead, signalling the final fall of the 'legislator' role for intellectuals.

And there now appears in Bauman's thinking a strand, already present but now acquiring rapidly increasing significance: the power of markets and consumerism, which for him 'has taken all the lids off human desires and has left no space for the limiting role of values, breeding instead an incessantly growing volume of dissatisfaction parallel to the unstoppably swelling volume of commodities' (*Legislators*: 124). It is the state, not intellectuals, that articulates values now, but in fact the state itself has begun to cede more and more ground to market forces. Markets have taken over from intellectuals. Bauman cites as his defining example the way in which good art is increasingly defined by what price it will fetch; the higher the price the better the art in the new art world.

As his narrative in *Legislators* unfolds, we see another characteristic aspect of Bauman's discourse on modernity and postmodernity: its totalising character. For he describes the hold of markets and consumerism as leaving no other 'limiting' forces (*Legislators*: 124). It is perhaps no surprise that nowhere does Bauman reference Lyotard, for Bauman's is the grandest of grand narratives of the modern type excoriated by Lyotard. It is interesting to note, too, as Habermas among others has pointed out, that Foucault, explicitly drawn upon by Bauman in formulating his depiction of modernity, also refused to sanction such grand narratives-while still engaging in them– and indeed claimed not to know what the term 'postmodern' meant, although Bauman, having drawn heavily on Foucault's analysis of the modern knowledge syndrome, omits mention of Foucault's scepticism towards grand narratives (Habermas 1984: 25) and 'the postmodern'.

Pluralism, relativism and the postmodern condition: further critical reflections on *Legislators and Interpreters*

A key feature of the new postmodern condition as defined by Bauman is a novel type of pluralism. This is not the version of pluralism portrayed by Kant, Weber, Habermas and all the 'moderns' in one form or another. Instead, Bauman keeps his distance from the usual idea of a pluralist differentiation in the discourses of modernity between the spheres of epistemology, morality and aesthetic judgement. In doing so, Bauman pursues something different, a new pluralism that has at its base something abhorrent to modernist discourse: relativism. In the postmodern intellectual universe 'all further search for supra-communal grounds of truth, judgement and taste is futile'. Moreover Bauman goes even further, drawing upon Kliever, by positing that *a promulgation of relativism is a 'moral duty of contemporary intellectuals'* (*Legislators*: 128–9, my emphasis). It is important to bear this advocacy in mind, for it will be necessary to return to it when discussing Bauman's subsequent attempts to distance himself from the idea of the postmodern.

Art, once again, provides for Bauman the template for postmodernity. While modernist art was constantly launching new movements with ever more *avant garde* manifestos, hoping always to explore another and further truth, for postmodern art – and here Bauman takes Calinescu (1987) as his guide – there are no advances, only directionless change. Moreover Bauman takes postmodern art to be 'deliberately eclectic in character, a strategy which can best be described as "collage" and "pastiche"' (Bauman conflates the two, although they are not necessarily the same). Now, in this new period, no aesthetic norms are deemed legitimate for deciding between good and bad art or between art and non-art (*Legislators*: 130–1). The category of 'pastiche' was one that had figured prominently in one of the most influential of all postmodern manifestos in architecture, by Jencks (1984), and this is where Bauman finds support for his view of pastiche as a key element differentiating modernism from postmodernism. Whether this can be taken to define postmodern aesthetics is an issue I will soon explore.

Bauman also identifies a form of nihilism, an anarchy of taste in postmodern art. No wonder, he says, that Yves Klein could create an art out of 'nothing' by inviting three thousand 'sophisticated members of the art public' to a private viewing of an empty art gallery (*Legislators*: 133). This type of nihilism, for Bauman, makes postmodernist art apolitical and conservative.

Modernist art, for Bauman, had the same epistemological underpinning as modernity. However outrageous the manifestos and products of modernist art seemed to contemporaries, with hindsight it should be clear, Bauman suggests, that even Cubism and Surrealism 'shared fully and whole-heartedly in this era's search for truth, its scientific methods of analysis, its conviction that reality can be – and should be – subjected to the control of Reason' (*Legislators*: 133–4). This is what allowed the art critics, for example, a perch from which to pronounce on works of art, however puzzling and shocking. But Bauman underlines that this also meant that the modernist art world was thoroughly elitist; the worth of modernist art could be judged only by experts, and it would not reveal its value to the untutored eye.

Postmodernist art, with its anarchism in aesthetics, pulls apart the alliance between artist and art critic that had sustained the elitism of modernism. Thus, the art critic as intellectual suffers a drastic deflation in status, a loss of legitimacy and confidence that according to Bauman has spread everywhere in the intellectual world, especially in 'those philosophical discourses that are concerned with issues of truth, certainty and relativism, and those which deal with the principles of societal organization' (*Legislators*: 140). Frustratingly, Bauman is parsimonious with his illustrations, but for the 'the principles of social organization' he presumably has in mind the widespread debate about the 'crisis of sociology' inaugurated by Gouldner (1971) and also reflected in books such as Hawthorne's *Enlightenment and Despair* (1976).

Bauman tellingly refers, though, to a judgement, modest and almost apologetic, by the philosopher and anthropologist Ernest Gellner, one of the most vociferous champions of Western modernity. Even Gellner had been reduced to admitting, in his own words, that there was no 'clear-cut choice' between Western and other modes of life; one could only make the limited claim that perhaps Western modernity, made prosperous through technological advances, '*probably* favours a liberal and tolerant' form of society (Gellner's emphasis, as quoted in *Legislators*: 141).

What role remains for Western intellectuals? Rather than being 'legislators' they should now act as 'interpreters' according to Bauman. Given the recognition of a plurality of 'traditions', 'communication across traditions becomes the major problem of our time' (*Legislators*: 143). Intellectuals need to become 'specialists' 'in translation between cultural traditions'. In effect, for Bauman, this becomes, as it did for Rorty, the 'art of civilized conversation'. This is all that remains in an intellectual universe that accepts, as Bauman rather strongly puts it, that 'all knowledge is ultimately grounded in essentially irrational, arbitrarily chosen assumptions, related deterministically or randomly to partly enclosed traditions and historic experiences' (*Legislators*: 144–5).

A significant difficulty in Bauman's account of postmodernity becomes apparent here. This new epoch is equated with the collapse of confidence in philosophical foundationalism and with various movements in the arts and architecture, and a simultaneous dethroning of intellectuals from a previously legislative role. However, given that only a few practitioners in the arts and architecture ever espoused postmodernist practices; that hardly any followed headlong into the anti-foundationalism of Rorty and the German philosopher Gadamer; that only one intellectual, Gellner, is cited as being less sure of the West's provision of a definitively better way of life; and that no evidence is provided for the loss of power and dominance of the West at the time: how could these fragmentary developments be given the grand, epochal title of 'postmodernity'? The answer is that throughout *Legisators*, Bauman is skating on a very thin sheet of evidential ice.

Bauman does not address the obvious question of whether his own thinking is based on 'irrational' and 'arbitrary' assumptions and if not, how he, Gadamer and Rorty escape these intellectual traps. I take up these issues again in a later section of Part II. For the present it is necessary to follow, albeit with a critical eye, the unfolding of Bauman's narrative.

The universalism of Enlightenment-derived philosophy, Bauman claims, has now been replaced by 'community' as the only 'secure foundation' for intellectuals. As interpreters, the only job left for intellectuals is ensuring the mutual intelligibility of cultures, and especially, it seems, communicating between Western and non-Western cultures with a particular emphasis on explaining the cultures of Others to the West. However, in a striking move, one not justified with any argument – although in making this assertion Bauman may be relying on Rorty without actually attributing the idea to him – Bauman suggests that *within* intellectual traditions it is entirely reasonable and legitimate for intellectuals to continue to act as legislators (*Legislators*: 145). This, like some others of Bauman's arguments in this text, is perplexing, but is discussed later.

Bauman does acknowledge one obvious question: exactly what constitutes a 'community' of cultural tradition? Where do the boundaries lie between such communities? This is a crucial problem, as Bauman recognises, because it is no longer possible to identify any particular community or cultural tradition with a *national* community. Bauman's enigmatic answer is that it is now up to *philosophers* 'to create communities and sustain them with the power of their arguments alone' (*Legislators*: 148).

Legislators ends with a pessimistic chapter, 'The Seduced', in which Bauman again pours scorn on the consumer culture in which everything, including print and television journalism has become dominated by the values of entertainment rather than serious discussion. Echoing an earlier lament by Bell, for Bauman the habit of instant gratification has prevailed in all spheres over the older Puritan ethic of abstention, moderation in consumption and avoidance of instant gratification. As this will become a major theme in all of Bauman's subsequent work, I will leave a fuller discussion for Part III of the book.

Legislators and Interpreters: extending the critique of Bauman's first exposition of postmodernity and postmodernism

Bauman's first foray into a postmodernist evaluation of Western modernity is undoubtedly a *tour de force*. It has a bold argument, elegantly and fluently written. But it is also flawed in a number of respects. I have indicated some seriously problematic aspects of his argument in my exposition of his narrative and will now focus on what I see as more of its shortcomings. It is best to begin with Bauman's understanding of modernism and postmodernism in culture and the arts.

Bauman on modernism and postmodernism

For Bauman, as we have seen, modernism was all of a piece with modernity's guiding assumptions of rationalism and the cultivation of order. But this account of the series of movements labelled 'modernist' cannot stand unchallenged.

To begin with, while modernity as analysed by Bauman has an overriding preoccupation with order, modernist artistic movements, while aware of social order, were heavily influenced both by the speed of change and adventure of modern cities and by the fleeting and the ephemeral as experienced in the modern world (Berman 1982: 15). *The point is that modernity is a far more contradictory phenomenon than it appears in Bauman's analysis – although he does refer to Simmel's ambivalence in relation to modernity – and Bauman overlooks the contradictions in the cultural movements that sprang up in the early part of the twentieth century such as Cubism and Dadaism in art, atonality in the music of Schoenberg or the fractured narratives of the literature of the day.*

It is not surprising that Bradbury and McFarlane (1976: 13), in discussing modernism in literature, refer to the 'pluralistic method' and the 'relativism and perspectivism' of modernism. It is clear that their delineation of modernism sees it as definitely breaking with the traditional view of the Enlightenment perspective on epistemology, as interpreted also by Bauman, where only one perspective could be seen as right – an interpretation of the Enlightenment that I have questioned, but for present purposes my critique is not relevant – and the task was to find it, rather than adopting a (modernist) strategy that favoured coming at reality from as many perspectives as possible.

Hence a second difficulty in Bauman's account. He sees a clear-cut difference between modernism and postmodernism, seeing in the latter a special emphasis on collage (and pastiche, on which more later). But Bradbury and McFarlane alert us to the existence of collage, pastiche, relativism and perspectivism within modernism; and another authoritative account of modernism, by Lunn (1985), also shows that distinguishing between modernism and postmodernism is fraught with difficulty. Perhaps most importantly, Lunn also points out that juxtaposition and montage were key elements in modernism, as were notions of the demise of the 'integrated individual subject'. Thus, in contrast to the coherent personalities of the realist novel, the modernist novel portrays anguished individuals struggling with internal psychic conflicts while 'in expressionist and cubist art the human form is either distorted or geometrically recomposed' (Boyne and Rattansi 1990: 7; Lunn 1985: 34–7). In various senses modernism was not at peace with modernity; as Bell had recognised, many modernist movements were critical of bourgeois society, and this became particularly clear after the carnage of the First World War. According to Harvey, there were differences between the temper of modernism in Europe and America (Harvey 1991: 27), with European modernism being more anti-bourgeois, though art historians have pointed out that many of the American modernists who became prominent in the 1950s had already been involved with an art critical of the Depression-era America of the 1930s (Harris 1993: 3).

As Bradbury and McFarlane put it, commenting on the contradictory character of modernism, 'It was the celebration of a technological age and a condemnation of it; an excited acceptance of the belief that the old regimes of culture were over, and a deep despairing in the face of that fear' (1976: 46). And the use of collage and montage, of course, blurs the lines between modernism and postmodernism.

The contradictoriness of modernity and modernism, and the

blurring of boundaries between what is to count as modernist and what as postmodernist, are indicative of a notable over-simplification by Bauman in his descriptions of both. It is interesting to note that Bell (1978) and Callinicos (1990), from opposite sides of the political spectrum, unite in seeing postmodernism in the arts as only slightly distinct from modernism.

Ironically enough, as Jameson (1991) and Huyssens (1984) have pointed out, in the post-Second World War period, although American abstract expressionism, in the art of Jackson Pollock for example, continued to express some of the alienation and anguish of earlier modernism, this type of art was taken up and officially legitimised in the Cold War against state-dominated Soviet communism; the US authorities could portray their tolerance for this type of critique as an example of their liberalism.

Bauman is right to believe that there was something different about the artistic movements and products that came to be labelled postmodernist, although he is wrong in regarding the two as totally distinct. He thus fails to provide an adequate account of the differences, and nor does he set out in any detail the historical changes that produced what came to be called postmodernism. Moreover, he does not get the origins of the term 'postmodern' right either, seeing it as emerging in architecture rather than literature and historiography.

Origins of the concepts of 'postmodernity' and 'postmodernism'

An early account of the history of the term 'postmodern' is in Ihab Hassan's various essays, collected together in his *The Postmodern Turn* (1987), where he locates the origins in a publication by the Spanish author Frederico De Onis in 1934. The term, however, had appeared even earlier, in 1917, in Rudolf Pannwitz's Nietzschean book on what he perceived as a crisis in European culture, and then was used in Arnold Toynbee's *A Study of History* in 1947 (Best and Kellner 1991: 5–6), being thence picked up by the cultural critic Bernard Rosenberg in a 1957 publication on mass culture. In the same year, the term 'postmodern' was used by the economist Peter Drucker, who gave the sub-title 'A Report on the New Post-Modern World' to his book *The Landmarks of Tomorrow*, which identified and welcomed trends that were later called 'post-industrialism' (Best and Kellner 1991: 7–8). Other than Best and Kellner, only Denzin (1991: 53), Smart (1992: 18) and Anderson (1998: 13) appear to have noticed that C. Wright Mills also used the term in his famous *The Sociological Imagination* of 1959. The term was becoming more commonplace in the literary and cultural criticism of Irving Howe and Harry Levin, and then it was used in the 1970s by Ihab Hassan himself and Leslie Fiedler, among others. The term was only then popularised in two influential commentaries on architecture, *The Language of Post-Modern Architecture* (1984) and *What is Postmodernism?* (1986), by Charles Jencks, who was particularly concerned to link it with notions of 'double-coding' and 'pastiche' in architectural styles that eclectically added elements of classical and other styles as ornaments, in a reaction against the concrete and glass brutalism of the International Style into which the modernism of Bauhaus had degenerated.

The meanings of 'postmodernism'

Bauman was only one among many who erroneously regarded the concept of postmodernism as having its origins in architecture rather than literary criticism. Be that as it may, by 1985 Hassan was concluding that the term 'postmodernism', which he had himself done much to popularise, 'has shifted from awkward neologism to derelict cliché without ever attaining to the dignity of concept' (1985: 119). And indeed there is a contradiction in a set of cultural movements claiming to be *united* by a 'self-proclaimed commitment to heterogeneity, fragmentation and difference' (Boyne and Rattansi 1990: 9).

Arguably, though, several features can be identified as giving what passed under the label of postmodernism *some* coherence, although these elements are missing in Bauman's account. First, in seeing postmodernism as apolitical and conservative, he fails to note that a key feature of many postmodernist projects was a critique of the elitism of modernism towards mass culture, and an attempt to bridge the divide between high and popular culture in a variety of ways, although we should note that there were some attempts in modernism at using popular or mass culture (Callinicos 1990: 15). Bauman correctly identifies the elitism of modernism, but not the postmodernist critique of this elitism. Examples of the artistic practices which combined high and mass culture can be found in Warhol's Pop Art, which recycled images from popular culture and objects in everyday use, a feature also of the art of Morley and Keifer (Crowther 1990: 252) and of Rauchenberg, who mixed old masters with superimposed modern images of trucks and helicopters (Crimp 1983: 45–6; Adamson and Pavitt 2011: 32–3). The mixtures of jazz and classical musical forms in the compositions of John Cage, Philip Glass and Keith Jarrett are also good illustrations of the relative distinctiveness of postmodern cultural products.

In *architecture* pastiche was something new, where modernism had become identified with the soulless concrete and glass structures of the International Style; thus in architecture the meshing of modern, classical and even Egyptian motifs in Stirling's Neue Staatsgallerie is often referred to (Jencks 1986: 18–19), and there are myriad examples of this sort of 'postmodernist' architecture, although Jameson argues that 'pastiche' is a deradicalised form of the earlier and more critical strategy of parody (Jameson 1991: 16–17).

Bauman and Jameson seem unaware that many postmodernist architecture projects also had a genuine populist intent, devising buildings and spaces in forms which gave them a human scale, different from the distant and forbidding towers of the International Style. Another distinctive feature of postmodernism was playfulness and humour (Jencks 1986: 4–5).

The mixing of historical fact and fantasy in Rushdie's novels, although owing much to the Latin American tradition of 'magical realism', may also be regarded as 'postmodern' (McHale 1987: 95–6; Hutcheon 1988; Berman 1992: 51–4); Rushdie's *Satanic Verses* and other writings are much concerned with ethnic-minority experience, and it is arguable, also, that the incorporation of feminism, as in Kelly's *Post-Partum Document* (Crowther 1990: 256–7), and a more general concern with modernity's Others, especially women, was a defining feature of postmodernist art (Owens 1983; Harvey 1991: 113).

Bauman's description of postmodernism in the arts as apolitical is also misleading in other respects. Most especially, by ignoring feminist postmodern cultural products, including the photography of Cindy Sherman and especially Barbara Kruger, one of whose photographs is a critique of consumerism with a poster of a Vincon carrier bag with the superimposed slogan, 'I shop therefore I am', Bauman misses the radical edge of postmodern aesthetics. Other photographic works by Kruger are explicitly feminist in intent, always with printed text that opposes the objectification of women, something illuminatingly discussed by Wolff (1990: 199).

However, the relationship between feminism and postmodern *social theory*, especially as typified by Lyotard, always exhibited considerable tension, with many feminists complaining that the grand narrative of women's oppression and emancipation was being consigned to the dustbin just as it had begun to have a public presence in philosophy and politics. As Sabina Lovibond asks, 'How can anyone ask me to say goodbye to "emancipatory metanarratives" when my own emancipation is such a patchy, hit-and-miss affair (Lovibond 1990: 161; but see Fraser and Nicholson 1988). Nevertheless, it is important to bear in mind, as Huyssen has pointed out, that in the arts modernism remained tied to the creativity of the male artist, and mass culture was seen as feminine (1986: especially 44–62).

In general postmodernism can be said to have opened up spaces for those excluded from the modernist canon, especially in the visual arts. Thus we cannot accept Bauman's judgement that postmodernism was apolitical and conservative *tout court*. With hindsight one can only conclude that, as with modernism, so in the case of postmodernism: there were both reactionary and progressive elements (Rosenau 1991; Good and Velody 1998; Hutcheon 2002).

Note, too, that the politics of postmodern art cannot be read off simply from a study of art objects devoid of the historical and political context of their reception. In the case of Warhol's Pop Art, for example, while it had little critical purchase on American politics – although in its earlier reception it had the effect of being a critical outsider to the institutionalised orthodoxy of museums of modern art (Jencks 1986: 6) – this may be attributed to the fact that it *preceded* the new Left and counter-cultural movements, while in Germany it was not seen simply as a celebration of commodification, but became part of a movement that attacked the division between high art and popular culture; thus Warhol's serial reproduction of Coke bottles and other objects fed into a political critique of the increasing commercialisation of mass culture (Huyssen 1986: 141–59). However, even in Germany, with the collapse of the student movement, Pop Art followed a more familiar American pattern, being incorporated into the Museum and the Academy.

Pluralism, relativism and the West

Bauman's pluralism and relativism in *Legislators* derive from both Gadamer's hermeneutical *Truth and Method* and, to a much greater extent, Rorty's neo-pragmatist critique of the universalist philosophical pre-suppositions underlying the Western tradition of philosophy, especially what Rorty variously calls the 'Cartesian–Kantian' tradition (1979: 9) and the 'Descartes–Locke–Kant' tradition.

Rorty has now confessed, with exasperation, that he regretted ever using the term 'postmodern', which he had done in sympathy with Lyotard's critique of metanarratives, for 'The term has been so over-used that it is causing more trouble than it is worth. I have given up on the attempt to find something common to Michael Graves's buildings, Pynchon's and Rushdie's novels, Ashberry's poems, various sorts of popular music, and the writings of Heidegger and Derrida' (1991: 1). Be that as it may, Bauman and many others in the 1980s and 1990s had taken Rorty at his word and drawn him into the ambit of the postmodern.

However, it is arguable that Bauman's appropriation of Rorty's arguments (1979) regarding the failure of universalism and the proposed role of philosophy as only one voice in the 'conversation of the West' results in what is the weakest set of propositions contained in *Legislators*. Part of the problem lies in Bauman's extension of Rorty's arguments about *philosophy* to all intellectual pursuits, including implicitly the social sciences, although Bauman, frustratingly, does not in fact mention any particular disciplines, preferring to talk more vaguely about intellectuals in general.

I will mention just a few of the many questions begged by Bauman's discussion of pluralism, relativism and the West. To begin with, Bauman fails to recognise that the simple fact of a culturally plural world does not necessarily imply any form of relativism (Connolly 2005: 38–67); the descriptor 'cultural pluralism' is itself, paradoxically, a truth about the world, and one that can allow a large number of inferences, and Bauman provides no reason why he deduces the need for relativism from this description of the world. Note, too, that whether Rorty is a 'relativist' and exactly in what senses – and Bauman seems to have Rorty as an inspiration for his relativism – is a matter of dispute. For a clear exposition of Rorty's position see Rorty (1989, 2000); for devastating critiques of Rorty see, among many others, Newton-Smith (1989), Geras (1995) and Bhaskar (2010). Rorty argues for anti-foundationalism, which is by no means the same as relativism, although relativism is one among many inferences that may be drawn from his and other anti-foundationalisms (anti-foundationalism being the perspective that there are no indubitable final or first grounds which can validate our beliefs). Rorty defends a form of what he calls 'ethnocentric' pragmatism – a position that he spells out in somewhat different ways in various writings – the implications of which for sociology need to be carefully spelled out, which Bauman fails to do.

Moreover Bauman does not distinguish the various sorts of relativism that one may wish to argue about in this context; the distinction between moral and epistemological relativism obviously comes to mind – and there is no necessary relation between them – providing further grounds for confusion when Bauman talks simply of relativism without further qualification and defence of the perspective.

Now, I have pointed out that relativism would call into question the grounds for his own descriptions, assertions and arguments, a matter which Bauman seems not to recognize, although at another stage of his discussion, as we have seen, he does add the view that *within* any particular cultural tradition intellectuals are able to act as 'legislators', which provides him with an escape route from self-defeating relativism. But this move in his argument only serves to raise further issues that he fails to address, chief among them being how legislators *within* communities of tradition are able to engage in foundational discourse, and how they escape relativism, given that no community is without its divisions, unless community is *defined* as having no divisions, which would constitute an unhelpful tautology.

This is connected to a similar but broader issue: although he recognizes that drawing boundaries around communities of tradition is fraught with difficulty, he nevertheless continues to draw one of the widest possible boundaries: between the 'West' and the 'non-West' without specifying the constituent elements of these large configurations, a problem that also confounds Rorty's discourse (Myerson 1994: 129). Thus the problem that looms large here is that there are likely to be possibly incommensurable, diverse traditions *within* Western and non-Western 'communities', so that no community of tradition can be treated unproblematically as a unified whole (Calhoun 1995: 54–5). And it is ironic that in treating the West as some sort of community of tradition, Bauman is doing so in a context in which he is at pains to point out that the West is conflicted between 'modern' and 'postmodern' intellectual and social moments, thereby neatly overturning his conception of a singular Western community of tradition.

Bauman also fails to note that within the West what in part has led to a questioning of hitherto hegemonic legislators is the emergence of a wide range of previously subjugated voices, among which those of women, racialised ethnic minorities, gays and lesbians and various counter-cultural groups have not only been prominent but, arguably, have played an important role in the very emergence of the postmodern stance that Bauman has adopted. The relationship between these new social movements and the emergence of the postmodern turn in social theory is better recognised in other accounts of this relationship, for example in essays by Mouffe (1989) and Seidman (1992).

Another tension, this one being somewhat ironical, is that Bauman's adoption of a postmodern perspective ignores the (at least partially plausible) argument of many commentators that, at least in part, postmodernism itself is a reflection and celebration of the consumerism Bauman is so critical of (Jameson 1991; Harvey 1991).

Bauman's elevation of 'interpreters' as the new intellectual hegemons raises another set of unanswered questions. What exactly does the practice of 'interpretation' mean and imply, and between exactly which groups is translation to be done? Can one have interpreters for the whole of the West and all of the non-West? Given the pluralism within the West and the non-West, is not one going to need interpreters to be bi- and tri-cultural and so on, and is there not going to be a need for cultural intermediaries who can mediate these practices? And who from 'other communities of tradition' is to be regarded as a legitimate cultural intermediary or interlocutor, that is, who is to accredit the legitimacy of the other partners in the interpretation?

As anthropologists began to realise only in the 1970s and 1980s, all classic and founding anthropological analyses had relied on *male* interlocutors and intermediaries, thus ignoring women's rather different status, experiences and standpoints, an issue that was highlighted only when the impact of feminist interventions and critiques was registered (Clifford 1986). And the mention of partners leads one to immediately recognise that while Bauman refers to conversation, he does not speak of *dialogue* and thus also the whole notion of an expansion of horizons, of learning from other cultures and communities of tradition.

Nor does he recognise that it is not merely a question of interpretation, but also a more difficult process, that is, *translation* between different cultural worlds (Asad 1986); and translation will always entail redescription and a change in both the translator and the translated (Calhoun 1992, 1995). To put it somewhat differently, accentuating a related point, although Bauman mentions Gadamer as one of his inspirations alongside Rorty, he misses a crucial part of Gadamer's project, which concerns dialogue and the widening of horizons of partners in dialogues (K. Simms 2015).

There is, too, the fundamental problem of the disparity of power between the West and the non-West, something of which Rorty (1992: 67) shows considerably more awareness than Bauman. More often than not the West has forcibly imposed its values and narratives on the non-West. Had Bauman extended his gaze beyond sociology and philosophy he would have had to confront the complicities of the sister discipline of anthropology – the cross-cultural social science *par excellence* – with imperialism (Asad 1973, 1986: 148, 163; Rosaldo 1986, 1989). Said had charged Foucault with French provincialism, Eurocentrism and ignoring feminism (1988: 9–10), accusations that of course apply to Bauman as well.

One final point: in elevating 'interpreters' to the position of eminence once occupied by 'legislators', Bauman is simply replicating the elitism of many Enlightenment intellectuals – something of which he is rightly critical –for there is no notion here of the need for a *democratisation* of culture, of 'interpreters' being drawn into dialogue with internal subalterns or Others. The absence of a concern with democracy and its relevance in the trilogy on modernity casts a long shadow over Bauman's work on postmodernity as well and sits oddly with his emphasis on pluralism and relativism.

Periodising modernity and postmodernity: some problems in Bauman

Despite the centrality of the category of modernity to Bauman's 'postmodern' trilogy, his analysis of it is characteristically ahistorical and abstract, features also highlighted by Kellner (1998). Bauman's narrative is more or less devoid of notions of stages of Western modernity, or competing intellectual traditions within the history of Western modernity, or even an acknowledgement of the specificity of Western modernity and the existence of other, non-Western modernities. Even within Western modernity, the specificity of European modernities compared with the modernities of the Americas is missing in Bauman's account.

What his narrative fails to acknowledge, therefore, is the essentially pluralist and contested nature of modernity. Order-making may have been the goal of the burgeoning state apparatuses from the eighteenth century onwards, but Bauman's account mistakes map for territory, the grand designs for the messy, contradictory realities and the to and fro of orders and disorders that have punctuated the historical formation of modern nation-states and the international system. It is hardly surprising that the reaction against the Enlightenment that animated Romanticism – and which fed so strongly into nationalism – is missing from Bauman's picture, as are the democratic struggles waged by subordinate groups, and even the schisms that were an endemic part of the history of Christianity.

Fundamentally, then, Bauman's narrative of modernity omits its endemic political and cultural pluralism. Thus, in a fashion similar to his exaggeration of the differences between modernism and postmodernism, he over-eggs the contrast between the supposed monolithic character of modernity and the pluralism of postmodernity. The entire building that Bauman labels 'postmodernity' is built on flimsy foundations. *Ambivalence* and *uncertainty* were embedded in *modernity* from the start, and not just for Jewish intellectuals in the early part of the twentieth century. Women, blacks, a variety of white groups like the Irish, southern Europeans such as Italians, colonised populations and especially their intellectuals, the labouring poor, were all ambivalent categories within Western modernity and its imperial outposts. To define *postmodernity* as a phase when ambivalence and uncertainty finally come into their own betrays a seriously deficient understanding of *modernity*.

It is not clear from Bauman's narrative exactly when intellectuals lost their authority as legislators. Sometimes, it seems, it happened with Napoleon. But in another parallel story in *Legislators* intellectuals lose their cultural power *only* when the market-regulating welfare state comes to be *dismantled*, ceding ever greater powers to market forces. That is, before the beginning of postmodernist discourse and the shrinking of the state, intellectuals supposedly did have a prominent role, one associated with an organic connection to the state.

In Bauman's various analyses of the transition from modernity to postmodernity these two, and in some versions three, defining, different histories of the rise and fall of intellectuals are dipped into as intellectual resources to shore up his periodisation of and division between modernity and postmodernity, allowing him considerable narrative latitude but at the obvious cost of coherence.

The confusion is compounded by Bauman's conceptualisation of modernity and postmodernity as involving both deep social, economic and political transformations, and changes in 'mentalities' or perspectives. As we will see, in his later works it is quite evident that modernity is both a historical stage, involving particular socio-economic and global structures, and a particular 'mentality'. Critics who saw in Bauman's writings the identification of a new stage beyond and after modernity could therefore be forgiven for their interpretation, especially because in *Legislators* and *Modernity and Ambivalence* Bauman explicitly advocates 'relativism', which came to be seen as a key defining feature of postmodernism in philosophy and social theory, although most 'postmodernists' were anti-foundationalists rather than wholesale relativists.

Sociology and postmodernity

If Bauman's stance in *Legislators and Interpreters* is not difficult to classify as 'postmodernist' in a fairly strong sense, his remarks on the specificity of the postmodern condition as characterised by uncertainty and ambivalence in *Modernity and Ambivalence* do little to dispel that impression. I will soon explore in greater depth how Bauman's analysis of the postmodern condition develops in a variety of works throughout the 1990s. For the time being, though, it is necessary to explore a key theoretical dilemma that confronted Bauman in the wake of his espousal of postmodernism in the 1980s and early 1990s.

How should he proceed as a sociologist now that postmodernism had obviously become a central part of the way in which he saw the world? Was his task to be the development of a postmodern (or postmodernist) sociology? And if so, what exactly would be involved in such an endeavour? The problem began to loom large because in both *Legislators* and *Modernity and Ambivalence* Bauman's sociological analysis is carried out in a conventional fashion, for example as a sociology of intellectuals as well as a sociological analysis of consumerism, and so forth. *Modernity and the Holocaust* too, although critical of positivist models of sociological explanation, is not difficult to assimilate within the canon of sociology, especially because of its reliance on Weberian concepts of bureaucracy, the Weberian (and Frankfurt School) theme of the domination of Western modernity by instrumental rationality and the fateful separation of science and ethics. His vocabulary in *Modernity and the Holocaust* of 'necessary' and 'sufficient' conditions for the occurrence of the Holocaust is arguably straight out of a positivist methodological handbook. And his analysis of what prompted so many Jews to collaborate with their murderous oppressors is a classic exercise in the sociological understanding of actions as underpinned by rational choices in exceptional circumstances.

How would a genuinely postmodernist sociology have differed in its explanatory strategies? Was it enough that his analyses had focused on the concept of 'modernity' and had incorporated a critique of the 'Enlightenment Project'? But here, of course, was the rub. Given that sociology itself was closely associated with the rise of modernity, and that many of its guiding epistemological, methodological and theoretical assumptions owed much to Enlightenment confidence in scientific rationality, it was surely not enough to critique modernity and the Enlightenment, for a critique carried fundamental implications as to how intellectual work should be accomplished, in a manner distinct from conventional sociology. Should not sociological practice change if Rorty's neo-pragmatism, Gadamer's development of hermeneutics, Wittgenstein's understanding of language and Derrida's deconstructionism were taken seriously as alternatives to the Enlightenment traditions that these authors had sought to challenge? There was, too, Bauman's adoption of Foucault's critique of modernity as an assemblage of disciplinary apparatuses, distinct from the traditional Enlightenment view of modernity as liberating, liberal and tolerant, although he neglects Foucault's important departure from conventional social analysis, to which he gave the Nietzschean title 'genealogy'.

Modernity and Ambivalence seemed to be setting the scene for a profound rethinking of sociology, one that would focus on contingency rather than necessity, particularity and locality rather than universality. It would be involved only in 'tradition bound interpretation', it would pronounce on the 'human condition' only in 'provisional' terms, and it would be acutely aware that 'man-made [sic] design' was not like the 'order of nature', but shot through with ambivalence (*Modernity and Ambivalence*: 231–2). In typical reificatory and over-generalising mode, Bauman denounces the whole of modernity:

> For most of its history modernity lived in and through self-deception. Concealment of its own parochiality, conviction that whatever is not universal in its particularity is but not-yet-universal, that the project of universality may be incomplete, but remains most definitely on, was the core of that self-deception ... The question is: is the fading of self-deception a final fulfilment, emancipation, or the end of modernity? (*Modernity and Ambivalence*: 232)

'Truth', moreover, is dismissed as no more than 'a social relation (like *power, ownership,* or *freedom*)' (*Modernity and Ambivalence*: 232, emphasis in original).

Bauman draws upon Rorty's *Contingency, Irony and Solidarity* (1989) to argue that 'the language of necessity, certainty and absolute truth cannot but articulate humiliation ... of the other', while the language of contingency creates a chance for kindness, for there is an acceptance 'that there are other places and other times that may be with equal justification (or equal absence of good reason) preferred by members of other societies' (*Modernity and Ambivalence*: 234–5). The 'postmodern condition', he concludes, thus 'discloses tolerance as fate', and tolerance may make it possible for the future to be one of 'solidarity' (*Modernity and Ambivalence*: 238).

A new form of sociology surely beckoned, in the same manner as Rorty had concluded that a new type of philosophy was necessary in a contingent world. This would be a sociology that would be postmodern in pointing out that a variety of narratives are possible, that many stories can be told (*Modernity and Ambivalence*: 238, 244). *Of course this raises the problem of Bauman's own narrative of modernity being only one of many possible ones without any means of deciding which one was 'better' or closer to the 'truth',* but Bauman fails to see the manner in which his own arguments could be turned against him; I set aside this issue for the time being, except to note that sociology's own pluralism, with its plethora of theories and perspectives, would even at the time when Bauman was writing would have qualified it as the postmodernist intellectual enterprise *par excellence* (Best 1994: 24), and that Bauman's postmodernist perspective was only one among many other postmodernist and already established traditions of sociological inquiry.

Sociologists, anthropologists, social psychologists and historians inspired by postmodernism had already begun to fashion distinctive methodologies and theorisations, as we shall see. Given Bauman's intellectual trajectory, and especially his espousal of relativism and the notion of 'interpreters' as the distinctive model of the postmodern intellectual, as also his adoption of a view of the world as being defined by contingency, uncertainty and ambivalence, it would seem that the next step could be no other than the project of a wholesale rethinking of conventional sociology, especially since he had always taken his distance from empiricist and positivist protocols in sociology.

Bauman confronts these dilemmas head-on in the essays that were collected together in *Intimations of Postmodernity* (1992a). And, perhaps surprisingly, although still claiming allegiance to what might be called the 'postmodern turn', Bauman takes a different stance from the one that might be expected after a reading of *Legislators* and *Modernity and Ambivalence*. *What was needed, he argued, was not postmodern sociology but a sociology of postmodernity.* The final essay in *Intimations* is indeed revealingly and decisively entitled 'A Sociological Theory of Postmodernity', and Bauman strongly implies that the following phrases are definitive of his position: the sociology of modernity would 'not [be distinguished by] new procedures and purposes of sociological work, as other [artistic] postmodern strategies would suggest, but by a new *object* of investigation' (*Intimations*: 111). Bauman continues in the same vein: the sociology of postmodernity – the latter being the new object of analysis – would 'not necessarily admit that its earlier pursuits were misguided and wasted'; there was no need to dismiss 'the old ways of doing [sociology]', nor was it necessary to discover 'new ways of doing it'. Thus, he concludes, sociology does *not* need to be 'post-Wittgensteinian' or 'post-Gadamerian': 'In other words, this strategy points towards a sociology of postmodernity rather than a postmodern sociology' (*Intimations*: 111). And Bauman goes so far as to describe postmodernity as 'a fully-fledged, viable social system [sic] which has come to replace the "classical" modern capitalist society and thus needs to be theorised according to its own logic', its '*systemness*' (*Intimations*: 52, emphasis in original), and thus, he says, 'the accuracy with which individual life-world, social cohesiveness and systemic capacity for reproduction fit and assist each other' (*Intimations*: 52–3). This evokes a similarity with Parsons and the old-style positivist and functionalist sociology of the social system so abhorrent to Bauman, so it is unclear why he adopts this stance, and it is worth remembering that Foucault was also in the habit of slipping into this mode of thinking (Walzer 1986: 57).

These are some of the ways in which his critique of functionalist sociology is constantly undermined by his own penchant for a totalising mode of analysis. Moreover, by identifying postmodernity as a *system* with its own distinctive 'inner logic', Bauman emphasises its difference from what he calls a classically modern system, thus providing ammunition for those who interpreted him as supporting the view that a radical rupture was in train, not merely a different stage of modernity. Here Bauman's analysis seems to be confronted by another self-contradiction, because he also wants to maintain that postmodernity – defined as we have seen as a system – actually lacks coherence, indeed is defined by 'incoherence' (*Intimations*: xxiv), which would make it impossible to define in singular terms as *a* postmodern condition, a singularity that is both implicit and explicit in Bauman's analysis.

The sociology of postmodernity, then, would simply be defined by taking consumerism seriously – thus moving away from focusing on a now outdated model of society as defined by the capital–labour contradiction – and would analyse the emergence of the 'new poor' in a 'post-full-employment' society, in which the poor were no longer a reserve army of labour to be groomed for a return to work. Sociology would now use its theories and methodology to explore how *seduction* works through consumerism and *repression* is held in reserve if seduction does not work, and how the seduction-repression strategy is displacing older modes of integration and social cohesion which operated by means of cultural legitimation (*Intimations*: 112).

Such a sociology would perform a critical function but its critique would be blunted by the fact that *the seduced would simply find this type of sociology 'incomprehensible'*, while those in power would find it 'annoying'; this sociology of postmodernity would thus be deeply unpopular, but 'the alternative is irrelevance'. Either unpopularity or irrelevance: 'This seems to be the choice sociology is facing in the era of postmodernity' (*Intimations*: 112). This is emphatically sociology as *a grand narrative*, one which makes a clear distinction between two historical epochs.

In this 'modernist' vein Bauman appears to endorse a view of sociology that implies some sort of 'false consciousness' on the part of the 'seduced', which seems to include the majority of ordinary members of Western societies. Why else would they find a sociology that exposes their seduction 'incomprehensible'? Also, the seduced seem to be therefore *totally* seduced; in Bauman's analysis there appear to be no points of resistance or a counter-hegemonic partial consciousness among this hapless majority of how they are being duped and seduced and where a critical sociology of consumerism might fall on some patches of fertile ground, might gain some traction, might further enhance a sense of uneasiness; this is a type of analysis that one would expect from someone who had genuinely absorbed the subtlety of Gramsci's profound re-thinking of cruder versions of Marxist theories of ideology (Mouffe 2013). This is in keeping with his view of postmodernity as a new, self-sustaining *system*. This is a grand narrative, of course, one which relies on epochal distinctions between modernity and postmodernity, and indeed Bauman argues that one important reason for his rejection of the project of a postmodernist sociology is that it would not have a conception of postmodernity, and *ipso facto* a concept of modernity, both of which he wishes to retain (*Intimations*: 40).

This consumerist, totalised postmodern world is a world *without ambivalence*, for consumers are totally seduced. Bauman neglects his own diagnosis of postmodernity as characterised by profound ambivalence, but this is not surprising given his penchant for totalistic analyses. Thus in his rendition either postmodernity is *completely* shot through with ambivalence, as strongly implied in *Modernity and Ambivalence*, or it contains a majority that is *totally* seduced, with no ambivalence towards the new social order. Thus ironically Bauman's position reveals an unacknowledged ambivalence or, more strongly put, a downright contradiction at the heart of his own thinking about postmodernity.

There is an equally disruptive ambivalence in Bauman's perspective on the relationship between sociology and postmodernity. Despite his protestations in *Intimations* that he is firmly in favour of a (modernist) sociology of postmodernity, there is enough in the essays in this volume to suggest otherwise: that is, that he appears equally concerned to develop a *postmodernist* sociology, marking a sharp break with sociology as usually conceived in the modern period.

Bauman sees the beginnings of this new, postmodernist sociology in the 1960s and early 1970s work of Harold Garfinkel and the ethnomethodologists – deriving their orientation from the phenomenological social philosophy of Alfred Schütz – who demonstrated the reflexivity and social skills required by ordinary members of society to 'bring off' successful social encounters (*Intimations*: 40), as against the view of the 'orthodox consensus' which saw members of society more or less mechanically playing out roles into which they had been socialised by the family, schools and other agencies of the social order.

Ethnomethodology, Bauman argues, is congruent with another turn in the social sciences, associated with the injunction of the anthropologist Clifford Geertz (1971, 1983) to social scientists to engage in 'thick description' in order to make other cultures intelligible (*Intimations*: 42), and with the social theories of Anthony Giddens and Alain Touraine, both of whom moved away from deterministic conceptualisations and began to emphasise the significance of a sociology in which action was as important as the orthodox emphasis on structure, and also with the looser conceptualisation of the social as system that characterised the later work of an erstwhile systems theorist, Eisenstadt (*Intimations*: 54–6). It is worth emphasising that Bauman calls for a new type of sociology not by citing much relevant empirical evidence but primarily on the grounds that other theorists like Giddens and Touraine have moved to a more voluntaristic stance on the structure/agency duality.

Bauman also argues that the very notion of 'society', theorised within orthodox sociology as identical to a nation-state, needs to be rethought, for in a postmodern world of globalisation the sovereignty of the nation-state is being undermined, and a strict differentiation between what is 'inside' and what is 'outside' a society is increasingly implausible (*Intimations*: 56–7). And the loss of state sovereignty is also of course being felt internally as the state is giving away greater power to market forces, while individualisation is becoming more pronounced.

Taken together, Bauman's remarks have profound implications for the conventional view of society and the social order: sociology can no longer rely on mapping regularities in behaviour and perceive strong trends and 'developmental sequences' (*Intimations*: 60) (although Bauman himself, of course, relies on a developmental sequence from modernity to postmodernity). And thus the very idea of a 'rational' sociology, which relies on analysing cause and effect in a mechanical manner, comes to be increasingly irrelevant (*Intimations*: 63). This is consistent with the ideas propounded in *Modernity and Ambivalence*, for in these sections of *Intimations* Bauman sees the postmodern condition as being characterised by

contingency, chance and ambivalence, and he is arguing for a new
sociology quite distinct from the modernist paradigm or 'orthodox
consensus' (which he confusingly identifies with specific socio-
economic conditions while also continuing to insist – in reificatory
fashion – that it is really a matter of a 'postmodern mind' rather
than social conditions) (*Intimations*: ix).

The focus of social analysis, he argues, should now be *agency*,
and the concept of society should be replaced by *sociality* to capture
the new 'dialectical play of randomness and pattern' (*Intimations*:
190). Bauman recommends a new sociology of complexity more
adequate to what he calls the postmodern 'habitat' (*Intimations*:
191–2), which is characterised by 'chronic indeterminacy' and,
from the point of view of social actors, 'rootlessness'. The enhanced
reflexivity of social actors in a world of much greater choice and
contingency requires a different sociology, more attuned to reflexivity and more of a participant than simply an observer, more engaged
in interpreting and clarifying rather than in judging common-sense
beliefs (remember that earlier in the book he had argued for sociology as a critique of the common sense of the 'seduced').

In emphasising complexity, sociality, randomness and a new
participatory mode for sociology, Bauman, in contrast to simultaneous calls for a conventional sociology of postmodernity, is also
arguing for a new *interpretative postmodernist sociology*, stripped
of grand narratives and more attuned to the lessons derived from
Rorty, Wittgenstein and Gadamer.

It is my view that Bauman's position on the relationship between
sociology and postmodernity is marked by a profound ambivalence
and at times is simply contradictory. *This contradictoriness is symbiotically connected to the contradictory manner in which he identifies the
character of postmodernity.* Sometimes it is a self-sustaining system in
which the seduced collude with their own entrapment in a consumerist dystopia, but at other moments in his analysis it is a form of
'sociality' at the mercy of contingency and ambivalence, in which,
instead of a system-like rigid social reproduction, what we find are
processes which are not 'pre-structured'; and instead of a neat fit
between the 'individual life-world, social cohesiveness and systemic
capacity for reproduction' (*Intimations*: 53), we encounter actors
who are constantly engaged in a loose form of 'self-constitution' and
'*self-assembly*' (*Intimations*: 191, emphasis in original); and what

Bauman calls the 'postmodern habitat' is a complex system which is radically unpredictable and one which defies any kind of statistical analysis of regular patterns of behaviour (*Intimations*: 191–2). Social actors have agency, they have autonomy, such that they are 'only partly, if at all constrained, in their pursuit of whatever they have institutionalized as their purpose'. 'To a large extent', he continues, 'they are free to pursue the purpose to the best of their mastery over resources and managerial capacity.' In case of doubt, he emphasises that 'They are free (and tend) to view the rest of the habitat shared with other agents as a collection of opportunities'; the 'postmodern habitat', then, is a space of 'chaos and chronic *indeterminacy*', a territory in which because of 'rival and contradictory meaning-bestowing claims', the agent is in a permanent state of ambivalence and has the freedom to behave differently and indulge in a pragmatic game of 'next moves'. 'The existential modality of the agents is therefore one of insufficient determination, inconclusiveness, motility and rootlessness' (*Intimations*: 192–3).

But, ipso facto, this is a world in which there is also freedom to not succumb to consumerism, and indeed this is what Bauman implies by saying that this is a social space of chaos, indeterminacy, contingency and ambivalence. Oddly enough, though, he does not mention the issue of unintended consequences of actions as adding to the complexity of this new, indeterminate space.

There seems to be no way of denying that Bauman has presented us with two radically different conceptions of the postmodern habitat or condition, one in which duped consumers internalise and simply play out a script dictated by the market, so much so that they would find a sociological critique of consumerism incomprehensible, and another in which social actors are highly self-reflexive, unpredictable and engaged in projects of self-assembly, confronted by a variety of meaning-endowing narratives from which they are free to choose. And presumably some of the competing narrative surely could be critical of consumerism and the dominance of market forces and the total commodification of social and cultural life, and could therefore seriously disrupt the systemness of postmodernity. The argument presented in *Intimations* is torn asunder by these dichotomous models of postmodern life, and as we shall see this contradiction continues to haunt Bauman's analyses from this time onwards.

The question of 'methodology' in sociology

To some degree the contradiction paralyses Bauman's thinking and prevents him from absorbing important lessons from Rorty, Wittgenstein and Gadamer. Although the final essay in *Intimations* plumps for contingency, ambivalence and self-reflexivity, he draws back from the obvious implication that a new way of doing sociology also requires a new methodology, different from positivist methods of quantification, statistical modelling and static attitude surveys and their associated survey questionnaires. The chaotic and unpredictable postmodern habitat surely demands new forms of investigation more attuned to self-reflexivity, self-assemblage and so forth.

But the other, more conventional pole of the antinomy by which Bauman is conflicted pulls him away from following other social scientists, and historians too, in trying to fashion new methodologies. While Rorty, Wittgenstein and Gadamer had called into question what Rorty called the 'spectator theory of knowledge' in which the observer could create a 'mirror' of reality and thus remain radically separate from the world that he or she was observing, Bauman fails to follow through in developing a post-empiricist sociology. In settling, in the final analysis, for a sociology of postmodernity rather than a postmodernist sociology, Bauman throws overboard the post-empiricist and post-positivist possibilities opened up not only by Rorty, Wittgenstein and Gadamer, but also by Foucault and Derrida. What Bauman fails to deal with is that the postmodern moment was one that brought into sharp relief the *crisis of representation* in the social sciences, philosophy and history.

In contrast, social anthropologists influenced by the new currents of thinking, as well by as new global and local situations, embarked on a series of important and valuable re-evaluations of their methods of inquiry and modes of writing, which hitherto had been taken for granted. The essays brought together by Clifford and Marcus in *Writing Culture* (1986), for example, provide fascinating illustrations of how social scientists could place themselves *within* their research, exploring the conditions of knowledge production in social anthropology in a postcolonial world as well as one in which Western governments were beginning to question the value of the social sciences, and of how the writing of monographs from field research involved a variety of literary devices, especially allegory. They also began to consider how their own monographs could be written in a more open, dialogical fashion, creating open texts with multiple voices (Marcus and Fischer 1986; Manganaro 1990; Jacobson 1991; James, Hockey and Dawson 1997), rather than as closed texts relying on a strict authorial privilege for the anthropologist as a supposedly disinterested observer, which is the classic 'realist' mode of writing in empiricist and positivist social research (Marcus and Fischer 1986; see also Brown 1995).

Bauman appears to have remained ignorant of these new developments, which deconstructed the strict empiricist separation of the social scientist from her or his subject matter and also reflected on how social-scientific texts used a variety of rhetorical and literary devices to create research texts, developments that had also engulfed the social sciences (Simon 1988; Nencel and Pels 1991) and the academic discipline of history, which had its own lively debates on the significance of the postmodern turn (Jenkins 1991, 1997, 1999; Munslow 1997; Evans 2000; Cannadine 2002; Breisach 2003; Southgate 2003; Thompson 2004; Gunn 2006), although that is exactly where one pole of his ambivalent response to the debates about postmodernity was pointing. Blackshaw's study (2003) of working-class masculinity, in Leeds, Bauman's home city, while reliant on Bauman's theorisation of modernity/postmodernity and solid modernity/liquid modernity, shows how the lessons of the poststructuralist turn in anthropology can be deployed in ethnographic research in sociology.

Paradoxically, one of the reasons for Bauman's lack of interest in and engagement with these new developments in the social sciences, philosophy of science and history is that he remained trapped in a positivist paradigm based on a strict separation between *theory* and *methods* or methodology. Bauman regarded methodological discussions in sociology as irrelevant to his concerns, but in fact they can be so conceived only if the theoretical and the empirical are regarded as separate domains. Post-empiricist and post-positivist philosophers such as Quine (1961) and the philosophers of science Lakatos (in Lakatos and Musgrave 1970), Kuhn (1962), Hesse (1980), Newton-Smith (1981) and Hacking (1983) have conclusively demonstrated that 'facts' are theory-dependent, thus making it impossible to regard methodologies simply as neutral ways of collecting data; in a post-empiricist conception 'data' is in part a creation of theories, making a consideration of methods of research a matter of crucial significance in any discipline. New theorisations and new methods of research have to be seen to be symbiotically connected. Only empiricists and positivists can deny this, and Bauman, by remaining dismissive of methodological reflections, therefore remains unwittingly trapped within empiricist and positivist modes of thinking.

Bauman's 'sociology of postmodernity' thus remains within a conventional paradigm; nothing in *Intimations* leads to a rethinking of the methods of sociological research, and indeed Bauman explicitly rules out new ways of doing sociology. His textbook *Thinking Sociologically*, the second edition of which was written jointly with Tim May, consciously and deliberately leaves out all consideration of research methods (Bauman and May 2001: 13) despite the fact that his choice of co-author is an expert on reflexive research methodology (May 2003, 2011; May and Perry 2010). He also fails to fully develop the significance of the post-empiricist and post-positivist point – one deeply embedded in the thinking of Rorty and Gadamer and the newer philosophies of science and social science and one intrinsic to many of Bauman's disagreements with conventional sociology – that the observer, whether sociologist, scientist, philosopher or ordinary actor, is part of the world observed, and therefore has to engage in a form of inquiry that is self-reflexive about the nature of this involvement and how it affects the inquiry (Seidman 1992: 67).

Bauman's espousal of the postmodern turn therefore remains half-hearted and under-theorised, and its implications for sociology are never properly thought through, allowing him, subsequently, great latitude in the way he approached and conducted sociological analyses, as we shall see.

With regard to methodology, Bauman could, for instance, have thought through the implications of Foucault's recommendation of 'genealogy', a suggestion made in postmodernist vein by Seidman (1992: 70) and Blackshaw (2003: 40).

Nevertheless, Foucault's recommendation of a form of analysis that eschews grand narratives of continuities in history, focusing instead on the complexity, contingency and fragility of historical and social formations, is obviously similar to Bauman's characterisation of the contingent, complex and unpredictable postmodern habitat, although for Foucault – and this might have given Bauman pause for thought in his totalising characterisation of modernity – this sort of complexity was not confined to a supposedly postmodern period but was always present, especially in modern history.

Moreover, as Smart (1983) has cogently argued, for Foucault genealogy as a method was intrinsically connected to social critique, an element that remains untheorised in Bauman's sociology of postmodernity, although there is an implicit critique of consumerism embedded within it. Foucault's mode of critical analysis would have expanded Bauman's horizons and given his analysis a wider critical canvas, for Foucault was concerned, in part, to rescue subjugated knowledges and voices that grand, global narratives had tended to marginalise, a form of analysis that also comes across in Blackshaw's much greater attention to Foucault in his ethnographic research on working-class masculinity (Blackshaw 2003). This after all remained a prominent element in one version of Bauman's sociology of postmodernity, as I will show, in the attention it brings to bear on the fate of what Bauman calls 'the new poor', and a properly theorised incorporation of Foucault's concerns might have brought home to Bauman the need to engage with ethnographies of the 'new poor' which would give voice to them, rather than treating them, as Bauman generally tends to do, simply as 'objects' of his sociology of postmodernity. In *Intimations* Bauman does espouse the idea of giving voice to subaltern populations (*Intimations*: 42), but this is not elaborated upon. However, Foucault's project of uncovering the relations between power and knowledge would, if Bauman had adopted and developed it in his work, have given greater attention to the ways in which sociology itself functioned to legitimate the interests of the powerful, especially in alliance with scientific and scientistic discourses, something that Bauman had to some degree acknowledged in his analysis of the Holocaust. Many sociologists seized the opportunities for a revised, postmodernist sociology and its research methods in a critical but constructive vein (see Best 1994; Ward 1996; Scheurich 1997; Alvesson 2002; Alvesson and Skoldberg 2010; Blackshaw 2003; Cooper and White 2012), but Bauman of course retained a disdain for discussions of methodology – stemming, paradoxically, from an unwitting imprisonment within empiricism as I have pointed out – so this element was never going to get the attention it deserved.

It is important to recognise that the newer poststructuralist anthropologists were also much concerned with exploring how their discipline could remain relevant to a cultural *critique*, especially of the West, via strategies of 'defamiliarisation' (Marcus and Fischer 1986; Rabinow 1986), which would bring home to Westerners that their ways of life were far from being the 'natural' patterns of behaviour, thus opening up *alternatives*, a project close to Bauman's heart, for he still retained a constant belief – as did Foucault in his genealogical mode – that social analysis can undermine, by defamiliarisation, the taken-for-granted 'truths' that eternalised and naturalised particular relations of power, advantage and hierarchy (see Smart 1983: 76–7; Poster 1984: 96–7; Barrett 1991: 157–68). Bauman explicitly commends 'defamiliarization' as a technique in *Thinking Sociologically* (Bauman and May 2001: 10) and a great many other works, and his continuing interest in the possibilities of critique during his postmodernist phase is evident in an essay on Baudrillard: 'Sociological diagnosis of the current figuration may not by itself guarantee reform, but without it prospects of critique would be gloomier still' ('The Sweet Scent of Decomposition',1993b: 45).

The impact of poststructuralism and postmodernism on a rethinking of methodology and forms of critique in sociology is evident in a range of texts (Steier 1991; Simons and Billig 1994; Goodman and Fisher 1995; Scheurich 1997; Abbinnett 1998; Alvesson 2002; Cooper and White 2012), and engendered wider debates in most sub-disciplines within sociology, especially those concerned with studying complex organisations (Hassard and Parker 1993; Boje, Gephart and Thatchenkery 1996; McKinlay and Starkey 1998; Hancock and Tyler 2001), health (Fox 1993, 1999) and welfare (Leonard 1997; Carter 1998). In anthropology questions of 'development' were rejuvenated by poststructuralism and postmodernism (Escobar 1995; Marchand and Parpart 1995; Gardner and Lewis 1996); postmodernist currents in geography, with its interests in urbanism as well as spatiality, were particularly strong (Minca 2001). Moreover, an interest in postmodernism spread to Japan (Miyoshi and Harootunian 1989), China

(Dirlik and Zhang 2000) and Latin America (Beverley and Aronna 1995).

Keith Tester, perhaps the most knowledgeable commentator on Bauman's work, has suggested in a note appended to an interview with Bauman (Bauman and Tester 2007: 30 n6) that both *Legislators* and *Intimations* represent Bauman's hesitant venture onto the postmodern terrain, followed by an implicitly more enthusiastic embrace in *Postmodern Ethics* (1993a) and *Life in Fragments* (1995). My interpretation disrupts this periodisation of Bauman's intellectual engagement with the postmodern turn: *Legislators*, with its advocacy of relativism, displays a more eager, uncritical adoption of postmodernism, while in *Intimations* Bauman draws back – somewhat regrettably in so far as he misses the opportunity for a potentially fruitful rethinking of aspects of sociology – and plumps for an unreconstructed sociology of postmodernity.

The possibilities missed by a too-hasty retreat are evident in the results of a more fruitful engagement by feminist sociologists with postmodernism (Fraser and Nicholson 1988; Nicholson 1995). The benefits of these constructive dialogues are perhaps nowhere better exhibited than in the emergence of sophisticated feminist sociological elaborations of reflexive, post-positivist and post-empiricist methodologies of research and their interconnection with the complexities of 'experience', knowledge and social theory. Feminist incorporations of postmodernist themes have enabled a move beyond some of the simplistic anti-realist positions in the latter without sacrificing the immense advantages of understanding all knowledge as discursively produced and socially and historically located, a sophistication that is particularly evident in Ramazonoglu and Holland (2002; Hesse-Biber 2014). Questions of embodiment, sexual difference, gender, emotions, trust, deconstruction, ethics, critique and accountability have combined with the rejection of simplistic modernist positions of the sociologist as subject investigating women as 'objects' of research, issues which have a significance for the whole project of a neutral, objective, value-free science of the social, and which could have enriched Bauman's sociological thinking. Even conventional historians have made better use of a dialogue with postmodernist currents, taking on board the need for greater self-reflexivity in method and conceptualisation, together with an awareness of issues of gender and ethnicity, with Richard Evans's intervention, *In Defence of History* (2000), being exemplary (see also Cannadine 2002; Raddeker 2007).

Eaglestone's remarkable *The Holocaust and the Postmodern* (2004; see also Milchman and Rosenberg 1998; Evans 2002) shows how a sophisticated postmodernist methodological understanding, one which refuses to cave in to the temptations of Rortyan or any other form of relativism, can undermine the claims of Holocaust deniers such as David Irving, while still being able to characterise the academic discipline of historical research and the presentation of its findings as a genre of writing and representation rather than a mere establishment of facts. In *Intimations* Bauman, caught on the horns of a dilemma regarding the significance of postmodernism, appears in the final analysis to play it safe and in so doing seems to settle for a relatively unreflective modernist sociology of postmodernity.

But in practice, or so I will argue, he appears to grasp both horns and attempts to ride out the antinomies between a postmodernist sociology and a sociology of postmodernity much like a rodeo rider on a bucking bull.

Bauman's 'right to inconsistency'?

Although in *Intimations* Bauman nowhere explicitly acknowledged that he had painted contradictory social portraits, such that some parts seem to advocate a postmodernist direction for sociology while in other passages and essays he plumped for a straightforward sociology of postmodernity, he was too astute a thinker to not realise that he was in fact continually sitting astride a possibly unbridgeable gulf.

In an insightful and incisive earlier essay on Giddens's theory of structuration ('Hermeneutics and Social Theory', 1989a) he had laid out the dilemmas of his own postmodern turn in an illuminating if not entirely reflexive manner – for he nowhere refers to his affiliation to the postmodern – by distinguishing, in embryonic form, between 'hermeneutic sociology' and 'sociological hermeneutics', a distinction that has been used by both Nijhoff (1998) and Blackshaw (2005) to mount a defence of Bauman's strategy for dealing with the possible antinomy between postmodernist sociology and a sociology of postmodernity.

There is, however, an important difference between Nijhoff's support for Bauman and Blackshaw's vindication of Bauman's stance: while Nijhoff, in his essay entitled 'The Right to Inconsistency', readily admits that Bauman is inconsistent, but wants to present this as a defensible position, Blackshaw bends over backwards – and sideways too – in following Bauman's convolutions and simply disavows that any inconsistency can be found. Blackshaw does use Bauman's trope of 'ambivalence' as part of his justification, and so arguably the difference between Nijhoff and Blackshaw as interpreters of Bauman is a matter of emphasis, but the emphasis matters, for the dividing line between 'inconsistency' and 'incoherence' is thinner than that between 'ambivalence' and 'incoherence'. In my view Bauman is much closer to incoherence than to ambivalence.

In an interview (Bauman and Blackshaw 2002) Blackshaw persuades Bauman to clarify the difference between 'hermeneutic sociology' and a 'sociological hermeneutics', and this is Bauman's response (here it should be borne in mind that although the quotation comes from Bauman's post-2000 liquid modern phase, Blackshaw's conflation of this with the postmodern turn is by and large justified, as will become clear later):

> hermeneutic sociology seems to me to be but one way among many good ways of doing a sociological job, while sociological hermeneutics (i.e. decoding the meaning of human actions in reference to social conditions) seems to be the job all sociology true to its vocation is bound to perform. This at any rate is what I try, however ineptly, to do all along. I attempt to make trends in human conduct and beliefs intelligible as collective results of the lay efforts to make sense of the socially produced conditions and to devise appropriate life strategies. You may say that making hermeneutics *sociological* is one more name for 'sociological imagination'. In my view, the two concepts should become in sociological practice coextensive. (Quoted in Blackshaw 2005: 71, emphasis in original)

The distinction between 'hermeneutic sociology' and a 'sociological hermeneutics' is not identical to a distinction between 'postmodernist sociology' and a 'sociology of postmodernity', but there are significant overlaps which become more visible when both Nijhoff (1998: 89) and Blackshaw (2005: 58–9) point out that

Bauman's use of literary illustrations and metaphor, rather than examples from empirical sociology, is a distinctive feature of his hermeneutic sociology, especially in his postmodern (and liquid modern) phase; thus, although at some points Bauman rejects the notion that the aesthetics of postmodernism has any lessons for sociology, his own practice of sociology has a significant element of aestheticisation as well as a refusal of conventional disciplinary boundaries between sociology, literature, rhetoric and philosophy.

Both Nijhoff and Blackshaw highlight Bauman's acceptance of an epistemological stance in which all interpretations are perspectival and never final, so that there is always room for disagreement and re-interpretation of – and in – any sociological analysis. However, while Nijhoff accepts that this can lead to inconsistency, for him this is acceptable, for Bauman simply 'arrogates' to himself the right to inconsistency (Nijhoff 1998: 87). By contrast, Blackshaw insists that however unsystematic Bauman may be in the way in which he approaches any sociological analysis, he produces accounts and explanations which are 'more compelling' than those produced within conventional, empirical 'non-literary' sociology (Blackshaw 2005: 68). But if Blackshaw thinks empirical sociology has much less to offer than Bauman's more intuitionist and unsystematic method, Nijhoff (1998: 90) insists that Bauman allows that 'empirical studies decide whether one or the other of these perspectives is more realistic'.

Neither Nijhoff nor Blackshaw, in mounting a defence of Bauman, acknowledges and deals with the contradiction I have identified in his pronouncements in *Intimations* between a deterministic sociology in which ordinary people are represented as dupes of consumerist ideology and who would not even recognise a critique of consumerism as having validity, and one in which social actors are depicted as self-reflexive agents able to articulate, visualise and choose between a range of practices and meaning-systems. This is an inconsistency and contradiction which produces incoherence and runs right through Bauman's sociology in his postmodern and liquid modern phases.

In the Introduction to *Intimations* Bauman attempts to paper over the cracks by referring to his essays in that volume as 'glimpses of the postmodern scene', 'each conscious of being partial and perceived from just one of the many possible observation points'

(*Intimations*: xxiv). The essays, he says, 'offer a picture produced by the rotation of a "hermeneutic circle": the successive re-cycling of a number of basic insights' (*Intimations*: xxv). But nowhere does Bauman grasp that he is not just offering different perspectives, and that at least in one key respect, he is providing sharply contradictory 'pictures', to borrow his own term.

It could be argued in his defence that Bauman is practising a postmodern refusal to be pinned down to an 'either/or' binary choice and is instead standing astride a 'both/and' position. Hutcheon, in a retrospective on the postmodern turn, has identified this type of move as the lasting and valuable legacy of postmodernism (2007: 17). There may indeed be productive contradictions that turn out to be in some ways complementary, thus leading to a genuine enlargement of insight, but I would aver that the contradiction I have identified in Bauman's writing is disabling: the impossibility of reconciliation between the two positions ends up in an analytical cul-de-sac. To borrow a term made both famous and notorious by Thomas Kuhn in his *The Structure of Scientific Revolutions* (1962), there is a degree of *incommensurability* between the two portraits that Bauman paints of the postmodern condition which seems impossible to overcome.

Aspects of Bauman's sociology of postmodernity: a critical commentary

The consumer society

In his (relatively conventional) sociology of postmodernity (rather than in his analysis of 'sociality' in the 'postmodern habitat') Bauman distinguishes his own position by identifying where the even more conventional 'orthodox consensus' – a term borrowed from Giddens – in sociology had gone wrong, thus ending up in crisis. Bauman could have taken a more postmodernist stance by referring to sociology's crisis as involving in part a crisis of representation, a move that postmodernist-inclined anthropologists and historians had made, but as we have seen Bauman steps back from taking this new road. Instead, he simply argues that the object of sociology, contemporary Western society, had undergone a profound transformation which academic sociology had failed to grasp. This viewpoint is clearly articulated in his critical commentary on Giddens ('Hermeneutics and Social Theory', 1989a), written at the same time as he was composing the essays that were brought together in *Intimations of Postmodernity*.

The problem with conventional sociology as Bauman sees it is simply that the world has changed, but sociology continues to operate with old, outdated conceptualisations ('Hermeneutics and Social Theory': 55): among other things, sociology continues to see 'society' as coeval with the nation-state; it is still obsessed with social class and sees the distributive struggle simply in terms of the capital–labour contradiction; power is still theorised as closely tied to the economy and economic conflicts; and political actors are seen as having preformed political interests. Implicit in these remarks are criteria by which one might judge Bauman's own sociology of postmodernity: how far does it move away from these nostrums?

While some of the historical analysis of how Western societies had been experiencing fundamental transformation is presented in *Memories of Class* (1982), a more up-to-date account is presented in *Work, Consumerism and the New Poor* (1998b), and to this one should add a range of insights into postmodernity that are presented in *Mortality and Immortality and Other Life Strategies* (1992b), *Postmodern Ethics* (1993a), *Life in Fragments* (1995), *Globalization* (1998a) and *In Search of Politics* (1999).

The consumer society

Work, Consumerism and the New Poor is a particularly useful text with which to begin, for in it Bauman provides a succinct overview, sketching out the key elements in his analysis of postmodernity. One central theme of the book is the transformation of Western European societies from 'producer' to 'consumer' societies. This is the first of many dualities that recur in the text. The producer society is not given any precise dating, but it is clear that Bauman here is speaking of Western Europe from the beginnings of industrialisation in the eighteenth century to some time in the 1950s. This was a society in which the bulk of the population became integrated through the discipline of factory work. A 'work ethic' was instilled by owners, the Church and the state. Dignity and identity were attained through work; work was a calling, a vocation, a duty, and many workers were able to build careers; they could identify a whole life's path through work (*Work, Consumerism*: 17). Workers spent their lives in Panopticon-like institutions, closely watched by supervisors. In a producer society work is not merely an economic phenomenon: it is a moral one. The notion of a work ethic therefore is also an ethic of work. But there was a cost, to the workers: most work was soulless; industrial production required what Bauman calls 'part-humans', involved in a 'blind drill' and requiring 'unthinking obedience'.

Bauman's exposition is pitched at a high level of abstraction, although he does – but only in this instance – distinguish between Western European and American societies, arguing that in the latter workers were integrated not so much by the work ethic as by the promise of something better to come, that is, upward social mobility. American workers worked simply to earn money, so that in some way or another they might move out and on, upwards, propelled by the 'spirit of enterprise' (*Work, Consumerism*:

20). However, it is remarkable that Bauman has nothing to say about the increasing participation of women in the labour force, nor does he comment on the role played by immigration in both Western Europe and the USA in lubricating the wheels of industry. Remarkable, but not untypical: this is simply part of the habitual manner in which Bauman's analyses remain blind to issues of gender and racialisation, as I have had to point out earlier.

Bauman moves abruptly from an account of the 'producer society' to what he calls 'our' consumer society. What characterises this new social form is that it engages its members primarily as consumers, not producers. At this stage no explanation is provided as to how the producer society becomes a consumer society; it just does. Interestingly, he refers to it as 'modernity mark two' (*Work, Consumerism*: 26) and also uses the notions of 'late-modern' and post-modern' as equivalents (*Work, Consumerism*: 24). But Bauman is keen to emphasise that this is a whole new type of society, for the differences between the producer and the consumer society 'are so deep and ubiquitous that they fully justify speaking of our society as a separate and distinct kind – a consumer society'; 'virtually every aspect of society, culture and individual life' is marked by consumerism (*Work, Consumerism*: 24). This formulation recalls those of *Intimations* where he talks of postmodern society as a *system*; hence now his emphasis on the *ubiquity* of consumerism. *Note the profound economism that is displayed in Bauman's analysis, for he argues that every aspect of life is governed by the principle of consumption.*

The demise of the old industrial factory jobs gives rise to more insecure work; flexibility becomes the 'catchword' (*Work, Consumerism*: 27). Life under consumerism is hectic. Individuals are seduced into a merry-go-round from which there seems no escape. Trends change quickly, and members of the consumer society have to be alert and flexible in the ways they construct their identities through consumer purchases so as not to be caught out by changes of fashion. The consumer society is as much a machine that devours its members as the producer society was, but this time by a continuous generation of new needs. Moreover, 'In a properly working consumer society consumers *seek actively to be seduced*. They live from attraction to attraction, from temptation to temptation, from swallowing one bait to fishing for another', driven by a 'compulsion' to consume (*Work, Consumerism*: 26, my emphasis).

What we see here is the *abolition of agency*, for this appears as a self-sustaining system. No agents are mentioned who produce this compulsion to consume, no advertising agencies, no large corporations, no banks. The credit card does appear in Bauman's account: indeed he steals a well-known credit card advertising slogan by writing of the way in which instant gratification is encouraged as consumers gorge on credit, resulting in a process in which 'waiting is taken out of wanting and wanting out of waiting', but the banks that have created the credit card make no appearance, nor the burgeoning hire-purchase schemes dreamt up by a combination of retailers and manufacturers. Indeed, manufacture of goods takes a back seat, for Bauman's gaze is fixed primarily on processes of consumption, except that this somehow happens without active agents. How is this 'compulsion', the addiction to consume, instilled, given that in the postmodern world 'authorities' involved in the consumption process 'spring up unannounced ... only to vanish instantly without notice' (*Life in Fragments*: 5)? How do we reach the stage where consumers 'seek actively to be seduced'? Consumers are the only active agents, then, but their actions are already pre-determined by compulsive desire, and so they are active only in a manner of speaking. In actuality they are wholly seduced. But are all members of society seduced? What evidence is there that everyone is a 'fashion victim' or that there is a compulsion to consume that induces an itch that is never satisfied or satisfactorily scratched? What exactly is the source of Bauman's supposed 'hermeneutic' insight into the consumer mind-set? Blackshaw in his explication of Bauman's method refers to 'something seen, something heard' (2005: 68) by Bauman, but the details of this arcane hermeneutic method remain undisclosed and thus utterly mysterious.

Lest I be accused of unfairness in taking these texts as typifying Bauman's mode of analysis, I will show later that similar economism, reductionism, over-generalisation and cavalier disregard for evidence reappear even in a text written in 2013 (see Rattansi 2014).

So Bauman refers to 'cultural fashions', but not to any of those who do the fashioning (*Work, Consumerism*: 28). What also becomes evident here is that Bauman homogenises consumer goods and acts of consumption in a tendentious manner. Bauman generalises the whole process of consumption as if it all resembled the market for clothing and its associated fashion industry. But there is a difference between buying cars, and even washing machines, and buying cheap, newly fashionable skirts and shirts. The consumer in Bauman's consumer society is a cypher, ungendered and devoid of ethnicity or other cultural markers except those defined by unnamed manipulators of needs. Of course, there is a differentiation by purchasing power. The 'stardom cult' ensures that extravagant and unattainable levels of consumption by sports stars, actors and other 'saints of the stardom cult' serve as examples of the good (consumerist) life (*Work, Consumerism*: 35). I will have much more to say on Bauman's conception of the consumer society later.

New postmodern identities

In *Life in Fragments* too Bauman has much to say about the corrosive effect of consumerism, individualism, the privatisation of everyday life and market domination on postmodern identities. In other words, Bauman's economism is again at the forefront of his analysis.

Thus, given the economic circumstances of the solid, hard relations of modernity in which work especially was relatively secure, the archetype of the modern identity was that of what Bauman refers to as 'the pilgrim', an identity that is also tied to the delay of gratification (*Life in Fragments*: 87). The pilgrim, typical of modernity, is a builder of life-long projects, always saving for the future, safe in the expectation that the savings will not devalue (*Life in Fragments*: 87).

But in the consumerist, market-driven, insecure postmodern world 'the rules of the game change in the course of playing'. The pilgrim's strategy of life-long attachments and identity-building would be totally inappropriate. 'The hub of postmodern life strategy is not identity building, but the avoidance of being fixed' (*Life in Fragments*: 89). Not for the last time, Bauman borrows the notion of the 'pure relationship' from Giddens: in postmodernity relationships are entered into only for the sake of what each person can get from them, and relationships are terminated as soon as one or both partners feel dissatisfied, just as consumer goods are kept only for as long as a new model of the gadget has not arrived on the market. Identities are adopted and discarded just like costumes; they are lightly worn. Instant obsolescence is always on the horizon. Life begins to be lived as a series of episodes; time is now irrevocably fragmented into disconnected bits. What defines the coming of postmodernity is the arrival of 'tourists', 'vagabonds', 'strollers' and 'players' (*Life in Fragments*: 91) who supplant modernity's pilgrims. These are 'life-styles'.

The 'stroller' is particularly suited to a world of time-sliced episodes, and is especially to be found in shopping malls, those temples of consumption. The 'heroic producer' has now become the 'playful consumer', who shops and strolls, but in a specially designed environment made safe by electronic monitoring and extensive protection by security guards. The 'vagabond' is again a product of economic changes, for with factories vanishing without notice and skills becoming outdated so quickly, the postmodern individual is without a settled place; while the pre-modern vagabond was masterless and out of control, the postmodern incarnation is rootless and forced to wander 'for the scarcity of settled places' (*Life in Fragments*: 94–5). The 'tourist' is a seeker after new experiences, but in safely packaged chunks. The tourist lives an aestheticised life, in an aesthetic space, but the strangeness of new environments is sanitised and rid of dangers; the shocks of the unfamiliar come 'in a package-deal of safety'. The player's is the world of risks. Life becomes a series of episodic games. Exactly who are the 'players'? Bauman does not say; he leaves it to the reader's imagination.

The problem for the postmodern individual is that each of these identities has to be adopted for some of the time and discarded as the situation demands. 'No wonder there is quite a generous pinch of schizophrenia in each postmodern personality' (*Life in Fragments*: 99).

Bauman, as usual, is frugal when it comes to examples of these types and any empirical literature on how these lives are lived. It is not clear where his hermeneutic insights are drawn (or overdrawn) from. The reader is invited to take Bauman's analysis or leave it. *The reader is treated much like a typical postmodernist consumer, tasting the wares that are offered, and keeping them for a while, or simply rejecting them as aesthetically displeasing. There is more than a suspicion that Bauman, in preferring to write in this mode, is,*

*wittingly or unwittingly, colluding with a postmodern condition that he
views in fact with considerable disquiet.*

And it perhaps bears reiterating that for the most part this is
an analysis which is highly economistic; the fundamental driving
forces of the emergence of identities as always open and unfinished,
and the arrival of episodic life-strategies and the new postmodern
life-styles, seem to be consumerism and the market-dominated
economy. At one point in *In Search of Politics* (1999: 138), in a
discussion of identities as always in process, Bauman refers to an
essay by Stuart Hall, but misses the point that Hall's portrayal is
derived from a poststructuralist decentring of the subject, not an
economistic analysis of consumerism.

But there are other significant problems with Bauman's typology of new postmodern identities. To begin with, one might ask:
why only four identities? Is the list meant to be exhaustive? Why
not the 'skate-boarder', and/or the 'roller blader'?

A more serious issue is that *the identities are taken for granted to
be male or masculine archetypes* (Jokinen and Veijola 1997). Why
does Bauman not think of the nanny or the au pair, both of whom
travel and live as 'strangers', but are usually female? Where does
the lesbian fit into Bauman's typology? Indeed she is nowhere to
be seen in Bauman's postmodern world of fluid identities, for he
simply ignores questions of gender and sexual difference; at the
very least, in the ways in which many are discomfited by lesbians,
gay men and transgendered individuals, they could have figured as
particular types of postmodern 'strangers' who disrupt the modern
binary of male/female and masculine/feminine.

There are other questions that arise: for example, can a woman
be a vagabond? Would she not be taken for a prostitute, or at least
a woman with dubious morals? Bauman's entire discourse on the
vagabond assumes a man, who can go anywhere, at any time,
beginning with the masterless men of the early modern period,
while the stranger too for Bauman is typically a male figure.
Women's ability to simply move around and settle wherever they
please is much more constrained even in the late twentieth and
early twenty-first centuries (Wolff 1993).

Moreover, even the implicitly male figures are drawn in a highly
selective manner. Jokinen and Veijjola highlight this by substitut-
ing the 'sex-tourist' for Bauman's generic tourist, the 'homeless

drunk' for Bauman's 'vagabond', the *'paparazzi'* for his stroller and the 'womaniser' for Bauman's player (1997: 34–8). In each case, a quite different type of 'spacing' and portrait emerges; moreover, the specificity of the maleness is thereby foregrounded, showing that the pretence at universality of Bauman's abstract typology conceals as much as, if not more than, it reveals.

In *Globalization* (1998a), Bauman adds some further reflections on his conception of postmodern identities. Now, the 'vagabond' has an additional element to his identity, for he is also seen as a 'flawed consumer' (*Globalization*: 96); in Bauman's analysis of postmodernity, given an all-pervasive consumerism, every identity is always seen in relation to this consumerist culture. The vagabond is both the tourist's worst nightmare and the figure that allows the tourist an even greater enjoyment, for he shows what the alternative form of travelling life may be like (*Globalization*: 98). More importantly, Bauman appears to recognise that his typology is both stark and threadbare, and so he now argues that most people occupy some sort of in-between state, as both tourist and vagabond (*Globalization*: 98–9).

But this raises the issue of 'hybridity'. Bauman too hastily adopts a viewpoint that sees hybridity as a privileged identity form that only globe-trotting, cosmopolitan, culturally sophisticated, transnational elites can adopt. In the process 'hybridization theorists' also come in for some scorn, for they too are connected with cosmopolitan elites 'who share a very different kind of experience of the world, connected to international politics, academia, the media and the arts' (*Globalization*: 100). What Bauman unfortunately, but typically, misses is the vital, stimulating debate abouy cultural hybridity that researchers of new ethnic identities were identifying as a growing and creative part of the new multi-ethnic mosaic of Western societies where postcolonial second-generation migrant youth were combining the identities of their parent cultures with the cultures of their new homelands (for an overview of research on these new identities see Rattansi 2000). In a widely influential essay Stuart Hall had dubbed these identities the 'new ethnicities' (S. Hall 1992a), both encapsulating and giving impetus to considerable new research. If any set of identities had the defining characteristics of the postmodern era, these new 'hybrid' ethnicities were the ones; alas, they escape Bauman's all-too-ethnocentric gaze.

Body-panic

In *Life in Fragments* and *In Search of Politics*, Bauman insists that the
collapse of collective institutions and identities in postmodernity is so
complete that the postmodern individual is forced to turn inwards,
and especially to the body. Postmodern times are times of body-
obsession and even 'body-panic' (*Life in Fragments*: 121). Another
stark duality emerges in this context, that between 'health' or the
healthy body, a requirement for the disciplined and regimented life
of modernity, and 'fitness' or the fit body, required to change course
at a moment's notice to sample yet another sensation promoted by
postmodern consumer culture. Bauman points to the popularity of
cooking and diet and slimming primers as a symptom of privatised
body-obsession. For the postmodern individual the intense need to
keep the body fit for consumerism breeds, he says, a 'siege mentality', making hygiene and cleanliness into life-long obsessions.
Above all, the 'postmodern practice of body training' is a necessity
in an epoch when each individual life is 'composed of excesses alone
and held together solely through finely balancing the tensions that
tear it apart' (*Life in Fragments*: 121; see also 176–7).

There is an important insight into contemporary forms of concern about body fitness in Bauman's discussion, but he misses the
point that much of this is also about health, and that, far from
being simply a result of the privatisation of fears and individualism, is often encouraged by state-funded campaigns about genuine
concerns over bodily health: anti-smoking measures, encourag-
ing the wearing of seat belts in cars, refraining from drink-driving
and over-drinking, limiting the consumption of high-fat foods and
taking enough exercise to avoid obesity are obvious illustrations of
policies that are in fact often portrayed as being opposed to private,
individual freedoms.

It is not surprising that Bauman's discussion of body-obsession
neglects issues of gender. Thus, in *In Search of Politics*, while lightly
mocking the popularity of 'Weight Watchers' groups (*In Search
of Politics*: 43–4), he completely fails to note the pressure put on
women by images of slim models in the mass media. For him, the
matter is only one of the endemic insecurity of postmodern life.
Thus, to adapt the title of that famous book by Susie Orbach (1984),
for Bauman 'fat' is definitely not a feminist issue in any sense.

However, it still comes as a shock that in *In Search of Politics* Bauman goes so far as to endorse the highly contentious view propounded by a John Seel that *the rise of 'gender politics' is a form of postmodern pathology, on a par with the fashion for tattoos and cosmetic surgery*, induced by the constant pressure to re-invent identities that is endemic in consumerism (*In Search of Politics*: 22).

But in reducing changes in identities in economistic manner simply to consumerism, Bauman neglects a whole raft of cultural and political transformations that were seminal in giving shape to the period he is writing about. He usually completely neglects changes in women's identities wrought by a variety of feminisms except when he sees them as part of a set of postmodern pathologies; he ignores the emergence of new identities growing out of the anti-racist and civil rights struggles of racialised minorities as well as the rise of novel gay and lesbian identities and the new ethnicities; none find a place in Bauman's picture of identities in the postmodern epoch. Gilroy (2000: 22) has interestingly drawn upon Bauman's emphasis on the body, but Gilroy's discussion of the forms of representation of black bodies serves only to highlight Bauman's neglect of the racialisation of black and brown bodies. He sees only the juggernaut, the all-devouring machine of consumerism. A more adequate analysis would at the very least have highlighted the manner in which women, ethnic minorities and gays and lesbians in fact challenged dominant imageries and imaginaries, for example in the mass media, including, especially, advertising, which remains one of the dominant agencies of the consumer society. I will discuss this again in the final part of the book.

Bauman provides no evidence to suggest that social class identities, so crucial in the 'producer society', had completely disappeared, leaving the field to domination by consumerist identities and ideologies, another issue to be discussed in the next part of the book. He addresses only the question of the fate of the work ethic. The work ethic, and the ethic of work, he argues, now give way to an *aesthetics* of work. The only work that has a semblance of a 'career', the 'elevated professions', is that which requires and embodies the same kind of 'good taste', 'sophistication' and 'discernment' that are needed for an 'appreciation of art' (*Work, Consumerism*: 33). Bauman, typically, gives no examples of this kind of work, and so we are left to wonder how occupations such as accountancy, banking, engineering and even law fit his description.

As I have pointed out, in his commentary on Giddens ('Hermeneutics and Social Theory') Bauman had complained that conventional academic sociology was too much dominated by economism and conceptions of preformed political identities; a decade later his own analysis shows that he had failed to break free from the nostrums that he had blamed for the crisis of sociology.

The degree of plausibility of Bauman's analysis of consumerism, with its central motif of individuals completely seduced by consumer culture, will be explored again in Part III of the book.

The rise and fall of the welfare state

In his account of 'the rise and fall of the welfare state' in *Work, Consumerism and the New Poor* Bauman reveals that he remained imprisoned within another dominant sociological framework that he had argued had contributed to the crisis of sociology, an economistic obsession with the capital–labour contradiction. The rise of the welfare state is primarily seen by Bauman as prompted by producer-society capitalism's need for keeping the unemployed fit for work, although pressure from labour movements is acknowledged (*Work, Consumerism*: 46–52); in other words, the welfare state is analysed in Marxist functionalist terms as necessary for the supply of a 'reserve army of labour', as well as an outcome of capital vs labour class conflict. The demise of the welfare state is seen primarily as the outcome of technological changes that reduced the need for industrial workers and the availability of cheaper labour in Asia (*Work, Consumerism*: 54), which enabled a solution to problems of profitability in advanced capitalism.

Not only does Bauman remain within the bounds of conventional political economy, but he also commits another fallacy that he had regarded as contributing to the crisis of sociology: treating the nation-state as synonymous with society. This is evident in his neglect of the contribution of the *international* oil crisis which contributed so much to recession, 'stag-flation' (the combination of stagnant economies and inflation which did so much to discredit Keynesian economics) and the crisis of profitability; the international dimensions were also evident in the growing competition between the major capitalist economies. These global dimensions were crucial in undermining the financial viability of the welfare state. And another key element in the cuts to public expenditure that precipitated the demise of the welfare state in the UK were the bail-out conditions laid down by the International Monetary Fund for its loan to the Labour government in 1976 (Clarke, Langan and Williams 2001: 67).

Thus, judged by the criteria laid down by Bauman himself for a new sociology adequate to the new postmodern period, his own sociological analysis seems severely wanting. This is equally evident in his account of the role of neo-liberalist economic and social doctrines in the demise of the welfare state. What is under-played in Bauman's understanding is the enormous ideological and cultural offensive that was mounted by a variety of agencies before Thatcherism and Reaganism triumphed, a process that was acutely dissected, for the UK, by Stuart Hall in particular (Hall and Jacques 1983) in essays widely influential on the left, but which are ignored by Bauman in *Work, Consumerism and the New Poor*, although he does recognise that some explanation for the success of neo-liberalism is necessary (*Work, Consumerism*: 51; the issue is only referred to in passing in *In Search of Politics*: 104) but not in the context of Hall's analysis of the Thatcherite project of creating hegemony. This is not just a matter of academic or scholarly nicety, for Hall's work was crucially informed by a reworking of Gramsci's insights into the construction of hegemony by ruling blocs; ignor-ing Hall's emphasis on the cultural and ideological struggle that was waged by right-wing think-tanks, politicians, governments and mass media in undermining the Keynesian-welfare consensus by someone who claimed Gramsci as a central source of inspiration is, to say the least, perplexing. And it produces in Bauman's work an arid economism.

There is another element in Bauman's explanation for the fall of the welfare state that requires attention. Bauman borrows (*Work, Consumerism*: 59–61) from Galbraith's *The Culture of Contentment* (1992) the view that the welfare state was a victim of its own success. Galbraith's thesis was that the welfare state ensured the growth of an affluent middle class, but that this new middle class came to the conclusion that they did not need the welfare state, for they wanted and could afford private insurance. But the extent to

which this analysis is more relevant to the American case is not discussed by Bauman; here his earlier attention to the historical and
economic specificity of the USA deserts him. He relies completely on
Galbraith, but any perusal of Galbraith's *The Culture of Contentment*
shows that he has only the most impressionistic knowledge of
Britain and the rest of Western Europe (Galbraith 1992: 152–3),
and in fact backtracks on Britain by noticing that by the time he
was writing, 'contentment' was fast disappearing in Thatcher's
Britain (and in Canada) (Galbraith 1992: 152). Galbraith also
fails to deal with the issue that the 'culture of contentment' in the
Scandinavian countries and in Germany did not lead to a similar assault on the welfare state, and Bauman, in simply endorsing
Galbraith's flawed analysis, commits the same error.

Equally important is the fact that Bauman reifies consumerism
as a causal factor, when in fact the idea of consumer choice in
welfare and health was part of the new right's ideological assault
on the guiding assumptions of the post-war British welfare settle-
ment and became institutionalized because of top-down legislative
and organisational transformations (Clarke, Langan and Williams
2001: 86–8).

But there are other problems with Bauman's (economistic)
political economy of the welfare state. First, he fails to give due
recognition to the fact that while the label 'welfare state' serves
as a useful shorthand description, it hides the plurality of 'welfare regimes', as Esping-Andersen (1989) in an influential analysis called them, which can be understood only by analysing the
historical specificities of the welfare states that developed in the
UK, Germany, France, the Scandinavian countries and the USA.
Bauman focuses on the British case but, because of the lack of a
comparative perspective, does not realise the uniqueness of Britain,
which did not fit neatly into any typology of welfare states, including Esping-Anderson's, which distinguished between 'conservative', 'liberal' and 'social democratic' versions; the British case
exhibited elements of all three.

This is not simply a matter of academic accuracy. In abstracting
from historical specificities Bauman misses the significant shaping of the British welfare state by imperialist and racist ideologies
which regarded support for the family by welfare as important for
the explicit purpose of reproducing the white British race so as

to better shore up imperial rule over 'lesser breeds' in the colonies (Clarke, Langan and Williams 2001: 32–3). And by building in restrictions against immigrants, beginning with the Aliens Act of 1905 which was designed to keep out Jews fleeing pogroms in Russia and Eastern Europe, the welfare state has in fact been closely bound up with the construction and reconstruction of welfare provisions that relied on very particular ideas of the British as a white, Christian, English-speaking nation (Clarke, Langan and Williams 2001: 33, 42–3); hence the anxieties fostered by the fact that welfare services could be delivered only by importing black and Asian nurses, and to meet other staffing needs, especially as there was a strong sentiment that white British women should be in the home and not drawn into the labour force (Clarke, Langan and Williams 2001: 61).

Moreover, in his account of the supposed role of the middle classes and their consumerism in undermining the welfare state, Bauman draws an exceptionally inept and inapt analogy with the backlash against affirmative action in the USA. Here one finds one of the few extended discussions of the case of a racialised minority in Bauman's work, but it takes a rather perverse form. Ignoring the *white* backlash against affirmative action programmes as well as the white racism that had led to the need for affirmative action in the first place, Bauman in effect argues that the whittling-away of these policies was due to the desire of the African American middle class – whose rise he attributes primarily to affirmative action programmes – to distance themselves from policies that implied that their success was due to policies that gave them undue advantage (*Work, Consumerism*: 59–61).

It is ironic that the only relatively extensive discussion of a racialised minority in *Work, Consumerism and the New Poor* occurs in a context where the African American minority is given pride of place in the backlash against affirmative action; racism against it is unacknowledged, an analogy then is made with white middle-class loss of support for the welfare state, and no attempt is made to acknowledge the different degree of affluence among the American – as compared with the Western European – middle class that made private insurance affordable and attractive. Moreover, Bauman ignores the crude tactics employed in bringing on side sections of the working class, a strategy which involved, in the UK, the sale of public housing to working-class tenants at below market cost and with additional financial support.

All in all, Bauman's analysis of the rise and fall of the welfare state is a poor advertisement for his version of 'sociological hermeneutics', besides betraying his implicit promise to break with the weaknesses of conventional, crisis-ridden academic sociology.

What, then, of the 'new poor'? Curiously, almost all of Bauman's discussion of the 'new poor' restricts itself to the *American* 'underclass'. Among other things, Bauman rightly points out that the diverse groups who find themselves lumped together as 'the underclass' are blamed for their own plight, for they are regarded as people to whom a variety of opportunities are offered to escape their fate, but their fecklessness, disinclination to work and other self-generated characteristics mean that they fester at the bottom of the social heap without hope of redemption. They are thus feared and loathed in equal measure, especially because they are also seen as highly likely to engage in criminal activities (*Work, Consumerism*: 63–73).

Even if the discussion is restricted to the American case, it is surprising that Bauman makes little reference to the debate within American sociology on the usefulness or otherwise of the category of the underclass, restricting himself to castigating the American mass media as the prime vehicle for popularising the term. Moreover, Bauman makes very little of the *racialisation* of the debate in the USA, which tended to focus disproportionately on African Americans and Hispanics. Both lacunae result in part from his failure to notice the seminal work of the eminent African American sociologist William Julius Wilson, who, in a number of research projects and publications, had challenged dominant popular assumptions about the underclass. His widely discussed book *The Truly Disadvantaged: The Inner City, the Underclass, and Public Policy* (1987) had highlighted the racialised character of the debate, and had also advanced an explanation that foregrounded the de-industrialisation of northern cities, the so-called 'frost-belt', as a prime cause of unemployment among black and poor white communities and the consequent effects on morale, educational aspirations, lack of opportunities for women and so forth which the mass media and right-wing authors such as Charles Murray had portrayed as being, instead, the result of wilful fecklessness, low intelligence and a host of other factors.

It is particularly surprising that Bauman makes little reference to similar debates in Britain, although a whole spate of publications and media panics had succeeded in raising public anxieties. By the time Bauman composed his *Work, Consumerism and the New Poor*, at least two important books by British sociologists had surveyed the debates and provided much-needed empirical information and a debunking of myths around the 'underclass' (Mann 1991; Morris 1994; see also Bagguley and Mann 1992). Especially, the assumption of a 'culture of poverty' which continually recycled the same families into feckless, indolent unemployment and criminality had been thoroughly debunked and would have provided much-needed grist to Bauman's mill on the way myths about the underclass served to stigmatise marginalised groups and shore up middle-class contempt for them.

Continuing on his American journey, Bauman argues that consumer culture has been central to the stigmatisation of the underclass, for the individualism and ideology of choice so central to consumer culture made it easier to blame the members of this underclass for simply having made the wrong choices wilfully and against all advice. Thus they could be dismissed simply as 'unfulfilled' and 'flawed consumers' (*Work, Consumerism*: 1, 38, 70, 73, 75), terms that Bauman came to use repeatedly in later work. However, Bauman is unclear as regards the degree to which this really is a *new* poor, or simply another version of similar marginalised groups always stigmatised since the rise of modernity.

Bauman concludes his analysis by reiterating a view propounded earlier in the book, that in an era of consumerism, with its related stigmatisation of the poor as flawed consumers, it is easier to dismantle the welfare state, for its institutions and policies are that much easier to present as a waste of tax-payers' money on the wilfully feckless, the slothful, the wicked and the corrupt (*Work, Consumerism*: 91).

He could have added, if he had read works by Mann (Mann 1991, 1994), Morris (1994), Bagguley and Mann (1992) and William Julius Wilson (1987), that however much sociology as a hermeneutic enterprise has to rely on common-sense understandings, in the case of the so-called 'underclass' debate, sociology had by and large acquitted itself honourably in subjecting the common-sense notion and its underpinning assumptions to consistent and incisive critique. Bauman's own critique is that much weaker for not having included the research and analysis of these other authors, especially with regard to the British case, but also in underplaying the racialisation and gendering of the debates (he mentions only in passing (*Work, Consumerism*: 76) the preponderance of African Americans awaiting execution in the US prison population; the issue of gender as usual goes unnoticed). And as Bagguley and Mann (1992: 123) complain, but Bauman does not but perhaps should have done, 'One never hears of the Wall Street underclass demoralised by their junk bond dependency culture [how prescient this now appears] ... Their divorces, white collar crime, drug taking, state welfare dependency [the reference here is to the vast sums saved through mortgage relief] and the casual sex.'

Insecurity, the nation-state and the demise of politics

Bauman's portrayal of the (usually white, male) citizen of the postmodern world is of a hurried and harried individual, beset with chronic anxiety and insecurity. In one part of his life he is a consumer whose appetite is limitless and probably now an addiction, armed with a credit card with high interest rates and mounting debt, assailed on all sides by tempting goods and experiences, each promising a hitherto unattained level of satisfaction. But the sheer level of choice is confusing and cause for further nervousness: what is the right choice out of innumerable versions of gadgets like cell phones, clothes like jeans, or microwave ovens or shoes (although Bauman is rarely specific enough to mention actual commodities)? The consumer is constantly looking to life-style gurus and his peer groups for cues and clues as to the right 'look' or the impressive gadget, never sure that the right purchase has been made.

For a worker, there is endemic insecurity at work. The increasing pace of globalisation means that his (I use the male pronoun advisedly, for Bauman focuses only on men) employer may decide to locate abroad in search of cheaper labour. New technologies may make his skill and livelihood redundant. Few jobs come with long-term guarantees of employment. He may be forced to learn an entirely new set of skills, younger workers may be willing to work for less pay, and he has to fight hard for chances of promotion up a career ladder threatened with instant obsolescence. But the media appear to gorge on celebrities with enviable amounts of sporting or other talent, money, glamorous parties, glorious holidays and amazing good looks.

The media are also full of scary stories about all sorts of crimes, from muggings in the neighbourhood to murders on cheap package holidays. Paedophiles, serial killers and mentally disturbed individuals seem to lurk everywhere, let out by all-too-liberal elites in thrall to doctrines that seem to go against common sense. Strangers and vagabonds abound. The world abroad is full of famines and wars, provoking an ambivalent response, Bauman argues, of compassion which soon turns into 'compassion fatigue' as another campaign to help the victims is launched, and exasperation at the inability of those 'Other', non-Western people to create stability and build fortifications against natural calamities. Meanwhile, the media reporting does not reveal that the war-ravaged countries are fighting with weapons supplied by the home country's hugely profitable armament industries, nor that so much of the poverty in those countries is due to 'structural adjustment programmes' imposed by bodies like the World Bank and the International Monetary Fund or development agendas hopelessly ill suited to their needs, but which sell these countries large amounts of over-sophisticated agricultural machinery which rusts in the sun but keeps jobs at home and bloat the profits of manufacturing corporations.

These and other insecurities, baffling events, ambivalences and absences of perspective, which cannot allow any coherent picture to be built up by the postmodern individual, are repeatedly mentioned by Bauman in *Life in Fragments*, *In Search of Politics*, *Globalization* and *Work, Consumerism and the New Poor*, from which I have drawn this composite picture of his harried and bewildering life. 'The sole grand narrative left in the field', Bauman says, is 'the accumulation of junk and more junk' (*In Search of Politics*: 5).

Several sets of pincer movements of uncontrollable fate attack the postmodern individual's sense of existential security: feelings of individual political impotence in the face of sclerotic, elite-dominated politics; globalisation in thrall to faceless 'global markets'; promises of technological 'fixes' that turn out to lead to unforeseen risks – in the late 1990s Bauman increasingly relies on Beck's warnings of an uncontrollable 'risk-society' (Beck 1992) – and a fear of Third World poor clamouring at the gates for charity or to be let in. It is no wonder that Bauman is able to claim that 'The most sinister and painful of contemporary troubles can best be collected under the rubric of *Unsicherheit* – the German term which blends together experiences which need three English terms – uncertainty, insecurity, and unsafety – to be conveyed' (*In Search of Politics*: 5). 'Free-floating fears' and 'diffuse anxieties' thus gravitate to questions of safety, but 'most measures undertaken under the banner of safety are divisive': they 'sow mutual suspicion', for they identify 'enemies and conspirators' everywhere. The postmodern individual, already suffering from loneliness, feels lonelier still when safety measures are put in place (*In Search of Politics*: 5–6).

The result: a series of paradoxes and dilemmas of postmodern politics. The measures to deal with safety take up all available resources, while spaces for debating the real issues keep shrinking. The agora, the public space where such debate might take place, is being down-sized and privatised. In any case, even if citizens had such places, and if debates occurred and decisions were made, the 'powers that be' which might carry out any reforms simply 'float' and 'flow' above such processes: 'the real power will stay at a safe distance from politics and the politics will stay powerless to do what politics is expected to do'. The real task is to cut the knot of 'deregulation and privatization of insecurity, uncertainty and unsafety', but this would require such radical social transformation – Bauman does not spell out what this might be – as to be 'beyond discussion'.

Quoting the famous Situationist Cornelius Castoriadis, Bauman argues that 'the trouble with our civilization' is that it stopped questioning itself' (*In Search of Politics*: 6–7). Sociology, though, can play a constructive role here, Bauman says (*In Search of Politics*: 7). Nevertheless, in *In Search of Politics* Bauman fails to point up any strategies that may revive the agora in contemporary postmodern sociality, and surprisingly makes no mention of the long-standing debates provoked by Habermas's famous and similar thesis on the demise of the public sphere (Habermas 1982; Calhoun 1993; and see Nash 2014 on the role of the public sphere in new conditions of globality). Moreover, his thinking is emaciated by the neglect of

issues of citizenship and rights, the merits and defects of liberal parliamentary democracy, problems of the legitimacy of authority and
the difficulties of reviving the agora in complex, large-scale modern
societies (Carleheden 2008).

To illustrate how 'free-floating anxieties' can condense around
actual individuals who seem to embody the enemy, Bauman takes
an account by the *Guardian* newspaper journalist Decca Aitkenhead
of a mob campaign against the alleged arrival of a paedophile in a
small town in the south-west of England. The 'mob' had gathered
around the local police station, although there was no certainty
that the paedophile was there. For both Bauman and Aitkenhead,
the paedophile is 'an excellent cause to bring together people who
seek an outlet for long-accumulated anxiety' (*In Search of Politics*:
10). At some later time, another cause will ignite local protest, but
the underlying reason for this mob action will be the same: the
possibility of condensing free-floating, accumulated fears and anxieties around a visible, embodied, named and identifiable figure. In
this case, it is the paedophile who has been 'placed on a spot where
private concerns and public issues' meet.

In the USA, the figure of the rapist Willie Horton, Bauman
says, met the required need and 'probably lost Michael Dukakis
the American presidency'. Dukakis was opposed to the death pen-
alty and believed in the possibility of rehabilitation via release for
short periods into the community; Willie Horton failed to return
from one such leave while serving a prison sentence on Dukakis's
watch as governor of Massachusetts, and while on the run raped a
woman. The liberal Dukakis was pilloried by journalists and haem-
orrhaged electoral support. Other politicians such as Clinton in the
USA and Jack Straw in the UK learned the lesson and promised to
get tough on offenders (*In Search of Politics*: 14).

The lesson that Bauman wants his readers to learn is that 'contemporary hardships and sufferings are fragmented; and so is the
dissent which they spawn'. 'The contemporary world is a container
full to the brim with free-floating fears and frustration desperately
seeking outlets. Life is over-saturated with sombre apprehensions
and sinister premonitions, all the more frightening for their non-
specificity, blurred contours and hidden roots' (*In Search of Politics*:
14). The inattentive reader of Bauman's *In Search of Politics* may
well agree with this analysis. And Bauman does seem to have a

point, although the whole narrative is loosely theorised and argued without reference to much evidence about differing levels of insecurity, issues which I will discuss later. For the present I will focus on other questions.

A closer reading of the relevant passages in *In Search of Politics* reveals some other, equally serious but typical Baumanesque omissions and weaknesses in the argument. Although quoting several times from Decca Aitkenhead's description that this 'mob' appeared to be entirely composed of women and that it was led by a woman (*In Search of Politics*: 10), and indeed the newspaper article carries the title 'These *women* have found their cause, but they're not sure what it is' (*In Search of Politics*: 203n, my emphasis), Bauman simply fails to notice that this may be significant. That is, these are not abstract, frightened every*man* postmodern loners, gathering together simply on any pretext to vent their fears. These are likely to be mothers – Aitkenhead and Bauman both note that there were 'grandmothers' involved – frightened for their children and grandchildren, especially given media campaigns by tabloid newspapers concerning paedophilia. This is a gendered fear, involving a moral panic about paedophilia. It cannot serve the purpose of Bauman's analysis without further specification of both the insecurities of mothers and grandmothers and the role of the mass media. These are not unfocused, free-floating fears, but insecurities grounded in very specific issues and controversies. Not for the first time, we find that Bauman's lofty abstraction means that he remains aloof from the everyday or quotidian, in this case gendered, realities. Blackshaw's Bauman-inspired research (2003) into the 'lads' with whom he grew up in Leeds, when discussing issues of insecurity and anxiety experienced by his group of friends, has to be mindful of the class- and gender-specific nature of the constant threats to their 'ontological security', a notion borrowed from the work of Giddens (1984, 1990, 1991) and put to good use by Blackshaw.

Turning now to the case of Willie Horton and the presidential campaign of 1988, Bauman fails to notice the intense racialisation surrounding the Republican advertising campaign that featured William Horton. Horton was a black man. 'Willie' was a nickname invented for the Republican advertisement and reminiscent of the practice of slave-owners' naming of slaves and black servants. The advertisements used a picture of Horton with a beard and looking unkempt, but it was never mentioned that he had been in a cell for several months where he was not allowed to shave. To illustrate the point about convictions during leave, white prisoners could have been used. As a large number of commentators – including many at the time – concluded, with evidence partly from interviews with Republican strategists, a deliberate move had been made to play the race card, and the Horton advertisement was debated in these terms at the time. The advertisement played on long-standing fears of the black man as rapist among white Americans, and also contained serious factual errors (see, inter alia, Feagin and Vera 1995; Mendelberg 2001; Brown et al. 2003). To miss the racial element in the Horton case, as Bauman does, is to fail to understand, as in the case of the paedophile Cooke in Britain, the historical and cultural specificity of the insecurities that were being manipulated or aroused. These are more than generalised 'postmodern' fears and anxieties.

Once again, in both cases, one observes how Bauman uses illustrations without grasping significant aspects, especially to do with racialisation and gender, which were crucial in providing the impetus to the events selected. And again, it is not unfair to conclude that Bauman's practice of 'sociological hermeneutics' has shown itself to be seriously deficient. Not to put too fine a point on it, this is just poor sociology. As so often, it is in relation to issues of racism against non-Jewish minorities in Western societies, and women, that Bauman's work consistently displays its blind spots (Rattansi 2016).

The episodic, fragmentary character of postmodern life, for Bauman, results from the dissolution of older forms of 'togetherness', both those involving the nation and more intimate relationships (*Postmodern Ethics*: 44–51). Instead of meetings of 'complete' selves, postmodern life consists of what Bauman dubs 'mis-meetings', where only part of the self is deployed, and only for the duration of the 'topic at hand' (*Postmodern Ethics*: 50–1). As usual, Bauman provides no illustrations of the nature – or evidence for the ubiquity of – these encounters. The reader is left to imagine what Bauman has in mind, but without any guarantee that the reader's and Bauman's imaginations are not caught up in a mis-meeting.

Neo-tribes

Now that the nation-state cannot provide a meaningful framework of meaning, Bauman argues, the field is left wide open to a
form of 'neo-tribalism', which supposedly leads to more violence,
partly because public attention in the blasé postmodern world can
be obtained only by ever louder public displays, which can in turn
lead to violence simply to shock the public out of inattention, and
partly because 'neo-tribal' groups are what Bauman calls 'postulated communities', lacking genuine institutions and traditional
restraints (*Postmodern Ethics*: 157–61). All these developments are
the result, Bauman says, of 'the privatization, deregulation and
de-centralization of identity-problems' typical of postmodern life
(*Postmodern Ethics*: 161, emphasis in original). Neo-tribalism seems
to involve a form of 'manifest togetherness'. 'Protest marches' and
the 'football crowd', for Bauman, are equivalent forms of this manifest togetherness. The gettings-together for a particular purpose –
political protest or watching a football match – are only 'pretexts',
a form of masquerade; the real reason for meeting is only the 'orgiastic' 'ecstasy' of 'over-stimulation' resulting from the physical
mass of human beings and the 'condensed, concentrated stimula-
tion' that arises when there is the homogeneity of 'the same colour
scarves wrapped around thousands of necks, the same jingle or
ditty chanted'. This is a uniform, homogeneous mass. Participation
is like a 'bank holiday trip' (*Postmodern Ethics*: 46–7). Among the
consequences is the creation of simple images of enemies, for neo-
tribes draw tight boundaries; a new cultural racism is one outcome
(*Postmodern Ethics*: 188–9).

The concept of neo-tribes is (presumably) borrowed from
Maffesoli's book *The Time of the Tribes* (2000; original French publication 1988); Bauman mentions Maffesoli, but does not reference
his books and articles (*Postmodern Ethics*: 47, 187), so the reader
is deprived of Maffesoli's full argument. Nor does Bauman provide
any reasons why Maffesoli's conceptualisation is worth deploying.
In this context, Bauman's analysis of the political protest march
is, to say the least, perplexing. It ignores vital aspects: did the students world-wide who protested against the Vietnam war simply
do it for 'orgiastic ecstasy'? Did the people who marched against
the Iraq invasion and war use that as a mask whose real purpose,

known only to commentators such as Bauman, was to experience the feeling of a 'bank holiday trip'? The notion that the majority of them were not and do not tend to be genuine and passionate about their cause is extraordinarily implausible. Protesting in groups usually does have, as a *secondary* effect, a joy of comradeship, a pleasure in being part of a group united in purpose, sometimes a festive atmosphere, perhaps with music and other entertainment as an accompaniment, meetings with friends and so forth. Bauman argues quite explicitly that these are the *real* reasons for the march, the political objectives but a masquerade.

Bauman seems to think that it is because of their neo-tribal character, supposedly lacking in institutions and tradition, that such occasions tend to be accompanied by violence. Such groups, he says, are 'hypochondriac and quarrelsome', leading only an 'ephemeral life', and face the danger of 'evaporating' very soon after the event (*Postmodern Ethics*: 187). This may apply to 1990s youth musical happenings called 'raves', but it is seriously erroneous to assume this for the Campaign for Nuclear Disarmament, anti-Vietnam and other anti-war marches, and protests against, for example, cuts in state welfare spending or even anti-immigration protests. All of these had and have a political and institutional base, large degrees of detailed planning and organisation and stewards to discipline the march, and of course there is usually a large and often intimidating police presence throughout the route. They are different not only from 'raves', but also from the spontaneous coming-together of a group of women in a small town on news of a paedophile in the vicinity. The concept of neo-tribes, with its primitivist, pre-modern connotations, is inappropriate for 'postmodern', let alone modern, conditions, and is too underdeveloped to allow a large number of disparate collectivities to be so labelled.

Bauman's comments on what he calls 'do-it-yourself violence', which results from neo-tribalist 'self-assertion', itself the outcome of 'the postmodern privatization of identity problems' (*Postmodern Ethics*: 158), cannot pass without comment. One reason Bauman gives for this 'DIY' violence is that neo-tribes, postulated communities that they are, tend to be plagued by uncertainty and anxiety, which make them prone to violence (*Postmodern Ethics*: 187). Can the violence that has often accompanied football matches be explained in this manner? As I have pointed out earlier, football crowds are referred to in one of Bauman's rare concrete illustrations of his use of concepts eclectically and inexplicably borrowed (*Life in Fragments*: 46–7).

There are several problems with such an explanation, which become obvious when the relevant sociological research and theorisation is consulted. First, as Dunning, Murphy and Williams (1988: 18) have pointed out, forms of crowd violence were common at football matches in Britain before the First World War; it is not a 'postmodern' phenomenon. Second, the changing character of the working class is connected in a complex manner to the transformation of the management of football clubs, one result of which is the emergence of the young working-class 'football hooligan' as an archetype – a figure not unknown in the nineteenth century – and consistent moral panics over football violence in which the mass media have played an important role (Dunning, Murphy and Williams 1988: 23–31 and passim; Armstrong 1998: 92–3; 170–1; Armstrong and Young 2000). Third, no account of football-related violence can ignore the role of issues surrounding working-class and middle-class masculinities (Dunning, Murphy and Williams 1988: 184–216; Armstrong 1998: 13–14, 155–64; Campbell and Dawson 2001). Finally, the types of policing and police tactics have now been shown to have a significant effect on whether any violence occurs (Stott and Pearson 2007).

Again, it is possible to see that although Bauman's postmodern stance should have led him away from abstract, 'grand narrative'-type generalisations about modernity and postmodernity, he provides just this sort of 'thin' analysis, ignoring cultural, historical, classed and gendered specificities which alone can illuminate the behaviour of particular types of neo-tribes and specific occurrences of violence.

In *Life in Fragments*, a form of postmodern racism is also commented upon by Bauman, one of the few occasions on which he addresses the issue outside his study of the Holocaust, although he also provides further thoughts on anti-Semitism. Drawing upon his earlier reading of the French structuralist anthropologist Lévi-Strauss, Bauman draws attention to the distinction between 'phagic' and 'emic' strategies which are adopted by cultural groups when confronted by strangers, the former being inclusivist – assimilating the strangers – while the latter is exclusivist, tending to treat the strangers as alien. Bauman insists that there is no in-between strategy: only 'such an either-or tactic offers a 'serious chance of controlling the social space' (*Life in Fragments*: 180). Bauman adds the notion of 'proteophobia', a condition of ambivalence, which continually co-exists with the other two, although he does not offer much by way of concrete illustration, the reader being implicitly left to fill in the absences, as I have done in my own research (Rattansi 1994, 2007). However, I have not drawn upon Bauman's abstract typology. I have relied more on poststructuralist deconstructions of the unified subject, something that Bauman curiously avoids doing and thus leaves himself stranded within an Enlightenment notion of the singular, unified subject of Enlightenment epistemology and political ontology. His ability to coin seductive conceptual terminology is reflected in the assertion that under postmodern conditions there is a constant tug of war between 'mixophilia' and 'mixophobia', these being presumably the equivalent of phagic and emic tendencies (*Life in Fragments*: 221).

However, Bauman repeats a common mistake by suggesting that the present is the period of 'identity-conflicts' as opposed to a modern politics that was bound up with national, class and status 'contradictions': as I have pointed out (Rattansi 2011), this distinction curiously misses the obvious significance of national and class identities that were bound up with earlier conflicts, which were no less concerned with identities. The idea that politics existed and can exist in the absence of the espousal and deployment of identities is patently absurd, for all social actors have identities that are inevitably brought into play in the arena of politics. The notion of 'identity politics' has been coined by a curious alliance of the left, liberals and right in an attempt to discredit the new social movements, especially feminism and anti-racism. In Bauman's oft-repeated disparaging remarks against the new social movements (also appearing in Rorty's writings, which Bauman cites in several works in this context including *Postmodernity and its Discontents*, 1997: 65–9) we can see a yearning for a grander, distinctly modernist narrative which would synthesise postmodern ills under a larger vision, although Bauman as so often remains suspended in ambivalence, for he is suspicious of movements that promise emancipation but end in repression: beware, he says, of a politics that promotes 'oppression in the guise of emancipation' (*Postmodernity and its Discontents*: 208). I will have more to say about this set of issues in my discussion of Bauman's notion of 'liquid modernity' in the next part of the book.

In the context of his discussion of neo-tribes Bauman mentions in passing the genocide of Africans in the Second Boer War and the 'savageries' of Belgians against the indigenous Congolese (*Life in Fragments*: 182) as support for his proposition that 'the modern era has been founded in genocide, and proceeded through more genocide' (inexplicably, there is no mention of the genocide of the indigenous peoples of the Americas), and he moves on to 'ethnic cleansing' in the former Yugoslavia as well as the cruel treatment by the state of Israel of Palestinians to argue, importantly, that 'victims are not always ethically superior to their oppressors'; the victims have just not had the opportunity to be cruel, being the weaker party in the circumstances. Some interesting but under-developed thoughts are offered on whether the twentieth century can be adequately described as a 'century of camps', with Auschwitz and the Stalinist Gulag as the gruesome symbols pointing up the continuing genocides that have marred the century, for example in Laos, Cambodia and Vietnam (*Life in Fragments*: 183), although Gilroy (2000: 87) is rightly critical of Bauman's brazen Eurocentrism when it comes to highlighting the key symbols of an age of camps.

Postmodern ethics: Bauman's Levinasian turn

Questions of ethics and morality were central to Bauman's concerns over a long period of his life. This is hardly surprising. Any intellectual project which has at its heart the constant desire to envisage a future different from the existing – the 'is' – in order to create social conditions which embody the dignity of an altogether greater freedom has to have a persistent concern with what 'ought' to be the case. The 'ought' immediately plunges the thinker into reflecting upon the nature of morality and ethics. This was intrinsic to Bauman's optimistic conception of culture as 'a knife pressed against the future' (Bauman and Tester 2001: 31). And this is given its most extended treatment in his *Postmodern Ethics* (1993a). The inspiration for Bauman's reflections in this and allied, shorter pieces was the work of the philosopher Emmanuel Levinas.

Bauman described his delighted discovery of Levinas's work as a 'Eureka' moment (Bauman and Tester 2001: 54). The cause of his excitement is not hard to fathom. Levinas's work was postmodern in the same sense that pervaded Bauman's sense of the postmodern. Levinas's ethical thinking attempted to go beyond the rationalism of Enlightenment and especially Kantian moral discourse. For Levinas, as for Bauman, modern, Enlightenment-derived morality was a matter of *duty*, of finding the right rules which could then be universally binding on ethical human behaviour; this was a deontological conception of morality. It was morality from on high, a form therefore of discipline which was in keeping with the disciplinary codes of conduct beloved of a modern sensibility. Bauman instead was seeking a morality that did not require reason to discover its structure of codes of behaviour, its foundational basis. And it needed to be one in which ethical behaviour was a matter of choice, not rule-bound duty. Moral choice meant the re-emergence of responsibility.

Levinasian thinking had another theme that undoubtedly attracted Bauman. Levinas was insistent that in properly ethical self–Other relations the Other should never be reduced to the Same; the Other's difference must always be respected. And relatedly in one of his major works, *Totality and Infinity* (1969), Levinas saw Western philosophy as an imperialist project, wanting to assimilate everything alien or foreign by a rationalist, intellectual operation. Only that which could be rationally grasped deserved to be respected; the rest could be discarded.

Paradoxically, this was often combined with a form of Eurocentrism in Levinas's work, where only Western philosophy mattered (Eaglestone 2010: 57–9), although this was not noticed or commented upon by Bauman, whose thought also of course suffers from a similar problem. There are two other aspects of Levinas's work which Bauman failed to mention, both being equally serious omissions on Bauman's part. First, Levinas was above all a Jewish, *theological* thinker for whom the absolute Other was God. This allowed him a certain licence in pronouncing about the immanent nature of humankind and enabled a form of phenomenological, transcendent thinking, aspects of which appear in Bauman but without the theological foundation. Thus similar pronouncements from Bauman, for example about the unconditional responsibilities of the self, appear to be simply *ex cathedra* assertions which can be perplexing, but make sense when they are seen as extracted from a thinker who relies on the ultimate authority of Jewish theology and the Bible. Second, Levinas has a distinctly masculine viewpoint. His self is male, a point made against him by thinkers such as de Beauvoir, Derrida and Irigaray (Davis 1996: 60–1; Chanter 2001). The female is often disparaged by Levinas, and is certainly seen in stereotypical terms as a presence, largely in the home, exhibiting traits such as 'weakness, tenderness, frailty, secrecy, voluptuousness, ambiguity, virginity, which raises the desire for violation and profanation, beauty, eroticism, lasciviousness' (from *Totality and Infinity*, quoted in Davis 1996: 60). Fathers and sons and fraternity are foregrounded in Levinas's reflections, such that not only is feminine the Other, but as the property of the male the female becomes assimilated to the (male) self, being reduced to the Same and thus violating his own injunction that to be moral is to respect the Other, never to reduce the Other to the Same, although some feminists have found valuable insights too in Levinas (Perpich 2010; Chanter 2001). Third, when Levinas discusses the Other's 'face' as initiating moral demands on the self, this is not an actual face of anyone; 'face' is deployed in a non-empirical, non-physical sense. Bauman did not make this clear. In Levinas's opaque prose the insubstantial nature of the Other's face creates much confusion and perplexity (Davis 1996: 135), and this was carried over into Bauman's work, as any reading of *Postmodern Ethics* will reveal.

In Bauman an additional, Levinas-derived puzzlement is caused by his assertion that morality is not rationally deduced or socially produced, but is immanent in human co-existence. Humans by nature live together, and this 'being with others' is the 'source' or the 'cause' of moral behaviour. My own equivocation between 'source' and 'cause' is self-consciously expressed to draw out a curiosity in Bauman's argument. Where does morality come from? Can there be a sociology of morals? The point here is that Bauman's antipathy to rationalism, as well as Durkheim's reification of morality as socially derived – to the extent that Durkheim collapses the distinction between social and moral facts, social and moral integration (Junge 2001: 107) – led Bauman to adopt wholesale Levinas's assertion that ethics itself needs no grounding: ethics is a 'first philosophy'. Human beings are, in the first place, not rational or biologically determined creatures: they are ethical beings who are impelled to be moral, to be concerned with issues of right and wrong, goodness and harm, justice and unfairness, just by their 'being with others' (Morgan 2011: 4).

Tester attempts to rescue Bauman's a-sociological account of the origins of morality by stating that morality in society is 'social' but 'pre-societal', while admitting that the 'subtlety of this distinction can easily get lost' (Tester 2004: 144). But the distinction remains opaque, and does nothing to dispel the sense that Bauman, in borrowing from Levinas, has simply reproduced a profoundly non-sociological and ultimately dogmatic, unsupported view of how moral norms emerge and operate within and among human groups (Lash 1996; Junge 2001; Hirst 2014). As Vetlesen (2005: 22) puts it, 'Coming from a sociologist, this is a truly startling claim. We are told that the ability to tell right from wrong is "ready formed"; hence it is already there, a given, akin to man's biological constitution.' It is no wonder that Lash complains about the lack of social grounding, and Junge about the need to build in notions of reciprocity as foundational, and that Hirst points out that Bauman's engagement

with Levinas has left him floundering between an a-social, dual
self–Other relation of the moral party of two and a sociologically
deterministic model of the individual caught up in neo-tribes and
the seductions of consumerism. To Junge's injection of reciprocity
into the moral process I would want to add the issue of *empathy* as
one requiring serious consideration if Bauman's moral thinking is
to carry conviction (see, for example, Vetlesen 1994; Slote 2007).
And instead of an a priori phenomenon of 'being for the Other' as
an existential given, it is at least worth exploring what the emerging contours of neuroscience and psychology have to say about
the forms of empathy, caring and co-operation that may possibly
be innate features of human constitution but require particular
forms of nurture to flourish (Hoffman 2000; Rifkin 2009; Decety
and Ickes 2011; Pagel 2012; Lieberman 2013; Bloom 2013; but
see also Kunz 1998 for an attempt at grounding empirical psychology in Levinas's ethical thought; for Bauman's belated recognition
of some problems in Levinasian ethics, see *Postmodernity and its
Discontents*, 1997: 45–53).

Proximity, Bauman argues, is crucial in creating a moral,
unselfish, unconditional response to the Other. Vetlesen, though,
rightly points out, partly in the context of criticising Bauman's use
of the Milgram experiments, that proximity is at best an ambiguous concept, having both spatial and psycho-social connotations
(Vetlesen 1994: 24–7). In addition the question arises of what
has been called 'distant suffering' (Boltanski 1999), for Bauman
often highlights what he regards as 'compassion fatigue' (see, for
example, *Postmodern Ethics*: 102, 149), especially in relation to
those whose misfortunes 'we' in the West experience only through
selective media images. On these he is particularly scathing about
what he calls 'carnivals of charity' and 'carnivals of cruelty'
which attend appeals for charity via media and other campaigns.
Bauman is surely right to emphasise the momentariness of attention involved in mass charity campaigns for the world's poor and
those afflicted by natural or other catastrophes, and he is justified in his complaints that Western media representations tend
to marginalise or completely ignore the extent to which refugee
crises, for example, are caused by armed conflict fuelled by weapons sold by the West, or the fact that crises of extreme poverty
often result from programmes of what Western agencies such as

the International Monetary Fund and the World Bank euphemistically dub 'restructuring'.

Indeed, Bauman's remarks in this context are of course part of a consistent concern for the world's marginalised populations and underdogs, and form an essential part of a sociological project animated by an ethics suffused with a concern to alleviate suffering and cruelty, and this is one reason why Rorty, whose moral thinking was equally concerned with minimising cruelty, has been such a congenial intellectual for Bauman. Note that Geras (1995) uses Rorty's views on the unacceptability of cruelty, especially, to clinch the argument that Rorty, despite his denials, has a notion of human nature that underlies his liberal ethical stance.

However, the issue of 'compassion fatigue' is far more complex than Bauman's rather glib discussion appears to acknowledge. One of the more sophisticated discussions of this supposed boredom and ennui is in fact provided by Tester (2001), who is generally very sympathetic to Bauman, but whose critique of one of the better-known studies of this supposed phenomenon, by Moeller (1999), also applies to Bauman's comments. Tester argues (and this applies to Bauman too, although Tester does not explicitly criticise his mentor) that Moeller 'never really defines what the phrase [compassion fatigue] means' and that in her argumentation 'compassion fatigue' never approaches anything resembling an analytic concept (Tester 2001: 37). Moreover, closer inspection of the supposed existence of compassion fatigue involves on Tester's part a sophisticated and nuanced investigation into the dilemmas facing journalists who report on humanitarian disasters as well as the diversity of responses of media audiences to images and commentary supplied by journalists (Tester 2001: 13–73). 'Compassion fatigue' emerges from Tester's account, as well as that of Wilkinson (2005: 136–56), as a reaction that does not exist in any simple, easily describable and explainable form. Any discussion would also have to take into account Cohen's analysis (2001) of the myriad strategies of denial and disavowal that individuals use in order to cope with the emotional demands of knowledge of atrocities and natural catastrophes. *Not for the first time, Bauman's role can be seen to be one of putting a discussion of these issues on the agenda of sociologists and others in an ethical frame, but his own analysis, as so often, fails to do justice to the complexities involved.*

There is another problem with Bauman's ethical demand regarding sympathy for the underdog and the poor. Did Bauman *think with suffering* or only write about suffering? Outhwaite (2010) suggests that Bauman was more interested in the production, not the experience, of suffering. Wilkinson (2007) has argued in a short but powerful essay that Bauman's whole style of writing about poverty and the poor, and those who suffer, detracts from his stated intention to create sympathy for them. First, as Wilkinson notes, and I too have argued, Bauman had a tendency to ignore ethnographic studies, in this case ones which can portray suffering and pain in graphic detail, instead providing brief statistical information, on global poverty for example, and thus framing issues in a manner that does not evoke the sympathy that he does seem to want to create among his readers. In this sense, Best (2016) is quite right in his sharp criticism that in Bauman's Levinasian ethical discourse the Other is given no voice, for it is Bauman who speaks for the Other and the Other is allowed a voice only through Bauman. This also, incidentally, makes for a strange relationship between Bauman and the work of Jeremy Seabrook, who was occasionally cited by Bauman but was apparently avidly read by him (Hogan 2002), for Seabrook's powerful work always attempts to give eloquent voice to the poor and the powerless of the world.

Second, Wilkinson argues that Bauman's abstract typologies of those who suffer, the 'vagabonds' for example, are denuded of their humanity and their pain when represented in these emaciated, abstract categories, and he contrasts Bauman's style with Arendt's agonising over the most effective way to write about evil, suffering and pain. Bauman, Wilkinson argues, displays little concern for the manner in which the discourses of social science may serve to hinder the creation of moral proximity, despite his repeated emphasis on the foundation of ethics in just such proximity; Bourdieu is regarded by Wilkinson as far more self-reflective in this regard. Third, Wilkinson points out that Bauman's characterisation of modernity as simply a totality dominated by instrumental and calculative rationality and the will to discipline fails to acknowledge the extent to which modernity has also created opportunities for an enlargement of sympathy. *He delivers a devastating verdict on the severe shortcomings of Bauman's writing on these issues that is worth extended quotation:*

Whilst working to frame human suffering for sociological attention
... he does not provide us with any moral or political defence of
the cultural representation through which he seeks to draw our
attention to the bounds of human affliction ... I suggest that, whilst
Bauman provides us with an idiosyncratic style of writing about
social injustice of the world, the problem of finding a sufficient
moral/rational explanation for the negative suffering in human life
does not appear to impact upon his approach to thinking. Whilst
writing about human suffering, he does not appear to be thinking
with suffering. (Wilkinson 2007: 253, emphasis in original)

For all his concern with ethics, responsibility for the Other and the
suffering of the world, Bauman's discourse and framing unfortunately fall well short of the standards which thinking and writing
about these issues should attain.

Part III

Floating, slipping, sliding, drowning, boiling and freezing: the perils of liquid life

With the benefit of hindsight, commentators have been able to note that many of those labelled as 'postmodernists' had often resisted being designated by that title or had not explicitly espoused it (Mathewman and Hoey 2006). And among those like Richard Rorty and Zygmunt Bauman, who had 'come out' as having a postmodernist allegiance of some kind, it was clear that they were busy distancing themselves from postmodernism as fast as they could in the 1990s and early 2000s (Bauman and Tester 2001; Bauman and Gane 2004). As I have argued earlier, I do not agree with Tester (Bauman and Tester 2007: n6) that Bauman's first explicitly postmodernist work, *Legislators and Interpreters*, was 'hesitant and cautious' in its commitment to the postmodern turn; for example, Bauman argues strongly in that book for relativism, a clarion call he is careful not to repeat, or at least not explicitly, in any other work. In *Intimations of Postmodernity* (1992a), in a key essay, he seems to step back from the brink by arguing for a sociology of postmodernity rather than a postmodernist sociology, although as I have pointed out Bauman also argues in *Intimations*, in contradictory manner, for a form of postmodernist analysis more suited to what he refers to as the novel postmodern 'habitat'.

My reading of Bauman's foray into postmodernism suggests that even in *Postmodernity and its Discontents* (1997) and *In Search of Politics* (1999) he gives little indication of what on the surface seems like a drastic change of direction and resulted in his announcement in 2000 of a new phase in his thinking, with a move from 'postmodern' as a description of the contemporary period in the West to 'liquid modern' in his *Liquid Modernity* (2000b).

Why did Bauman become a postmodernist?

However, before pursuing Bauman's sudden retreat from postmodernism it is necessary to ponder the reasons why Bauman found the postmodern turn attractive. In a case of Minerva's owl flying at dusk, it is only now possible to narrate his journey into postmodernism because I have laid out what his postmodern turn consisted of, and his entry into it can be properly charted and explained only now that the lines and products of his postmodern phase are clear. The reader may remember that I had earlier said that it was only in retrospect that the reasons for the attractions of postmodernism for Bauman would become clear.

As should be clear from my argument earlier in the book, it is not surprising that Bauman's first major foray into the terrain of postmodernism was announced in a volume, *Legislators and Interpreters*, which is above all a wide-ranging critique of the Enlightenment. The Enlightenment, or a particular, selective interpretation of it, was a key target of the postmodernists who attacked its supposed hyper-rationalism and militant universalism. Bauman had already absorbed the Frankfurt School's Critical Theory version of the critique of Enlightenment as set out, in the aftermath of the Holocaust, by Horkheimer and Adorno in their *Dialectic of Enlightenment* (1997, first published 1947). Moreover, a key influence on Bauman's critique, as I have also underlined, came from the work of Michel Foucault, especially his *Discipline and Punish* (1984), in which Foucault offers a contrary perspective on the Enlightenment and Western modernity, choosing to highlight – instead of liberty and tolerance – the disciplinary, Panopticon-like institutions that combined power, specialised knowledge and surveillance, such as the prison, school, hospital and army.

In interviews with Gane (2004) and Tester (2007), Bauman points out that what attracted him about the postmodern turn, especially in architecture, was its clear articulation that a rationally planned order, free of ambiguity, ambivalence, contradiction and 'messiness', was simply born of humanity's conceit; the hubris embedded in the Enlightenment dream of a rational order based on clear, straightforward axioms derived from a scientific study of human nature and society was, for Bauman and all postmodernists, an impossibility. The outcome of this rationalist drive was not a liberal, democratic fulfilment of individualism, but a power/knowledge complex that disciplined not just the mind but the very body of the individual and developed new, more effective means of surveillance and control never before seen in human history. The new disciplinary society encouraged and began to rely upon the development of new 'disciplines' of knowledge: psychology, psychiatry, medicine and sociology, and these in effect provided a new priesthood which, like the old, put itself at the service of those who came to occupy elite positions in the new, post-feudal social order.

It has sometimes been remarked that key, highly influential postmodernists like Lyotard and Baudrillard often tended to be former but now disillusioned Marxists whose dreams of a new, better post-capitalist society had been shattered by the inability of the student revolts of 1968 – especially in France – to spark a socialist revolution, a failure in which official Western communist parties and trade unions had colluded with the 'bourgeois' state. Moreover, the stubborn survival of bureaucratic brutalism in the Soviet Union and the ruthless crushing of progressive revolts against official Communism first in East Germany and Hungary and then in 1968 in Czechoslovakia by the Soviets had served to convince these Marxists that their Marxism, with its teleological and eschatological grand narrative of human history as nothing more than a story of class struggle which would result in a liberated, un-alienated, rationally ordered society, was itself the root cause of their illusions.

The headlong rush into postmodernism was thus seen by such critics as an over-reaction against rationalism and the continuing reality of class conflict. And the resulting 'irrationalism', whether founded on a new enthusiasm for Nietzsche, an anti-foundationalist pragmatism nurtured by figures such as Rorty or a newly minted enthusiasm for the later Wittgenstein and a relativist interpretation of Kuhn's ambiguous *Structure of Scientific Revolutions* (1962), allegedly sat well with intellectuals, who could therefore abandon a principled, rationally grounded critique of capitalism and enjoy their membership of an affluent new middle class and their novel media fame. They could now indulge themselves with apolitical aesthetic pleasures and celebrate the new, 'anything goes' permissiveness of wild postmodernist adventures in art, literature, cinema, architecture and a philosophy that blurred the distinctions between literature and philosophy, literary criticism and political critique (Callinicos 1990: 162–71; see also Eagleton 1996: 1–44; and see also Owen 1997, and Lopez and Potter 2005).

Some of these descriptions apply only too well to Bauman the postmodernist. In the 1987 *Legislators*, as we have seen, Bauman draws upon Rorty's critique of the Western rationalist tradition and Foucault's notion of modernity as a disciplinary complex, and is clearly influenced by the critique of hyper-rationalism and modernism in postmodernist architecture. Equally important to Bauman's embrace of the postmodern turn was his utter disillusionment with Soviet-style socialism, for he regarded the failure of this 'communism' as synonymous with the more general failure of modernity in so far as modernity, for him, involved above all the achievement of a *rational* organisation of society, and thus an end to messiness, waste, and ambivalence. The 'war cry' of the communist revolution was, as Bauman puts it, '"The Kingdom of Reason – now"' (from the essay 'Communism: A Postmortem', reprinted in *Intimations*: 166). Thus, as he says in another essay on the collapse of communism also reprinted in *Intimations*, 'Living without an Alternative', 'communism took the precepts of modernity most seriously and set out to implement them in earnest' (*Intimations*: 179). It attempted to rationally plan and manage the economy and society, to create 'a harmonious totality', to create a system of 'global management' (*Intimations*: 178). This was none other than the vision of social order bequeathed to humanity by the Enlightenment; its failure thus had to be seen as a signal of 'the final retreat of the dreams and ambitions of *modernity*' (*Intimations*: 178, emphasis in original).

For Bauman, the citizens of the Soviet Union and Eastern Europe rejected modernity in favour of a postmodernity of choice and freedom, but this for Bauman meant overwhelmingly a new social order that prioritised nothing nobler than *consumer* choice and the provision of a cornucopia of consumer goods. He ignores the desire for freedom of expression and other democratic rights that had been equally powerful among dissenters in the Soviet Union and Eastern Europe. In these essays on the collapse of communist states Bauman makes abundantly clear that he is no celebrator of this new postmodern condition of consumerism that was embraced by so many of those involved in the overthrow of communism.

The nod to Foucault in Bauman's use of the notion of 'the modern power/knowledge syndrome' serves, unwittingly, to highlight a curious absence in Bauman's discussion of the collapse of communism: there is no discussion of Marxism, which after all was the legitimating ideology of actually existing socialism. Apart from a passing reference to Lenin (*Intimations*: 166–7), Bauman simply says nothing about the questions that are raised for Marx and Marxism when systems that deified Marx and Lenin, and were constructed with Marxism as the official ruling ideology, collapsed; nor does he comment on Marxism's huge investment in modernity, in rational planning, and he pointedly does not draw upon the resources of Western Marxism to critique consumer capitalism; indeed he rarely uses the concept of capitalism in any systematic way except as an anodyne substitute for talking about the West or consumerism (see, for example, *Intimations*: 168).

By the time Bauman finished *Memories* (1982), he had become ready to see the crisis of the Western capitalist system as a crisis in a variant of *modernity*, which is why in his postmodern phase, as Varcoe and Kilminster also argue (1996: 226), Bauman offers little systematic analysis of *capitalism*. The problem as Bauman now saw it was not capitalism, but a type of modernity in its consumerist phase. In an interview conducted by Varcoe and Kilminster and reprinted in *Intimations*, Bauman, asked about his relation to Marxism, distances himself from it without offering a serious critique, although he does single out the Italian Marxist Antonio Gramsci and also Simmel – but not Adorno, surprisingly – as key influences on his own thought, especially in convincing him of the importance of 'culture' (*Intimations*: 206–7).

Hence, too, the attraction of Foucault, who had similarly eschewed Marxist analysis and struck out on his own trajectory of examining post-Enlightenment power/knowledge complexes such as schools, prisons, the army and mental asylums, with class playing only a minor role in the narrative; and also because Foucault rejected totalising, modernist theory in favour of Nietzsche and the method of genealogy (Smart 1983: 73–107; Foucault 1977), with an interest in local and dispersed discourses and practices of opposition, which also sat well with Lyotard's suspicion of grand narratives and support for local narratives. Foucault himself acknowledged that there were important overlaps between his work and that of the Frankfurt School of Critical Theory (Jay 1984: 22), especially its critique of the legacy of the Enlightenment and of the system of domination that underlay what it regarded as the veneer of liberal freedoms provided in Western capitalist societies. Thus, although it is important to avoid falling into the trap of assimilating Foucault's analysis of power/knowledge to Critical Theory's critique of domination (Miller 1987; Poster 1984), the ground had been well prepared for Bauman's own highly sympathetic reading and deployment of Foucault in his postmodern phase.

Thus Bauman's turn to postmodernism was influenced by his own disillusionment with Marxism's master categories of class and capitalism, the collapse of communism, the development of critiques of modernism in architecture and spheres of culture and the arts, the emergence of theorists such as Foucault and Lyotard who voiced their suspicion of totalising discourses and grand theories of history, and the replacement of a politics based on production and class by manifold so-called 'single-issue' campaigns and struggles over the environment and myriad issues of human rights. But there were perhaps other drivers too, as Dennis Smith (1999: 122) suggests: 'Furthermore, Bauman was coming to a pensionable age and his career as a full-time university teacher was drawing to a close. It is not unreasonable to suspect Bauman heard the sound of scaffolding collapsing all round. He needed a new base, a new identity and a new horizon.' As we will see later, when Bauman abandoned the language of postmodernity for that of liquid modernity, some commentators expressed similar cynicism, if that is an appropriate description of Smith's interpretation.

Bauman, as I have already discussed, evinced little interest in the new 'postmodern' politics; he was lukewarm towards feminism and anti-racism, for example, and failed to grasp their importance (*Intimations*: 198). As I have argued in Part II, in this he seemed to be blinded by a residual totalising Marxism, as well as a commitment to class politics, for his objection to the new 'postmodern' politics mirrored those of Marxists such as Hobsbawm (1996) and others who disparaged so-called 'identity politics' because they supposedly failed to engage in a wider, more encompassing politics of changing the overall distribution of wealth and income (*Intimations*: 198). As I have also discussed earlier, Bauman now saw the main division in consumerist modernity as one between *seduction*, for those who can afford to consume the variety of goods on offer, and *repression*, for those unable to pay to consume to any significant degree, who therefore become outcasts who need to be kept under surveillance, shamed, punished and incarcerated, if necessary, so that the postmodern consumerist merry-go-round can continue unhindered.

Bauman's poorly disguised contempt for 'postmodern politics' contrasts, oddly enough, with the more favourable interpretation that even Marxist critics were willing to grant to the achievements of postmodernism: Harvey, for example, praises new projects of urban renewal, especially some that benefited inner-city ethnic minorities, which used postmodern architectural aesthetics (Harvey 1991: 88–98), and the opening that postmodernism provided for the voices of women, blacks, gays and colonised peoples (Harvey 1991: 42, 46, 47–51; 113–14; see also Gibbins and Reimer 1999).

Bauman, as we have seen, had an ambivalent relation to the postmodern turn, being attracted to its critique of rationalism and universalism but critical of any celebration of affluent consumerism, and he was usually hostile to the new social movements of women, blacks, gays and others. It is thus not surprising that in his interviews with Gane (2004) and Tester (2007) Bauman seemed to see little merit in the achievements of the postmodern turn, whether in academe or politics.

The whys and wherefores of the demise of postmodernism

While books endorsing some or other idea of the 'postmodern' have been published as late as 2014 (Dasgupta and Kivisto 2014), and while Costas Douzinas used the concept productively in 2007 (Douzinas 2007), Hardt and Negri's *Empire* (2000) and Connor's edited collection *The Cambridge Companion to Postmodernism* (2004) used the notion of the postmodern without always the sense that the usage of the term was about to expire, there is some merit in the suggestion that the beginning of the new millennium marked a sudden downturn in the fortunes of the notion of the 'postmodern' (Mathewman and Hoey 2006). Interviewed in 2007 by Tester about his flight from postmodernism, Bauman laments that 'Entering a discourse [postmodernism] bent on becoming the talk of the town (the urban salons to be precise) meant giving hostages to fate from the start.' He continues, 'Soon, all my efforts to protect the intended meaning turned out to be hopeless. I had been "filed away", and having read the label on the file's cover, who would care to contemplate the subtleties inside?' (Bauman and Tester 2007: 23).

So what exactly did Bauman come to reject in the way the idea of the postmodern had developed? One feature was the manner in which those who had embraced the term had become – Bauman argues in an interview with Gane – celebrators of the new era rather than subjecting it to critique (Bauman and Gane 2004: 18). But Bauman provides no names: who exactly did he have in mind? Critiques by self-confessed modernists such as Norris (1990) and Best and Kellner (1997), would suggest that a key figure in Bauman's sights as a celebrator of the new postmodern times would be the French intellectual Jean Baudrillard. But Bauman is, at best, ambivalent about Baudrillard, whom he defends (*Postmodern Ethics*: 45 n1) against Norris's objection (Norris 1990) that Baudrillard, having adopted a postmodernist stance, leaves himself without any modernist, epistemological resources to mount a critique of the present. The most notorious celebrators of the present were conservatives like Francis Fukuyama, who was no 'postmodernist' and indeed quite the opposite (Williams, Sullivan and Matthews 1997: 162–9); these commentators saw in the post-communist world order the 'end of history' (Fukuyama 1993), and Bauman makes no mention of Fukuyama and his cheerleaders. We are thus only left with a question: who exactly was Bauman rejecting as the unsavoury 'bedfellows' (Bauman and Gane 2004: 18) with whom he was unwilling to share his bed?

As an answer to this question is not forthcoming from Bauman, it may seem wiser to move on to a discussion of the more fathom-able reasons that Bauman provides for moving on from a commit-ment to 'postmodernity'. However, before doing so it is necessary to confront the question: why did 'postmodernism' disappear from the scene so suddenly at the beginning of the twenty-first century, almost as if it had never happened?

Mathewman and Hoey (2006) suggest that the notorious 'Sokal affair' may have played its part in discrediting postmodernism. Sokal, a physicist with left-leaning sympathies, had found the (mis) use of examples from physics by many postmodernists galling. In addition, his sense of a rightward shift in the political outlook of most postmodernists had provoked him into submitting to the jour-nal *Social Text* an article that purported to provide a postmodernist reading of modern physics but which was, by his own later admis-sion, full of half-truths, falsehoods and nonsense (Sokal 1996). But the editors of *Social Text*, as ignorant of modern physics as other postmodernists, had gone ahead with publication of the mis-chievous submission. Sokal's hoax received widespread publicity and by and large seemed to have had the intended effect, for it allowed those unsympathetic to postmodernism effective ammuni-tion against its pretensions (Mathewman and Hoey 2006: 530). But none of the postmodernists subsequently skewered in Sokal and Bricmont's *Intellectual Impostors* (1998) – Lacan, Kristeva, Baudrillard and Virilio – had ever accepted the term 'postmodern-ist' as a valid description for themselves. Moreover, as Mathewman and Hoey argue, the idea and image of postmodernists as a homoge-neous group of reactionaries was probably the creation of Marxist critics and lacked plausibility when put under serious scrutiny.

There was, however, greater political complexity to these

debates than Mathewman and Hoey recognise. While Sokal's was a left-inspired critique, there was at the same time in the USA a fierce battle raging within the natural sciences, in science studies, the humanities and the wider political arena: while environmentally concerned scientists had been raising the alarm about industrial technology's impact on the environment, right-wing politicians, humanities-based academics and right-leaning scientists had been attacking postmodernists and environmental scientists for their *leftist* politics and for subverting the credibility of mainstream humanities. Led by Newt Gingrich in the US Congress and in academia by texts such as *Higher Superstition: The Academic Left and its Quarrels with Science* by Gross and Levitt (1994), there was a right-wing backlash against postmodernism as well (see Ross 1996), which added to the weight of the critique of postmodernism.

But at least four other causal elements need to be considered if we are to understand why the postmodern current suddenly lost its force. First, in architecture (which after all had been so pivotal in putting postmodernism on the agenda in the first place), postmodernism had exhausted its potential, and practitioners were turning away to a modern-revival style (Venturi 2007); Goulimari (2007: 2) goes so far as to assert that association with postmodernism in architecture was now 'tantamount to professional suicide'. Secondly, as Bauman himself points out (Bauman and Gane 2004: 17), 'postmodern' could only ever be a stop-gap notion, lacking any positive content, pointing as it did to something that was ending rather than providing a guide to what was coming into being. Moreover, it had the disadvantage of implying that modernity was coming to an end, although in reality it was the case that the changes were to a large extent part and parcel of a new phase within modernity (Bauman and Gane 2004: 18). Third, the new phase of modernity was already being given positive content in ideas such as Beck's conception of 'reflexive modernity' and Giddens's 'late modernity'. Both Beck and Giddens had also contributed to a growing literature in which 'globalisation' was becoming the new master category in social analysis, shunting postmodernism away from the centre stage of debates in sociology, political studies, political economy and international relations. And Beck (2000c), in particular, had argued vociferously for a shift of perspective within sociology, given an increasingly interdependent global world, away from analyses confined to national societies (what he called 'methodological nationalism', which had continued within the postmodern turn) and to the global as the central context for sociological analyses (see also Urry 2000).

Moreover, the global political context was rapidly changing and had begun to give rise to new grand narratives, thus undermining one of the key positive elements of the postmodernist claim that the intellectual and political world had experienced a decisive shift away from modernist grand narratives. Of the three key instances of the return of the grand narrative, one has already been mentioned: Fukuyama's astonishingly naïve proclamation of 'The End of History' (1993: 199), which self-consciously relied on a Hegelian grand story of the triumph of the West's liberal democratic capitalism in the wake of the collapse of Soviet-style communism. This absurd claim was soon debunked, but the collapse of communism was a spectacular historical event which undoubtedly gave some credence to the idea of an overarching story about the rise and rise of the West. This narrative of the West's self-aggrandisement gained traction from another grand story that underpinned it: neoliberalism. Placing the possessive individual so astutely identified by Macpherson (Macpherson 1965) as a key figure in liberalism from the seventeenth century onwards at its centre, neo-liberalism (admittedly espousing a variety of claims and expressed in differing institutional measures), as propagated by the economists Hayek and Friedman and given great political influence by Thatcher in the UK and Reagan in the USA – and enshrined in some of the economic nostrums of the European Union – lauded the free market and the state's withdrawal from as much economic and welfare activity as possible (see, among many others, Harvey 2007). Neoliberalism's tenacious survival in the face of the catastrophic financial crisis of 2008, which many expected to be its nemesis (Crouch 2011), has only served to reinforce an interpretation that regards it as yet another grand narrative that undermined the postmodern climate of scepticism towards these sorts of overarching 'universal' truths about humankind and its history. Remember too, that neo-liberalism has had a powerful global reach through the brutal 'structural adjustment' programmes imposed on debt-ridden poorer nations by the World Bank and the International Monetary Fund. As against neo-liberalism, another grand narrative has gained traction: that of 'human rights'. The discourse of human rights is the source of much controversy (Douzinas 2007; Nash 2014). But its deployment as a form of opposition to the global march of neo-liberal discourses and practices is not in doubt, and may be regarded as part of the nexus of reasons why the debates over postmodernism spluttered to an end.

Finally, there was the set of events set in train by the spectacular attack on the Twin Towers on 11 September 2001, now and forever known as '9/11'. As Akbar Ahmed (2007) puts it, some hefty fatal blows to postmodernism were struck by 'George W. Bush at the White House and Osama bin Laden in the caves of Tora Bora', for they both 'advocated and came to embody their own versions of a Grand Narrative which saw opposed ideas as false and evil' (Ahmed 2007: 141). In the West, Bush's narrative had already found its intellectual underpinnings in Samuel Huntington's 'Clash of Civilizations' thesis (1993, 1996) and in various publications which homogenised the story and the 'rage of Islam', especially influential being the writings of Bernard Lewis (Ahmed 2007: 141). And so it came to be that various types of 'the West vs Islam' narratives gained ground, one example being Benjamin Barber's *Jihad vs. McWorld,* which had originally been published in 1996 (Barber 1996) but which was given great impetus by 9/11 and thus issued in a second edition in 2003. Both the West and Islam purported opposition to an 'Axis of Evil' as Bush famously proclaimed: the Islam of Bin Laden and the Taliban lined up against an axis supposedly composed of Jews, Christians, Israel, the USA and all 'infidels' within Islam, mostly Shia Muslims, a sub-group within Islam.

The demerits of these grand narratives, including bland versions of the globalisation debate, together with the fact that, in any case, Lyotard's idea of the disappearance of grand narratives had been poorly defined (see Malpas 2002: 24–8 for an attempt at clarification) and had had few adherents except for those who had identified it with the demise of Marxism; and given the reality that postmodernism in architecture and the arts generally had exhausted itself, meant that the sandcastle of postmodernism was swept aside in an unstoppable tidal wave; but it may as well be said, to use another well-worn phrase, that postmodernism died with a whimper rather than a bang. It simply fell off the stage with little ceremony or protest. The fact that many who had been attacked for their postmodernism had never embraced the term of course did little to help the postmodernist cause. Poststructuralism, one of postmodernism's components, especially the influence of Foucault, has certainly survived in a variety of academic guises. And the 'cultural' and 'linguistic' turns that were also central to postmodern theory, as well as the anti-essentialism and 'decentring of the subject' (Henrique, Holloway and Urwin 1984; Rattansi 1994). have now been more or less assimilated into mainstream academic theorising. So it cannot be said that postmodernism failed in any simple sense. But there seem to be no postmodernists left now, and, one might be forgiven for thinking, definitely not in the person of Zygmunt Bauman, who now prefers the positive concept of 'liquid modernity'. However, appearances here may be deceptive, as we shall soon see. To begin with, though, we come back to a long-standing problem in Bauman's theorisation.

'Liquid' modernity vs 'reflexive' modernity: Bauman's problem of agency, again

Bauman's conception of agency has been a source of some debate, and has often been tied in to a concern over whether he is fundamentally a pessimist or an optimist (Dawson 2012). Earlier in the book I have had occasion to draw attention to some of the points at which Bauman's sociology wipes out agency, for example when he relies on abstract reifications of social forms such as 'modernity' and 'postmodernity', or when consumers are treated as being so driven by the urge to consume that they effectively have no choice. Dawson has argued, however, that once Bauman's Levinasian understanding of morality is taken into account, together with his conception of culture and the inevitability of moral choice, not only is he an optimist but he has an adequate notion of the powers of individual agency. However, the problems with this manner of interpreting Bauman are at least two-fold. First, it relies on accepting the cogency of Bauman's Levinasian conception of morality; but as I have argued earlier, Bauman's embrace of a Levinasian ethical standpoint runs aground in a sea of objections. Second, as I have also pointed out earlier, there are far too many occasions on which Bauman argues strongly that in contemporary times consumerism has such a hold on individuals that, as he puts it in an essay in *Intimations of Postmodernity*, ordinary members of society will not even be able to recognise and accept a critique of consumerism, so complete is their seduction by consumerism's questionable charms.

In part, Dawson relies on Bauman's assertion that the liquid phase of modernity results in an expansion of moral choices in the 'life world' (Dawson 2012: 559). But Bauman himself undermines this interpretation, as can be seen in his comment about his attitude to Beck's notion of 'reflexive modernity' in response to a question from Gane (Bauman and Gane 2004: 18–19), and about why he had chosen to speak of liquid rather than reflexive modernity. Gane's question is well put, for at first sight there are similarities between Beck's conception of greater individualism and individuation in what he also calls a second modernity and Bauman's equally strong assertion of liquid modernity as a time of greater individualism than ever before.

But whereas for Beck the individualism also results in greater *reflexivity* in individuals as they confront the risks and ethics of their choices (Beck 1992) – *Bauman insists that Beck overestimates the cognitive capacities of individuals caught up in the maelstrom of liquid modernity* (Bauman and Gane 2004: 18): '"Reflexive"? I smelled a rat here. I suspected that in coining this term we are projecting our own (professional thinkers') ... puzzlement into imaginary popular prudence – whereas that world out there is marked by the fading and wilting of the art of reflection (ours is a culture of forgetting and short-termism ... the two arch-enemies of reflection).' In this instance Bauman is only repeating an argument he had made in *The Individualized Society* (2001b: 9–10), where he had emphasised that the reflexivity of ordinary people, of which 'much has been made recently', ignores the fact that most people are simply not reflective enough to understand how the 'odds are piled against them'; small wonder, he says, that people simply carry on in a placid manner accepting the status quo even though they come off so badly in the game of life. There is no need for a dominant ideology or any 'brainwashing' by the mass media, for ordinary people are simply too unreflective to understand how the rules of the game of life operate routinely, behind their backs, to ensure that they are the losers. As in *Intimations*, so in *The Individualized Society*: Bauman repeats the argument that even if the unfairness of the rules is pointed out to people, the argument will remain beyond their grasp: as he puts it, borrowing a well-worn phrase, 'one can take a horse to water, but one cannot make it drink' (*The Individualized Society*: 10).

This sort of judgement betrays a considerable elitism on Bauman's part: intellectuals, he implies, may be able to reflect upon and ponder deeply on the dilemmas of the social world, but ordinary members of society, trapped in what he elsewhere often calls a 'nowist' culture, are too busy rushing hither and thither, chasing consumer goodies and generally trying to cope with individualised life, to effectively stand back and think through the sham choices of consumer society.

While in principle Bauman's conception of culture implies that there will always be resistance, in effect he cuts the ground from under the feet of the vast majority of social actors: the resistance will simply not happen. It is little wonder that he 'smells a rat' when Beck grants to ordinary people a greater degree of reflexivity than in the earlier phase of modernity: for Bauman, Beck is simply projecting onto ordinary people a capacity for critical reflection that only *some* intellectuals seem able to achieve. Small wonder, too, that I have referred to Bauman as 'an Adorno for liquid modern times' (Rattansi 2014) and that I believe that for all his eclecticism, it is appropriate to see Bauman as continuing in the pessimistic tradition of the Frankfurt School's Critical Theory.

'Metaphoricity' in Bauman's sociology

As I have emphasised in the Introduction and elsewhere in this book, Bauman's deployment of metaphors is a defining feature of his sociology, and most commentators have argued that Bauman's sociology has a 'literary edge' giving it a number of strengths, and should not be judged in a conventional sociological manner. The 'liquid' metaphor is only one among myriad metaphors that litter Bauman's sociology, among them being 'vagabonds', 'tourists', 'legislators', 'interpreters', 'weeds', 'strangers', 'players', 'strollers', 'solid modernity' and 'liquid modernity', and his description of the modern nation-state as a 'gardening' state rather than a 'game-keeping' state, or humans as 'artists of life', politics as a 'camping site', usually connected with his 'will to dualism', and hence also the dualist metaphoric juxtapositions of 'proteophoia' and 'fixeophobia', 'mixophilia' and 'mixophobia', 'phagic' and 'emic', 'allosemitism' and 'philo-semitism'; this is by no means an exhaustive list. Thus, before turning the spotlight on the merits or otherwise of the 'liquid' metaphor, it is necessary to discuss the role of metaphors in sociology. Note here that Bauman appeared to come late to a proper recognition of metaphoricity in his work, perhaps prompted by interlocutors such as Jacobsen, Tester and others; before this belated acknowledgement Bauman was more likely to refer to his metaphors as 'ideal types' (*Life in Fragments*: 49) He used the idea of 'ideal types' later, too, in his liquid modern phase (*Consuming Life*, 2007: 23–4, 27–8).

Be that as it may, it is clear enough that metaphors are central to the human use of ordinary language (Lakoff and Johnson 1980), but also that the natural sciences cannot do without them either, for example in likening light to 'waves' (Hesse 1967), although in the history of Western philosophy an early bifurcation occurred when Plato condemned metaphors while Aristotle in his *Poetics* regarded them as essential to any form of thinking. Bauman rightly points out in an interview with Jacobsen that sociology cannot do without metaphors: even the idea of 'society' started life as a metaphor (Jacobsen 2013a: 17), but sociologists stopped noticing that it was a metaphor for 'fellowship' and other such terms when the metaphor became so successful that it assumed a reality of its own.

Bauman point out, 'Metaphorical juxtaposition is an act of selection and discrimination: some features are drawn into limelight, some others cast in shadow ... In all cases, metaphor "prejudices" the perception of the object it tries to comprehend ... Each metaphor is for that reason reductionist' (Jacobsen 2013a: 17–18). This seems more like an ideal type than a metaphor, strictly speaking, but I do not wish to side-track my discussion. Justifiably, Bauman argues that metaphors are necessary because language does not 'mirror' reality, there is always a 'disparity between words and things', and that metaphors are useful not only because they illuminate certain aspects of reality, but because what they leave out can also have great fertility in further investigations (Jacobsen 2013a: 18).

Bryant (2013) also makes the point that only empiricists and positivists decry the use of metaphors. For them, there is 'a sharp contrast between metaphors and statements that can be judged in terms of truth, veracity or accurate depiction. This can be seen as essentially a positivist view', he continues, 'based on the assumption that reality is accessible in some direct manner, a possibility that is precluded or at least distorted if metaphors are involved' (Bryant 2013: 26).

Commentators who praise Bauman's use of metaphors, such as Blackshaw, Tester, Mark Davis and others, have argued not only that metaphors give Bauman's sociology its special literary character, but also that this literary quality precludes Bauman's being judged – to a greater or lesser degree – in conventional manner by the empirical veracity of his analyses. But if metaphors were not special to Bauman's sociology, but were the bread and butter of any sociology and especially post-empiricist and post-positivist sociology, then it would be possible to argue that Bauman's sociology should not be judged by its empirical grounding and reach only if one adopted the positivist and empiricist view that metaphors and conventional sociological concepts are more separate than they actually are. In other words, Blackshaw, Davis, Tester and others make too strong a distinction between Bauman's metaphor-laden sociology and conventional sociology. *Ipso facto*, judging Bauman's work by whether it stands up to empirical research, even if we admit that facts are always dependent on theory and metaphor, can be rejected only if one adopts an empiricist and positivist view of sociological research. Blackshaw and others think they are making a non-empiricist and non-positivist case by distinguishing between Bauman's sociology and conventional sociology, but in fact they are falling into an empiricist and positivist trap by insisting on a wide gulf between a sociology that relies heavily on metaphors and one that remains close to empirical research findings. As I argued in my Introduction, I reject as implausible the distinction that Davis, for instance, makes between 'analytical reach' and 'empirical grasp', and it is now possible to see how and why this division as a strict separation must be refused; some of Bauman's critics, Ray (2007) for example, also fall into a positivist trap by making too rigid a separation between the metaphoric and the empirical. Although some of Bauman's metaphors have an important ethical function, it would actually be doing Bauman an (empiricist and positivist) injustice not to judge his sociology by looking at the empirical research produced by sociologists, historians and anthropologists. In other words, the conclusion to be drawn when considering what Jacobsen calls the 'metaphoricity' of Bauman's sociology (Jacobsen 2013b) is the opposite of what commentators like Blackshaw imply: one of the ways in which Bauman's metaphoric sociology must be judged is on empirical grounds, although it is arguable that some forms of positivistic sociology may be so far removed from Bauman's manner of conducting his sociological investigations that they become inappropriate when judging the value of Bauman's sociology. But certainly, the products of ethnographic sociology, and as we shall see other forms of empirical sociology, certainly cannot be considered out of bounds completely: hence my puzzlement that Bauman not only failed to refer to conventional sociology, but in his attempt to present life as it is lived paid such scant attention to ethnographic accounts. That he never appears to refer to Lefebvre's magisterial *Critique of Everyday Life* (2014, first published 1961) is just one puzzle among many when it comes to the sources Bauman regarded as useful and appropriate.

It should become even clearer now why I have been critical

of Bauman's disdain for discussions of methodology in sociology: I can make the point even more strongly now that separating 'theory' and 'research methods', which Bauman did, and in which he was supported by commentators such as Blackshaw and Jacobsen, can be sanctioned only in an empiricist and positivist sociology which sharply demarcates theories and concepts from 'facts', such that the way 'facts' are gathered – that is, 'research methods' – can safely be ignored because how sociological findings are generated is of no particular interest if one is engaged in a Bauman-type socio-literary project. In reality, 'methods' of research are crucial to any discussion of the value of whatever type of sociology one is engaged in doing, for they influence heavily what kind of metaphors are appropriate and useful. This is why I concur with Davis – Director of the Bauman Institute, if a reminder is necessary – when in another work he chastises Bauman for the vagueness of his concepts-metaphors and the lack of empirical grounding and referencing of his metaphors of 'tourist' and 'vagabond' (Davis 2008: 109).

The usefulness of one form of selectivity and reductionism rather than another, to cite from Bauman's own discussion of what work metaphors do in sociology, cannot be judged on 'literary', aesthetic and personal grounds only: they must be put against appropriate findings from sociological and other empirical research. As Bauman put it, the 'truths' of fiction and literature are the 'truths' of literature and should not be conflated or assimilated or confused with the 'truths' of other forms of commentary on human affairs including sociology (Bauman, Jacobsen and Tester: 2013: 24–5). 'Novel-writing and sociology-writing, each technique has its own techniques and modes of proceeding and its own criteria of propriety, which sets them apart from each other' (Bauman in Jacobsen, Marshman and Tester 2007: 39; Bauman and Mazzeo 2016).

It is thus not surprising that when Bauman himself doubted claims that he sensed were implausible he asked (with reference to Jackson's *Redefining Prosperity*) in *This is Not a Diary* (2012: 105): 'I wonder on what *facts* that supposition rests; there is a lot of *evidence* [no references are given by Bauman for *his* facts], that in a recession some people are forcefully ... and much to their despair disqualified as credit-worthy and eliminated from the consumer orgy' (my emphasis). In the same text Bauman commended Wilkinson and Pickett's *The Spirit Level* (*This is Not a Diary*: 102–3). However, one of the key defining features of Wilkinson and Pickett's text (2009) is of course its wholesale use of statistical methodology, which is more usually regarded by Bauman and authors such as Blackshaw as having no particular virtues, indeed quite the opposite. And with regard to multiculturalism, Bauman went so far as to demand 'proof' of its benefits (*Culture in a Liquid Modern World* 2011b: 48).

I can only conclude that there is no necessary incompatibility, let alone incommensurability, between the 'literary edge' of metaphoricity in sociology and statistical and other empirical research methods, and we have this on Bauman's own authority.

On the 'liquid' metaphor: what is this liquid in 'liquid modernity'?

The interview with Gane (Bauman and Gane 2004) reveals quite clearly that Bauman wanted to distance himself from postmodernism not only because he did not like (unnamed) postmodernist bedfellows, but also because he wanted to put aside any lingering doubts that might have been entertained about his views on modernity: modernity was not ending, although he had been interpreted as arguing the opposite. Now, I have earlier pointed out that there was enough ambiguity in Bauman's pronouncements on the radical novelty of postmodernity as a 'social system', and on its 'sociality' as a radically new 'habitat' requiring a new kind of sociology to give those who wished to see in his thinking an 'end of modernity' thesis enough grounds for their judgement. It is also the case that there were occasions on which Bauman could not have been clearer that in his view postmodernity was a phase within modernity, that is, that we are now living in 'modernity without illusions', and that *that* is what he meant by postmodernity. Coining the concept of 'liquid modernity' was a way of putting the matter beyond any doubt, while also giving a positive content to the new reality.

Mark Davis (2013: 6) is insistent that Bauman's decision to use the metaphor of liquidity 'can be seen as an artistic, literary decision rather than a scientific one'. However, in the light of my discussion above, it is possible to conclude that this is only part of the story: there are empirical, sociological reasons as well, and indeed Bauman's usage, as will emerge later, appeals to socio-historical and economic changes as key reasons why the current phase of modernity (in the West, at least, though Bauman rarely enters this caveat) should be referred to as liquid modernity.

Bauman's choice of and explication of the 'liquid' metaphor cannot be considered immune to critical interrogation simply because it may in part be regarded as a 'literary' decision. The choice is a literary-cum-sociological-empirical one, and various questions may legitimately be put to probe its appropriateness, plausibility and possible limitations. It may as well be noted in this context that others have doubted whether Bauman's change of terminology away from the postmodern is simply an intellectual decision: Jay (2010: 97) argues that Bauman appeared to have realised that the postmodern phase 'was losing favour', thus prompting a change of vocabulary, while Best (2013: 102) is more scathing: 'what Bauman is engaged in here is a reconfiguration or rebranding of his *sociology of postmodernity* to satisfy changing market conditions' (emphasis in original).

But the 'liquid' metaphor throws up a number of questions. Liquids come in various degrees of viscosity, but Bauman assumes that 'liquid' simply implies the opposite of 'solid', and that its chief characteristic is fluidity. This may be true of water, but it is not true of honey or treacle to the same degree. Moreover, while individuals can move rapidly within water, honey and treacle are sticky and difficult to move through, coat the traveller, leave marks and are an environment in which detaching from other travellers is more difficult: a liquid modernity seen as composed of honey or treacle rather than water would not create conditions and possibilities for the rapid fragmentation and disembedding of social ties that are available in water. Honey, moreover, has different degrees of viscosity and fluidity depending on its temperature, and is therefore susceptible to influences beyond its own structure. Remember too that glue is a liquid until exposed to air, allowing further metaphorical and analogical reflections on social relations. Water can freeze and, in doing so, expand; and it melts at varying rates depending on the temperature.

There are also substances that are between solid and liquid: mud is a good example, being a slimy, sticky mixture of solids and liquids. One might, in sociological-metaphorical usage, want to suggest that the poor and excluded are 'knee deep in mud' and the very poor and destitute are 'up to their necks in mud', with the metaphor of one's 'name being mud' – and the metaphor of 'slinging mud' at opponents – a useful addition to the ways in which poverty is made to carry connotations of stigma and lack of 'respectability'. Latterly, Bauman (*This is Not a Diary*: 79) deployed the idea of magma, molten lava that has solidified, but one can hardly speak of being knee deep in magma, or slinging magma at opponents, so this is not a metaphor that has much mileage.

Furthermore, given that for Bauman space and time were
important to liquid modernity in the sense that the speed of movement allows spaces to 'shrink', why should the whole space of
liquid modernity be composed of a homogeneous liquid? There are
a variety of physical and social spaces as different physical settings
for different types of social activities with different degrees of freedom: homes and families; offices, call centres and their workforces;
factories – even liquid modernity has many – and factory workers
and managers in a variety of managerial hierarchies; school buildings and playgrounds; it is easy to multiply examples with different
types of physical and social configurations. Social ties in the home
and family are, to use the metaphor from honey, usually more
sticky and durable than those in the school or workplace.

Thus a very significant problem with the way in which Bauman
uses the 'liquid' metaphor is that the social is homogenised in a
highly implausible manner, with all contradiction, unevenness –
one is tempted to add 'ambivalence' to the list – washed away (Ray
2007: 70). Or, as Best (2013: 117) pointedly asks: 'Is it the same
liquid Bauman has in mind across all his post-2000 writings? Is
the liquid Bauman has in mind water? If so, is it hot water or cold
water? ... If the people in liquid modernity are in hot water they
are in great danger. Are the liquid moderns ... swimming against
the tide or going with the flow? ... Can the liquid be frozen into
a solid? Can it evaporate? Can human agents redirect the flow?
Can we simply build bigger and stronger tanks?' And as the title
of my Part III suggests, movements of individuals can metaphorically be of many different kinds: slipping, sliding, falling over or
drowning; the individuals may even freeze in the cold. Bauman's
use of his 'liquid' metaphor and its implications for social relations
and individual movement is disappointingly unimaginative. There
is another relevant, related differentiation that Bauman ignores:
there is a distinction to be made between the liquid, which may or
may not flow, and the individuals in it, who may or may not flow,
with or against the current.

And, one might ask, can the liquid appear free-flowing on the
surface but contain far higher levels of viscosity and stickiness at
lower levels? Or, as Ray (Ray 2007: 67–8) inquires, might it not be
the case that underneath the apparently free-flowing social movement of individuals that Bauman observes there are more enduring

social structures of class, nation, local communities and so forth which may have loosened somewhat but still retain entrenched? Lee (2005), on the other hand, points out that processes of social dis-embedding may be subject to re-embedding.

In *Moral Blindness* (Bauman and Donskis 2013: 78) Bauman's correspondent Leonidas Donskis coins the notion of 'liquid totalitarianism' to characterise contemporary China and Putin's Russia. However, no plausible reasons are provided for this invention, and in his reply Bauman does not question the appropriateness of this term. But if Putin's 'managed democracy' (Donskis's phrase) and China's state capitalism can both be described with the 'liquid' metaphor, what are the limits to the extension of this metaphor? Would it be appropriate to describe Twenty20 cricket as 'liquid cricket'? What would be served by this extension of the metaphor? And given that before the invention of Twenty20 cricket one-day internationals might have been regarded as liquid cricket, how is one to differentiate between the liquidity of Twenty20 and one-day internationals? No answer exists in Bauman's oeuvre, and this is not surprising because the metaphor is very loosely conceptualised. It is no wonder that Bauman himself has been able to write about phenomena that he calls 'liquid', in *Liquid Love* (2003) and *Liquid Surveillance* (with Lyon, 2013), as well as *Management in a Liquid Modern World* (with I. Bauman, Kociatkiewicz and Kostera, 2015) and *Liquid Evil* (with Donskis, 2016). Presumably there are few limits to social phenomena that can now be labelled 'liquid'. There is an arbitrariness to the usage of 'liquid' which renders the metaphor susceptible to vacuity.

With these question marks hanging over Bauman's metaphor of liquidity, we can now explore how he fleshes out the distinction between solid and liquid modernity which replaces the one between modernity and postmodernity, and probe the plausibility and novelty of Bauman's new narrative.

'Solid' modernity

Liquids, unlike solids, cannot easily hold their shape. Fluids, so to
speak, neither fix space nor bind time. While solids have clear spatial dimensions but neutralize impact, and thus downgrade the significance of time (effectively resist its flow or render it irrelevant),
fluids do not keep to any shape for long and are constantly ready
(and prone) to change it; and so for them it is the flow of time that
counts more than the space they happen to occupy ... In a sense,
solids cancel time: for liquids, on the contrary, it is mostly time that
matters. When describing solids, one may ignore time altogether:
in describing fluids to leave time out of account would be a grievous
mistake ... Fluids travel easily. We associate 'lightness' or 'weight-
lessness' with mobility and inconstancy: we know from practice
that the lighter we travel the easier and faster we move. These are
reasons to consider 'fluidity' and 'liquidity' as fitting metaphors
when we wish to grasp the nature of the present, in many ways
novel, phase in the history of modernity. (*Liquid Modernity*, 2000b:
2, emphasis in original)

Bauman was well aware of a major pitfall in using these analogies for characterising what he saw as a crucial faultline between
'solid' and 'liquid' in the history of modernity: Marx and Engels in
a now famous passage in *The Communist Manifesto* (1848) referred
to their period of capitalism as one in which change was so rapid
that 'all that is solid melts into air' (let us set aside the little difficulty
that when solids *melt* they do not become gaseous). If 'modernity'
was liquid then, how can we be living through a novel phase of
modernity now?

Bauman's answer is that in Marx's time, and throughout the
phase of 'solid modernity', socio-economic change, although rapid
and ubiquitous, was always only a temporary state of affairs, with
one solid set of social relations soon replaced by another solid social
stage. So, although the first stage of melting led to the 'melting' of
feudal social relations, the installing of the capitalist economy and

the dominance of what Weber called 'instrumental rationality', this soon began to solidify into a particular form of heavy capitalist modernity. This is a stage that has often been called within the regulationist school of political economy, borrowing from Gramsci, the 'Fordist' stage of capitalism. Taking Henry Ford's assembly-line production of automobiles as a typical feature, this is seen as a stage of capitalism of large manufacturing enterprises operating with a minute and inflexible division of labour, soul-destroying, repetitive jobs for manual workers and a strict hierarchy dividing manual workers from managers (*Liquid Modernity*: 115).

Thus this was 'the era of *hardware*, or *heavy* modernity – the bulk-obsessed modernity, "the larger the better" kind of modernity, of the size is power, "the volume is success" sort ... Heavy modernity was the era of territorial conquest. Wealth and power was firmly rooted or deposited inside the land – bulky, ponderous and immovable like the beds of iron ore and deposits of coal' (*Liquid Modernity*: 113–14, emphasis in original). This was therefore a phase of modernity in which both workers and capital were by and large tied to place and forced to confront each other without any route of escape. The 'commonality of fate' of both workers and capital, tied to particular spaces, meant that despite many conflicts, the two simply had to find ways of co-existence.

If the solids were deliberately melted, this was in order to create better versions. In other words, there were definite standards for what would constitute progress, and an ever-expanding horizon of progress could be envisaged as a linear process. But this was a case of replacing one cage with another, for 'people were released from their old cages only to be admonished and censured in case they failed to relocate themselves ... The task confronting free individuals was to use their new freedom to find the appropriate niche and to settle there through conformity' (*Liquid Modernity*: 7). Whether it was social class, family or neighbourhood, the rules of behaviour were clear and it was difficult to break out of pre-determined patterns and boundaries. Foucault's use of Jeremy Bentham's Panopticon as an 'archmetaphor' for this type of modernity was therefore particularly apt (*Liquid Modernity*: 9–11).

The most obvious problem with Bauman's characterisation of 'solid modernity' is the very high level of abstraction at which the analysis is carried out, and here the problem is similar to the one in

Work, Consumerism and the New Poor where Bauman distinguishes, in very similar fashion, between a modern society of producers and a postmodern society of consumers. Can, say, two hundred and fifty years of social history and the variety of institutional configurations of Western societies be captured by this single, homogenising metaphor of solidity? He cites, favourably, Beck's description of class, family and neighbourhood as 'zombie' categories and institutions in liquid modernity: dead but surviving in a peculiar post-death state. They were properly alive and useful only in the solid modern period (*Liquid Modernity*: 6). But were class, family and neighbourhood similar enough across such vast swathes of space and time?

The metaphor of solidity fails to capture the political and cultural changes experienced in Western societies between, say, the early 1800s and the 1950s; as Bauman gives no precise periodisation there is no reason to exclude perhaps even the tumultuous 1960s as simply another blip in solid modernity. The sociological usefulness of the metaphor is threadbare; it is – to turn the tables on Bauman – a lightweight metaphor that simply cannot support the weight Bauman wishes it to bear.

For example, one huge change that took place was the social *movement* of women from the home to the workplace; another was the large-scale, physical, population *movement* from the West's former colonies to the metropolis in the period after the Second World War; another was the retreat of the West from its colonial territories, and thus a momentous shrinking in the *spatial* reach of Western power; and the extension of democratic and citizenship rights to all adults in Western populations meant that the Panopticon 'archmetaphor' was clearly undermined in significant respects. In other words, to use another of Bauman's metaphors, there have been enough significant fluidities and flows, varying between historical periods and across territories, to cast serious doubt on the appropriateness of the 'solid' metaphor, even if re-embedding has also taken place, for the re-embedded 'solid' may be less solid and may differ in other significant respects that simply escape the 'solid/liquid' metaphor altogether.

One notable instance of the muddy nature of the re-embedded solidities has been the position of women and ethnic-minority workers in the labour market and the class structure; there may have been movement from the home to the workplace and from the colonies to the metropolis respectively, but the women tended to be concentrated in part-time, less secure 'women's work', whether in the typing pool or the garment-making industry, and black people, Asians and other ethnic-minority workers were concentrated in lower-level manual occupations, whatever their educational and professional qualifications, and consistently suffered twice the rate of unemployment as white male workers. *What Bauman has to say about the heavy or solid phase of modernity, in relation to workers, applies largely to white males.* Again, the neglect of gender and race severely restricts the applicability of Bauman's metaphor, which, not to put too fine a point on it, seems otiose, or certainly of limited use.

'Liquid' writing and liquid modernity: some ethical considerations

Bauman repeated his nostrums on liquid modernity with only slight variation and often with verbatim repetition (Walsh and Lehmann 2015) across a vast number of mostly lightweight books – some *very* lightweight books such as *Liquid Times* (2013b, 115 small pages, no index), *Culture in a Liquid Modern World* (2011b, 121 pages, no index), *This is Not a Diary* (2012, no index, mostly based on ruminations on news items and commentaries in newspapers) – journal articles, chapters in edited collections and interviews, from the publication of *Liquid Modernity* in 2000 onwards. Although some elements are highlighted over others in particular publications and although as Bauman's reading of other authors continued he borrowed, transformed and added new ideas, the basic outline of his views remained constant. What will follow, then, is a summation for which I have drawn upon a wide range of his publications but will cite or quote from only some. It is also worth emphasising at the outset of this brief exegesis that there are few significant differences between Bauman's characterisations of solid and liquid modernity and his earlier distinction between modernity and postmodernity. It is thus not surprising that Blackshaw (2005), for example, in giving a sympathetic exposition of Bauman's work in his book, simply merges the two sets of distinctions, and writes without making any differentiation between modernity and postmodernity on the one hand and solid and liquid modernity on the other.

The point about his incessant repetition across breathlessly written and rapidly published books – some of them simply consisting of wide-ranging and not particularly scholarly or rigorous reflections based on email exchanges, such as *Living on Borrowed Time* (written with Rovirosa-Madrazo, 2010), *Moral Blindness* (with Donskis, 2013), *Liquid Surveillance* (with Lyon, 2013), *State of Crisis* (with Bordoni, 2014), *Management in a Liquid Modern World* (with I. Bauman, Kociatkiewicz and Kostera, 2015), *Of*

God and Man (with Obirek, 2015a), *On the World and Ourselves* (with Obirek, 2015b), *Liquid Evil* (with Donskis, 2016), *In Praise of Literature* (with Mazzeo, 2016) – and articles on liquid modernity bears further discussion. There is a sense in which Bauman is *knowingly* colluding with a consumerist culture in which readers supposedly live in hurried time and a 'nowist' culture in which memories are short and the newest is best. Rapid repetition for him is important, as is the apparent part-newness of each publication, because he wants to get his 'message in a bottle', as he puts it, out as often as possible, not knowing who is going to come across it as it finishes its journey along turbulent seas and rivers; the more bottles with similar messages that are launched at great speed, the greater the chance that more people will actually receive the message (Bauman, Jacobsen and Tester 2013: 48; passages here are quoted verbatim from a 2007 publication, Bauman, Jacobsen, Marshman and Tester 2007: 34–5). Of course, the irony is that in his publication practice Bauman was *reinforcing* 'nowist' and consumerist culture by swimming with the tide and enhancing the rapidity of the flow.

He even complains that in consumerist culture and liquid modernity there is a huge excess of information (*Wasted Lives*, 2004b: 25–6; *Consuming Life*: 39–40; *Does Ethics Have a Chance in a World of Consumers?*, 2008: 162) or, as he puts it in the later *Moral Blindness*, there is now a 'tsunami of information, opinions, suggestions, recommendations, advice and insinuation that inevitably overwhelms us' (Bauman and Donskis 2013: 42). If so, how *ethical* is his practice of repetition and rapid publication, in quickly published books one following another, while at the same time he complains about too much information being available in liquid modernity?

There is a related question: if Bauman's 'liquid modernity' is mostly 'postmodernity' in new packaging this raises ethical issues in relation to the practice of creating an appearance of a newness that, like so many supposedly new goods in consumer culture, simply alters surface features of the old. In *Moral Blindness* (Bauman and Donskis 2013: 15) Bauman complains that one of the *evils* of consumerist liquid modernity is that 'the time between purchase and disposal tends to shrink', and 'all consumer goods ... are eminently exchangeable'. The same, unfortunately, may be said of the (ex)changing of 'postmodernity' for (to) 'liquid modernity' and also the great degree of verbatim repetition in his works (Walsh and Lehmann 2015), in which case Bauman appears to have been colluding with a liquid modern *evil* that he warned against. This is by no means a trivial issue, for a persistent and vehement critic of consumerism such as Bauman arguably has an ethical responsibility to not make the situation worse if he or she can help it.

Liquid modernity: the bare essentials

Liquid modernity, not unlike postmodernity, is a time of 'interregnum', Bauman says, one in which existing institutions, because of 'deregulation, fragmentation and privatization', have been denuded of larger visions and the capacity to bring about change, resulting in a profound loss of trust in dominant institutions (Bauman and Donskis 2013: 84; Bauman and Bordoni 2014: 98; Bauman, Jacobsen and Tester 2013: 89). It is a 'between and betwixt' period 'when the old ways of having things done no longer work properly, but new and more effective ways have not been made available' (Bauman and Bordoni 2014: 83).

The two key features of the liquid phase of modernity for Bauman are *globalisation* and *individualisation*. Bauman's analyses of these interrelated phenomena are generally economistic, a point endorsed but not criticised by Tester in his well-informed exegesis of Bauman's social thought (Tester 2004: 164). Globalisation is primarily seen to be the outcome of the freeing of capital controls and the unleashing of market forces, initially in Western economies, but to be in danger of rapidly engulfing the globe. And market forces are also the drivers behind individualisation. The power of market forces is caused by and is further reinforced by the retreat of the state in individual Western nation-states. As welfare nets have huge holes punched in them, and as citizenship is hollowed out, turning citizens into consumers and 'customers', rather than individuals having citizenship entitlements, individuals find themselves having to fend more and more for themselves as best they can. They are encouraged to go and shop for solutions, both literally and metaphorically, and are led to believe that in fact they are now being given more choices than they had. 'Choice', imported from the terminology of market-driven culture, seeps into every social nook and cranny and provides the illusion of greater freedom.

Being left alone to 'choose' as both the public sector and social bonds are dissolved by the market leads to great insecurity among individuals. Individualised liquid modernity (*The Individualized Society*: 51), like the postmodernity described in *Intimations of Postmodernity* and most especially *In Search of Politics*, is characterised by the same acute anxiety and insecurity which Bauman had dubbed *Unsicherheit* (*In Search of Politics*: 5), a combination of 'uncertainty, insecurity and unsafety'.

Moreover, individuals also find themselves subjected to *surplus manipulation*:

> Surplus manipulation is at its most vicious when it turns the blame for the imperfections of the culturally produced life formulae and the socially produced inequality of their distribution on the self-same men and women for whose use the formulae are produced ... It is then one of those cases when (to use Ulrich Beck's expression) institutions 'for *overcoming* problems' are transformed into 'institutions for *causing* problems'; you are, on the one hand, made responsible for yourself, but on the other are 'dependent on conditions which completely elude your grasp' (and in most cases your knowledge); under such conditions, 'how one lives becomes the *biographical solution of systemic contradictions.*' Turning the blame away from institutions and onto the inadequacy of self helps to either defuse the resulting potentially disruptive anger, or to recast it into the passions of self-censure and self-disparagement or even rechannel it into violence and torture aimed against one's own body. (*The Individualized Society*: 5)

Bauman here is quoting from books by Ulrich Beck – *The Reinvention of Politics* (1997) and *Risk Society* (1992) – and one by Ulrich Beck and Elizabeth Beck-Gurnsheim, *The Normal Chaos of Love* (1995). The notion of 'surplus manipulation' implies that there might be a *normal* or equitable level of manipulation, a puzzling idea crying out for clarification. Although Beck's concept of 'reflexive modernity' had implied a greater degree of awareness of social conditions than Bauman's usual understanding of ordinary people, as I have argued earlier, in the passage Bauman quotes above they both seem to agree that ordinary members of society are living in social conditions that '*completely* elude' their grasp (my emphasis); but while social conditions are never completely transparent to those who endure them, neither should they be seen as completely opaque to them. What we see here is a return to Bauman's mode of thinking which I highlighted earlier, in which ordinary citizens as consumers are completely deluded and duped into an unthinking consumerist orgy.

Again, in liquid modernity, as in postmodernity, the public sphere is hollowed out, which is why individual problems are never traced to their social origins and nor are public, collective solutions sought. Liquid modernity sees the 'demise of politics as we know it', and 'Politics with a capital P, the activity charged with the task of translating private problems into public issues ... is nowadays grinding to a halt' (*Liquid Modernity*: 70).

The separation of real power, now possessed by economic elites, from the state and politics is a constant theme in Bauman's liquid modern writings, as indeed they are in his postmodern phase, especially in *Globalization* and *In Search of Politics*. As well as in *Liquid Modernity*, above, he repeats the point, for example, in *Living on Borrowed Time* (Bauman and Rovirosa-Madrazo 2010: 55, 89; *Liquid Surveillance* (Bauman and Lyon 2013: 112); and most of his other works in the liquid modern phase (see Bauman and Bordoni 2014: 115–17).

It is in the context of the demise of 'real politics' and the public sphere that Bauman launches an attack on the mass media and popular culture that is repeated across a wide range of works throughout his 'liquid' writings. He criticises the ubiquity of 'chat shows' and 'celebrity culture'. Chat shows often feature ordinary people disclosing their private troubles, and also feature celebrities who discuss how they have solved their own life problems. The 'public' then take their cue from the lives of celebrities, who often go on to write autobiographies and self-help books which insecure, anxious individuals turn to in their millions for help, rather than making public demands for a change in the social conditions that are at the root of their problems. Bauman (*Liquid Modernity*: 66–7) cites the example of the famous actor Jane Fonda and her *Workout Book* as a prime illustration of this process at work. Indeed, celebrity culture is so insidious and permeates popular culture so deeply that children grow up just wanting to be 'famous', no matter for what (*Consuming Life*: 13).

The ubiquity of television means that for Bauman, in liquid modernity the Panopticon model appropriate for solid modernity is now replaced by the notion of the 'Synopticon' (an idea borrowed from Mathieson 1997) in which, instead of the few watching the many as in the case of the Panopticon, now 'the many watch the few', and it is in this process that they become dependent on mass-mediated popular culture for illusionary solutions to their very real problems of how to negotiate life in liquid modernity (*Liquid Modernity*: 30).

Of course, experts in life-styles and life-politics, health and so forth also come into their own, as Bauman had pointed out in his postmodern phase in *Postmodern Ethics* and *Life in Fragments*. In *Liquid Love*, too, Bauman has much to say about the role of 'relationship experts', and he has scathing judgements to offer on them as well as on what he sees as the fragility of bonds in relationships of love in which people have what he calls 'top pocket' relationships which they 'can bring out when they need them' but push deep into the pocket when they do not (*Liquid Love*, 2003: x). Intimate relationships within couples, for Bauman, have been totally invaded and corroded by commodification; I will explore these issues when I discuss once again the question of consumerist culture.

In such conditions old forms of *identity* undergo a dramatic change. While in solid modernity identities such as class and gender were supposedly a *given*, in liquid modernity they become a never-ending *task* (*Liquid Modernity*: 33). It is no wonder, then, that 'we' replace a 'few *depth* relationships with a mass of thin and shallow *contacts*' (*Identity*, 2004a: 69). The technology of mobile phones has an insidious role. It hastens the transition from real, face-to-face communities to 'virtual' communities, which are only 'pretend' communities with an 'illusion of intimacy' (*Identity*: 25).

As the 'society of producers' turns into a 'society of consumers', Bauman argues that social groups should increasingly be characterised as 'swarms' (*Society under Siege*, 2002: 7). This is little different from the 'neo-tribes' which made their appearance in his postmodern phase, further enhancing the sense that liquid modernity is postmodernity re-packaged for further consumption (see *Intimations*: 190–1; Best 2013: 117–19). Swarms, somewhat like Bauman's conception of football crowds discussed earlier, are collections of individuals with little structured organisation and few dissenters. They get together on occasions, disperse, and come together 'attracted by changing and moving targets' (*Consuming Life*: 76). They are like liquids, with little determinate shape.

It might be thought that given Bauman's obvious distaste for swarms and what he called the 'postulated communities' of liquid modernity (*Liquid Modernity*: 169), he would have welcomed the attempts by 'communitarians' to re-invigorate communities with stronger cohesion and bonds as an important antidote. But he found their attempts underwhelming, self-contradictory and counter-productive. They are self-contradictory because they invoke the very mechanism of choice that has in fact been at the heart of the problem in the first place. It is because of the greatly enlarged freedom to choose that the problem of community has arisen in the first place (*Liquid Modernity*: 170).

The search for community is understandable. Liquid moderns face a situation of *precariousness – précarité*, as the French sociologist Pierre Bourdieu has called it (*Liquid Modernity*: 171). This is particularly strong in the world of work and employment, with the growth of unemployment, the increase in short-term working patterns and the rapid growth of what Standing in a path-breaking book has called the 'precariat' (Standing 2011; see also Standing 2014; Bauman and Donskis 2013: 63–5). Add to these 'uncertain old-age prospects', but also the 'hazards of urban life', and the result is 'diffuse anxiety' – an idea familiar from Bauman's postmodern phase – such that 'born again' communitarians strike a chord in millions of people. But the 'seductive security' offered by communitarians is for Bauman not only illusory but dangerous, for it hardens the boundaries around groups – 'communities' – and this can only lead to a demonisation of those outside the glittering, blissful harmony supposedly on offer from communitarians (*Liquid Modernity*: 172). This danger becomes particularly evident when the idea of community idealised by communitarians is closely inspected. For Bauman, the ideal-typical community of 'born again communitarianism' is the ethnic or national community, and that is a serious problem. Ethnic and national exclusivities create strangers, outsiders.

Bauman goes out of his way to emphasise the dualism that is evident in this analysis: '*It is a typically either/or situation: the boundaries dividing "us" from "them" are clearly drawn and easy to spot, since the certificate of "belonging" contains just one rubric, and the questionnaire which those applying for the identity card are required to fill in contains but one question and a "yes" or "no" answer*' (*Liquid*

Modernity: 176, my emphasis). Whatever, one might legitimately ask, has happened to 'ambivalence' towards others? Ambivalence seems to have been a victim of what Mark Davis (2008) has called Bauman's 'will to dualism'.

Small wonder that 'multiculturalism' – as he understands it – provokes Bauman's ire. He equates it with the practice of 'political correctness' (a notion which Bauman adopts despite the fact that it has been a right-wing mud-slinging term invented to discredit ethnic and sexual minorities' and women's demands for due cultural and legal recognition) and argues that it does no more than collude with inequalities produced by globalisation within nation-states (*Community*, 2001a: 106–7). In *Culture in a Liquid Modern World* (2011: 59), Bauman charges multiculturalism with turning a positive valuation of cultural difference into a generalised 'indifference' to other cultures, relying upon just one French critic of multiculturalism and without mentioning the overall climate of French hostility to multiculturalism. No actual evidence is cited to show that this is the case wherever any form of multiculturalism has been tried in Western Europe.

What Bauman understands by the notion of multiculturalism is a caricature of the actual variety of conceptualisations and practices that are encompassed by it. I do not have the space in this book to present a critique of Bauman's views on multiculturalism and can only refer the reader to my book on the subject for a more nuanced and positive appraisal of some forms of multiculturalism (Rattansi 2011; see also Taylor and Gutman 1994).

Whether with regard to multiculturalism or other social developments, in his liquid modern phase Bauman is even more dismissive of demands for any kind of empirical evidence. Those who ask for even a modicum of systematic evidence are dismissed as 'methodology addicts' (*Liquid Love*: 2) as I have remarked earlier, although Bauman himself demands 'proof' of the benefits of multiculturalism (*Culture in a Liquid Modern World*: 48), a very strong empiricist and positivist demand that contradictorily goes against the grain of his critique of mainstream sociology.

If multiculturalism is no more than collusion with globalisation – and my book on the subject shows how facile this view is (Rattansi 2011) – what is wrong with globalisation? Bauman repeats his critique of globalisation in many places (in *In Search of Politics*: 170;

Globalization, 1998a; *Liquid Modernity*: 185–6; and many other publications). Globalisation above all means the freeing of capital from the shackles of the nation-state. Nation-states cannot control out- and in-flows of capital; capital and its elite owners seek out the most profitable territories with the cheapest and most desperate workforces. Contemporary capital fits the liquid modern world, for it travels light, while workforces and labour are 'heavy', being much more dependent on and rooted in place. Factories and other workplaces can easily be relocated and important functions can be outsourced, leaving behind a 'downsized', 'lean' labour force afraid and insecure about the next round of downsizing and outsourcing. The nation and the state increasingly part company. The state too is downsized, its capacities and 'family silver' sold off to private investors and welfare nets hauled back as far as possible, with a citizenry with fewer rights now unable to mount much of a defensive challenge. While in the period of solid modernity capital and labour were locked in a place-bound marriage, now capital can divorce from labour at will, promiscuously forging relationships with far-flung labour forces and threatening the new nation-states and their populations with instant divorce proceedings. In the process there is an exponential increase in inequality within nations as elites roam the globe in search of tax havens. The influx of cheap imports feeds a consumerist, credit-fuelled 'orgy' which keeps domestic populations in the richer countries docile and distracted.

This is a world in which the 'social engineering' and planning typical of solid modernity become unfeasible (*Society under Siege*: 33–7). 'No more salvation by society', a phrase coined by Peter Drucker, is repeatedly quoted by Bauman to signal the new world of diminished state capacities and the strong power of markets to undercut attempts at controlled social change (*Society under Siege*: 33; *Culture in a Liquid Modern World*: 57; Bauman and Bordoni 2014: 9). Profound questions about the possibilities for social transformation are involved here, raising doubts about the degree to which Bauman's is still a sociology of 'hope'; I discuss the relevant issues again later.

In *Liquid Fear*, Bauman introduces the notion of 'negative globalization'. This refers to the forced opening-up of all societies, including the poorest ones, to 'open market forces', whether they think this is best for their populations or not (*Liquid Fear*, 2006:

97). The agencies of negative globalisation are the USA together with the World Bank, the International Monetary Fund and the World Trade Organization, although Bauman fails to provide any analysis of the policies of these organisations. The results of negative globalisation, as the term implies, are wholly deplorable. It creates inequality and injustice in the societies which have these policies imposed on them and it colludes with neo-liberalism in creating huge disparities of income and wealth, an issue that Bauman tackles in *Does the Richness of the Few Benefit Us All?* (2013a). It gives rise to 'resentment and vengeance', perverse nationalisms, fascism, religious fanaticism and terrorism. It creates a world in which there is no escape or hiding place from the forces and effects of negative globalisation. Ultimately, it leads to a 'new world disorder' in which *'Global lawlessness and armed violence feed each other'* (*Liquid Fear*: 97, emphasis in original). Negative globalisation generalises fear, risk and uncertainty on a planetary scale. This is a world in which terrorism thrives (*Liquid Fear*: 102; Best 2010). Far from eradicating uncertainty and risk, actions such as the invasion of Iraq end up glorifying and enlarging terrorist organisations like al-Qaeda (*Liquid Fear*: 103).

Negative globalisation in the form brought about by global neo-liberalism creates 'wasted lives' (*Wasted Lives*). The 'new poor' are not only in Western societies but are spread globally; neo-liberal modernisation, meaning the spread of free markets and the retrenchment of welfare, creates huge numbers of new 'outcasts' who cannot find employment, proper shelter or health care. The waste generated by various forms of industrial and electronic manufacturing, polluting the environment, land and sources of safe water, goes hand in hand with the creation of whole populations of the poor whose lives are also a form of waste.

The growth in the number of refugees is one consequence of various forms of negative globalisation. 'Refugees are human waste' for which no state wants to take responsibility, handing over their care to humanitarian organisations with a 'moral righteousness' which is belied by the callousness of the way in which states wash their hands of these abject populations (*Wasted Lives*: 76–7; *Strangers at our Door*, 2016).

Within liquid modern Western societies, business organisations and managerial hierarchies also undergo a profound

transformation, according to Bauman, drawing in particular upon
the 1999 French edition of Boltanski and Chiapello's *The New
Spirit of Capitalism* (English translation 2007). Employees have
been falsely 'empowered' in the business organisations of liquid
modernity. Instead of facing a disciplinary regime of management, employees now have to vie for attention from managers to
prove that they were worth hiring in the first place (*Society under
Siege*: 34; Bauman and Tester 2001: 89). The advent of mobile
phones means that employees are constantly on call and potentially under surveillance (Bauman and Lyon 2013: 59). There is a
rise in businesses' short-term projects, increasing the job insecurity
felt by employees. Bauman dubs this form of managerial discipline
'integration-by-succession-of-short-term-projects' (*Society under
Siege*: 35). Thus not only work identities but, with the invasion of
the liquid modern market into all spheres of life, identities in general now undergo transformation: 'A flexible identity, a constant
readiness to change and the ability to change at short notice ...
appear to be the least risky of conceivable life strategies' (*Society
under Siege*: 36).

The size of connections and networks becomes more significant
than the mere possession of professional skills. In the new world
of work 'Living in a network, moving through a network, shifting from one network to another with growing speed and facility,
travelling light and being constantly on the move – all this means
to be and to stay on top'. The term 'society' becomes increasingly
redundant, to be replaced by 'network' (*Society under Siege*: 40–1).

But in the association of insecure and changing networks that
replaces society, one main element of 'collateral damage' is trust.
Liquid modernity suffers from a large deficit of trust (*Liquid Fear*:
67–9; Bauman and Donskis 2013: 104). Insecurity in work and
the constant need to change networks lead especially to a mis-
trust of strangers and the entrenchment and growth of stereotypes
(*Collateral Damage*, 2011a: 70). 'Trust nobody', Bauman says, is
the watchword for liquid modern individuals (*Liquid Fear*: 68).
'Fear is here to stay' (Bauman and Donskis 2013: 97). In liquid
modernity temporary trust is brought into being on occasions of
'targeted solidarity' such as horrific disasters or 'the sudden death
of an idol', or during occasions of 'targeted patriotism' like 'world
cups' and 'cricket tournaments'. The rest of the time 'the "others"

(others as *strangers*, anonymous, faceless others met daily in passing, or milling around densely populated cities) are sources of a vague, diffuse threat ... No solidarity is expected from them and none is aroused by seeing them ... Keeping your distance seems the only way to proceed' (*Liquid Fear*: 68–9, emphasis in original). Liquid modern individuals, for Bauman, suffer from acute anxiety and fear and are thus highly prone to depression (Bauman and Donskis 2013: 100).

When Bauman turned to particular events, which was not very often, he showed an awareness that in fact it is the poor who are most at risk of many urban hazards, even in the case of 'natural' disasters like the Katrina hurricane and consequent flooding which hit New Orleans. The well-off were able to escape on planes and in cars; the poor found themselves stranded (*Liquid Fear*: 77–81). Arguably, the rich and the poor suffer quite different proportions of 'diffuse anxiety', for the rich always have the advantage of rapid mobility out of danger; it is therefore a pity that Bauman nevertheless insisted on deploying the rhetoric of 'we' ('we suffer from diffuse anxiety' or 'we suffer from lack of trust', for example) in a generalised manner when he was writing, as he usually did, in a highly abstract style.

Bauman argues that the corrosion of trust consequent upon growing insecurity, the invasion of the market and individualisation has profound *ethical* consequences. While the chief driving force of 'adiaphorization' in solid modernity was bureaucracy, in liquid modernity it is the market (Bauman and Donskis 2013: 40). Adiaphorisation involves a process whereby certain acts and groups of people are placed outside the sphere of morality, as Jews were during the Holocaust, with bureaucrats being also convinced that the ends justify the means, so that moral considerations simply do not enter the calculations of the consequences of actions. Now, in liquid modernity, this 'evil' of adiaphorisation becomes market-driven. The sheer pace of life in a 'nowist' culture means that pangs of conscience and moral controversies diminish in significance (Bauman and Donskis 2013: 41). What matter are the rapidly changing results of 'ratings wars', and profitability.

If nothing takes root, moral anxieties and scruples are driven out, because 'reference points and guidelines that seem trustworthy today are likely to be debunked tomorrow as misleading or corrupt ... Whatever is "good for you" today may be reclassified as your poison tomorrow ... There seems to be no secure island among the tides ... We no longer possess a home' (Bauman and Donskis 2013: 42). 'Compassion fatigue', which Bauman had identified as a moral hazard in postmodernity, is not surprisingly also a moral danger in the re-named liquid modernity (Bauman and Donskis 2013: 43). The problematic nature of Bauman's argument about compassion fatigue has already figured in my discussion of Bauman's postmodern phase and need not detain us again.

Liquid modernity is characterised by a fateful coupling of state- and media-induced fears against outsiders with enhanced *surveillance* of citizens by the state (*Wasted Lives*: 90–1; Bauman and Lyon 2013). The risks, uncertainties, fears and supposedly dangerous 'strangers' and 'aliens' generated within liquid modernity are exaggerated by the state and mass media. There is a huge proliferation of closed-circuit television, X-ray machines and pre-emptive strikes. When threats fail to materialise into actual events, this is taken as evidence of the success of mass surveillance (*Wasted Lives*: 91).

Together with the notion of the 'Synopticon', Bauman borrows the concept of 'ban-opticon' from Jean-Luc Nancy and Giorgio Agamben to signal that to a considerable degree liquid modernity is a post-Panopticon phenomenon (Bauman and Lyon 2013: 64–6). Drones as small as insects can sit on window sills and spy without being noticed, and can move around as necessary; this is what allows surveillance to be called 'mobile' and therefore *liquid* surveillance, a new liquid modern phenomenon. The launching of weaponised drones from a distance also creates a moral or ethical distancing, a process of adiaphorisation, which allows soldiers to destroy human life without pangs of guilt. If innocents are killed, this can be brushed aside as a 'technical' failure (Bauman and Lyon 2013: 89).

But the drone also combines with new information technologies and the use of the internet to generate almost unmanageable amounts of data about liquid modern individuals. Credit cards, online purchasing via sites such as Amazon and posts on Facebook leave traces that allow profiles and classification of individuals to be built up (Bauman and Lyon 2013:24–6, 63, 125–7 and passim).

Thus consumerism and liquid surveillance dovetail with each

other. As in postmodernity, so in liquid modernity individuals not only purchase commodities but sell themselves and become commodities, for example on Facebook (Bauman and Lyon 2013: 33). The willingness of individuals to collude with surveillance was, for Bauman, particularly disturbing (Bauman and Lyon 2013: 73, 127, 136). Individualisation breeds loneliness, and building up a large list of 'friends' on Facebook creates an illusory community for individuals, although these are 'networks' that do not guarantee any help if it is needed, something that was available in older forms of community whatever their disadvantages. Postings on Facebook are a form of ersatz 'recognition' in a lonely world (Bauman and Lyon 2013: 23, 25, 39–40; Bauman and Donskis 2013: 109). For lonely, 'homeless' individuals 'the fear of disclosure has been stifled by the joy of being noticed' (Bauman and Lyon 2013: 23); the search for recognition means that liquid moderns are willing to reveal the most intimate secrets of their lives especially on 'TV talk shows, tabloid front pages and the covers of glossy magazines' (Bauman and Lyon 2013: 28; Bauman and Donskis 2013: 108). But the result of self-disclosure on Facebook, the traces available in credit card use, searches on Google and confessions in the mass media together constitute a paradise for those interested in selling commodities, with populations being classified into crude segments for the purposes of marketing (Bauman and Lyon 2013: 67–8, 136).

As in postmodernity, so in liquid modernity there is a fundamental division between the seduced and the repressed; this coincides with groups who 'fence' themselves into gated communities and shopping malls, and the excluded who are 'fenced out' but put into 'camps' and for whom older Panopticon modes of surveillance and incarceration in ghettos and prisons are still alive and well (Bauman and Lyon 2013: 55–6, 64–5).

Although new forms of social media such as blogs, text messaging and the like do help protest movements such as Occupy, which have created encampments on Wall Street and were also very useful in organising the mass protests of the Arab Spring, Bauman remained generally sceptical about the possibilities for protest and emancipation opened up by the internet and other information technologies. In particular, he bemoaned the lack of a vision for an emancipated and genuinely democratic future among those who come out in protest (Bauman and Lyon 2013: 49–51; Bauman and Bordoni 2014: 99), although Bauman himself very seldom suggested, described or praised alternatives: the proposal for a basic income in *In Search of Politics*, and praise for the Slow Food Movement in *Does the Richness* (*Does the Richness*: 66–7), based on an article in *Wikipedia*, are notable though poorly thought-through exceptions.

Aspects of liquid modernity: critical reflections

Earlier in this book I have presented a series of critical reflections on Bauman's diagnosis and critique of postmodernity. Here I shall continue that task, but with regard to some of the ideas he now groups under the umbrella of a critique of liquid modernity. Given the overlapping meanings of 'postmodernity' and 'liquid modernity' in Bauman's work, there is a danger that my earlier criticisms might simply be repeated. However, there are enough relatively new ideas and commentaries on human predicaments and social trends presented by Bauman in his liquid modern phase for this danger to be largely avoided, especially because my earlier critical reflections deliberately omitted certain aspects of Bauman's ideas to enable separate treatment in this section on liquid modernity.

Limitations of space necessitate a selective critical assessment of Bauman's voluminous output in his liquid modern turn. Given the almost overriding, repetitive presence of his critique of consumerism (he was indeed *obsessed* with consumerism), my lengthiest considerations will focus on this aspect of his diagnosis of the malaise of liquid modernity.

Before embarking upon a critical commentary on aspects of Bauman's analysis of liquid modernity, it should be emphasised that there are many elements of his critique that 'hit the bull's eye', as he is fond of saying in his email exchanges and interviews (see, for example, Bauman, Jacobsen and Tester 2013: 11), and can be found in other critiques of life under what Bauman calls liquid modernity. Globalisation in its current phase has made serious inroads into the sovereignty enjoyed previously by nation-states; today's rich elites are grotesquely rich and have a tendency to barricade themselves behind high walls and armed guards; consumerism, new social media and market forces have penetrated deep into social relations, forcing individuals to market themselves to an unprecedented degree; increasing numbers in the labour forces of Western societies are experiencing an anxiety-provoking precariousness and new forms of control in the workplace, while private and state surveillance have reached worrying proportions; shopping has become a significant aspect of social and individual life, the identities of individuals are increasingly developed in the arena of consumption and style rather than work, and some individuals do develop an addiction to shopping; consumerism, the new information technologies and the rapid flows of capital and the exponential increase in financial transactions have hastened the pace of life, and individuals often feel overwhelmed by the proliferation of consumer goods and the rapid appearance of newer models as well as built-in obsolescence; there has indeed been an exponential rise in the information available, particularly via the internet, and choices between goods and their corresponding lifestyles are subject to bewildering change; under the influence of inroads made by the privatisation and outsourcing of national and local state services and neo-liberal ideology, the public sphere and welfare safety nets are constantly being reined in, adding to insecurity as well as lack of public accountability; the mass media all too often amplify fears of supposedly uncontrolled immigration and exaggerate the pace of increase in 'strangers' and 'aliens'; there is a 'new world disorder' which has many causes, and what Bauman has called 'negative globalization' is a very real phenomenon; collapsing or weakened nation-states, terrorism, civil wars and refugees are patently significant issues in the twenty-first century and have contributed to heightened feelings of insecurity, anxiety and fear; excessive consumption is depleting the world's natural resources, and new risks are constantly being produced by technological innovations which are supposed to help create safety, better health or better consumer goods; 'celebrity culture', with its many attendant ills, is also is a real phenomenon as 'celebrities' such as footballers, television and film actors, entertainers and so forth, with their high incomes, conspicuous consumption and endorsement of consumer goods serve to embed ever more deeply the veneration and consumption of desirable brands and 'designer labels' in a race to keep up; those who are unable to keep up, especially the young, are often 'shamed' and stigmatised by their peers; the young, often dubbed 'generation X' and 'generation Y', face high costs of living, mounting debts, precariousness at work and very high rates of unemployment, a new phenomenon in Western societies where in the past the young had always expected to do better than their parents' generation.

Bauman was by no means alone in pointing to the rise of these new levels of inequality, insecurities, anxieties, addictions, risks and planetary dangers; by now a large number of authors have made similar arguments (James 2007, 2008; Wallop 2013; Lawson 2009; De Graaf, Wann and Naylor 2005; Standing 2011; Wilkinson and Pickett 2009; Dorling 2015; Stiglitz 2012; Skidelsky and Skidelsky 2012; Klein 2014; Giddens 2009).

In the light of the fact that critiques of consumerism, in particular, are very common, in my view it is fair to ask whether Bauman's analyses offer anything especially insightful that is not available in myriad publications, newspaper and journalistic accounts and documentaries on consumerism. Part of the issue here is that very often Bauman himself relies on no more than the accounts of journalists in broadsheet newspapers, or he presents unsystematic critiques of 'agony aunts', for example, who offer advice on relationships and other matters. If so, does he offer sociological insights that are not widely available in books that reach wider audiences than his own repetitive books published by Polity Press, an academic publisher?

It is my contention that because Bauman too often read only very selectively, or ignored altogether and disparaged the more systematic research efforts of sociologists, anthropologists and other social scientists into consumerism, the mass media and popular culture, his analyses too often fail to offer genuinely original and particularly revealing insights that might, by so doing, also highlight for a wider audience the contribution that sociology, cultural studies and anthropology can make to a more nuanced and complex understanding of the issues involved. In the process, although he offers useful analyses, he is also guilty of a damaging selectivity; that is, he ignores important factors such as gender, race and ethnicity as well as contradictory and oppositional elements in consumerism and popular culture. He therefore fails to engage sufficiently with 'common sense' and ignores developments that might actually help the hapless individuals caught up in the swirling and turbulent forces that are shaping the social, political and cultural trends of the twenty-first century. As is his usual practice, it is again notable that in his liquid modern phase Bauman rarely quotes from actual ordinary individuals who are living through liquid modernity, for he eschews deeper ethnographic and other research accounts, even those provided by serious investigative journalists, relying instead on highly abstract and over-generalised assertions, combined with journalistic commentaries and unsystematic critiques of life-style experts and television shows. So, although he explicitly wishes to have a dialogue with 'common sense' (an issue I have discussed earlier, but for example see, inter alia, Bauman, Jacobsen and Tester 2013: 9), as in many of his postmodernist writings and now even more so in his liquid modern phase, he provides little convincing evidence concerning what the 'common sense' is in relation to the topics he addresses. For instance, he is highly critical of the mass media, but rarely studies the large amount of valuable research conducted on the content and complex effects of the media that he abhors but also relies on for primary material. He has a tendency to impute meanings to narratives and entertainment programming in the mass media, whether on coverage of refugees or television talk shows, but neglects to take even a cursory look at any of the by now large amounts of 'audience research' evidence, a great deal of which cannot be dismissed as simply the product of mindless 'methodology addicts'. He derides systematic social research, unfairly characterising the bulk of 'sociological practices' as involving treating social actors as 'statistically concocted *homunculi*' and arguing without evidence that sociological research results 'in a trained incapacity to grasp human beings in their mind-bogglingly complex entirety' (Bauman, Jacobsen and Tester 2013: 19).

His abstract over-generalisations result in over-simplifications. This is particularly true of his liquid modern phase. In liquid modern mode Bauman claims to have withdrawn from having a dialogue with his fellow researchers, wishing instead to engage directly with the individuals who live through the ills of liquid modernity (Bauman, Jacobsen, Marshman and Tester 2007: 37), and although he claims to incorporate 'what fellow sociologists find and suggest' into his work, he now does this in even more cavalier fashion than before, as we shall see. One consequence is that his liquid modern writings have a tendency to replicate the over-simplifications of an earlier generation of Frankfurt School critics of 'mass culture' such as Adorno (Rattansi 2014). Much of

Bauman's critique of consumerism can also be found in a slightly different form in the critiques of mass culture of the Frankfurt School, including not only Adorno but especially Herbert Marcuse, for example in his *One-Dimensional Man* (1964), and in the work of Erich Fromm, an early member of the Frankfurt School who drifted away from his colleagues, but in the 1970s wrote a critique of consumerism in his *To Have or To Be* (Fromm 1976).

Bauman was probably one of the earliest of post-Second World War sociologists to put the critique of consumerism at the heart of his diagnosis of the problems of life in the late twentieth and early twenty-first centuries, and for this he deserves credit and praise. But his analyses of this phenomenon and, as we shall see, globalisation and other malaises of modernity leave much to be desired. In particular, they do not always add enough of what might be said to constitute genuinely sociological understanding of the ills that plague 'liquid' modern life. There is no unfairness involved in judging Bauman's assertions and observations in this manner, for he himself remains committed to sociological understanding (see, inter alia, Bauman, Jacobsen and Tester 2013: 36; Bauman and Tester 2001: 40), especially in going beyond the 'common sense' narratives that circulate within popular culture in television shows and newspaper reporting. Jacobsen and Tester, in their introduction to the interviews with Bauman that resulted in *What Use is Sociology?*, airily dismiss what they call 'the banality of findings' (Bauman, Jacobsen and Tester 2013: 3) produced by sociology and, by implication, from other social sciences, but as I will show, this conclusion is facile and ill-judged.

In critically assessing aspects of Bauman's interpretation of 'liquid modernity', I will begin with a discussion of his analysis of consumerism, which I have already critically explored in a preliminary manner in my reflections on *Work, Consumerism and the New Poor* but which can now be subjected to a deeper interrogation. I make no apology for devoting considerable space to consumerism, for this is of course central to Bauman's critique of contemporary life.

The question of consumerism, again

Bauman's distaste for consumerism did not start with his postmodern phase, although it came to be particularly highlighted during it and in his liquid modern writings. As early as 1982, in *Memories of Class*, Bauman had complained about consumerism in what he at the time regarded as a capitalist rather than postmodernist society (*Memories*: 178–80). Capitalist profit-seeking, he had argued, had created a society dominated by the buying of status-endowing 'positional goods', the search for a meaningful life had been reduced to 'the excitement of supermarket sales', and the 'natural need for experience and challenge' was caricatured into 'the motorised crowd congesting the coastal motorways'. Consumerism, he had concluded, had already made the search for alternative ways of living 'irrealistic', and all critique now sounded 'hollow' (*Memories*: 178). Pessimism had already entered into his thinking, for he now saw no real prospects for a critique of the present that would have serious traction.

Moreover, the concept of 'flawed consumers', especially as applied to the rebellion of black British youth, was already in play in Bauman's thinking. He contemptuously dismissed the early 1980s urban rebellions by black youths in Liverpool's Toxteth and London's Brixton, who were protesting especially against racist policing but also against racial discrimination in other spheres (Benyon and Solomos 1987), as 'the consumer society's equivalent of the luddites' quixotic attempt to stem the tide of the industrial revolution'. For Bauman, these young black people were simply expressing a 'destructive rage' because their 'consumer dreams were torn in pieces' (*Memories*: 179). *This complete failure to understand the racism faced by Britain's black and Asian minorities has remained as strong a feature of Bauman's thinking as his critique of consumerism; not surprisingly, it re-emerges when he comments on the urban disorders of 2011, which I shall discuss later.* Note here only that in seeing the protests of black youths as simply those of thwarted consumers Bauman in effect was endorsing the views of Mrs Thatcher and the then Conservative government that these young black people were no more than criminals, a description that was discredited by the officially commissioned *Scarman Report* (Scarman 1982; Benyon 1984).

However, before discussing Bauman's analyses and critiques of consumerism in more depth, it is worth setting out, albeit briefly, some of the key elements of Bauman's critique of the role of consumerism in contemporary Western culture, which I have collated from a wide range of his works, including the previously considered analysis in *Work, Consumerism and the New Poor*, but more especially from his liquid modern publications such as *Consuming Life* (2007), *Does Ethics Have a Chance in a World of Consumers?* (2008), *Moral Blindness* (written with Donskis, 2013) and *Does the Richness of the Few Benefit Us All?* (2013a).

Individuals are so overwhelmed by consumerism, Bauman claims, that their most important identity is that of consumer rather than, say, citizen, and this process of interpellation by which individuals become, overwhelmingly, consumers begins in childhood; people come to believe that solutions to life's problems are to be found in the purchase of more and more commodities in the market, seeing shopping as a form of therapy for life's ills, from ageing to not finding the right partner or friends, to be rectified if only the right commodities can be identified and purchased; consumerism can lead to pathologies such as addiction to shopping; addictions are only an extreme form of a more chronic condition in which it is the acts of shopping and purchasing that satisfy, while the actual commodity that is purchased soon loses its lustre as newer models become more enticing; the extraordinary proliferation of models and versions of the same commodity creates high levels of anxiety, for it becomes ever more difficult to decide which is the correct version to buy; anything deemed to be a wrong choice leads to shame and embarrassment, especially within the individual's own reference and peer groups; there is therefore a great proliferation of 'experts' who supposedly can guide the individual in making the 'right' choice, from 'life-style' advisers to scientists and advertisers; in contrast to Freud's notion of 'the reality principle' as a governing mode of organising one's life, in liquid modernity (and postmodernity) it is 'the pleasure principle' that now predominates and there is a desire for 'instant gratification', fed by the availability of abundant credit in the form of credit cards which, however, result in the piling-up of personal debt; the rapid turnover of gadgets and other commodities and the desire and compulsion to buy them lead to a 'nowist' and 'hurried' form of living characterised by 'pointillist' time which, especially, erases the past and creates an eternal present as well as an unfulfilling longing for a future with newer commodities, while at the same time undermining the idea of progress; individuals see themselves as commodities to be properly clad and with the right qualities and possessions to be attractive in the market; the latter is particularly evident in activities like internet dating, where the presentation of an attractive self with the right attributes and possessions becomes paramount; this form of commodification is accompanied by a loss of social skills when actual individuals have to be encountered, for individuals become more skilled at presentation via the internet than at actual socialising; commodification invades intimate life such that partners, wives and husbands are tolerated only for so long as they provide satisfaction, to be discarded like mobile phones or other gadgets for another partner who seems to promise greater fulfilment of desires; exclusion from the resources required for whatever is regarded as an adequate level and type of consumption, in other words becoming 'flawed consumers', causes great shame, agony and embarrassment and may lead to criminality; consumerism produces huge amounts of excess and waste; excess is also involved in the production of a veritable 'tsunami' of information in which individuals drown and are left bewildered; individuals in consumerist liquid modernity suffer from a form of 'melancholy' in which they sense 'the infinity of connection', but are 'hooked up to nothing'; this 'melancholy' is related to addiction to shopping where individuals are forced to choose but find themselves adrift in a world where there are no trustworthy guides and criteria, and hence they are constantly 'hedging their bets', but are helpless when trying to separate 'the relevant from the irrelevant, and the message from the noise'. I have already referred to another feature of 'the consumerist syndrome', the loss of ethical compasses in a world where advice and knowledge change rapidly and what might have been considered the morally right course of action with regard to the self and others is subject to obsolescence and contradiction.

This may not be a comprehensive discussion of Bauman's critique of consumerism, but there is enough here to give a strong flavour of what Bauman finds objectionable about what he also calls the 'consumerist syndrome', which in its wording sees consumerism as a pathology, for 'syndrome' is typically used in connection with diseases. Nevertheless, many of Bauman's mis-givings about consumerism have considerable force, and as I have pointed out earlier, have now been expressed by many authors (see, among innumerable others, James 2007; De Graaf, Wann and Naylor 2005; Barber 2007; Schwartz 2005; Lawson 2009; Salecl 2010), although they have not met with universal assent either (Warde 1994a, 1994b), a question to which I shall return.

Some typical statements from a late work by Bauman, *Does the Richness of the Few Benefit Us All?*, illustrate the cast of his thinking and, given that his earliest critique of consumerism dates from the 1980s, give an indication of continuities in his thinking as well as the manner in which his thinking has seldom taken new directions or perspectives. From the many passages in the book on the way consumption has taken over the lives of Westerners I will quote only some. 'We are all consumers now, consumers first and fore-most, consumers by right and duty' (*Does the Richness*: 59). 'From cradle to coffin we are trained and drilled to treat shops as pharma-cies filled with drugs to cure or at least mitigate all the illnesses and afflictions of our lives ... Fullness of consumer enjoyment means fullness of life. I shop therefore I am. To shop or not to shop is no longer the question' (*Does the Richness*: 60; see also 54). Shopping numbs sensibilities to such an extent that feelings of outrage at present-day inequalities and other ills are assuaged by the pur-chase of more and more commodities. 'Electronic gadgets' provoke particular ire in Bauman. For him they have an erotic and roman-tic charge; they are easily acquired substitutes for genuine love, which requires 'commitment, the acceptance of risks, a readiness for self-sacrifice' the choice of an 'unmapped, rough and bumpy track' in the hope of sharing 'life with another' (*Does the Richness*: 50–1). But 'electronic gadgets do not just serve love: they are designed to be loved in the way that is offered to other love objects but that they seldom allow' (*Does the Richness*: 50). They take over our psyches to the extent that they set standards 'for both enter-ing into and exiting love affairs' with other human beings. But the 'electronically concocted version of love is, in the last account, not about love; products of consumer technology catch their clients with the bait of ... narcissism. They promise to reflect well on us.'

There are two further aspects of Bauman's critique that are significant and deserve attention. First, Bauman claims that in contemporary consumerist societies it is consumerism itself that is the dominant ideology and the chief integrating force binding individuals into something resembling fragmented, but nevertheless relatively enduring social bonds and cultural cohesiveness, that can legitimately be called 'society'. In consumerist societies, consumerism as a phenomenon becomes alienated, much as labour was in the 'society of producers', becoming 'an extraneous force which sets the "society of consumers" in motion and keeps it on course as a specific form of human togetherness, while by the same token setting specific parameters for effective individual life strategies and otherwise *manipulating* the probabilities of individual choices and conduct' (*Consuming Life*: 28, my emphasis). Consumerism is so pervasive and all-powerful that it has developed the capacity 'to absorb all and any dissent', and indeed it 'recycles' dissent and makes it 'a major resource of its own reproduction, reinvigoration and expansion (*Consuming Life*: 48).

The second aspect concerns the vital question of how consumerism has been able to get such an overriding grip on people's innermost selves that they are willing to succumb readily to any and all enticements and to enthusiastically give themselves over to 'the consumerist syndrome'. Bauman's answer to this question is clearly spelled out in *Does the Richness* and other publications, especially *Consuming Life*. Although Bauman gestures towards the role of advertising and the injunctions of politicians to citizens to consume more – he refers to President Bush's advice to people to 'go shopping' in the wake of the 9/11 attacks but in the process gets the date wrong, for Bush made that statement in 2006 (see Smart 2010; Rattansi 2014) – his basic analysis is economistic and borrows heavily from the dissection of the 'fetishism of commodities' in Marx's first volume of *Capital*, which was then generalised in the Hungarian Marxist George Lukacs's and the Frankfurt School's critique of 'reification' (see Jarvis 1998; Bronner 2011: 35–50).

Thus in *Does the Richness* Bauman is clear that although there is a constant process of 'drilling' of consumerism (by unnamed agents) into human subjectivity, the chief mechanism is to be found in the way *commodification in the economy is transplanted into human consciousness, more or less without mediations, so that commodification and consumerism invade and are embedded in all aspects of social, cultural and political life*. 'It is ... [the] pattern of client-commodity or user-utility relationship which is grafted upon human-to-human interaction and drilled into us all, consumers in a society of consumers, from early childhood and throughout our lives.' This process, stemming from commodification, 'bears a major responsibility for the current frailty of human bonds and the fluidity of human associations and partnerships'; commodification results in the 'brittleness' and 'revocability' of 'human bonds' and also leads to the chronic anxiety over 'exclusion, abandonment and loneliness haunting so many of us these days and causing so much spiritual anxiety and unhappiness' (*Does the Richness*: 84–5; *Consuming Life*: 19–21).

Let us begin with this last argument, which suggests that commodification in the economy is transplanted onto all human relationships. Not to put too fine a point on it, this is a blatant form of economic determinism and one which writes out human reflexivity, on the part of consumers and those who devote huge sums of money and much creative talent and energy in marketing commodities (see Warde 1994b; Wernick 1991; A. Davis 2013; Nava et al. 1997; M. Davis 2013, among many others). Ethnographic studies of advertising, for example by Miller (1997, 1998, 2001) and Nixon (2009), show the complexity and reflexivity of the processes which characterise advertising campaigns. At the other end of the chain, Bauman completely neglects the creative aspects involved in practices of consumption. In effect, he treats consumers as cultural dupes, something that was also very evident in *Intimations* where, as I have demonstrated, Bauman regards individuals as so much in thrall to consumerism and other ideologies that they would simply laugh off or be annoyed by sociological critiques.

However, in the first place, he could perhaps have read one of his favourite authors, Simmel, with greater care. As one astute student of consumer culture has noted (Sassatelli 2007: 64–5), Simmel showed considerable awareness of the creative manner in which consumption practices were being deployed to create distinctive identities in an increasingly anonymising urban environment. And Miller (2009: 62) has pointed to Simmel's acute awareness of the contradictory nature of money and consumption. Michel de Certau, in his magisterial study of everyday life (1984), is also a more perceptive observer of the creativity involved in matters of consumption, and it is a pity that someone like Bauman with an avowed interest in the common sense of everyday life makes no reference to him. Moreover, myriad studies, beginning with the pioneering research of the British Birmingham Cultural Studies school, have shown how young people take mundane articles of everyday consumption, whether scooters or safety pins, and give them novel and sometimes oppositional meanings in their own sub-cultures (Jefferson and Hall 1976). Of course, advertising agencies and capitalism more generally have a way of assimilating, recuperating and re-marketing for sale items that may have ostensibly functioned in oppositional mode (Heath and Potter 2005); the grotesque appropriation of the iconic image of Che Guevara to sell frivolous garments or name cocktail bars is an obvious example, but it is also worth acknowledging, as Mara Einstein reveals in an eye-opening study (2012), that giant corporations have cynically latched onto the idea that it is very profitable to advertise that buying their products can help the poor by attaching themselves to worthwhile global causes. Nevertheless, that does not negate the argument that consumer goods are constantly being used and re-used in a manner not originally intended by their producers, for example in the form of incongruous juxtapositions of items of clothing to create dissonant and original styles. Nor is it the case that 'newness' trumps all before it: consumer culture also includes shoppers who shop for antiques, vintage clothing and second-hand items in charity shops. These and many other instances of variety and reflexivity in consumer habits should lead to a conception of 'the active consumer' (Sassatelli 2007: 126; Warde 1994a) rather than the cultural dupe who populates Bauman's work.

Moreover, Bauman exaggerates the extent to which consumerism and individualism dovetail with each other. An alternative perspective highlights how consumer goods can act as a glue, a substance, which, as I have suggested earlier, acts as a counterpoint to Bauman's conception of liquidity. As Trentmann (2016: 520–1) has pointed out, 'Consumption has acted as a glue between generations in three ways'. Trentmann refers first to the many objects that older people keep with them as reminders of their children; second, to the very wide variety and the great diffusion of goods and leisure activities which have promoted greater 'tolerance and respect' for differences between the life-styles of children and their parents; and third, to the transfer of resources, including consumer durables and funds for housing and furnishings, that parents and grandparents are increasingly providing for their children and grandchildren. Also, when women shop, even for mundane household goods, they often attach to the activity a sense of love for their children or partners and even sacrifice their own consumption in order to buy for the family (Edwards 2000: 120–1).

The reader of Bauman will find little that refers to the fact that the majority of shopping expeditions are for the mundane purchase of household necessities (Miller 2012: 69), especially by women, nor anything about the ambivalences and drudgery involved in much of everyday shopping (Miller 2012: 64–8; Sassatelli 2007: 97). Nor does Bauman acknowledge that shopping for cheap throwaway fashion or gadgets, on which he models his conception of consumerism, is rather different from buying cars and household appliances, which are usually made with careful thought and with regard to household budgeting by all but the most affluent, an issue that, it may be recalled, I have raised in relation to Bauman's *Work, Consumerism and the New Poor* in Part II.

Moreover, Bauman neglects the fact that in consumption there are pleasures of a social and bodily kind involved, as well as the forging of attachments (Warde 1994a, 1994b): the consumption involved in a night out with friends and family, whether to a restaurant or to go dancing, is an enjoyable experience, and it is no wonder that it is so frequently indulged in. Consumerism does not just fragment social relationships; it can cement family ties and friendships. Shopping can be both wearisome and pleasurable, and the purchasing of goods in markets has been going on for millennia and has acted as a social and celebratory practice for just as long.

How should one 'defamiliarise' consumerism? Given the centrality of defamialiarisation to Bauman's project of sociological analysis one might expect that in his writings on consumer culture this might figure as an important element. But it does not. However, there is a simple technique that could begin such a task, one that comes to mind from Marcuse's assertion in *One-Dimensional Man* (1964) that 'the mere absence of all advertising ... would plunge the individual into a traumatic void'. Bauman could ask his readers to imagine walking around in city streets that contain no advertising posters and hoardings: this might bring home the ubiquity of the messages of advertisers urging ordinary individuals to consume and how much these form a taken-for-granted backdrop to everyday life. I experienced this when I visited Moscow and what was then called Leningrad in the early 1980s, and what seemed drab at first also soon became liberatory in many respects as it focused attention on architectural novelties and details, in contrast with my usual walks through central London.

The absence of this type of defamilarising strategy goes hand in hand with the absence of references to movements of resistance and opposition to consumerism, an issue I will focus on in the last part of the book. Here I will finally add that Bauman seldom examines in any depth, first, the production process by which commodities of mass consumption are produced. Given the outcries over very poor labour conditions in sweat-shops in poorer countries, it is surprising that Bauman even fails to refer in any detail to the investigative work of one of his supposedly favourite authors, Jeremy Seabrook (Hogan 2002), whose many writings on relevant subjects include the brilliant *Song of the Shirt* (2015) on garment workers in Bangladesh, articles from which project have been available for some time, as have articles on this subject from myriad reports and authors. Other illustrations that could be drawn upon include Alexander Harney's exposure (2008) of abysmal, super-exploitative working conditions in China, where many items for the mass consumer market are produced, as well as the exploitation of undocumented Chinese workers in the UK (Pai 2008). It would even be salutary for his many readers, second, for Bauman to have laid out for them the unethical and corrupt practices that have made Coca-Cola a deeply embedded commodity in everyday life around the globe (see, for example, Thomas 2009). Third, a focus on the huge power of retail giants like Walmart (Fishman 2007) or the British company Tesco (Simms 2007) could all be 'eye-openers' (a phrase Bauman is fond of) for his readers. Goldacre has published numerous articles leading up to his important book *Bad Pharma: How Drug Companies Mislead Doctors and Harm Patients* (2014). Even recommending books and articles such as these to his readers would extend and support Bauman's critical but more often than not unsupported generalisations on the malaise of consumerism. That he does not do so is puzzling to say the least, and certainly his failure to do so does his many appreciative readers a disservice.

An especially important insight is to be found in Tonkiss's argument (2006: 100–1) that the new phase of niche marketing and consumption that developed in the 1980s was at least as much a product of changing production technologies and methods as a consumer-driven phenomenon, for computer-aided design and just-in-time production allowed rapid changes in style, not just of garments but of also cars and other commodities, and producers who were moving over to these new technologies had to mount marketing campaigns exhorting the pleasures and advantages of rapidly changing fashions and customisation of products, which led in turn to new ways of carving up consumers not based on old categories of class and age but in terms of distinct 'life-styles'. Terence Conran, an important British designer and retailer, has a point when he says, 'People do not know what they want until you give it to them' (quoted in Salecl 2010: 145); this is an acute insight into the creation of new 'needs'.

On the other hand, Ritzer's analysis of what he calls McDonaldisation (see, for example, Ritzer 1998) brings sharply into focus that old-Fordist methods of mass production in the food and other service sectors are very much alive, making any hard and fast distinction between 'solid' and 'liquid modernity' untenable, certainly in the manner in which Bauman over-generalises the two phases. Similarly, call centres, a huge growth industry in post-Fordist times as a result of outsourcing to the Global South, have factory-like conditions of work with strict, almost Taylorist forms of control, especially now that even the number of key-strokes on a keyboard has been opened up to monitoring (Williams et al. 2013: 34–5).

Bauman's contention that what now holds contemporary Western societies together is simply the ideology and practice of consumerism appears at first blush baffling. Not only does this ignore nationalism and patriotism, which are also a significant taken-for-granted backdrop to everyday activities as Billig (1995) has demonstrated, and as can be seen in debates in Western Europe and the USA about multi-ethnicity, multiculturalism and national identity (Rattansi 2011), and in the UK over the defence of the Falklands – upon which Bauman did not comment as far as I am aware – and about the issues of Scottish independence and an English parliament and of the decision to leave the European

Union: there is also the question of attachments to the political and cultural freedoms that are deeply rooted in Western liberal democracies. And there are long-standing connections between consumerism and both these phenomena, for the branding of goods has been tied to national pride and identity (Cadbury's as 'British chocolate' and the idea of 'Swiss' or 'Belgian' chocolate, to take obvious examples; see Trentmann 2016 among many others); and consumer choice has also been explicitly promoted in advertising as related to a broader culture of voting and political freedom and choice in liberal democracies. This is why Bauman was only half right when he surmised that the overriding impulse that brought down the old communist regimes was their failure to provide enough consumer goods and that those who tore down the Berlin Wall were primarily motivated by the desire to consume Western goods (*Intimations*: 170). Bauman's lack of understanding of the desire for democracy, however, is a long-standing trait which I have already commented upon.

What underlies Bauman's belief that Western affluent societies are now chiefly held together by the ideology of consumerism is his assumption that all individuals now see themselves first and foremost as consumers. Their first and key identity, according to Bauman, is defined by being a consumer. But he provides no evidence that this is indeed how all individuals construe their identities. Bauman can only maintain this stance on the assumption that he understands what consumption actually means to the consumer. But consumers attach various meanings, for example, to the clothes they are wearing, and the ways in which these clothing styles are judged may vary considerably. As Edwards (2000: 46) suggests, an expensive suit does not mean that the man wearing it wants it to signify that he is well off: many men wear pricey suits because their workplace identity as, say, a manager, demands it. The man may much prefer to wear casual clothes; and as he walks down the street, it is entirely possible for some people to dislike this mode of dress and disapprove of what they think he is trying to signify: they may be thinking, 'What a plonker', as Edwards humorously puts it (2000: 46). Individuals can have multiple identities, and which one comes to the fore depends on the context, for in the voting booth or on a demonstration an individual's identity as consumer will not be the dominant one unless the demonstration, say, is actually in favour of a consumer boycott, but even here this implies a refusal and protest. Identities, as Bauman well knows, are complex, contradictory and provisional, and he more or less says so in *Identity*: thus it is by no means clear that it is the consumerist syndrome that is holding (affluent Western) societies together: individuals also see themselves simultaneously as citizens, men or women, English or British or Scottish or German or American, as belonging to a particular social class and so forth. Complex societies are bound together as well as fragmented by any or some or all of these identities, and more, depending on the context, and the consumerist identity may become salient only in the activity of purchasing commodities and shopping, rather than always drowning all other identities in a deluge of unthinking consumerism.

The neglect of the role of branding in consumerist culture is another surprising omission in Bauman's myriad critiques of consumerism, especially in the wake of the international success of Naomi Klein's *No Logo* (2000, second edition 2010), although only a modicum of research into consumerism reveals the significance of brand culture. Branding is part of the rather complex manner in which the manufacturing of goods – that is, 'production' – is linked to the consumer and practices of 'consumption'. Branding has developed as a result of aggressive marketing strategies by manufacturers and retailers and involves a great deal of psycho-demographic, life-style, attitudinal and motivational and other research by marketing departments and advertising agencies (Lury 2011: 142). In turn, branding, it could be argued, is connected to the way in which from the 1970s onwards retailing has become ever more central to the circuit linking production and consumption (du Gay 1996: 97–8; Pettinger 2016). A key aim of branding, as Lury (2011: 142) among a host of other writers on consumerism has pointed out, is the construction for consumers of 'an imaginary lifestyle' within which 'the *emotional* and *aesthetic* values of the product' are developed. The branding of products has now extended to corporate branding, and even individuals are increasingly being described in popular media and self-help publications as 'brands'; there are frequent discussions about whether a person's 'brand image' has been damaged or enhanced by, say, hitherto secret video tapes or other information being put in the public domain.

It may be that Bauman's lack of interest in the exponential growth of branding and designer labels is partly explained by his general indifference to the role of emotions in social life, despite his occasional remarks on the 'romantic' and 'erotic' aspects of electronic gadgets. After all, Hochschild had pointed out as long ago as 1983 in her *The Managed Heart*, a book that has had a significant impact in the sociology of consumption and sociology more generally, that companies are using techniques whereby employees are encouraged to attempt to develop emotional empathy with customers (Pettinger 2016: 144–61). Taking account of gender is crucial in understanding the emotional labour involved in selling (Pettinger 2016: 151). Women in particular have been recruited into sectors where there is interactive service provision, partly stemming from the stereotyping that assumes that women have greater facility with emotion than men, although men are not completely absent from such selling environments.

For Bauman the consumer is a hurried and harried individual, caught up in 'pointillist' time, and for him it is consumer culture and the availability of mobile phones and such like that are responsible for the contemporary 'hurried' life. It has indeed become part of the common sense of life, especially in Western cultures and Japan, that we live in grotesquely speeded-up times. The French critic Virillio (2001, 2002) is only one among many – Manuel Castells (1996) and John Urry (2001) are notable other examples – who are often described as 'speed theorists', sharing this label with Bauman and his conception of liquid modernity. But this common sense needs challenging, and if Bauman had indeed been genuinely interested in contesting common sense that is precisely the intellectual route one would have expected him to take. But this would have required a deeper study of the sociological literature which now has been brought together and contributed to by Sharma (2014) and Wajcman (2015), among other researchers. Sharma demonstrates not only the differential pace of life of different groups of workers – business executives and managers, taxi drivers, yoga practitioners who serve corporate clients, for instance – but also how speeding up is in fact part of corporate strategies of control over employees, not merely the consequence of the black box of 'consumerism'. Wacjman is even more critical of over-generalising speed theorists, including Bauman, for her research also reveals in particular the complex and contradictory effects of digital technology on the pace of life. A striking aspect of Wacjman's study is the differential impact on women and men, because women, bearing the major part of the burden of housework, find themselves living more harried lives than their male partners (Wacjman 2015: 116–17; see also Hochschild 1997, 2012).

This now brings us more centrally to the issue of gender and consumerism, some important aspects of which I have already discussed, although I document, in what follows, that we also need to understand another feature of the development of Western societies if we want to analyse 'the consumerist syndrome', and that is the issue of imperialism, which by and large has been an obviously neglected theme in Bauman's work (Rattansi 2016).

Gender, imperialism and consumerism

Gender appears in Bauman's analyses only incidentally, for example in *Consuming Life* (2007: 60), where he draws upon a discussion by one of his favourite journalists, Decca Aitkenhead of the *Guardian* newspaper, to make the point that young girls feel pressured to appear sexually attractive; but note that Bauman here is concerned not so much with gender and sexualisation per se, but with the early age at which individuals come under peer pressure, for he goes out of his way to insist that 'There are no separate drilling strategies for boys and girls' because '*the role of consumer is not gender-specific*' (*Consuming Life*: 55, my emphasis).

As the above quotation makes very clear, for Bauman there is no need to pay any particular attention to gender when it comes to the question of consumerism. It is my view that Bauman commits a serious error of judgement in disregarding the role of gender.

In my discussion of modernity and the Enlightenment earlier in the book I have already pointed to the manner in which Western modernity began to structure and solidify around divisions of 'culture' and 'nature' in which women, by and large, came to be located as part of 'nature' and thus as an inferior category in this duality, an issue barely registered in Bauman's thinking. But there were other binaries of power, discipline and function within which women found themselves increasingly imprisoned.

Two are of particular significance. With growing industrialisation and urbanisation came growing disruptions to earlier family
patterns and the emergence of a distinction between 'public' and
'private'. But this overlapped with the binary between 'production' and 'consumption', and women, fatefully, found themselves
increasingly confined to the 'private' and to 'consumption' (see,
especially, Slater 1997; Thornham 2000; Sassatelli 2007; Smart
2010; Lury 2011, among a host of others). Of course, women,
especially from the growing working classes, continued to work
outside the home, but it is undeniable that the home, child-rearing
and consumption, especially with regard to the provision of meals,
clothing and items pertaining to domesticity, were increasingly
seen as women's domain.

This was a contradictory phenomenon, especially with regard
to 'nature', for women were also seen as a vital 'civilising' and
nurturing force. And in Britain, for example, this became part of a
complex intertwining between class, nation, education and empire
(Skeggs 1997: 42–9). Women soon found themselves charged
with maintaining order among the working class as well as nurturing healthy males for a strong nation and the British Empire. The
fostering of a strong moral ethos also became seen increasingly as
part of women's civilising and nurturing role.

From the 1850s onwards the rise of the department store, aimed
especially at women, became a particularly important part of the
retail sector of the Western economy. The architecture and internal design of the stores drew upon the open staircases, large win-
dows, mirrors and ornate iron work that had been fashioned for
the great exhibitions and other spectacles that were also becoming
a significant part of the cultural landscape, and also signified
modernity (Nava 1996, 2007). The department store became one
of the few places other than the church where middle-class women
could wander on their own, unaccompanied by men (except for the
mainly male shop assistants). Women were thus central to the rise
of consumerism.

But the increasingly exotic goods and artefacts on display at
exhibitions and in the department store demonstrate how the
rise of consumer culture was connected to the imperialism of the
metropolitan powers. Transnational trade and colonialism were
intertwined in a central manner with the rise of consumer cul-

ture in Europe and America, as the surpluses generated by slavery and imperialist exploitation of natural resources contributed substantially to increased consumption among the upper and middle classes, mediated by the shopping expeditions of women, who now also increasingly came under the influence of magazines which guided them as to the appropriate manner in which to consume the newly available goods (Thornham 2000: 139).

Advertising grew rapidly. But again, this was not only gendered, but racialised. Thus women, as guardians of hygiene, were bombarded with advertisements for goods such as soap, though there was here what McClintock has called the emergence of 'commodity racism', with advertisements for Pears soap being particularly notorious for suggesting that the 'dirty' black skins of Africans could be lightened by soap while at the same time lightening 'the white man's burden' by bringing a civilisation of cleanliness to the colonies (McClintock 1994: 132; see also Mackenzie 1989). 'Natives' were depicted as happy in their servitude in advertisements for goods from the colonies, such as cocoa, coffee, tea and sugar. McClintock (1994, 1995) argues that as international competition intensified between the colonial powers, so advertising and marketing strategies became more aggressive and sophisticated, contributing in no small measure to the establishment of consumer culture in the metropolitan powers. Branding too was an outgrowth of this form of advertising, McClintock argues, and the soap industry in particular was marked by the rise of large corporations, thus being in the forefront of a growing trend in Western capitalism. Note that contemporary advertisements for a prominent British brand of tea, PG Tips, carried until recently an image of a docile Indian woman picking tea, while there is a form of what Ware has called 'missionary discourse' in advertising material for the supposedly ethical brand 'The Body Shop' in which the founder, Anita Roddick, is depicted in a poor region of the globe bringing the civilising influence of 'green capitalism' (Ware 1992: 243–8).

None of these fascinating and necessary insights regarding the entanglements between modernity, gender and race in the formation and *modus operandi* of Euro-American consumer culture can be found in any of Bauman's innumerable narratives and critiques of consumer culture.

But there is more. As I have pointed out, Bauman is well

aware that in contemporary consumer societies individuals see
themselves as commodities and indeed are forced to see themselves
and market themselves as such. However, it is crucial to grasp that
men and women are positioned differently in this process, for not
only do women have to sell themselves as commodities, but they
have to go to far greater lengths than men in performing a by
and large devalued labour of femininity in making themselves into
desirable commodities by way of applying make-up and buying
clothes. Moreover, they are also constantly used to sell commodities, for example in advertisements for anything from cars to holidays, sports events to gardening tools and men's deodorants. They
are thus doubly commodified. And a great many women work in
occupations, such as receptionists or in boutiques, where the display of women's sexuality is an intrinsic part of the job, making for
further commodification (Thornham 2000: 134).

Historically it has been women who have found themselves
disciplined and oppressed by images of perfection, especially in
magazines and advertisements, although an emphasis on the fit,
young, toned and tanned body is now also being held up to men as
an ideal. Bauman has been insightful in noting the way in which
control over the body is one of the few areas of faux autonomy left
to individuals who then become obsessed by fitness and looks (*Life
in Fragments*: 116–22). But not surprisingly he pays little attention
to how this is gendered, such that women, assailed by images of
slim, indeed thin, body perfection have become prone to eating disorders of various kinds (James 2007: 30) a male phenomenon only
evident in men's rates of obesity, but for different reasons, although
cases of anorexia and bulimia are not unknown in men.

As I have remarked, men are now also targeted by advertising in
ways which were formerly reserved for women. In the UK this is a
phenomenon that emerged in the 1980s, as magazines like *GQ* and
Arena were marketed as life-style guides for a 'new man' now urged
to be more interested in fragrances, accessories such as expensive
watches and new styles to reflect a changing workplace, especially
in the advertising industry itself, characterised by less hierarchical management structures and an emphasis on personal creativity rather than the earlier model of 'the organization man' (Nixon
1996). A more lower-class version was the 'lad's magazine', exemplified by *Zoo* and the now defunct *Nuts*, more explicitly sexist and

aimed at men who were more interested in sport and other traditional working-class male interests. I have already referred to a
telling instance of Bauman's gender-blindness that occurs in his
In Search of Politics (1999) in a discussion of women protesting
against a paedophile. In *In Search of Politics* (43–4), again, this time
to illustrate contemporary preoccupations with the body in consumer culture, Bauman fails to note that the narrative, based on
a particular branch of Weight Watchers and a tabloid newspaper
story about the supposed weight gain of the actor Kate Winslett,
star of the film *Titanic*, is profoundly gendered.

Finally, I offer a brief comment on Bauman's category of
'flawed consumers'. Again, I wish to draw attention to the manner
in which issues of race and gender are side-lined by Bauman,
although in this case the question of class in its relation to gender is
also important as a missing dimension.

Bauman defines 'flawed consumers' as 'those weeds of the consumerist garden, people short of cash, credit cards and/or shopping enthusiasm, and otherwise immune to the blandishments
of marketing' (*Consuming Life*: 4): in other words, people who
either cannot or do not wish to join the consumerist merry-go-
round. Those who cannot consume are what he has also called the
'new poor' (*Work, Consumerism*): as we have seen, those forcibly
excluded by lack of resources from the new consumerist paradise-
cum-nightmare of endless consumption and having to bear the
shame and humiliation of not having the accoutrements of the
life-style held up to all as the good life.

But what Bauman fails to notice is that the category of the 'flawed
consumer' in public discourses is profoundly gendered. As Skeggs
(1997) and others have pointed out, the categories of 'rough'
and 'respectable' working classes and the middle class have been
habitually constructed primarily through the appearance, domestic
habits and child-rearing practices of lower-class wome. Women's
way of consuming was, and to a great degree continues to be, a
mode of defining class location: to be feminine, women had to be
middle-class, engaging in forms of appropriate personal consumption, clothes especially, and also in the particular manner of deco-
rating the home with approved furnishings. In the contemporary
period, as Skeggs's insightful ethnography (1997) of young working-class women demonstrates, there is an acute consciousness

among them about how consumption choices, especially in modes of dress and make-up, can habitually exclude them from what are seen as middle-class patterns of adornment and behaviour; this results in feelings of class shame and humiliation as well as resentment. Working-class men can gain respect and self-esteem from a form of hard masculinity, in other words by being ultra-masculine, but it is difficult for working-class women to be ultra-feminine, and glamorous, because the very definitions of these characteristics are class-coded. It is worth mentioning that Owen Jones's rightly praised recent critique of the demonisation of the working class, *Chavs* (2009), also fails to notice the particular gendering of the category of 'Chav', a label for a despised section of the working class.

It will come as no surprise that Bauman also fails to recognise the racialisation of what he regards as the race-neutral character of his category of the 'flawed consumer'. As in his *Memories of Class* several decades earlier, so now this is evident in his too-hasty remarks on the 2011 urban disorders in the UK (Bauman 2011). For Bauman those who took part in the disorders were no more than 'flawed consumers' who took this opportunity to obtain desirable, expensive goods by looting, the only way in which they could join the consumerist culture to which they were completely in thrall. There is an important truth here, as becomes evident in what is perhaps the most thorough research analysis so far available, conducted jointly by the London School of Economics and the *Guardian* newspaper, entitled *Reading the Riots* (Lewis et al. 2011; Jefferson 2012). But to focus only on this aspect is to miss another equally salient aspect of the disorders: the resentment of young men, especially black and Asian young men, at being repeatedly stopped and searched and generally subjected to what they saw as racist police harassment (Lewis et al. 2011: 19). Given that this was exactly how Bauman had treated the urban rebellions of 1980–81, as I have shown earlier, it documents how little Bauman's understanding of issues of racial discrimination, including that by the police, against black and Asian minorities has developed. For someone who reads the broadsheet newspapers so assiduously, this is extraordinarily surprising: this issue has been highlighted time and again in such news media and on television, and most especially in the wake of the *Scarman Report* of 1982 and then the Macpherson Inquiry's report of 1999, which branded the police as 'institutionally racist'. And as with the 1980–81 disorders, by seeing in the 2011 disorders only looting and witless destruction, Bauman in effect colludes with the Conservative government's branding of these disorders as solely *criminal*, rather than as also containing elements of protest against heavy-handed racially discriminatory policing. The 2011 disorders had in fact been sparked in the wake of the shooting of a young black man in Tottenham in London and only then had spread to other areas.

Nevertheless, whatever the complexities of consumerist culture that are ignored by Bauman, there is little doubt that commodification is insinuating itself into more and more spheres of lives in Western cultures, including even the most intimate of relations. Anyone who doubts this would do well to read the excellent description of this ever-growing process in Arlie Hochschild's insightful and somewhat alarming *The Outsourced Self: What Happens When We Pay Others to Live Our Lives for Us* (2013). This is a book that is justifiably congenial to Bauman's vision of the world, and it comes as no surprise that in one of his last works he finds room for a discussion of *The Outsourced Self* (Bauman, Bauman, Kociatkiewicz and Kostera 2015: 130–4). It is also important to acknowledge that the huge proliferation of choice in consumer goods can create anxiety (Schwartz 2005), although Schwartz provides evidence to suggest that particular personality types that he dubs 'maximisers', who seek the ideal commodity, are more likely to suffer the full force of consumerist anxieties than 'satificers', who are prepared to settle for the 'good enough' commodity or partner syndrome. But there is a more generalised need to seek out authorities including celebrities, who endorse products, and 'life-coaches' who can guide the consumer to make the right choices, as Bauman always emphasises (see also Salecl 2010: 33, 49).

Moreover, the elevated sphere of art, too, has been subject to ever-more commodification. Julian Stallabrass (2006) has punctured the pretensions of the YBA ('Young British Artists') phenomenon by exposing the driving forces of celebrity culture, branding and simple greed that have undergirded the rise of artists such as Damien Hirst and Tracey Emin. The blatantly commercial buying of high art by corporations as 'investments' or the purchase of wine for similar purposes is so widespread now as to require little documentation.

And there is much persuasiveness in Salecl's very Baumanesque point (2010: 31; see also Ehrenreich 2009) when she says, in relation to the exponential growth of 'self-help' books, that in this extraordinary proliferation 'social critique is increasingly replaced by self-critique'.

The burden of my critical commentary on Bauman's analyses, however, is that these trends are more complex, ambivalent and contradictory, as well as subject to more oppositional currents, than Bauman acknowledges. 'Self-critique' is far from being the only game in town.

Globalisation and its discontents: Bauman's world-view critically assessed

As with consumerism, so with globalisation: Bauman has written tens of thousands of words on the subject without his views developing in any significant respect, in the case of globalisation, from the late 1990s to the present day. From the 1998 book *Globalization* to the 2014 *State of Crisis* (written with Bordoni) Bauman's basic 'message-in-a-bottle' is the same: the territorially based nation-state has become a weak and impotent agent, emasculated by the powers of a global, 'extra-territorial elite' and impersonal global markets which threaten at the slightest provocation to move capital and jobs to more accommodating polities and cheaper, more docile workforces. If Marx and Engels wrote in their youth in a famous passage in *The Communist Manifesto* that the state was no more than a committee for managing the common affairs of the national bourgeoisie, then for Bauman one hundred and fifty years on states are simply the handmaidens of an international bourgeoisie, although Bauman, embarrassed now by explicit Marxist vocabulary, refers coyly to a nameless extra-territorial elite that gorges on surpluses nationally generated, but moved around the globe at will and almost without effort. The world is their 'space of flows', a notion borrowed from Manuel Castells's *The Rise of the Network Society*, in which they are sharks swimming unhindered and ever ready to feed off local populations, leaving behind them devastated cities, communities, refugees, 'vagabonds' and national public spheres deregulated and eviscerated beyond recognition, all to please hard-faced shareholders and billionaires who hold the

fate of the nation in their huge, soiled, grubby and greedy hands
and sharks' teeth.

And as with consumerism, so with globalisation: there are
important kernels of truth in Bauman's gloomy homilies. But
they are tendentious over-simplifications, as I will show, albeit
briefly. However, we must recognise, to begin with, that for all his
general insistence upon the significance of 'culture', 'hope', the
need not to give in to the mantra of TINA ('there is no alternative'), Bauman's globalisation is a process without agents, for its
profound Marxisant economism writes out agency in a manner
familiar from so much of his thinking and writing (Gane 2001a:
86); for him even the elites are not wholly in control, though in
emphasising this Bauman has a point. In doing so without qualification, though, he makes it somewhat self-fulfilling. As Hay and
Marsh (2000) and many others have pointed out, if the *perceived*
threat of capital flight exists in relation to, say, a change in interest rates, then that in itself, whether true or not, will constrain
national government. What they call the 'first wave' of globalisation discourse – in which Bauman remains trapped – propagated
the view that national governments were helpless in the face of a
world so strongly globalised, with spaces of flow and space-time
compression developing so rapidly, that resistance was futile. As
they put it, this phase of globalisation theory had itself a disempowering effect (Hay and Marsh 2000: 9). Bauman is a 'hyperglobalist', in Held and his co-authors' powerful coinage (Held et al.
1999), which is drawn upon adroitly in Gamble's *Politics and Fate*
(2000). The problem with hyperglobalists is that they are indeed
fatalists. They see no room for a relatively autonomous realm of the
political, a form of agency that can have real effects. Game, set and
match to economic determinism. We have been left stranded in this
space with Bauman time and again, as I have shown (see also Gane
2001b: 273–4). For Bauman the current in this space of flows is so
homogeneously strong that swimming against it in any shape or
form is impossible.

As against the 'first wave' globalisation discourse, Hay and
Marsh and many others provide a more complex, nuanced view
summed up thus: '... our claim is that there are multiple processes of globalization, that these interact in specific and contingent ways, that such processes are unevenly developed over space

and time, are complex and often resisted and, moreover, that they are *simultaneously social, cultural, political and economic*' (Hay and Marsh 2000: 3, my emphasis; see also Giddens 1999: 10; Beck 2000c: 19).

By the time Bauman was getting into his unstoppable stride, the first wave of globalisation discourse had already been challenged by Held, Giddens, Beck and others, although Bauman has taken little notice. For example, Berger and Dore (1996) had already edited an important collection, *National Diversity and Global Capitalism*, which had challenged the idea of a homogeneous global space of flows. They had begun to document that different nation-states had different stances and policies in relation to global capital, and Wade had contributed to the volume an important corrective to first-wave globalisation by pointing out that 'reports of the death of the national economy are greatly exaggerated'. What he pointed out, echoing Mann's earlier argument, was that the national state remained an important locus for capital accumulation and that international agencies structured and constrained what Bauman considered to be the unhindered global flows of capital. Linda Weiss had published a significant article in *New Left Review* (1997) and then a book in which she had critically examined what she called 'the myth of the powerless state' (Weiss 1998). She pointed out in some detail, with comparisons between the Swedish, German and Japanese cases, that states *adapted*, and not in a uniform manner, to globalising forces rather than simply ceding all autonomy. By so doing she challenged a framework that viewed the state as simply a 'victim' of internationalising trends. Moreover, she also documented, as others have done (Chang 2007), the very great degree to which the rise of Asian economies has involved state intervention. This brings out the broader argument that globalisation is state-driven too, and is not just an effect of the activities of large corporations, neatly overturning the hyperglobalist argument favoured by Bauman in which the state is viewed as a bystander in the process of globalisation apart from the original decision to open the world to global capital flows, thus knowingly and deliberately amputating its own powers.

Bauman posits a powerful and homogeneous current of globalisation with effects, especially, on security at work and in work conditions, as unions and other forms of collective labour are constantly under threat of losing jobs to countries where wages are low. However, Bradley and her colleagues, who researched in some depth the economy and job markets in the north-east of England, have pointed out (Bradley et al. 2000) that the nature of local labour markets is influenced by a wide variety of factors, of which the inward and outward flow of globally foot-loose capital is only one. The state, again, is important, for one of the key creators of jobs was the public sector. This is not something that can simply be glossed by talk of 'glocalization', a notion that Bauman has found useful but that in his usage remains unelaborated, or is written about in his work only in the context of local problems created by global forces: '"Glocalization"', he says, 'means local repair centres servicing and recycling the output of the global problem industry' (Bauman and Bordoni 2014: 125). This sort of formulation is typical of Bauman's treatment of the local in his hyperglobalist discourse, which is belied by the kind of research undertaken by Bradley and her colleagues.

Moreover, *internationalisation* rather than globalisation was the thesis advanced by Hirst and Thompson (1996) in a widely discussed and influential book. Through its various editions, including the last in 2009, they argue that national economies still remain the basic economic unit and that national states retain important powers in how they regulate their economies. Multinational corporations remain important players beside the goliaths of transnational corporations, and the point about multinationals is that many of their most important operations, including management, research and development, core production and sales are located in the company's main national base. Importantly, foreign direct investment flows, although they have increased hugely, tend to be between the three major economic blocs of North America, Europe and the Asia-Pacific. And so much of trade happens within a national economy or a trading bloc. In the case of the USA in particular, it is important to recognise that a large proportion of its trade takes place within the borders of its own national economy.

None of this is meant to imply that nothing has changed. There is now a new density to globalisation, which has seen a manifold increase in four aspects identified by Held and his colleagues (Held et al. 1999): the extensity of global networks, the intensity of global interconnectedness, the velocity of global flows and the 'impact propensity' of global interconnectedness, in which the huge strides made in information technology play an important but not overwhelmingly large role.

Hirst, Thompson and Bromley (2009) and now Jessop (2016: 194–8) have been particularly keen to lay low the shibboleth of impotent national states and international organisations in the face of global market forces and capital flows. As Hirst, Thompson and Bromley suggest, major economic powers, the G8, now with China and India, 'have the capacity, if they coordinate policy, to exert powerful governance pressures over financial markets and other economic tendencies' (Hirst, Thompson and Bromley 2009: 3). Jessop contests the 'zero-sum' approach of hyperglobalists, arguing instead that an increase in the power of global markets does not automatically mean any diminishing of the powers of sovereign nation-states (Jessop 2016: 198), because globalisation is a complex and contradictory set of processes in which there is no homogeneous de-territorialisation.

'Globalisation', Hirst, Thompson and Bromley conclude, has become a hugely inflated term, and those like Bauman who see it as an accomplished fact need to step back and take a more nuanced and complex view. In particular, they, like Gamble, Weiss, Castles (2007), Jessop, and Held (see especially Held 2004), are dismayed by the prophets of gloom who, in effect, reinforce the mantra of TINA because *they give to globalisation a misleadingly entrenched facticity that only leads to a toothless fatalism and pessimism.*

Take the example of the welfare state. Bauman's thesis of relentless neo-liberal deregulation of the public sphere implies a uniform retrenchment of welfare in all of the richer countries of Europe and in the USA. The first point to underscore in this context is that the pressures of neo-liberal ideology have led, in practice, to a *re-regulation* rather than simply to de-regulation (Standing 2011: 26; see also Gane 2012: 128–30), with neo-liberal policies requiring a corresponding expansion in state legislation and oversight, including the setting of 'targets' and an extensive monitoring apparatus, to check and enforce the achievement of targets, for example in the delivery of health and educational services; there has been an expansion in state apparatuses involved in 'auditing' (Power 1999). Sectors of the state have been subject to various forms of commodification via privatisation, but this has usually required greater state activity. Moreover, there is no homogeneity of restructuring in welfare regimes (Hay and Wincott 2012). European national states have implemented widely varying types of modifications to welfare benefits, reinforcing the view that the relationship between globalisation and deregulation is far more complex, with varying degrees of autonomy available to national states: there is no uniform 'separation of power from politics' as implied in Bauman's constant refrain. Moreover, as Keane notes in his magisterial treatise on democracy (2009: 713–16), there is cause to believe that there are many 'monitory' structures and processes by which public bodies are held accountable, in which democracy has increased in recent periods; Keane also documents the many instances in which public protests have led to changes, whether through the Civil Rights struggles which empowered and reduced discrimination against African Americans or movements for equal pay for men and women in many companies and workplaces. Not surprisingly, he warns against unwarranted cynicism towards democracy (2009: 747), for it carries great self-fulfilling dangers for the future of democracy just at the time when a great many inroads have been made, despite the depredations of neo-liberalism, against the power of corporations and so forth, in the struggles to expand the remit of democratic accountability throughout the globe. Williams and his co-authors also point out that despite the influence of neo-liberal ideologies on the process of globalisation, it has been possible to develop international frameworks on minimum labour and environmental standards (Williams et al. 2013: 14). They emphasise the need to conceptualise globalisation as a process with many agents, including workers and their organisations.

None of this is to underestimate the power of, especially, genuinely transnational corporations, twenty of whom can be included in the forty largest economies on the planet. Their lobbying powers are extensive and deeply dug into the agencies of national governments and international bodies. As George (2015) puts it, they 'represent neo-liberal practice in its purest form', demanding deregulation, freedom from government oversight and weak trade unions or preferably none at all, and they have succeeded in taking over many public services on the supposed grounds that private ownership and enterprise will always be more efficient and cost-effective for citizen-users, who now become 'customers' (see also Clarke et al. 2007; Marquand 2015); and they continually demand and often get freedom to trade and invest without tariffs.

Moreover, Bauman (*Does the Richness*) and others are quite right in highlighting the grotesque inequalities within countries that follow upon neo-liberal-inspired low taxation and the selling-off of publicly owned assets. The revelations in the 'Panama Papers' have shown the degree to which the rich have been able to use tax havens to avoid paying taxes, although some of this has long been well known (Shaxson 2011). Inequalities between the rich and the poor, globally, remain high, which is why some 795 million people (one in nine) are chronically malnourished (UNWFP 2015), the difference in average life expectancy between low-income and high-income countries varies between 81.6 years at the top and 51.6 years at the bottom (UNDP 2015), and the richest 10 per cent of the world's adult population account for 85 per cent of all global assets, although it may be that some inequalities between countries have declined (Bourguignon 2015; Therborn 2006). Many of the trends in inequalities can be attributed to neo-liberal policies pursued and imposed by global institutions such as the International Monetary Fund and the World Bank, with their cheerleaders in the USA and the UK (George 2010: 69–160).

There is much merit in Bauman's passionate denunciation of such trends. However, one major problem is that he sees them as more or less inevitable and cannot posit any means of progressive transformation. But there is a second difficulty in Bauman's account of neo-liberalism and its ideological impact, which emerges clearly in *Does the Richness* of 2013. As I have shown in more detail elsewhere (Rattansi 2014), Bauman's argument becomes mired in self-contradictions, claiming that 'everyone' believes in the neo-liberal ideologies of 'trickle down' and 'natural talents' being properly rewarded in exceedingly high remuneration while at the same time citing evidence, from the High Pay Commission of the UK and other sources, that in fact the majority of people actually reject both aspects of neo-liberal ideology. The contradictory argument reveals a lack of rigour that, as I have shown in the discussion of Bauman's contradictory arguments regarding postmodernist sociology, damages Bauman's reputation. This may be evidence of a certain intellectual laziness or perhaps a tendency to write too hastily; in any case, such practices are unacceptable in a globally revered and influential sociologist.

On the question of rising inequalities, there is another element that needs attention. Picketty's research (2014), for example, shows the degree to which wealth continues to be held within families over many generations. In effect, this means that a too hard and fast distinction between solid and liquid phases of modernity (as with the persistence and expansion of McDonaldisation) is simply untenable. Bauman's conceptualisation of this differentiation is loose enough to allow a 'get out of jail' card to be played here, enabling him to escape, but that is precisely the problem: the two phases of modernity are conceptualised with such lack of rigour that all exceptions can be potentially excused on the grounds that these stages of modernity are only ideal types or suggestive metaphors. The continuities in the fate of the poor across generations (see, for example, the revealing BBC documentaries on 'The Secret History of My Family' 2015) and now the declining opportunities for social mobility in 'liquid modernity' (Putnam 2015; Sutton Trust 2006, 2016; Social Mobility and Child Poverty Commission 2014) mean that the real lack of liquidity in liquid modernity is seriously belied by trends of continuing and hardening solidities (Gane 2001b: 274). A key continuous solidity between the supposedly different phases of solid and liquid modernity lies also in the persistent inequalities experienced by ethnic minorities in Europe (Kahanec and Zimmermann 2011) and by African Americans, especially, in the USA (Lee 2011; Rattansi 2007). Underneath the surface currents of fast-flowing 'liquid modernity', the economic and cultural effects of racialised and class inequality show a stubborn solidity and a mud-like stickiness; women's inequalities in pay and conditions also span the solid–liquid divide. These persistent patterns over long periods of the twentieth century and now the twenty-first century only serve to confirm my argument that Bauman's 'liquid' metaphor is too blunt an instrument with which to dissect the complexities of 'flows' in contemporary modernity.

Readers of Bauman's many pronouncements on 'extra-territorial elites' who hold national states to ransom would be forgiven for thinking that these elites in fact constitute some sort of transnational ruling class, although Bauman does not use precisely this formulation, instead referring to 'a cosmopolitan upper class' which 'owns' the 'world economy' (Bauman and Tester 2001: 151). Sklair (2000, 2002) has been perhaps the most serious scholar to posit the existence of, in his case, a 'transnational capitalist class' composed of multinational corporate executives, national and international bureaucrats, politicians, globalising professionals and the mass media, who seem to epitomise Bauman's 'extra-territorial elites'. But Bauman shows no interest in investigating the composition, networks and functioning of his loosely formulated notion of extra-territorial elites. He would have found much nourishment in Sklair's research (see also Rothkopf 2009; Wedel 2009, 2014; Carroll 2010; Hart-Landsberg 2013). However, as Williams and his colleagues have documented (Williams et al. 2013: 69), Sklair (and by implication Bauman) seriously underplays the divisions of corporate and national interests that divide the transnational capitalist class. Again, unsubstantiated over-generalisation in Bauman's work is found wanting when subjected to more rigorous and research-grounded inspection. The issue is of more than academic interest, for Bauman-type formulations both over-simplify and disempower by magnifying the power and unity of dominant elites. This is not to doubt that there are many interconnections between global elites, exemplified by the World Economic Forum meetings at Davos, but to argue that these require careful documentation and analysis of the kind provided by Carroll (2010), Wedel (2009, 2014) and others, and with due attention to often serious internal rifts and conflicts of interest.

In this context it is worth noting that despite the great crash of 2008–09, brought about in large part by the activities of a poorly regulated financial sector in the USA and UK but also globally (Lapavitsas 2013), and indeed in part because of it, the wealth and income going to the elites has continued to grow. But it is becoming ever more concentrated even within the elites, so much so that there is much discussion of the 1 per cent of the population who now own the bulk of the wealth in wealthy countries as well as poor ones, and who earn ever larger chunks of the income that is globally produced by the world's population (see, for example, Dorling 2014; Weeks 2014; Di Muzio 2015).

What needs to be recognised in all the discussion of the withdrawal of the state, which is a strong theme in Bauman's work, is the degree to which it is the state itself that has been involved in facilitating the transformation of economies and cultures that are dominated by neo-liberalism. To take one illustration, the much-vaunted success of many large companies like Apple in introducing new technologies like the iPhone has been heavily dependent on initial investment in research and financing by the state (Mazzucato 2013: 102–10). And in a different vein, as Stiglitz (2012: 28) and Doogan (2009: 33–5) among others have pointed out, although markets are of course involved in the creation of inequality, they can do so only because the state shapes the market in distinctive ways; this is why Stiglitz is able to argue that 'much of the inequality that exists today is a result of government policy, both what the government does and what it does not do. It is governments that decide what is and what is not fair competition, which sectors and companies get public subsidies of various kinds, who pays taxes and what proportion of their income and wealth is taxed, which technologies to support, which infrastructural projects to undertake, and how income is distributed.' The state is centrally involved in what Stiglitz calls 'rent seeking', that is, 'hidden and open transfers and subsidies from the laws that make the marketplace less competitive, lax enforcement of existing competition laws, and statutes that allow corporations to take advantage of others or to pass costs on to the rest of society' (Stiglitz 2012: 39). This may seem like an obvious point to make, but the reason for highlighting it is to challenge the kind of thinking that Bauman indulges in which assumes a radical separation of 'power from politics' tout court, and thus implies the impotence of government and politics. Governments are involved, in a sense, at every step of the way in the creation of the grotesque inequalities that we witness today, and of course governments bailed out the financial sector when its excesses led to the crash beginning in 2008. The state may have withdrawn from some sorts of regulation, but its active regulation is nevertheless crucial in shaping market forces, technology and the nature and extent of employment and unemployment. Even in neo-liberal economies there is of course an interpenetration between state and market, the public and the private sectors, as Gamble (2014: 50) emphasises in his analysis of the 2008 financial crisis – indeed, so much so that governments of the day took the blame for the crisis by being voted out of office, although they had taken action to prevent the financial sector from imploding. And as Gamble had said in an earlier work (2009: 95), 'neo-liberals ... did not reduce very much the scope and scale of the state. They merely redirected its energy and targets. The state remained very intrusive in the lives of its citizens, particularly through the continued programme of reform and reorganization launched in public sectors around the world.' In other words, they did this by way of re-regulation (see also Power 1999). Not surprisingly, Gamble draws the conclusion (2009: 97), echoed by Crouch (2013), that the state *can* reorganise the economy, markets and other spheres in a direction away from neo-liberal theorems and practices. *Bauman's writings encourage pessimism because of their economic determinism with regard to the state and globalisation, but also because he is parsimonious when it comes to alternatives,* an issue discussed in the Conclusion below.

As we have seen, Bauman also consistently argues that the world of liquid modernity is full of 'free-floating' insecurity, anxiety and fear, partly as a result of the hollowing-out of the public sphere, and partly because of increasing job insecurities. These free-floating fears are constantly fed by the mass media with their constant diet of reporting on immigrants and asylum-seekers, the ubiquity of crime and so forth. Bauman provides no evidence for his assertion that as they go about their daily business of living, all people everywhere (in the West) are constantly in a state of fear and anxiety, because evil lurks everywhere and may be hard to spot (*Liquid Fear*: 67–8) and are ever ready to pounce on scapegoats, especially those who can be represented in one way or another as 'strangers'. When he does provide an illustration of this process at work, via the reporting of anger against the presence of a paedophile, it turns out, as I have shown, that this is not a generalised sense of fear, but a specific and gendered one. In *In Search of Politics*, again, Bauman mentions the way in which the Willie Horton case cost Michael Dukakis the American presidency, and again I have had to point out that the Horton issue played on well-established racialised sexual fears among white Americans. One might argue more generally that fears tend to be of this sort, whether about jobs, sexual predators or immigrants, and that these affect specific parts of the population at different times and in different spaces. The fears that arise about crossing the street in a neighbourhood where there is active street-based gang warfare affect only those living in these neighbourhoods, or those who live in particularly violent social housing blocks, and so forth. Thus even in the lives of the working classes or the poor, fears are localised. Women experience fears regarding sexual assault that by and large men do not. The middle and upper classes, for most of the time, do not suffer from the kinds of anxiety that plague those not so well off. There is no evidence of an abstract, general state of anxiety having a hold on an entire citizenry. The fears experienced by 'denizens' are again different (Standing 2011: 93–6) and need to be understood as such, not assimilated to some unnamed general 'liquid fear' that supposedly oozes into every nook and cranny of all (Western) societies. It will be recalled that in his discussion of Hurricane Katrina, which devastated New Orleans, Bauman shows an awareness that it was the poor who suffered most, while the rich either lived in areas higher up or were able to escape by car and air. Risks and fears, are unevenly distributed: a general, totalised and undifferentiated state of liquid fear simply does not exist, even in European capital cities subject to the threat of terrorism by Isis or so-called Islamic State.

An important related issue addressed by Bauman, in *In Search of Politics* especially, is the collapsing trust in political institutions. This needs to be understood as a particular problem that has a variety of causes, many to do with the long-standing and continually growing sclerosis in party politics and liberal representative politics, most recently analysed by Mair (2013) and Tormey (2015), but prefigured in an important contribution by Crouch on what he called 'post-democracy' (*Post-Democracy*, 2004; see also Marquand 2004; Hay 2007; Wolin 2010; Marquand 2015). One symptom of this democratic deficit is the mismatch between the rise in 'life-politics' on the one hand and conventional representative democracy on the other, which has given rise to the 'New Social Movements'. As will be recalled from the discussion of postmodernity, Bauman does not have much sympathy for the new social movements, although they have attracted large numbers of feminists, greens, anti-racists, those against the arms trade, human rights activists, those struggling in the sphere of animal welfare and rights and many more. Conventional political forms have been unable to respond in adequate fashion to the issues that have arisen in this new 'life-politics', and this, together with a variety of other factors including the professionalisation of politics, corruption scandals and the influence of 'big money' in elections, has led to decreasing trust in liberal democracies.

However, Bauman has tended to reduce this whole question to one of globalisation and its baleful effects in making governments impotent. The separation of power and politics as a result of globalisation is the only analysis that Bauman provides (see, for example, *In Search of Politics*: 97–9, 120–1). Globalisation and the diminished powers of states in the face of global markets, financialisation and transnational corporations are no doubt part of the reason for diminishing levels of trust in conventional party and parliamentary politics, but the analysis must address issues that have arisen in the political sphere at the level of politics too, rather than being reduced to the economic forces of globalisation, as Crouch, Wolin, Mair, Tormey, referenced earlier, and also Gamble (2000) have emphasised.

The growth of far-right movements all over Europe, the 'Tea Party' and Donald Trump phenomena in the USA and the Jeremy Corbyn, Syriza and Pedemos phenomena also need a multi-causal treatment as part of the transformations and unmet demands that have undermined trust in conventional liberal politics (Skocpol and Williamson 2016; Ford and Goodwin 2014; Wodak 2013; Pai 2016).

Bauman extends his mantra of the separation of power from politics to a global level, so much so that in his world-view all states on the planet have now been left impotent in the face of globalisation: thus his conclusion that, as he puts it, 'On a negatively globalized planet, all the most fundamental problems ... are *global*, and being global they admit of no *local* solutions' (*Liquid Fear*: 128, emphasis in original). 'The reunion of power and politics will have to be achieved, if at all, at the planetary level' (*Liquid Fear*: 128). But as the authors of *Globalization and Work* argue (Williams et al. 2013: 14), *local factors are important as constituent elements of the global*. Workers, managers, trade unions and a variety of community activists all play a part in responding to globalisation, and the manner in which they act influences 'the nature of globalization and how it functions'.

If Bauman's broad generalisations about rising anxiety and precariousness are instead made in more sociologically specific ways as operating in particular spheres of social and economic life and affecting particular segments of the population in specific ways, they can be made to hold more water, to deploy his 'liquid' metaphor. Work is one such sphere where precariousness can be documented and analysed, with 'globalisation' being one important causal factor – technological change and state policies are others – although globalisation itself has to be understood in a complex manner rather than simply as an unstoppable juggernaut that denudes the process of human agency.

Changes in the nature of work, and attendant consequences for greater insecurity at work, had already been emphasised by Beck (1992; see also Beck 2000a), especially, but also by Bourdieu, from whom Bauman had borrowed the French term *précarité*, and by Castells (1996), and their influence on Bauman is evident in in his post-2000 liquid modern phase. Beck and Castells have been criticised by many for their indiscriminate generalisations (Edgell: 2006: 119–21). Moreover, as Doogan (2009: 204–5) notes in relation to Bourdieu's use of *précarité* – and this is replicated in Bauman's borrowing of the concept – the analysis exhibits a tendency to assume that all the changes in work patterns and globalisation had already been accomplished, thus leaving little room for opposition, when in fact this was a process in train, and subject to unevenness as well as hiccups; to accept this as a *fait accompli* is self-fulfilling, for this is part of the *ideology* of neo-liberalism, that there is no alternative, when in fact different possibilities were and are still available. I have made the same argument in relation to Bauman's well-worn pronouncements on the separation of power and politics – also to be found in Bourdieu – which are now conjoined by both Bauman and Bourdieu to theses on the precariousness of work.

Although many caveats need to be borne in mind, there is some general agreement among researchers that the post-Fordist phase of capitalism – Bauman's liquid modernity, at least in part – has led to global changes in the 'de-standardisation' of work. As semi-skilled jobs have shrunk in number, the labour force globally has seen a growing polarisation between better-paid, secure work and ever larger numbers of unskilled, part-time and temporary jobs in which workers have no workplace rights to holiday pay and sickness leave, suffer poorer work conditions and so forth (Williams et al. 2013). But note that women and ethnic minorities suffer disproportionately high degrees of precariousness at work, a social phenomenon characteristically ignored by Bauman.

Now, even middle managers have had to accept more insecurity and poorer conditions (Ehrenreich 2006; Alvesson and Willmott 2013: 110, 115). Standing's *The Precariat* (2011) has to date perhaps been the most widely discussed contribution to the thesis of growing insecurity and degradation in working conditions, especially for those at the lowest end of the class structure globally. For the UK it has been estimated that some 15 per cent of the population falls into this category (Savage 2015: 171). Standing, it has been suggested, over-states the role of globalisation, transnational corporations and outsourcing to the Global South in producing these conditions, for successive governments have played an important role in eroding security and other conditions in the workplace (Williams et al. 2013: 13; see also Doogan 2009; but see Standing 2011: 32).

There is considerable debate over Boltanski and Chiapello's thesis of the development of more horizontal styles of work organisation (Boltanski and Chiapello 2007; see du Gay and Morgan 2013; Doogan 2009: 30–3), which Bauman borrows, and it is particularly noteworthy that even among those researchers explicitly influenced by Bauman's idea of liquid modernity and writing in *Liquid Organization: Zygmunt Bauman and Organization Theory* (Kociatkiewicz and Kostera 2014), there is some scepticism as to the extent to which organisational change along the lines posited by Boltanksi and Chiapello and by Bauman has actually taken place. There may be some 'liquid organisations' in the business world, but many tend to be in high-tech sectors; there is not necessarily a general trend for businesses to be organised along more horizontal lines, for organisations have both 'liquid modern' and 'solid modern' characteristics, again demonstrating the necessity of detailed empirical research. Foucault, moreover, is as useful if not more so in understanding how contemporary organisations encourage and enable technologies of the self, such as 'emotional intelligence', among managers (see the contribution by Clegg and Baumeler in Kociatkiewicz and Kostera 2014).

Again, research suggests that Bauman's general thesis of precariousness and anxiety for the whole citizenry is over-stated. Nevertheless, there are important truths in Bauman's various diagnoses of the malaise of 'liquid modernity', which other sociologists and political economists refer to as variants of post-Fordist capitalism: a range of groups in the occupational structure of the Global North are finding that job-security as well as other conditions of work are deteriorating, and the neo-liberal state has, by its actions, further eroded feelings of security not only in the workplace but by retrenchment in welfare. Outsourcing of production to countries in the Global South, where wages are lower, has contributed to de-industrialisation, job-insecurity and poorer work conditions in the Global North. However, even here, the picture is more complex than the one painted by Bauman: the Scandinavian countries, especially, have still managed to retain greater state-sponsored affluence and security for larger sectors of their populations than in the rest of Western Europe, even in the face of ever more intensive globalisation. Bauman's pessimism when confronting globalisation is both exaggerated and disempowering.

Bauman's theses on individualisation have also been found wanting by sociological researchers. It will be recalled that for Bauman globalisation and individualisation are the two defining parameters of liquid modernity, and I have provided an exposition of Bauman's analysis of individualisation earlier in Part III, in the section describing Bauman's general conception of liquid modernity. The problems with Bauman's understanding of individualisation are manifold. First, there is no rigorous definition of the phenomenon except as one of 'disembedding'. Second, as usual, the extent of the phenomenon remains unclear, but is generally exaggerated to the whole population and is posited as having taken extreme and irresistible forms. As Bauman puts it (*The Individualized Society*: 46–7), 'Let there be no mistake: now, as before, individualization is a fate, not a choice: in the land of individual freedom of choice the option to escape individualisation and to refuse to participate in the individualizing game is emphatically *not* on the agenda' (emphasis in original). Third, the absence of re-embedding once individuals have been atomised by market forces, precariousness and the withdrawal of welfare safety nets is attributed to the fact that class, family and community have now become 'zombie' categories – a notion borrowed from Beck – such that they are now effectively dead, but live on in ghostly form. But this sort of individualisation thesis, common to Bauman and Beck, has been challenged in a wide range of research. Jamieson (1998:65, 78–79 and passim), Atkinson (2007, 2008, 2010), Savage (2000), Savage and Butler (2013), Savage, Bagnall and Longhurst (2004), Brannen and Nilsen (2005), Smart (2007: 20–1, 63–79), Beer and Koster (2009) Chambers (2012: 39–41) and the researchers from an Economic and Social Research project into identities in the twenty-first century brought together in Wetherell (2009), among many others, have shown that class, family and various forms of communal ties and belonging retain a much greater degree of salience in people's objective and subjective lives than Bauman and Beck seem to realise (see also Gane 2001b: 274). Atkinson's critique of Bauman echoes mine. He says of Bauman that his analysis of individualisation is '*incredibly simplistic and detached from the intricacies of everyday life*' and that his is '*an intellectual edifice constructed out of acutely unsound materials*' (Atkinson 2008: 10, 14, my emphasis). Smart (2007: 20) is also critical of the lack of research evidence in what she calls Bauman's 'apocalyptic' view of the disintegration of relationships in contemporary societies. Skeggs (2004: 54) and Savage (2000: 108) have simply concluded that Bauman and Beck appear unwittingly to be generalising from their own middle-class experiences to the whole society.

As with globalisation, so with individualisation: although containing some useful broad insights, on closer inspection Bauman's descriptions and diagnoses are shown by research to be overdrawn and need to be understood as relevant only in more limited and nuanced terms.

To return to globalisation, one notable feature of Bauman's voluminous output on globalisation is the absence of any serious consideration of the relations between globalisation and culture. Some aspects of this issue, as I now go on to suggest, are intertwined with Bauman's Eurocentrism. Bauman's limitations with regard to individualisation, as we shall see, are also relevant to his Eurocentrism.

Bauman and Eurocentrism, again

'*We* are all individuals now; not by choice, though, but by necessity … self-identification, self-management and self-assertion, and above all self-sufficiency in the performance of all these three tasks, are *our* duty whether or not *we* possess the resources which the performance of the new duty demands' (*The Individualized Society*: 105, my emphasis). 'Individualization is here to stay; *all* who think about the means to deal with its impact on the fashion in which *we* conduct our lives must start from acknowledging this fact' (*The Individualized Society*: 10, my emphasis). 'From cradle to coffin *we* are trained and drilled to treat shops as pharmacies filled with drugs to cure or at least mitigate *all* the illnesses and afflictions of *our* lives ... Fullness of consumer enjoyment means fullness of life. *I* shop therefore *I* am. To shop or not to shop is no longer the question' (*Does the Richness*: 60, my emphasis). '*We* have been trained and drilled to believe that ... Abilities ... are unequally distributed by their nature', a belief that prompts 'us' to 'reconcile *ourselves* to the eerie, uncannily swelling inequality ... by alleviating the pain of surrender and resignation to failure, while stretching the odds against dissent' (*Does the Richness*: 70–1, emphasis in original).

These are typical pronouncements from Bauman, especially in his liquid modern phase. They dovetail with another recursive rhetorical move, one in which large agglomerations such as 'modernity', 'modern society' and the modern or postmodern 'mind' are anthropomorphised to give them agency and strip it from individuals and smaller collectivities, a trait on which I have commented before.

At least three questions immediately arise from a moment's reflection on such judgements by Bauman. What is the identity of the 'we' and 'I', and who is excluded in these pronouncements? Who is included in the readership of these portentous statements? Given that Bauman appears to have a very wide readership, a fact that he was well aware of, in a wide range of countries at various stages of development, are his books meant to resonate with all who read them, whether in Kathmandu or London, Kigale or New York and Berlin? Finally, whose 'modernity' is being included? In the context of the passages on individualisation, Bauman cites Richard Sennet's *The Fall of Public Man* (sic), Bourdieu's remarks on *précarité* and the American television sitcom *Ally McBeal* (*The Individualized Society*: 6, 11).

There is a strong prima facie case for concluding that Bauman is addressing primarily a Western European and American audience, and that for all his talk of 'all of us', he is in fact addressing and including only a small portion of the globe's population. Not to put too fine a point on it, he is only conversing, and seems interested only in the problems facing those like him – women too are absent – who live in the affluent West. In that case, Bauman is guilty of 'Eurocentrism', 'Euro-Americanism' or 'West-centrism', depending on which of his statements are spotlighted. And as I have demonstrated in greater detail in his analyses of consumerism, his gaze is obdurately male in addition to privileging the already privileged and affluent West or Global North.

By and large, the Global South and even the southern and eastern countries of Europe – Italy, Spain, Greece, Bulgaria, Romania and his native Poland – make only rare appearances and play bit parts in Bauman's narratives. His all-too-few concrete illustrations of his arguments are usually plucked unsystematically from British, French and American newspapers and authors and television shows and films, as evidenced above. Sometimes Scandinavian countries make an appearance, but in anecdotal and unscholarly references. Latin American countries were referred to, together with the Nordic north, in *Consuming Life* (2007) in the context of some hopeful developments in stemming the tide of neo-liberalism (*Consuming Life*: 142–3), hopes that soon dissipated. India and China get a brief mention in an interview with Galecki (Galecki 2005), where Bauman expresses ecological dismay at thought of every Indian and Chinese family owning a car; and inevitably the Middle East enters the discourse only in the context of a discussion of 'our' insecurity in the face of threats from Islamic terrorists (*Liquid Fear*: 101–11)), although Sikh terrorists in India enter the narrative in the same context (*Liquid Fear*: 111).

This is by no means an exhaustive account of all the times that countries outside the gilded West or North make an appearance in Bauman's writings and impinge on his imagination; I am merely documenting that, as others have also noted (Jay 2010: 100), Bauman's world seems to be suffocatingly small, habitually excluding the vast majority of the globe's population.

But pinning the charge of Eurocentrism, Euro-Americanism or West-centrism on Bauman, while superficially an easy manoeuvre, could flounder on the difficulty of giving precise definitions to these terms. The discussion kick-started by Said's *Orientalism* tended to conflate Eurocentrism with racism and imperialism

(Hobson 2012: 3), and I think it can safely be said that Bauman was no racist or imperialist, however widely those labels might be stretched. For Blaut (2000: 4), Eurocentrism, although encompassing a wide range of standpoints, unites under its umbrella 'false claims by Europeans that their society or region is, or was in the past, or always has been and always will be, superior to other societies or regions'. Bauman escapes this charge partly by default, because he engages in so little comparative historical and sociological work, and partly because it is hard to find such a strong judgement of Western superiority in his historical and other analyses. Wallerstein (1997) in his intervention in the debate has provided five criteria for judging a discourse as Eurocentric, including the assumption that the West's lead in developing industrial capitalism can be defined, with hindsight, as a welcome outcome because capitalist modernity has been by and large a good thing for the world. The difficulty that Wallerstein's listing exercise encounters is that it does not make clear how many of the five criteria have to be present to condemn a discourse as Eurocentric (McLennan 2006: 67). And in relation to Bauman, his anti-capitalism is almost axiomatic, making it difficult to lumber him with the Eurocentric tag.

Drawing instead on Connell (2007) and Bhambra (2007, 2014), it is my view that it is more plausible to argue that there are several defining features of Eurocentrism in sociology. The first is that the world is basically viewed through the optic of the West. This carries the implications that 'modernity' is defined as essentially Western: the modernity or otherwise of the Rest is judged according to the institutional and cultural configuration of Western institutions, and these usually do include, though not necessarily explicitly, liberal forms of parliamentary democracy and the observance of human rights as defined in the West as a good thing. On this criterion Bauman can be seen to be Eurocentric in the sense that in all his writings on modernity, postmodernity and liquid modernity he seems never to imagine that modernity is anything but Western; the idea that there might be other forms of modernity is simply not entertained (Lee 2005). Modernity is Western modernity *tout court*. He seems unaware of the debates about 'multiple' (Eisenstadt 2002) and 'alternative' (Gaonkar 2001) modernities – whatever their limitations (Sachsenmaier, Riedel and Eisenstadt 2002; Bhambra 2014: 33–7) – that have been raging within sociology. Moreover, he asserts, astonishingly (Bauman and Tester 2001: 31), that Europe's uniqueness lies in its unity in the face of 'cultural pluralism' and its ability to 'communicate across cultural (or any other divides)': among the many counter-examples that can be cited, I need only mention postcolonial India for Bauman's Eurocentrism to be laid bare. Outhwaite (2010: 10) suggests that Bauman himself would want to argue that 'what do they know of Europe, who only Europe know?' The evidence suggests, instead, that Bauman would be most unlikely to say any such thing, given his lack of curiosity, knowledge and understanding regarding non-European cultures.

But he is critical of human rights discourses and he is sceptical about the virtues of Western-style liberal democracy in so far as he thinks that some or other form of socialism would be preferable, and so on these secondary counts Bauman cannot be regarded as Eurocentric. Nevertheless, on the wider issue of the geo-economic-cultural location of modernity it is hard to see how Bauman can be absolved of the charge of Eurocentrism.

Closely related to the above, it is my view that the term 'Eurocentrist' should be applied to those who tend to see the world primarily from *inside* Western modernity: little or no attempt is made to see the West from the eyes of non-Westerners, especially by reading non-Western, non-European authors or examining the contents of non-Western cultural products such as films, novels or indeed scholarly works in history, sociology and anthropology. For all Bauman's interest in literature, cinema and television, the single reference to non-Western novels or visual products in his works is to the fiction of Borges, and there are none to academic works written by non-Westerners – the omission of Edward Said, as I have had occasion to point out, being an egregious example. Bauman, like Bourdieu, Beck and Giddens (Connell 2007; Bhambra 2014), looks out at the world through a distinctly European and sometimes Euro-American lens.

Further, and this follows closely from the first two points above, it is my argument that we should regard as Eurocentric authors who tend to generalise Western modernity's characteristics out-wards when they analyse non-Western societies. Connell specifi-cally targets Bauman's *Globalization* (1998a) as a prominent and obvious instance of this sort of generalisation from the West to the Rest (Connell 2007: 54–5): 'In this text, Bauman describes an increase in social diversity, growing difficulty in forming social norms, the impossibility of rational planning, the predominance of consumption over production, and the transformation of politics into spectacle and media manipulation.' But, as Connell remarks, what is this if not a generalisation to the whole globe of the condition of postmodernity (and *ipso facto*, liquid modernity)? She argues that many other authors, including the radicals Hardt and Negri (2000) and Beck in his various works on globalisation in which 'risk society' becomes 'world risk society' (see also the penetrating critiques of Beck's 'cosmopolitanism', Wallerstein's 'world systems theory' and Mann's historical sociology in Bhambra 2014: 43–50, 63–79), also indulge in this form of Eurocentrism in which there is a reification of trends to the global level from analyses that are not genuinely about non-Western societies, but are an extension of concepts that have previously been worked out in the understanding of metropolitan societies and are then unreflexively deployed as a grid with which to understand the Rest (Connell 2007: 51–5).

It is especially relevant to point out in this context that both Brooks (2011) and Belliappa (2013), on the basis of research in Asian societies, have provided compelling evidence that the thesis of 'individualization' as formulated in recent Western sociology has only limited purchase when transplanted and deployed in understanding these non-Western societies.

Another feature of Eurocentrist discourse is the blind-spot it exhibits in relation to how the West became the dominant region of the globe. Given that China, India and Western Europe, but especially China and Europe, were at similar levels of economic development up to at least the fifteenth century, what enabled the rise of the West to pre-eminence? The deficiency of Eurocentric narratives of this form of uneven development can be simply and bluntly stated: Eurocentric authors tend to ignore or grossly underplay the role of the expansion of European imperialism and the establishment of overseas colonies, which gave the West access to vast amounts of gold, silver and other primary commodities while also providing a captive market for its manufactured commodities (Blaut 2000; Goody 2006, 2012; Connell 2007). The specialness or uniqueness of the West in explaining what is often called 'the European miracle' is seen to reside in features solely or almost solely internal to the West. The rise of the West is seen as an endogenous affair, and is attributed to either its geology and environment, the particularly independent character of its cities, or the early development of civil political arenas that could balance central state power, and so forth. But these accounts are unconvincing, as Blaut (2000), Connell (2007), Goody (2012, Bhambra (2007), Pomeranz (2000) and many others have now demonstrated. However, by the same token, Eurocentric authors misconstrue the nature of globalisation, for the violence to indigenous non-Western peoples and their societies that has been involved in Western dominance, and the continuing inequalities that have marked contemporary globalisation are also ignored or underplayed or poorly understood. As Connell argues, this results in an anodyne view of the process of globalisation in which authors such as Bauman and Beck 'certainly *recognise* differences between the global rich and the global poor, but [their] concept of globalization gave them no coherent way of *explaining* these differences (Connell 2007: 60, emphasis in original). Arguably, the literature on globalisation is unnecessarily coy about using the term *imperialism* to describe the origins and continuing patterns of global inequality (Tully 2008). Connell also indicts sociologists of globalisation for an 'under-determination by evidence', for authors such as Bauman and Beck operate more by 'emblematic instances' and 'panoramic gestures' (Connell 2007: 61) than by considered scholarship on the origins and complexities of processes of globalisation. The lack of attention to the imperial and colonial origins of Western dominance means that the contemporary dominance of the West, especially as against its former colonies, simply goes unexplained (Slater 2004; Gregory 2004; Tully 2008). Little attention, too, is paid to the constant and consistent manner in which the West, especially the USA and its close allies, has deliberately and with considerable violence thwarted progressive movements and governments throughout the world (for recent analyses, see Blum 2014; Kennard 2016). This enables the identification of another trait of Eurocentrism: the overwhelming sense that globalisation is something that happens to the Rest, rather than the latter having any agency with regard to the processes involved. Inevitably, this underplays acts and movements of resistance in the Global South, but also in the Global North. Bauman's dismissive view of the new social movements and the

Occupy and anti-globalisation movements of the North, as well as the Arab Spring and labour movements in the Global South which, as I have shown, have actively shaped and resisted neo-liberal globalisation and its associated authoritarianisms is indicative of a perception of globalisation which minimises the agency of the underdogs of the West and those of the Rest. Unsurprisingly, Bauman is more comfortable writing about refugees fleeing the Global South, as he does in *Wasted Lives* and *Strangers at our Door* (2016) than about those who stay, resist and fight the depredations of neo-liberal globalisations.

On several grounds, then, Bauman, although he is of course not alone in this among Western sociologists (see Connell 2007; Rodriguez, Boatcă, and Costa 2010; Bailey 2013; Bhambra 2014), remains trapped in a narrow Eurocentrism which considerably diminishes his capacity for understanding and explaining the contemporary world. In relying exclusively on what Connell calls the 'metropole' for his 'intellectual tools and assumptions' he ends up treating 'the majority world as object'. Any chance of sociology working as a 'shared learning process' and dialogue is prevented from being on the agenda (Connell 2007: 68). Authors such as Bauman and Beck show what Connell calls an 'erasure' of non-metropolitan experience. Thus there is a powerful sense in which, in Bauman's thinking and voluminous writings, there is an unwitting collusion with imperial power that seriously undermines claims that his is a view from below, championing the global underdogs. That is his intention, but his Eurocentrism prevents him from being an effective champion. It has also prevented him from exploring long-standing debates about contemporary forms of cultural imperialism (see, for example, Tomlinson 1999; Sparks 2007; Pieterse 2009) despite his avowed interest in matters cultural. Moreover, his 'male gaze', as I have shown in considerable detail throughout this book, further limits the vision of the world that emerges from his pen.

It may be that some of his later works are written in a manner that makes them suitable for reading on a bus or train, as Beilharz (2016) has recently suggested, but this cannot be a legitimate excuse for the exceptional Euro-American selectivity of the entire corpus of his work, for it helps neither the hapless male or female reader on the train in London or New York nor the seeker after insights on a bus in Nairobi, Rio and Mumbai who turns to one of the world's most celebrated sociologists for a reliable and knowledgeable guide to today's seemingly bewildering and very unequal world.

The texts of authors such as Bauman (and Beck), Connell (2007: 62) warns, 'put a metaphorical arm round the reader's shoulder and speak confidentially about the problems "we" now face', but by doing so what they are in actuality effecting is a 'performative unity' between metropolitan author and metropolitan reader 'which accounts for much of the declamatory style in globalization texts. It implies a shared knowledge that can simply be recalled by panoramic gestures and emblematic instances. There is little need for laborious examination of evidence when the reader already has the news.' There is little doubt that this is how the ubiquitous 'we' in Bauman's writings functions. One of his last books is entitled *Strangers at our Door* (2016). The message in this bottle is obviously addressed to the metropolitan, Western 'us', not the 'stranger' refugees and asylum speakers of whom Bauman speaks. It is *about* them, not *for* them: they are the *objects*, we (Westerners, in this case primarily Europeans) are the *subjects*.

Conclusion: a sociologist of hope or a prophet of gloom?

To rehearse my critique of Bauman in this Conclusion would be too tedious and is unnecessary. I have already set out my arguments in some detail, and the main themes of the book have also been signalled in my Introduction. But although I have primarily focused on the flaws in Bauman's thinking, he would hardly have found such a broad and enthusiastic readership if, in some ways, he had not connected with troubling issues in readers' lives. His Eurocentrism, though, means, arguably, that he speaks more to those in the Global North than to those in the Global South, and his white, male gaze sets limits to the questions about publicly produced but privately felt troubles that his sociology illuminates. His focus on the *production* of suffering rather than the *experience* of suffering, as Outhwaite (2010: 7) has put it, has meant that it is difficult for his work to evoke empathy in his readers with the underdogs of the world, however much he thinks the care for the Other should be at the heart of moral life.

In this Conclusion I will focus primarily on one final issue that I have not yet dealt with, except by implication: was Bauman an optimist or a pessimist? Is his a sociology of hope or a discourse of disillusionment and a prognosis of doom? In an earlier piece (Rattansi 2014) I sensed that Bauman had succumbed to an Adorno-esque pessimism that had been the fate of the tradition of Critical Theory, to which, despite his eclecticism, he seemed to belong. In this book I have quoted many passages from Bauman's last writings and interviews which paint an unmistakably dystopian picture of contemporary times.

Nevertheless, some of the most valuable parts of his thinking focus on the social conditions and contemporary social changes, especially consumerism and individualisation – however much he exaggerated both tendencies – that undermine serious moral engagement (a process of moral blindness and ethical numbness that he of course refers to as 'adiaphorization') with the pressing issues of inequality, powerlessness, inhumane social engineering, genocide and what he calls modernity's outcasts. It is entirely in keeping with his burning moral outrage and his awe-inspiring energy that in 2016, at the age of ninety-one, he managed to write a powerful indictment of the West's feeble and vacillating response to the so-called 'migrant crisis' which has erupted as a result, partly, of the West's own arrogant and disastrous meddling, in the guise of 'humanitarianism' but also for vengeance for 9/11, in the Arab world: his *Strangers at our Door* contains a searing indictment of this meddling and its aftermath and is as powerful a work as he ever wrote. And he still worried about what he had earlier called 'compassion fatigue' and in *Strangers at our Door* refers to as 'refugee tragedy fatigue'; he writes with great moral outrage at the dangers that this may dull our senses to the tragedy unfolding at Europe's borders: the tragedy of 'drowned children', 'overcrowded concentration camps', 'barbed wire fences', 'governments vying with each other to add the insult of treating the migrants as hot potatoes to the injuries of exile' and 'narrow escape and the nerve-wracking perils of the voyage to safety'. The danger, Bauman sensed, is that these will turn into the 'dull routine of normality' and pass into a collective amnesia that fails to remember the Afghan refugees wanting asylum in Australia and 'hurling themselves against the barbed-wire fences of Woomera or confined to the large detention camps built by the Australian government on Nauru and Christmas Island' (*Strangers at our Door*: 2).

It is hard to think of any contemporary sociologist who would express his or her moral and heartfelt outrage in these terms. Although most sociologists have long since abandoned the notion that their work is 'value-free', few practise a form of sociology that continually fuses sociological analysis with ethics. The greatest strength of Bauman's work has undoubtedly been that it has always carried an ethical charge; it is no wonder that he was delighted when Tester said in an interview with him (Bauman and Tester 2001: 47) that his work was 'dripping with ethical commitment'. 'I am so pleased', Bauman responded.

Of course, many sociologists would regard the constant intrusion of ethical demand into sociological analysis as unhelpful in creating the forms of objectivity that can create public credibility in the eyes of those who have the power to bring about change as professionals and as office holders in the state; but it is precisely this power that Bauman was suspicious of, for he himself had been the victim, and he had seen too many victims, of top-down social engineering; as he warned, the 'trap' against which there should always be vigilance is 'that of promoting oppression in the guise of emancipation' (*Postmodernity and its Discontents*, 1997: 208).

While the totalitarianism that Bauman had experienced and suffered from – Nazism and Soviet-style Communism – do not now exist, Bauman was always on the look-out for new dangers to personal and collective freedoms. In his consistent and persistent questioning of social and political developments that undermine freedom, dignity and injustice Bauman remains an unparalleled figure in modern sociology. He is a worthy disciple of the Critical Theory tradition. That he even bothered to think about justice in general terms set him apart from contemporary sociologists, although his answer to the question of what was a just society is a masterclass in obfuscation: A 'just society is a society which thinks it is not just enough, which questions the sufficiency of any achieved level of justice' (Bauman and Tester 2001: 63).

Bauman's views constantly vacillated between optimism and pessimism. Despite the pessimism of so much of his work (Rattansi 2014), Bauman remained hopeful. As long as sociologists keep 'sounding the alarm' (Bauman, Jacobsen and Tester 2013: 108–9), sociology's critical message will always find an audience and a better world will always be a possibility, a 'chance' as he often put it (see, for example, *The Individualized Society*: 95).

But sociology has a real fight on its hands, for the 'world as we know it', Bauman argues, is

> a caddish/boorish world ... If Victorians crammed piano legs into stockings, we put pianos on legs previously to be savoured only on the pages of pornographic magazines. We use daily, publicly and ostentatiously, a kind of language once confined to the gutters and dens of vice. We no longer respect rights to privacy and intimacy. Maybe the Englishman's home is still his castle, but a castle open 24/7 to visitors, and inhabited by people fearing the absence or dearth of snooping onlookers, as the most awesome of Egyptian plagues. We revel at the sight of the also-run apprentices having been shown the door, and of residents of Big Brother's house voted out after a week-long string of routine humiliations and ridicule.

We respect neither dignity of others nor our own. When we hear the word 'honour', we reach for a dictionary (that is, in case we swot for 'Who wants to be a millionaire' or the 'Weakest link' quiz). And gratuitous ... mud-slinging has reached unprecedented heights of facility – courtesy of protection offered by the anonymity of internet calumny, slander and libel. It is as if the 'right to slander' has become the one human right most likely to be universally respected and tooth-and-nail defended by law-guarding agencies ... Respect and ... trust are the two attributes of what used to be called 'civilized society' that are conspicuously missing from human interactions ... In fact, stripping individuals of respect and the grounds of trust in each other is in my view the paramount ... stratagem in casting the 'core concerns of society' ... off limits of society's attention, care, action – and, indeed, concern. (Bauman, Jacobsen and Tester 2013: 111)

It is hard to think of a better example of Bauman's later dystopian vision, his totalising and dismissive critique of contemporary social trends, his contempt for popular culture (especially television and the internet), which was worthy of a contemporary Adorno (Rattansi 2014) yet contained within it a moral outrage and an ethical demand that things should and can be different (see also Bauman and Donskis 2013: 27–8, 54–8).

Pessimism, the mass media, popular culture and the search for the democratic agora

Bauman's frequent outbursts against the 'infotainment' that 'news' programmes on television and in tabloid newspapers have now become, the banality and confessional mode of talk shows and the evils of the internet, to take just three examples to illustrate his ire against the mass media and popular culture, demand discussion, although not in any detail, for that is a task that would occupy more space than is available in this book. However, I want to draw attention to several key points. Note, first, that Bauman implored sociologists to watch television, and indeed he regarded it as 'one of the sociologist's prime duties'. *Why?* Because, he answered, this is how most ordinary people spend 'a good chunk of their lives and acquire a good chunk of their knowledge of the world' (Bauman, Jacobsen and Tester 2013: 134). But *how* should the sociologist view television, with what sociological antennae and what critical faculties? Bauman assumed an unmediated relationship both between the sociologist and the mass media and between 'most people' and the media. But nobody *simply* 'watches' television: the audience is an *active* part of a *communicative process* that has been exhaustively studied by sociologists, social psychologists and cultural anthropologists, in research that has revealed a complex web through which meanings are constructed and negotiated by members of the audience and the texts of mass media, whether written in newspapers and magazines or presented as 'shows' on television. There are no simple 'effects' of the media on passive consumers (Bird 2003; Street 2011: 101–30), although this is how the audiences are presumed as consumers in Bauman's tirades against the mass media, in keeping with the Frankfurt School's early critique of mass culture. In one of his last works, published in 2016, he went so far as to refer to broadcasting and advertising as forms of 'brainwashing', the 'filling of brains' by 'soft power', but a 'curse' which 'we' accept as a 'blessing in disguise' (Bauman and Donskis 2016: 37–8). Bauman assumed without any evidence that the viewers of CNN have been 'trained' by that broadcaster to 'watch without understanding and listen without comprehension' (Bauman and Donskis 2016: 40). In another set of email exchanges, with Ezio Mauro, published as *Babel* (Bauman and Mauro 2016: 67–8), Bauman cited approvingly Neil Postman's 1985 critique of the mass media and popular culture, *Amusing Ourselves to Death*, agreeing with him that the whole population has now become 'distracted by trivia' and that 'serious public conversation' has become 'a form of baby-talk'. But research on talk shows (Wood 2009), to take one of Bauman's main targets in media and popular culture, shows that contrary to what Bauman believed, women, who are the main viewers of talk shows, are an active and critical audience, self-reflexively 'talking back' at the content of the shows, although it has to be noted that there are a variety of talk-show formats, with different types of content and effects (Gill 2006: 150–79). Mark Davis is sharply critical (2008: 96–100) of Bauman's much-repeated critical responses to popular British television shows such as *Big Brother* and *The Weakest Link*. Bauman regurgitated his critical remarks on these shows in the 2016 *Babel* (Bauman and Mauro 2016: 138), which seems

to suggest that he had not read the critique of his views penned
by Davis, the founder and Director of the Bauman Institute. To
Bauman, these television shows epitomised liquid modernity, for
they underscored notions of *personal* success which rely on a ruthless *exclusion* of losers. For Davis (2008: 98–9), the shows also
emphasise inclusion, the 'reaffirmation of normative social bonds',
and encourage a discussion of the social and moral dilemmas and
anxieties of living in a liquid modern society.

Second, Bauman, as always, failed to provide defamiliarising
materials and techniques which would help his readers to adopt a
more critical stance towards the mass media. One strategy could
have been to *familiarise* his readership – that is, make them aware
– of how much of the media content is advertiser-driven, in television, magazines and newspapers, or how the programming and
editorial lines are influenced by the corporate conglomerates that
own not just large sections of the mass media, but also a variety
of other types of businesses, and how much editorial and other
content is influenced by the political and cultural proclivities and
economic interests of 'media moguls' such as Rupert Murdoch
and Silvio Berlusconi (Meehan 2005; Street 2011: 159–208).
Bauman made no attempt to become aware of these issues himself,
and therefore failed to act as a proper critical sociologist should
by providing a deeper understanding of how media content is
produced. This of course is a familiar failing in Bauman's thinking and writing on consumerism: that is, the absence of analyses
of the production and retailing of the commodities at the heart of
consumerism, including, not surprisingly, the consumption of the
products of the mass media.

Third, Bauman, despite his avowed interest in 'culture', characteristically failed to treat the products of the mass media as *cultural*
and therefore meaning-producing products which are *framed* and
encoded in particular ways; this is particularly important in understanding how 'news' programming works, as can be seen in the
discussion of research in Street (2011: 21–76). Even news and current affairs programming – Bauman's 'infotainment' – follows the
conventions of genre (news can be seen to work via constructing
plots, creating (melo)dramas and so forth). Because Bauman failed
to deconstruct the ways in which the content of television, magazines and newspapers is socially constructed, coded and made to

fit into particular genres, while at the same time being constrained by the need to attract advertising and make profits, he did his readers a disservice; he was being a poor sociologist, simply railing at trends in the media without lifting the veil and peering underneath to make himself and his readers aware of how the media actually work and to what effect, and of how they function in very complex ways in the culture of 'liquid modernity' (see, for example, Edwards and Cromwell 2005).

Finally, it is important to point out that while the internet has its 'dark side', which was primarily what Bauman focused on, its mushrooming growth, involving also the exponential growth of citizen-led 'monitoring' and activist websites, has greatly widened the opportunities for exposing official corruption and conspiracy (see, especially, Keane 2013 and Castells 2012). It is not at all surprising that the explosive myth-busting 'Wikileaks' (Assange 2015), to take just one instance, gets hardly any mention in Bauman's *email* exchanges on the subject of the internet, while the critical role of the new social media in popular citizen protests and events like the Arab Spring and Occupy (Castells 2012) is downplayed. For all his reliance on articles in *Wikipedia*, Bauman failed to note the extraordinary cyber-invention of democratic content that it signifies.

The internet is a contradictory phenomenon and only in its infancy. But in keeping with his pessimism Bauman could see mainly its dark side (for which see, for example, Carr 2010; Morozov 2011; Keen 2015; Turkle 2011, 2015), not its positive potential for an expansion of what Keane (2013: 77–108) has called 'monitory democracy' and Castells (2012) has dubbed 'networks of outrage and hope'. The point is also that Bauman's constant search for the agora and the pessimism provoked by not finding that democratic public space for debate in the age of 'the separation of power from politics' is now outdated, for there are innumerable agoras, that is, citizen-inspired and -led websites and associated movements that are thriving and attracting global allegiances and fostering globally co-ordinated protests, as commentators such as Keane (2013) and Castells (2012) have highlighted, although both are well aware that those in positions of power of course are busy trying to shut down these democratic initiatives. But even the Chinese authorities have been having difficulty in containing internet-based protest

(Keane 2013: 196–212). Bauman, however, dismissed – as usual, without any evidence – internet-based activism as a sort of couch-potato activism that he dubbed 'slacktivism' (Bauman and Mauro 2016: 154), thus shoring up a pessimistic view of the internet generation 'as interconnected loners' who have been 'formatted' by the media and advertising (Bauman and Mauro 2016: 80).

A universal basic income: an idea whose time has come?

Perhaps the only policy proposal that Bauman made in his mature years was one for a universal basic income, in 1999 (*In Search of Politics*: 180–90). He traced the idea back to Thomas Paine, although some have seen earlier hints of such thinking in Thomas More's writings in the sixteenth century. For the present period, Bauman drew principally on the 1991 proposals suggested by the well-known German centre-left political economist Claus Offe (*In Search of Politics*: 183–4), for whom this was a pragmatic move to offset growing job insecurities and the possible effects of future automation. And it is indeed the new fears of an era where rapid advances in artificial intelligence and robotics will possibly make a large number of jobs susceptible to automation that are now, at least in part, giving new life to the idea (Srnicek and Williams 2015; Bregman 2016). Given the 'separation between power and politics', though, Bauman remained pessimistic about the proposal for a basic income ever coming to fruition (*In Search of Politics*: 190–2).

Bauman's pessimism notwithstanding, only seventeen years after the publication of *In Search of Politics*, the Swiss were voting in a referendum, on 5 June 2016, on a proposal for a basic universal income, while pilot projects are planned in Finland, Utrecht in the Netherlands and Ontario in Canada. Swiss citizens rejected the proposal for a universal basic income of 38 per cent of GDP per capita, with 76.9 per cent voting against and 23.1 per cent saying yes to the proposal.

A socialist case for the proposal continues to be made, based on a payment being made out of increased general taxation, although some (Susskind and Susskind 2015) have warned that even some of the professions could face being replaced by artificial intelligence and robotics. A feminist case has also been made, combining the basic income with a fifteen- or twenty-one-hour working week so as to abolish the distinction between part-time and full-time work, which often disadvantages women. These and other supporting arguments are made in a variety of texts (Srnicek and Williams 2015; Bregman 2016) which are likely to be part of a growing literature, especially as research on the pilot projects planned in Finland, Utrecht and Ontario becomes available. The idea is also being discussed by Labour parties in Britain and New Zealand.

Bauman's pessimism and the poverty of alternatives to TINA

At the same time as Bauman raged against TINA ('there is no alternative'), it is only too obvious that he seldom offered any concrete alternatives to the present. In what sense could his be a sociology of hope? How could he claim to be defamiliarising a taken-for-granted, reified, naturalised world when he felt that consumerist delusion had seeped so deeply into culture and personality that a sociologist who presented a critique of the present to deluded consumerists would be not only disbelieved but laughed at in derision? This is where, as I have also pointed out, Bauman neglected Gramsci's insight that common sense contains oppositional as well as conformist elements, therefore always allowing for the possibility of critique from the ordinary populace and from intellectuals fusing into genuine protest and social transformation. Add to this the general ambivalence towards agency that I have highlighted in Bauman's work, and the stage is set for a world that is hospitable only to pessimism.

The irony is that when people did organise in what have come to be called the new social movements of feminism, anti-racism, environmentalism and so forth, and when the Arab Spring and the Occupy movement expressed exuberant outrage, Bauman consistently poured cold water on their protests on the grounds that they had no comprehensive alternative (Bauman and Donskis 2013: 62–3, 68–9, 83, 113–14) and that the new social movements (not Occupy, for obvious reasons) have diverted attention away from overall economic inequality in their 'identity politics'. But even Occupy was castigated for not having an overall plan for social and economic transformation. In his later writings he referred to protest movements as 'protest moments' (Bauman and Donskis 2016: 88).

The 'precariat', on the other hand, was seen as too divided and demoralised to pose any threat to the established order (Bauman and Bordoni 2014: 23–4), and there is no doubt some truth in his judgement. It cannot play the part of the universal historical agent that Marx assigned to the proletariat, for 'the figure of the "historical agent" is completely irrelevant. It can be dropped from the agenda, Bauman argued, without guilty conscience, and above all without regrets and 'the bitter after-taste of loss' (*Liquid Fear*: 169). By downplaying the new social and protest movements, though, Bauman failed to recognise that the stage is now dominated by a wide variety of historical agents. His blindsight simply abolished agency from the picture, thus underscoring his dark, pessimistic vision of the present and the future.

Bauman came to believe that Popperian-style piecemeal, pragmatic social engineering was the only possibility in the face of the failure of the modern 'gardening' utopias of Communism and Nazism (*Intimations*: 221). His Popperianism is evident, too, in his double commitment to both socialism and liberalism (Bauman and Tester 2001: 153–5), although he gave no indication as to what socialism now implied in terms of institutions and principles. At one point elsewhere he said that 'the welfare state [is] ... one of the greatest gains of humanity and achievements of civilized society' (*The Individualized Society*: 82). But is this the most we can hope for? Elsewhere he praised Scandinavian social democracy and the pink tide in Latin America, and was highly critical of New Labour and the 'modernisation' agenda of the Third Way in the UK (*Consuming Life*: 142–4). *It is not unfair to infer that his preference was for a heavily statist and top-down version of the just society, a 'gardening', modernist vision, rather than the multiple-sited, new social movement media vision of what one might call liquid democracy.* As the conventional welfare state has always been the goal of British empiricist reform-minded sociology, exactly what is more radical about the political implications of Bauman's version of critical sociology or 'sociological hermeneutics' remains unclear (Bauman, Jacobsen and Tester 2013: 49–52).

It is altogether too tempting to say that Bauman was having his cake and eating it too, for he denounced activists and protesters of all shades for not having overall plans for reform while denying their very possibility and indeed desirability in postmodern and liquid modern times, and refusing to spell out even in broad terms what alternatives, except for the welfare state, one might reflect on. His thinking retained streaks of utopianism (Jacobsen 2008), but it pointed to no radical utopia beyond the welfare state. His critique of the discourses and movements focusing on human rights (see for example *Liquid Modernity*: 36) is embarrassingly thin (instead, for more thoughtful contributions see, among a host of others, Nash 2014; Holder and Reidy 2013), although it seems to be in keeping with his general aversion to discussing democracy, an issue that cannot be altogether separated from questions of human rights.

It is especially notable that apart from a reference to a *Wikipedia* article on 'The Slow Food Movement' (*Does the Richness*: 66), Bauman resolutely refused to engage with the large number of critics and activists who have suggested alternatives to consumerism and organised counter-cultural movements against it (Littler 2009; Lawson 2009: 165–244; Humphery 2010; Binkley and Littler 2011).

It is no wonder that he remained pessimistic. He admitted (Bauman and Donskis 2013: 182) that on his travels, often at the end of his talks, he was invariably asked 'Dear Sir, why are you such a pessimist?' Bauman answered that he still believed that European culture gives grounds for optimism (Bauman and Donskis 2013: 182–3), in an answer that merely highlights his Eurocentrism, for he writes out the rest of the world as providing a 'chance' for humanity. But his pessimism wins out, for he said in the same set of epistolary exchanges with Donskis (Bauman and Donskis 2013: 47) that he stood with Adorno's own pessimistic views and endorsed Adorno's paradoxical argument that in the present period 'For the intellectual, inviolable isolation is the only way of showing some measure of solidarity'; the only advantage the intellectual has is that he has 'insight' into his predicament (for ultimately unconvincing defences of pessimism, see Scruton 2012 and Sim 2015). In supporting this judgement, Bauman also betrayed an elitism that he in fact shared with Adorno, for there is here the presumption that only intellectuals have these insights. If one dismisses the intellectual abilities of the majority, who are not intellectuals, to come to an understanding of the present, then it is hard to see why there would ever be grounds for optimism, for the majority would always remain deluded by ruling ideologies such as consumerism and managerialism (Bauman, Bauman, Kociatkiewicz and Kostera 2015: 17).

However, *Management in a Liquid Modern World* (Bauman, Bauman, Kociatkiewicz and Kostera 2015), a set of conversations in which Bauman's daughter Irena also participated, shows that her father's pessimism did not rub off on his daughter, for her contributions are full of references to optimistic projects and she remains optimistic, too, about the capacities of the state as an agency for transformation (Bauman, Bauman, Kociatkiewicz and Kostera 2015: 40; see also 38–9 for Irena's support for socially progressive initiatives in direct response to her father's pessimism).

A crisply argued case for a basic universal income and other positive proposals for the contemporary era has been made by Danny Dorling in *A Better Politics: How Government can Make us Happier* (2016: 100–9; see also Jhabvalla et al. 2015). Not only does Dorling's short text propose a whole raft of feasible policies, but it illustrates, first, that Bauman-type pessimism *disempowers* citizens because it makes them fatalistic (although note that both Sim (2015) and Scruton (2012) have put positive cases for pessimism, with Sim being more persuasive) while Dorling's sort of argument empowers them to make concrete, feasible, positive proposals which keep hope genuinely alive; second, that national and local initiatives can still be effective, that is, Bauman's notion that only global solutions mattered ('The Triple Challenge', 2010: 200–5) is misleading; third, that carefully and systematically collected empirical evidence by economists, geographers, epidemiologists and psychologists is essential to the formulation of persuasive, progressive policies to alleviate human suffering, which after all seemed to be the wish underlying all of Bauman's version of sociology (Wright 2010; Hahnel and Wright 2016; Levitas 2013); and fourth, that to retain ethical commitment, as Dorling's research and writing does, does not require abandoning careful, methodologically defensible research. Condemning 'methodology addicts' and practising a cavalier attitude to empirical research are simply not helpful in a world where scrutiny of evidence in political argument is playing an ever-important role in the age of well-funded think-tanks and the internet. Close attention to empirical claims is all the more important in a post-Brexit and post-Trump world which – it is widely feared – is entering an era of 'post-factual' politics.

Bauman's greatest strength, his eloquent moral commitment, will inspire in an effective enough manner only if it is accompanied by feasible proposals to combat TINA.

References

Abbinnett, R. (1998), *Truth and Social Science: From Hegel to Deconstruction*, London: Sage

Adamson, G. and Pavitt, J. (2011), 'Postmodernism: Style and Subversion', in Adamson, G, and Pavitt, J. (eds), *Postmodernism: Style and Subversion, 1970–1990*, London: Victoria and Albert Museum

Adler, J. (2000), 'Good against Evil? H. G. Adler, T. W. Adorno and Representation of the Holocaust', in Fine, R. and Turner, C. (eds), *Social Theory after the Holocaust*, Liverpool: Liverpool University Press

Adorno, T. and Horkheimer, M. (1997), *Dialectic of Enlightenment*, London: Verso (first published in German in 1947: English 2nd edn, New York: Seabury Press, 1972)

Ahmed, A. (2007), 'Postmodernism and Islam: Where to after September 11?', in Goulimari, P. (ed.), *Postmodernism: What Moment?*, Manchester: Manchester University Press

Alvesson, M. (2002), *Postmodernism and Social Research*, Buckingham: Open University Press

Alvesson, M. and Skoldberg, K. (2010), *Reflexive Methodology: New Vistas for Qualitative Research*, 2nd edn, London: Sage

Alvesson, M. and Willmottt, H. (2013), *Making Sense of Management: A Critical Introduction*, London: Sage

Anderson, P. (1998), *The Origins of Postmodernity*, London: Verso

Arendt, H. (1994), *Eichmann in Jerusalem*, revised and enlarged edn, London: Penguin Books (first published 1965)

Armstrong, G. (1998), *Football Hooligans: Knowing the Score*, Oxford: Berg

Armstrong, G. and Young, M. (2000), 'Fanatical Football Chants: Creating and Controlling the Carnival', in Finn, G. and Giulianotti, R. (eds), *Football Culture: Local Contests, Global Visions*, London: Frank Cass

Arnold, D. (1993), *Colonizing the Body: State Medicine and Epidemic Disease in Nineteenth Century India*, Berkeley: University of California Press

Asad, T. (ed.) (1973), *Anthropology and the Colonial Encounter*, London: Ithaca Press

Asad, T. (1986), 'The Concept of Cultural Translation in British Social Anthropology', in Clifford, J. and Marcus, M. (eds), *Writing Culture: The Poetics and Politics of Ethnography*, Berkeley: University of California Press

Ashcroft, B., Griffiths, G. and Tiffin, H. (eds) (1995), *The Post-Colonial Studies Reader*, London: Routledge

Assange, J. (2015), *The WikiLeaks Files: The World According to US Empire*, London: Verso

Atkinson, W. (2007), 'Beck, Individualization and the Death of Class: A Critique', *British Journal of Sociology*, 58 (3): 349–66

Atkinson, W. (2008), 'Not All that is Solid has Melted into Air (or Liquid)', *Sociological Review*, 56 (1): 1–17

Atkinson, W. (2010), *Class Individualization and Late Modernity*, Basingstoke: Palgrave Macmillan

Baehr, P. (2010), 'Banality and Cleverness: *Eichmann in Jerusalem* Revisited', in Berkowitz, R., Katz, J. and Keenan, T. (eds), *Thinking in Dark Times: Hannah Arendt on Ethics and Politics*, New York: Fordham University Press

Bagguley, P. and Mann, K. (1992), 'Idle Thieving Bastards: Scholarly Representations of the Underclass', *Work, Employment and Society*, 6 (1), 113–26

Bailey, T. (ed.) (2013), *Deprovincializing Habermas*, New Delhi and Abingdon: Routledge

Baranowski, S. (2010), *Nazi Empire*, Cambridge: Cambridge University Press

Barber, B. (1996), *Jihad vs. McWorld*, New York: Times Books (2nd edn 2003)

Barber, B. (2007), *Consumed: How Markets Corrupt Children, Infantilize Adults and Swallow Citizens Whole*, New York: Norton

Barrett, M. (1991), *The Politics of Truth*, Cambridge: Polity Press

Bauer, Y. (2002), *Rethinking the Holocaust*, New Haven: Yale University Press

Bauman, J. (1986), *Winter in the Morning*, London: Virago

Bauman, Z. (1969), 'Modern Times, Modern Marxism', in Berger, P. (ed.), *Marxism and Sociology: Views from Eastern Europe*, New York: Appleton-Century-Crofts

Bauman, Z. (1976a), *Socialism: The Active Utopia*, London: Allen and Unwin

Bauman, Z. (1976b), *Towards a Critical Sociology*, London: Routledge

Bauman, Z. (1978), *Hermeneutics and Social Science*, London: Routledge

Bauman, Z. (1982), *Memories of Class*, London: Routledge

Bauman, Z. (1987), *Legislators and Interpreters: On Modernity, Postmodernity and Intellectuals*, Cambridge: Polity Press

Bauman, Z. (1989a), 'Hermeneutics and Social Theory', in Held, D. and Thompson, J. (eds), *Social Theory and Modern Societies: Anthony Giddens and his Critics*, Cambridge: Cambridge University Press

Bauman, Z. (1989b), *Modernity and the Holocaust*, Cambridge: Polity Press

Bauman, Z. (1991), *Modernity and Ambivalence*, Cambridge: Polity Press

Bauman, Z. (1992a), *Intimations of Postmodernity*, London: Routledge

Bauman, Z. (1992b), *Mortality and Immortality and Other Life Strategies*, Cambridge: Polity Press

Bauman, Z. (1993a), *Postmodern Ethics*, Oxford: Blackwell

Bauman, Z. (1993b), 'The Sweet Scent of Decomposition', in Rojek, C. and Turner, B. (eds), *Forget Baudrillard?*, London: Routledge

Bauman, Z. (1995), *Life in Fragments*, Cambridge: Polity Press

Bauman, Z. (1997), *Postmodernity and its Discontents*, Cambridge: Polity Press

Bauman, Z. (1998a), *Globalization*, Cambridge: Polity Press

Bauman, Z. (1998b), *Work, Consumerism and the New Poor*, Buckingham: Open University Press

Bauman, Z. (1999), *In Search of Politics*, Cambridge: Polity Press

Bauman, Z. (2000a), 'The Holocaust's Life as a Ghost', in Fine, R. and Turner, C. (eds), *Social Theory after the Holocaust*, Liverpool: Liverpool University Press

Bauman, Z. (2000b), *Liquid Modernity*, Cambridge: Polity Press

Bauman, Z. (2001a), *Community*, Cambridge: Polity Press

Bauman, Z. (2001b), *The Individualized Society*, Cambridge: Polity Press

Bauman, Z. (2002), *Society under Siege*, Cambridge: Polity Press

Bauman, Z. (2003), *Liquid Love*, Cambridge: Polity Press

Bauman, Z. (2004a), *Identity*, Cambridge: Polity Press

Bauman, Z. (2004b), *Wasted Lives: Modernity and its Outcasts*, Cambridge: Polity Press

Bauman, Z. (2006), *Liquid Fear*, Cambridge: Polity Press

Bauman, Z. (2007), *Consuming Life*, Cambridge: Polity Press

Bauman, Z. (2008), *Does Ethics Have a Chance in a World of Consumers?*, Cambridge: Polity Press

Bauman, Z. (2010), 'The Triple Challenge', in Davis, M. and Tester, K. (eds), *Bauman's Challenge: Sociological Issues for the 21st Century*, Basingstoke: Palgrave Macmillan

Bauman, Z. (2011a), *Collateral Damage*, Cambridge: Polity Press

Bauman, Z. (2011b), *Culture in a Liquid Modern World*, Cambridge: Polity Press

Bauman, Z. (2011c), 'The London Riots: On Consumerism Coming Home to Roost', *Social Europe Journal*, 98: 110–13

Bauman, Z. (2012), *This is Not a Diary*, Cambridge: Polity Press

Bauman, Z. (2013a), *Does the Richness of the Few Benefit Us All?*, Cambridge: Polity Press

Bauman, Z. (2013b), *Liquid Times*, Cambridge: Polity Press

Bauman, Z. (2016), *Strangers at our Door*, Cambridge: Polity Press

Bauman, Z., Bauman, I., Kociatkiewicz, J. and Kostera, M. (2015), *Management in a Liquid Modern World*, Cambridge: Polity Press

Bauman, Z. and Blackshaw, T. (2002), 'Sociological Hermeneutics', *Network* (newsletter of the British Sociological Association), Durham: British Sociological Association

Bauman, Z. and Bordoni, C. (2014), *State of Crisis*, Cambridge: Polity Press

Bauman, Z. and Dawes, S. (2011), 'The Role of the Intellectual in Liquid Modernity', *Theory, Culture and Society*, 28 (3): 130–48

Bauman, Z. and Donskis, L. (2013), *Moral Blindness: The Loss of Sensitivity in Liquid Modernity*, Cambridge: Polity Press

Bauman, Z. and Donskis, L. (2016), *Liquid Evil*, Cambridge: Polity Press

Bauman, Z. and Gane, N. (2004), 'Liquid Sociality', in Gane, N. (ed.), *The Future of Social Theory*, London: Continuum

Bauman, Z., Jacobsen, M., Marshman, S. and Tester, K. (2007), 'Sociology as Vocation and Dialogue', in Jacobsen, M., Marshman and Tester, K. (eds), *Bauman beyond Postmodernity*, Aalborg: Aalborg University Press

Bauman, Z., Jacobsen, M. and Tester, K. (2013), *What Use is Sociology?*, Cambridge: Polity Press

Bauman, Z. and Lyon, D. (2013), *Liquid Surveillance*, Cambridge: Polity Press

Bauman, Z. and Mauro, E. (2016), *Babel*, Cambridge: Polity Press

Bauman, Z. and May, T. (2001), *Thinking Sociologically*, 2nd edn, Oxford: Wiley-Blackwell

Bauman, Z. and Mazzeo, R. (2016), *In Praise of Literature*, Cambridge: Polity Press

Bauman, Z. and Obirek, S. (2015a), *Of God and Man*, Cambridge: Polity Press

Bauman, Z. and Obirek, S. (2015b), *On the World and Ourselves*, Cambridge: Polity Press

Bauman, Z. and Rovirosa-Madrazo, C. (2010), *Living on Borrowed Time*, Cambridge: Polity Press

Bauman, Z. and Tester, K. (2001), *Conversations with Zygmunt Bauman*, Cambridge: Polity Press

Bauman, Z. and Tester, K. (2007), 'On the Postmodern Debate', in Goulimari, P. (ed.), *Postmodernism: What Moment?*, Manchester: Manchester University Press

Baumel, J. (1998), *Double Jeopardy: Gender and the Holocaust*, London and Portland, OR: Valentine Mitchell

Bayly, C. (2004), *The Birth of the Modern World 1780–1914: Global Connections and Comparisons*, Oxford: Blackwell

Beck, U. (1992), *Risk Society*, Cambridge: Polity Press (first published 1976)

Beck, U. (2000a), *The Brave New World of Work*, Cambridge: Polity Press

Beck, U. (2000b), 'The Cosmopolitan Perspective: Sociology of the Second Age of Modernity', *British Journal of Sociology*, 51 (1): 79–105

Beck, U. (2000c), *What is Globalization?*, Cambridge: Polity Press

Beckwith, F. and Jones, T. (eds) (1997), *Affirmative Action: Social Justice or Reverse Discrimination*, New York: Prometheus Books

Beer, P. and Koster, F. (2009), *Sticking Together or Falling Apart? Solidarity in an Era of Individualization and Globalization*, Amsterdam: Amsterdam University Press

Beilharz, P. (2000), *Zygmunt Bauman: Dialectic of Modernity*, London: Sage

Beilharz, P. (2016), 'Zymunt Bauman at 90', *Thesis Eleven*, 133 (1): 118

Bell, D. (1960), *The End of Ideology*, Glencoe: Free Press

Bell, D. (1973), *The Coming of Post-Industrial Society*, London: Basic Books

Bell, D. (1978), *The Cultural Contradictions of Capitalism*, New York: Basic Books (first published 1976)

Belliappa, J. (2013), *Gender, Class and Reflexive Modernity in India*, Basingstoke: Palgrave Macmillan

Benyon, J. (1984), *Scarman and After*, London: Pergamon Press

Benyon, J. and Solomos, J. (eds) (1987), *The Roots of Urban Unrest*, London: Scarman Centre

Bergen, D. (2013), 'What do Studies of Women, Gender, and Sexuality Contribute to Understanding the Holocaust?', in Goldenberg, M. and Shapiro, A. (eds), *Different Horrors, Same Hell: Gender and the Holocaust*, Seattle: University of Washington Press

Berger, P. (ed.) (1969), *Marxism and Sociology: Views from Eastern Europe*, New York: Appleton-Century-Crofts

Berger, S. and Dore, R. (eds) (1996), *National Diversity and Global Capitalism*, Ithaca: Cornell University Press

Berman, M. (1982), *All that is Solid Melts into Air*, London: Verso

Berman, M. (1992), 'Why Modernism Still Matters', in Lash, S. and Friedman, J. (eds), *Modernity and Identity*, Oxford: Blackwell

Bernstein, R. (1996), *Hannah Arendt and the Jewish Question*, Cambridge: Polity Press

Best, S. (1994), 'Foucault, Postmodernism and Social Theory', in Dickens, D. and Fontana, A. (eds) (1994), *Postmodernism and Social Inquiry*, London: UCL Press

Best, S. (2010), 'Liquid Terrorism: Altruistic Fundamentalism in the Context of Liquid Modernity', *Sociology*, 44 (4): 678–94

Best, S. (2013), *Zygmunt Bauman: Why Good People Do Bad Things*, Farnham: Ashgate

Best, S. (2016), 'Voice and the Generalised Other in the Ethical Writings of Zygmunt Bauman', in Jacobsen, M. (ed.), *Beyond Bauman*, London: Routledge

Best, S. and Kellner, D. (1991), *Postmodern Theory: Critical Interrogations*, Basingstoke: Macmillan

Best, S. and Kellner, D. (1997), *The Postmodern Turn*, New York: Guildford Press

Beverley, J. and Aronna, M. (eds) (1995), *The Postmodernism Debate in Latin America*, Durham, NC: Duke University Press

Bhabha, H. (1994), *The Location of Culture*, London: Routledge

Bhambra, G. (2007), *Rethinking Modernity: Postcolonialism and the Sociological Imagination*, Basingstoke: Palgrave Macmillan

Bhambra, G. (2014), *Connected Sociologies*, London: Bloomsbury Academic

Bhaskar, R. (2010), *Philosophy and the Idea of Freedom*, London: Routledge

Billig, M. (1995), *Banal Nationalism*, London: Sage

Binkley, S. and Littler, J. (2011), *Cultural Studies and Consumerism: A Critical Encounter*, London: Routledge

Bird, E. (2003), *The Audience in Everyday Life: Living in a Media World*, London: Routledge

Blackshaw, T. (2003), *Leisure Life: Myth, Masculinity and Modernity*, London: Routledge

Blackshaw, T. (2005), *Zygmunt Bauman*, London: Routledge

Blackshaw, T. (2006), 'Too Good for Sociology', *Polish Sociological Review*, 3 (155): 293–306

Blaut, J. (2000), *Eight Eurocentric Historians*, New York: Guildford Press

Bloom, P. (2013), *Just Babies: The Origins of Good and Evil*, London: Bodley Head

Blum, W. (2014), *Rogue State: A Guide to the World's Only Superpower*, London: Zed Books

Boje, D., Gephart, R. and Thatchenkery, T. (eds) (1996), *Postmodern Management and Organization Theory*, London: Sage

Boltanski, L. (1999), *Distant Suffering: Morality, Media and Politics*, Cambridge: Cambridge University Press

Boltanski, L. and Chiapello, E. (2007), *The New Spirit of Capitalism*, London: Verso (first published in French in 1999)

Bourguignon, F. (2015), *The Globalization of Inequality*, Princeton, NJ: Princeton University Press

Boyne, R. and Rattansi, A. (1990), 'The Theory and Politics of Postmodernism', in Boyne, R. and Rattansi, A. (eds), *Postmodernism and Society*, Basingstoke: Macmillan

Bradbury, M. and McFarlane, J. (eds) (1976), *Modernism: A Guide to European Literature 1890–1930*, Harmondsworth: Penguin

Bradley, H., Erickson, M., Stephenson, C. and Williams, S. (2000), *Myths at Work*, Cambridge: Polity Press

Brandom, R. (ed.) (2000), *Rorty and his Critics*, Oxford: Blackwell

Brannen, J. and Nilsen, A. (2005), 'Individualisation, Choice and Structure: A Discussion of Current Trends in Sociological Analysis', *Sociological Review*, 53 (3): 412–28

Bregman, R. (2016), *Utopia for Realists: The Case for a Basic Income, Open Borders, and a 15-Hour week*, London: The Correspondent

Breisach, E. (2003), *On the Future of History: The Postmodernist Challenge and its Aftermath*, Chicago: University of Chicago Press

Bronner, S. (2011), *Critical Theory*, Oxford: Oxford University Press

Brooks, A. (2011), *Social Theory in Contemporary Asia*, Abingdon: Routledge

Brown, M., Carnoy, M., Currie, E., Duster, T., Oppenheimer, D., Shultz, M. and Wellman, D. (2005), *Whitewashing Race: The Myth of a Color-Blind Society*, Berkeley: University of California Press

Brown, R. (ed.) (1995), *Postmodern Representations: Truth, Power and Mimesis in the Human Sciences*, Urbana: University of Illinois Press

Browning, C. (2001), *Ordinary Men: Reserve Battalion 101 and the Final Solution in Poland*, new edn with Afterword, London: Penguin Books

Browning, C. (2005), *The Origins of the Final Solution*, New York: Arrow Books

Bryant, A. (2013), 'Bauman's Challenge: Metaphors and Metamorphoses', in Davis, M. (ed.), *Liquid Sociology: Metaphor in Zygmunt Bauman's Analysis of Modernity*, London: Routledge

Burchell, G. (1996), 'Liberal Government and Techniques of the Self', in Barry, A., Osborne, T. and Rose, N. (eds), *Foucault and Political Reason: Liberalism, Neo-Liberalism and Rationalities of Government*, Chicago: University of Chicago Press

Burton, A. (2000), 'Who Needs the Nation? Interrogating "British" History', in Hall, C. (ed.), *Cultures of Empire: Colonizers in Britain and the Empire in the Nineteenth and Twentieth Centuries*, Manchester: Manchester University Press

Calhoun, C. (1992), 'Culture, History, and the Problem of Specificity in Social Theory', in Seidman, S. and Wagner, D. (eds), *Postmodernism and Social Theory*, Oxford: Blackwell

Calhoun, C. (ed.) (1993), *Habermas and the Public Sphere*, Cambridge, MA: MIT Press

Calhoun, C. (1995), *Critical Social Theory*, Oxford: Blackwell

Calinescu, M. (1987), *Five Faces of Modernity: Modernism, Avant-Garde, Decadence, Kitsch, Postmodernism*, Durham, NC: Duke University Press

Callinicos, A. (1990), *Against Postmodernism: A Marxist Critique*, Cambridge: Polity Press

Campbell, B. and Dawson, A. (2001), 'Indecent Exposures, Men, Masculinity and Violence', in Perryman, M. (ed.), *Hooligan Wars: Causes and Effects of Football Violence*, Edinburgh: Mainstream Publishing

Cannadine, D. (ed.) (2002), *What is History Now?*, Basingstoke: Palgrave Macmillan

Carey, D. and Trakulhun, S. (2013), 'Universalism, Diversity and the Postcolonial Enlightenment', in Carey, D. and Festa, L. (eds), *Postcolonial Enlightenment*, Oxford: Oxford University Press

Carleheden, M. (2008), 'Bauman on Politics – Stillborn Democracy', in Jacobsen, M. and Poder, P. (eds), *The Sociology of Zygmunt Bauman: Challenges and Critique*, Aldershot: Ashgate

Carr, N. (2010), The *Shallows: How the Internet is Changing the Way We Think, Read and Remember*, New York: Norton

Carroll, W. (2010), *The Making of a Transnational Capitalist Class: Corporate Power in the 21st Century*, London: Zed Books

Carter, J. (ed.) (1998), *Postmodernity and the Fragmentation of Welfare*, London: Routledge

Cassirer, E. (1951), *The Philosophy of the Enlightenment*, Princeton, NJ: Princeton University Press

Castells, M. (1996), *The Rise of the Network Society*, Oxford: Blackwell

Castells, M. (2012), *Networks of Outrage and Hope: Social Movements in the Internet Age*, Cambridge: Polity Press

Castles, F. (ed.) (2007), *The Disappearing State?*, Cheltenham: Edward Elgar

Cesarani, D. (2005), *Eichmann: His Life and Crimes*, London: Vintage Books

Chakrabarty, D. (2000), *Provincializing Europe: Postcolonial Thought and Historical Difference*, Princeton, NJ: Princeton University Press

Chambers, D. (2012), *A Sociology of Family Life*, Cambridge: Polity Press

Chang, H.-J. (2007), *The East Asian Development Experience*, London: Zed Books

Chanter, T. (ed.) (2001), *Feminist Interpretations of Emmanuel Levinas*, University Park: Pennsylvania State University Press

Charlesworth, A. (2004), 'The Topography of Genocide', in Stone, D. (ed.), *The Historiography of the Holocaust*, Basingstoke: Palgrave Macmillan

Chatterjee, P. (1993), *The Nation and its Fragments: Colonial and Postcolonial Histories*, Princeton, NJ: Princeton University Press

Chatterjee, P. (2006), *The Politics of the Governed*, New York: Columbia University Press

Clarke, J. (1997), *Oriental Enlightenment: The Encounter between Asian and Western Thought*, London: Routledge

Clarke, J., Langan, M. and Williams, F. (2001), 'The Construction of the British Welfare State', in Cochran, A., Clarke, J. and Gerwitz, S. (eds), *Comparing Welfare States*, London: Sage

Clarke, J., Newman, J., Smith, N. and Vidler, E. (2007), *Creating Citizen-Consumers: Changing Publics and Changing Public Services*, London: Sage

Clifford, J. (1986), 'Partial Truths', in Clifford, J. and Marcus, M. (eds), *Writing Culture: The Poetics and Politics of Ethnography*, Berkeley: University of California Press

Clifford, J. and Marcus, M. (eds) (1986), *Writing Culture: The Poetics and Politics of Ethnography*, Berkeley: University of California Press

Cohen, S. (2001), *States of Denial: Knowing about Atrocities and Suffering*, Cambridge: Polity Press

Cohn, B. (1996), *Colonialism and its Forms of Knowledge: The British in India*, Princeton, NJ: Princeton University Press

Colley, L. (1992), 'Britishness and Otherness: Who Are the British Anyway?', *Journal of British Studies*, 31 (4): 309–29

Collingham, E. (2001), *Imperial Bodies: The Physical Experience of the Raj 1800–1947*, Cambridge: Polity Press

Connell, R. (2007), *Southern Theory*, Cambridge: Polity Press

Connolly, W. (2005), *Pluralism*, London: Duke University Press

Cooper, K. and White, R. (2012), *Qualitative Research in the Postmodern Era*, London: Springer

Crimp, D. (1983), 'On the Museum's Ruins', in Foster, H. (ed.), *Postmodern Culture*, London: Pluto Press

Crouch, C. (2004), *Post-Democracy*, Cambridge: Polity Press

Crouch, C. (2011), *The Strange Non-Death of Neo-Liberalism*, Cambridge: Polity Press

Crouch, C. (2013), *Making Capitalism Fit for Society*, Cambridge: Polity Press

Crowther, P. (1990), 'Postmodernism and the Visual Arts: A Question of Ends', in Boyne, R. and Rattansi, A. (eds), *Postmodernism and Society*, Basingstoke: Macmillan

Dasgupta, S. and Kivisto. P, (eds) (2014), *Postmodernism in Global Perspective*, London: Sage

Davidson, I. and Penslar, D. (eds) (2005), *Orientalism and the Jews*, Waltham, MA: Brandeis University Press

Davin, A. (1978), 'Imperialism and Motherhood', *History Workshop Journal*, 5 (1): 9–66

Davis, A. (2013), *Promotional Cultures*, Cambridge: Polity Press

Davis, C. (1996), *Levinas: An Introduction*, Cambridge: Polity Press

Davis, M. (2008), *Freedom and Consumerism: A Critique of Zygmunt Bauman's Sociology*, Aldershot: Ashgate

Davis, M. (ed.) (2013), *Liquid Sociology: Metaphor in Zygmunt Bauman's Analysis of Modernity*, London: Routledge

Davis, M. and Tester, K. (2010) (eds), *Bauman's Challenge: Sociological Issues for the 21st Century*, Basingstoke: Palgrave Macmillan

Dawson, S. (2012), 'Optimism and Agency in the Sociology of Zygmunt Bauman', *European Journal of Social Theory*, 15 (1): 555–70

de Certau, M. (1984), *The Practice of Everyday Life*, Berkeley: University of California Press (first published 1980)

De Graaf, J., Wann, D. and Naylor, T. (2005), *Affluenza: The All-Consuming Epidemic*, San Francisco: Barret Koehler

Decety, J. and Ickes, W. (eds) (2011), *The Social Neuroscience of Empathy*, Cambridge, MA: MIT Press

de Djin, A. (2012), 'The Politics of Enlightenment: From Gay to Israel', *Historical Journal*, 55 (3): 785–805

Delacampagne, C. (2001), 'The Enlightenment Project: A Reply to Schmidt', *Political Theory*, 29 (1): 80–5

Denzin, N. (1991), *Images of Postmodern Society: Social Theory and Contemporary Cinema*, London: Sage

Di Muzio, T. (2015), *The 1% and the Rest of Us*, London: Zed Press

Dirks, N. (ed.) (1992), *Colonialism and Culture*, Ann Arbor: University of Michigan Press

Dirlik, A. and Zhang, X. (eds) (2000), *Postmodernism and China*, Durham, NC: Duke University Press

Donald, J. and Rattansi, A. (eds) (1992), *'Race', Culture and Difference*, London: Sage

Doogan, K. (2009), *New Capitalism? The Transformation of Work*, Cambridge: Polity Press

Dorling, D. (2014), *Inequality and the 1%*, London: Verso

Dorling, D (2015), *Injustice: Why Inequality Persists*, 2nd edn, Bristol: Policy Press (first published 2010)

Dorling, D. (2016), *A Better Politics: How Government can Make Us Happier*, London: London Publishing Partnership

Douzinas, C. (1987), 'Human Rights and Postmodernity', in Goulimari, P. (ed.), *Postmodernism: What Moment?*, Manchester: Manchester University Press

du Gay, P. (1996), *Consumption and Identity at Work*, London: Sage

du Gay, P. (1999), 'Is Weber's Bureau Bauman's Bureau?', *British Journal of Sociology*, 50 (4): 575–87

du Gay, P. (2000), *In Praise of Bureaucracy: Weber – Organization – Ethics*, London: Sage

du Gay, P., and Morgan, G. (eds) (2013), *New Spirits of Capitalism?*, Oxford: Oxford University Press

Dunning, E., Murphy, P. and Williams, J. (1988), *The Roots of Football Hooliganism*, London: Routledge

Eaglestone, R. (2004), *The Holocaust and the Postmodern*, Oxford: Oxford University Press

Eaglestone, R. (2010), 'Postcolonial Thought and Levinas's Double Vision', in Atterton, P. and Calarco, M. (eds), *Radicalizing Levinas*, Albany: State University of New York Press

Eagleton, T. (1996), *The Illusions of Postmodernism*, Oxford: Blackwell

Edgell, S. (2006), *The Sociology of Work*, London: Sage

Edwards, D. and Cromwell, D. (2005), *Guardians of Power: The Myth of the Liberal Media*, London: Pluto Press

Edwards, T. (2000), *Contradictions of Consumption*, Buckingham: Open University Press

Ehrenreich, B. (2006), *Bait and Switch: The Futile Pursuit of the Corporate Dream*, London: Granta Books

Ehrenreich, B. (2009), *Smile or Die: How Positive Thinking Fooled America and the World*, London: Granta Books

Eisenstadt, S. (ed.) (2002), *Multiple Modernities*, New Brunswick: Transaction Publishers

Eisenstein, M. (2012), *Compassion Inc.: How Corporate America Blurs the Line between What We Buy, Who We Are and Those We Help*, Berkeley: University of California Press

Elkins, C. (2005), *Imperial Reckoning: The Untold Story of Britain's Gulag in Kenya*, New York: Henry Holt

Escobar, A. (1995), *Encountering Development: The Making and Unmaking of the Third World*, Princeton, NJ: Princeton University Press

Esping-Andersen, G. (1989), *Three Worlds of Welfare Capitalism*, Cambridge: Cambridge University Press

Evans, R. (2000), *In Defence of History*, 2nd edn, London: Granta

Evans, R. (2002), *Telling Lies about Hitler: The Holocaust, History and the David Irving Trial*, London: Verso

Eze, E. (ed.) (1997), *Race and the Enlightenment*, Oxford: Blackwell

Feagin, J. and Vera, H. (1995), *White Racism*, London: Routledge

Fearn, N. (2006), 'Profile: Zygmunt Bauman', *New Statesman*, 16 January

Fein, H. (1979), *Accounting for Genocide*, New York: Free Press

Festenstein, M. and Thompson, S. (eds) (2001), *Richard Rorty: Critical Dialogues*, Cambridge: Polity Press

Fine, R. (2000), 'Hannah Arendt: Politics and Understanding after the Holocaust', in Fine, R. and Turner, C. (eds), *Social Theory after the Holocaust*, Liverpool: Liverpool University Press

Finkelstein, N. (1997), 'Daniel Jonah Goldhagen's "Crazy" Thesis: A Critique of Hitler's Willing Executioners', *New Left Review*, 224

Fishman, C. (2007), *The Wal-Mart Effect: How an Out-of-Town Superstore Became a Superpower*, London: Penguin

Ford, R. and Goodwin, M. (2014), *Revolt on the Right*, London: Routledge

Foucault, M. (1977), 'Nietzsche, Genealogy, History', in Foucault, *Language, Counter-Memory and Practice: Selected Essays and Interviews*, New York: Cornell University Press

Foucault, M. (1984), *Discipline and Punish*, Harmondsworth: Penguin Books

Fox, N. (1993), *Postmodernism, Sociology and Health*, Buckingham: Open University Press

Fox, N. (1999), *Beyond Health: Postmodernism and Embodiment*, London: Free Association Books

Fraser, N. and Nicholson, L. (1988), 'Social Criticism without Philosophy: An Encounter between Feminism and Postmodernism', *Theory, Culture and Society*, 5 (2–3): 373–94

Frisby, D. (1986), *Fragments of Modernity*, Cambridge: Polity Press

Frisby, D. (2002), *George Simmel*, 2nd edn, London: Routledge

Fromm, E. (1976), *To Have or To Be?*, New York: Harper and Row

Fukuyama, F. (1993), *The End of History and the Last Man*, London: Penguin

Gabriel, Y. and Lang, T. (2006), *The Unmanageable Consumer*, 2nd edn, London: Sage

Galbraith, J. (1958), *The Affluent Society*, Harmondsworth: Penguin

Galbraith, J. (1992), *The Culture of Contentment*, London: Penguin

Galecki, L. (2005), 'The Unwinnable War: An Interview with Zygmunt Bauman', *Open Democracy*, 1 December 2005, www.opendemocracy.net/globalization-vision_reflections/modernity_3082.jsp (accessed 3 February 2017)

Gamble, A. (2000), *Politics and Fate*, Cambridge: Polity Press

Gamble, A. (2009), *The Spectre at the Feast: Capitalist Crisis and the Politics of Recession*, Basingstoke: Palgrave Macmillan

Gamble, A. (2014), *Crisis Without End? The Unravelling of Western Prosperity*, Basingstoke: Palgrave Macmillan

Gandhi, L. (1998), *Postcolonial Theory: A Critical Introduction*, Edinburgh: Edinburgh University Press

Gane, N. (2001a), 'Chasing the Runaway World: The Politics of Recent Globalization Theory', *Acta Sociologica*, 44 (1): 81–9

Gane, N. (2001b), 'Liquid Modernity and Beyond', *Acta Sociologica*, 44 (3): 267–75

Gane, N. (2012), *Max Weber and Contemporary Capitalism*, Basingstoke: Palgrave Macmillan

Gaonkar, P. (ed.) (2001), *Alternative Modernities*, Durham, NC: Duke University Press

Gardner, K. and Lewis, D. (1996), *Anthropology, Development and the Postmodern Challenge*, London: Pluto Press

Gascoigne, N. (2008), *Richard Rorty: Liberalism, Irony and the Ends of Philosophy*, Cambridge: Cambridge University Press

Gay, P. (1973), *The Enlightenment: An Interpretation*, New York: Norton

Geertz, C. (1971), *The Interpretation of Cultures*, New York: Basic Books

Geertz, C. (1983), *Local Knowledges*, New York: Basic Books

George, S. (2010), *Whose Crisis, Whose Future?*, Cambridge: Cambridge University Press

George, S. (2015), *Global Sovereigns: How Global Corporations are Seizing Power*, Cambridge: Polity Press

Geras, N. (1995), *Solidarity in the Conversation of Humankind: The Ungroundable Liberalism of Richard Rorty*, London: Verso

Geras, N. (1998), *The Contract of Mutual Indifference: Political Philosophy after the Holocaust*, London: Verso

Gibbons, L. (2000), 'Race against Time: Racial Discourse and Irish History', in Hall, C. (ed.), *Cultures of Empire: Colonizers in Britain and the Empire in the Nineteenth and Twentieth Centuries*, Manchester: Manchester University Press

Gibbins, J. and Reimer, B. (1999), *The Politics of Postmodernity*, London: Sage

Giddens, A. (1984), *The Constitution of Society*, Cambridge: Polity Press

Giddens, A. (1990), *The Consequences of Modernity*, Cambridge: Polity Press

Giddens, A. (1991), *Modernity and Self-Identity*, Cambridge: Polity Press

Giddens, A. (1999), *Runaway World: How Globalization is Reshaping Our Lives*, London: Profile Books

Giddens, A. (2009), *The Politics of Climate Change*, Cambridge: Polity Press

Gill, A. (1995), *Ruling Passion: Sex, Race and Empire*, London: BBC Books

Gill, R. (2006), *Gender and the Media*, Cambridge: Polity Press

Gilman, S. (1992), 'Black Bodies, White Bodies: Towards an Iconography of Female Sexuality in Late Nineteenth Century Art, Medicine and Literature', in Donald, J. and Rattansi, A. (eds), *'Race', Culture and Difference*, London: Sage

Gilroy, P. (2000), *Between Camps: Nations, Cultures and the Allure of Race*, London: Penguin

Goldenberg, M. (2013), 'Sex-Based Violence and the Politics and Ethics of Survival', in Goldenberg, M. and Shapiro, A. (eds), *Different Horrors, Same Hell: Gender and the Holocaust*, Seattle: University of Washington Press

Goldenberg, M. and Shapiro, A. (eds) (2013), *Different Horrors, Same Hell: Gender and the Holocaust*, Seattle: University of Washington Press

Goldhagen, D. (1996), *Hitler's Willing Executioners: Ordinary Germans and the Holocaust*, New York: Abacus

Good, J. and Velody, I. (eds) (1998), *The Politics of Postmodernism*, Cambridge: Cambridge University Press

Goodman, R. and Fisher, W. (eds) (1995), *Rethinking Knowledge: Reflections across the Disciplines*, Albany: State University of New York Press

Goody, J. (2006), *The Theft of History*, Cambridge: Cambridge University Press

Goody, J. (2012), *Metals, Culture and Capitalism: An Essay on the Origins of the Modern World*, Cambridge: Cambridge University Press

Gordon, C. (ed.) (1980), *Foucault, Power/Knowledge: Selected Interviews*, New York: Vintage Books

Gordon, D. (2001), 'On the Supposed Obsolescence of the French Enlightenment', in Gordon, D. (ed.), *Postmodernism and the Enlightenment*, London: Routledge

Gouldner, A. (1971), *The Coming Crisis of Western Sociology*, London: Heinemann

Gouldner, A. (1973), *For Sociology: Renewal and Critique in Sociology Today*, London: Allen Lane

Goulimari, P. (2007), 'Introduction', in Goulimari, P. (ed.), *Postmodernism: What Moment?*, Manchester: Manchester University Press

Gray, J. (1995), *Enlightenment's Wake: Politics and Culture at the Close of the Modern Age*, London: Routledge

Griffin, R. (2007), *Modernism and Fascism: The Sense of a New Beginning under Mussolini and Hitler*, Basingstoke: Palgrave Macmillan

Gross, P. and Levitt, N. (1994), *Higher Superstition: The Academic Left and its Quarrels with Science*, Baltimore: Johns Hopkins University Press

Gruner, W. (2010), 'The History of the Holocaust: Multiple Actors, Diverse Motives, Contradictory Developments and Disparate (Re)actions', in Wiese, C. and Betts, P. (eds), *Years of Persecution, Years of Extermination: Saul Friedlander and the Future of Holocaust Studies*, London: Continuum

Gunn, S. (2006), *History and Cultural Theory*, Harlow: Pearson Longman

Habermas, J. (1982), *The Structural Transformation of the Public Sphere*, Cambridge, MA: MIT Press

Habermas, J. (1983), 'Modernity – an Incomplete Project', in Foster, H. (ed.), *Postmodern Culture*, London: Pluto Press

Habermas, J. (1984), *The Philosophical Discourse of Modernity*, Cambridge: Polity Press

Hacking, I. (1983), *Representing and Intervening: Topics in the Philosophy of Natural Science*, Cambridge: Cambridge University Press

Hahnel, R. and Wright, E. (2016), *Alternatives to Capitalism: Proposals for a Democratic Economy*, London: Verso

Hall, C. (1992), *White, Male and Middle Class: Explorations in Feminism* and *History*, Cambridge: Polity Press

Hall, C. and Rose, S. (eds) (2006), *At Home with the Empire: Metropolitan Culture and the Imperial World*, Cambridge: Cambridge University Press

Hall, S. (1992a), 'New Ethnicities', in Donald, J. and Rattansi, A. (eds), *'Race', Culture and Difference*, London: Sage

Hall, S. (1992b), 'The West and the Rest: Discourse and Power', in Hall, S. and Gieben, B. (eds), *Formations of Modernity*, Cambridge: Polity Press

Hall, S. and Jacques, M. (1983), *The Politics of Thatcherism*, London: Lawrence and Wishart

Hancock, I. (2004), 'Romanies and the Holocaust: A Re-Evaluation and Overview', in Stone, D. (ed.), *The Historiography of the Holocaust*, Basingstoke: Palgrave Macmillan

Hancock, P. and Tyler, M. (2001), *Work, Postmodernism and Organization: A Critical Introduction*, London: Sage

Hardt, M. and Negri, A. (2000), *Empire*, Cambridge, MA: Harvard University Press

Harney. A. (2009), *The China Price: The True Cost of Chinese Competitive Advantage*, London: Penguin Books

Harris, J. (1993), 'Modernism and Culture in the USA, 1930–1960', in Wood, P., Frascina, F., Harris, J. and Harrison, C., *Modernism in Dispute: Art since the Forties*, New Haven: Yale University Press

Hart-Landsberg, M. (2013), *Capitalist Globalization: Consequences, Reistance, and Alternatives*, New York: Monthly Review Press

Harvey, D. (1991), *The Condition of Postmodernity*, Oxford: Blackwell

Harvey, D. (2007), *A Short History of Neoliberalism*, Oxford: Oxford University Press

Hassan, I. (1985), 'The Culture of Postmodernism', *Theory, Culture and Society*, 2 (3): 119–31

Hassard, J. and Parker, M. (eds) (1993), *Postmodernism and Organizations*, London: Sage

Hawthorne, G. (1976), *Enlightenment and Despair: A History of Sociology*, Cambridge: Cambridge University Press

Hay, C. (2007), *Why We Hate Politics*, Cambridge: Polity Press

Hay, C. and Marsh, D. (eds) (2000), *Demystifying Globalization*, Basingstoke: Palgrave

Hay, C. and Wincott, D. (2012), *The Political Economy of Welfare Capitalism*, Basingstoke: Palgrave Macmillan

Haynes, S. (2002), 'Ordinary Masculinity: Gender Analysis and Holocaust Scholarship', *Journal of Men's Studies*, 10 (2): 143–63

Heath, J. and Potter, A. (2005), *Nation of Rebels: How Counter Culture Became Consumer Culture* New York: Harper Collins

Hedgepeth, S. and Saidel, R. (eds) (2010), *Sexual Violence against Jewish Women during the Holocaust*, Waltham, MA: Brandeis University Press and New England University Press

Heilbronner, O. (2004), 'German or Nazi Antisemitism?', in Stone, D. (ed.), *The Historiography of the Holocaust*, Basingstoke: Palgrave Macmillan

Held, D. (1980), *Introduction to Critical Theory*, London: Hutchinson

Held, D. (2004), *Global Covenant: The Social Democratic Alternative to the Washington Consensus*, Cambridge: Polity Press

Held, D., McGrew, A., Goldblatt, D. and Perraton, J. (1999), *Global Transformations*, Cambridge: Polity Press

Helm, S. (2015), *If this is a Woman: Inside Ravensbrück, Hitler's Concentration Camp for Women*, New York: Abacus

Henrique, J., Holloway, W. and Urwin, C. (1984), *Changing the Subject: Psychology, Social Regulation and Subjectivity*, London: Routledge

Herf, J. (1986), *Reactionary Modernism: Technology, Culture and Politics in Weimar and the Third Reich*, Cambridge: Cambridge University Press

Herf, J. (2006), *The Jewish Enemy: Nazi Propaganda during World War II and the Holocaust*, Cambridge, MA: Harvard University Press

Hesse, M. (1967), *Models and Analogies in Science*, Notre Dame, IN: University of Notre Dame Press

Hesse, M. (1980), *Revolutions and Reconstructions in the Philosophy of Science*, Sussex: Harvester

Hesse-Biber, S. (ed.) (2014), *Feminist Research Practice: A Primer*, London: Sage

Hilberg, R. (1985), *The Destruction of the European Jews*, New York: Holmes and Meier (first published in German in 1983)

Hilberg, R. (1993), *Perpetrators, Victims and Bystanders: The Jewish Catastrophe 1933–1945*, New York: Harper Perennial

Himmelfarb, G. (2008), *The Roads to Modernity: The British, French and American Enlightenments*, New York: Random House

Hirschman, A. O. (1977), *The Passions and the Interests: Political Arguments for Capitalism before its Triumph*, Princeton, NJ: Princeton University Press

Hirst, B. (2014), 'After Levinas: Assessing Zygmunt Bauman's "Ethical Turn"', *European Journal of Social Theory*, 17 (2): 184–98

Hirst, P. and Thompson, G. (1996), *Globalization in Question*, Cambridge: Polity Press (2nd edn 1999)

Hirst, P., Thompson, G. and Bromley, S. (2009), *Globalization in Question*, 3rd edn, Cambridge: Polity Press

Hobsbawm, E. (1996), 'Identity Politics and the Left', *New Left Review*, 217

Hobson, J. (2012), *The Eurocentric Conception of World Politics*, Cambridge: Cambridge University Press

Hochschild, A. (1983), *The Managed Heart: Commercialisation of Human Feeling*, Berkeley: University of California Press

Hochschild. A. (1997), *The Time Bind*, New York: Wiley

Hochschild, A. (2012), *The Second Shift: Working Families and the Revolution at Home*, London: Penguin

Hochschild, A. (2013), *The Outsourced Self: What Happens When We Pay Others to Live Our Lives for Us*, New York: Picador

Hoffman, M. (2000), *Empathy and Moral Development: Implications for Caring and Justice*, Cambridge: Cambridge University Press

Hogan, T. (2002), 'The Spaces of Poverty: Zygmunt Bauman "After" Jeremy Seabrook', *Thesis Eleven*, 70 (1): 72–87

Holder, C. and Reidy, D. (eds) (2013), *Human Rights: The Hard Questions*, Cambridge: Cambridge University Press

Humphery, K. (2010), *Excess: Anti-Consumerism in the West*, Cambridge: Polity Press

Huntington, S. (1993), *The Third Wave: Democratization in the Late Twentieth Century*, Norman: Oklahoma University Press

Huntington, S. (1996), *The Clash of Civilizations and the Remaking of the World Order*, New York: Simon and Schuster

Hutcheon, L. (1988), *A Poetics of Postmodernism*, London: Routledge

Hutcheon, L. (2002), *The Politics of Postmodernism*, London: Routledge

Hutcheon, L. (2007), 'Gone Forever, but Here to Stay: The Legacy of the Postmodern', in Goulimari, P. (ed.), *Postmodernism: What Moment?*, Manchester: Manchester University Press

Huyssen, A. (1986), *After the Great Divide: Modernism, Mass Culture and Postmodernism*, Basingstoke: Macmillan

Hyams, R. (1990), *Empire and Sexuality: The British Experience*, Manchester: Manchester University Press

Israel, J. (2010), *A Revolution of the Mind: Radical Enlightenment and the Intellectual Origins of Modern Democracy*, Princeton, NJ: Princeton University Press

Israel, J. (2014), *Revolutionary Ideas: An Intellectual History of the French Revolution from 'The Rights of Man' to Robespierre*, Princeton, NJ: Princeton University Press

Jacobsen, M. (2008), 'Bauman on Utopia – Welcome to the Hunting Zone', in Jacobsen, M. and Poder, P. (eds), *The Sociology of Zygmunt Bauman: Challenges and Critique*, Aldershot: Ashgate

Jacobsen, M. (2013a), 'Blurring Genres: A Conversation with Zygmunt Bauman on Metaphors, Science versus Art, Fiction and Other Tricks of the Trade', in Davis, M. (ed.), *Liquid Sociology: Metaphor in Zygmunt Bauman's Analysis of Modernity*, London: Routledge

Jacobsen, M. (2013b), '"Metaphormosis": On the Metaphoricity of Zygmunt

Bauman's Social Theory', in Davis, M. (ed.), *Liquid Sociology: Metaphor in Zygmunt Bauman's Analysis of Modernity*, London: Routledge

Jacobsen, M. and Marshman, S. (2008), 'Bauman on Metaphors – a Harbinger of Humanistic, Hybrid Sociology', in Jacobsen, M. and Poder, P. (eds), *The Sociology of Zygmunt Bauman: Challenges and Critique*, Aldershot: Ashgate

Jacobsen, M., Marshman, S. and Tester, K (eds) (2007), *Bauman beyond Postmodernity*, Aalborg: Aalborg University Press

Jacobsen, M and Poder, P. (2008), 'Introduction', in Jacobsen, M. and Poder, P. (eds), *The Sociology of Zygmunt Bauman: Challenges and Critique*, Aldershot: Ashgate

Jacobson, D. (1991), *Reading Ethnography*, Albany: State University of New York Press

James, A., Hockey, J. and Dawson, A. (1997), *After Writing Culture: Epistemology and Praxis in Contemporary Anthropology*, London: Routledge

James, C. L. R. (2001), *The Black Jacobins*, Harmondsworth: Penguin (first published 1938)

James, O. (2007), *Affluenza*, London: Vermillion

James, O. (2008), *The Selfish Capitalist: The Origins of Affluenza*, London: Vermillion

Jameson, F. (1984), 'Introduction', in J.-F. Lyotard, *The Postmodern Condition*, Manchester: Manchester University Press

Jameson, F. (1991), 'Postmodernism, or the Cultural Logic of Capitalism in *Postmodernism, or The Cultural Logic of Late Capitalism*, London: Verso (first published in *New Left Review*, 1984)

Jamieson, L. (1998), *Intimacy: Personal Relationships in Modern Societies*, Cambridge: Polity Press

Jarvis, S. (1998), *Adorno*, Cambridge; Polity Press

Jay, M. (1984), *Adorno*, London: Fontana

Jay, M. (2010), 'Liquidity Crisis: Zygmunt Bauman and the Incredible Lightness of Modernity', *Theory, Culture and Society*, 27 (6): 95–106

Jefferson, T. (2012), 'Policing the Riots: from Bristol and Brixton to Tottenham, via Toxteth, Handsworth, etc.', *Criminal Justice Matters*, 87(1): 8–9

Jefferson, R. and Hall, S. (eds) (1976), *Resistance through Ritual*, London: Hutchinson

Jencks, C. (1984), *The Language of Post-Modern Architecture*, London: Academy Editions

Jencks, C. (1986), *What is Post-Modernism?*, London: St Martin's Press

Jenkins, K. (1991), *Re-Thinking History*, London: Routledge

Jenkins, K. (ed.) (1997), *The Postmodern History Reader*, London: Routledge

Jenkins, K. (1999), *Why History? Ethics and Postmodernity*, London: Routledge

Jessop, B. (2016), *The State*, Cambridge: Polity Press

Jhabvalla, R., Mehta, S., Standing, G. and Davala, S. (2015), *Basic Income*, London: Bloomsbury

Jokinen, E. and Vejjola, S. (1997), 'The Disoriented Tourist: The Figuration of the Tourist in Contemporary Cultural Critique', in Rojek, C. and Urry, J. (eds), *Touring Cultures*, London: Routledge

Jones, A. (2006), *Genocide: A Comprehensive Introduction*, London: Routledge

Jones, A. (2009), *Gender Inclusive: Essays on Violence, Men and Feminist International Relations*, London: Routledge

Jones, O. (2009), *Chavs: The Demonization of the Working Class*, London: Verso

Junge, M. (2001), 'Zygmunt Bauman's Poisoned Gift of Morality', *British Journal of Sociology*, 52 (1): 105–19

Kahanec, M. and Zimmermann, K. M. (eds) (2011), *Ethnic Diversity in European Labour Markets*, Cheltenham: Edward Elgar

Kalpagam, K. (2014), *Rule by Numbers: Governmentality in Colonial India*, New York: Lexington Books

Keane, J. (2009), *The Life and Death of Democracy*, London: Simon and Schuster

Keane, J. (2013), *Democracy and Media Decadence*, Cambridge: Cambridge University Press

Keen, A. (2015), *The Internet is Not the Answer*, London: Atlantic Press

Kellner, D. (1988), 'Postmodernism as Social Theory: Some Challenges and Problems', *Theory, Culture and Society*, 5 (2–3): 239–70

Kellner, D. (1998), 'Bauman's Postmodern Turn', *Theory, Culture and Society*, 15 (1): 73–88

Kennard, M. (2016), *The Racket: A Rogue Reporter vs the American Elite*, London: Zed Books

Kershaw, I. (1985), *The Nazi Dictatorship: Problems and Perspectives of Interpretation*, London: Edward Arnold

Kershaw, I. (1997), '"Working towards the Führer": Reflections on the nature of the Nazi Dictatorship', in Kershaw, I. and Lewin, M. (eds), *Stalinism and Nazism: Dictatorships in Comparison*, Cambridge: Cambridge University Press

Kershaw, I. (1998), 'Hitler's Role in the Final Solution', in Kershaw, I., *Hitler, the Germans and the Final Solution*, New Haven: Yale University Press

Kilminster, R. and Varcoe, I. (eds) (1996), *Culture, Modernity and Revolution: Essays in Honour of Zygmunt Bauman*, London: Routledge

Klein, N. (2000), *No Logo*, New York: Picador (2nd edn 2010)

Klein, N. (2014), *This Changes Everything: Capitalism vs the Climate*, London: Allen Lane

Knott, S. and Taylor, S. (eds) (2005), *Women, Gender and Enlightenment*, Basingstoke: Macmillan

Kociakiewicz, J. and Kostera, M. (eds) (2014), *Liquid Organization: Zygmunt Bauman and Organization Theory*, London: Routledge

Kolakowski, L. (2005), *Main Currents of Marxism*, New York: Norton (first published 1978)

Kuhn, T. (1962), *The Structure of Scientific Revolutions*, Princeton, NJ: Princeton University Press

Kunz, G. (1998), *The Paradox of Power and Weakness: Levinas and an Alternative Paradigm for Psychology*, Albany: State University of New York Press

Lakatos, I. and Musgrave, A. (eds) (1970), *Criticism and the Growth of Knowledge*, Cambridge: Cambridge University Press

Lakoff, G. and Johnson, M. (1980), *Metaphors We Live By*, Chicago: University of Chicago Press

Lapavitsas, C. (2013), *Profiting Without Producing: How Finance Exploits Us All*, London: Verso

Lash, S. (1996), 'Postmodern Ethics: The Missing Ground', *Theory, Culture and Society*, 13 (2): 91–104

Lawson, N. (2009), *All Consuming*, London: Penguin Books

Lawson, T. (2010), *Debates on the Holocaust*, Manchester: Manchester University Press

Lee, R. (2005), 'Bauman, Liquid Modernity and Dilemmas of Development', *Thesis Eleven*, 83 (4): 61–77

Lee, R. (2011), 'Modernity, Solidity and Agency: Liquidity Reconsidered', *Sociology*, 45 (4): 650–64

Lefebvre, H. (2014), *Critique of Everyday Life*, London: Verso (first published 1961, 2nd edn 1981)

Leonard, P. (1997), *Postmodern Welfare: Reconstructing an Emancipatory Project*, London: Sage

Levi, P. (1979), *If This is a Man and The Truce*, London: Abacus

Levi, P. (1988), *The Drowned and the Saved*, London: Abacus

Levi, P. (2013), *The Drowned and the Saved*, London: Abacus

Levinas, E. (1969), *Totality and Infinity*, Pittsburgh: Duquesne University Press

Levine, P. (2006), 'Sexuality and Empire', in Hall, C. and Rose, S. (eds), *At Home with the Empire: Metropolitan Culture and the Imperial World*, Cambridge: Cambridge University Press

Levitas, R. (2013), *Utopia as Method: The Imaginary Reconstitution of Society*, London: Palgrave Macmillan

Lewis, P., Newburn, T., Taylor, M. and C. Mcgillvray (2011), *Reading the Riots: Investigating England's Summer of Disorder*, London: London School of Economics

Lieberman, M. (2013), *Social: Why Our Brains are Wired to Connect*, Oxford: Oxford University Press

Littler, J. (2009), *Radical Consumption: Shopping for Change*, Maidenhead: Open University Press

Lloyd, G. (1984), *The Man of Reason*, Minneapolis: Minnesota University Press

Lloyd, G. (2013), *Enlightenment Shadows*, Oxford: Oxford University Press

Loomba, A. (1998), *Colonialism/Postcolonialism*, London: Routledge

Lopez, J. and Potter, G. (eds) (2005), *After Postmodernism: An Introduction to Critical Realism*, London: Continuum

Losuro, D. (2014), *Liberalism: A Counter-History*, London: Verso

Lovibond, S. (1990), 'Feminism and Postmodernism', in Boyne, R. and Rattansi, A. (eds), *Postmodernism and Society*, Basingstoke: Macmillan

Lower, W. (2013), *Hitler's Furies: German Women in the Nazi Killing Fields*, London: Chatto and Windus

Lozowick, Y. (2002), *Hitler's Bureaucrats: The Nazi Security Police and the Banality of Evil*, London: Continuum

Lunn, E. (1985), *Marxism and Modernism*, London: Verso

Lury, C. (2011), *Consumer Culture*, Cambridge: Polity Press

Lyotard, J.-F. (1984), *The Postmodern Condition*, Manchester: Manchester University Press (first published in French in 1979)

Lyotard, J.-F. (1988), *The Differend*, Minneapolis: University of Minnesota Press

Mackenzie, W. (1989), *Imperialism and Popular Culture*, Manchester: Manchester University Press

Macpherson, C. (1965), *The Political Theory of Possessive Individualism*, Oxford: Oxford University Press

Maffesoli, M. (2000), *The Time of the Tribes*, London: Sage (first published in French in 1988)

Mair, P. (2013), *Ruling the Void: The Hollowing of Western Democracy*, London: Verso

Malachowski, A. (ed.) (1990), *Reading Rorty*, Oxford: Blackwell

Malpas, S. (2002), *Jean-François Lyotard*, London: Routledge

Mamdani, M. (1996), *Citizen and Subject: Contemporary Africa and the Legacy of Late Colonialism*, Princeton, NJ: Princeton University Press

Manganaro, M. (1990), *Modernist Anthropology: From Fieldwork to Text*, Princeton, NJ: Princeton University Press

Mann, K. (1991), *The Making of an English Underclass?*, Buckingham: Open University Press

Mann, M. (2004), *Fascists*, Cambridge: Cambridge University Press

Mann, M. (2005), *The Dark Side of Democracy: Explaining Ethnic Cleansing*, Cambridge: Cambridge University Press

Marchand, M. and Parpart, J. (eds) (1995), *Feminism, Postmodernism and Development*, London: Routledge

Marcus, G. and Fischer, M. (1986), *Anthropology as Cultural Critique: An Experimental Moment in the Human Sciences*, Chicago: University of Chicago Press

Marquand, D. (2004), *Decline of the Public: The Hollowing Out of Citizenship*, Cambridge: Polity Press

Marquand, D. (2015), *Mammon's Kingdom: An Essay on Britain, Now*, London: Allen Lane

Marshall, B. (1994), *Engendering Modernity: Feminism, Social Theory and Social Change*, Cambridge: Polity Press

Mathewman, S. and Hoey, D. (2006), 'What Happened to Postmodernism?', *Sociology*, 40 (3): 529–47

Mathieson, T. (1997), 'Foucault's Panopticon Revisited', *Theoretical Criminology*, 1 (2): 215–34

May, T. (2003), *Social Research: Issues, Methods and Process*, Milton Keynes: Open University Press

May, T. (2011), *Social Research: Issues, Methods and Process*, 4th edn, Milton Keynes: Open University Press

May, T. and Perry, B. (2010), *Social Research and Reflexivity*, London: Sage

Mazzucato, M. (2013), *The Entrepreneurial State: Debunking Public Sector vs Private*, London: Anthem Press

McClintock, A, (1994), 'Soft-Soaping Empire: Commodity Racism and Imperial Advertising', in Bird, J., Curtis, B., Masm, M., Putnam, T., Robertson, G. and Tickner, L. (eds), *Travellers' Tales: Narratives of Home and Displacement*, London: Routledge

McClintock, A. (1995), *Imperial Leather: Race, Gender and Sexuality in the Colonial Contest*, London: Routledge

McHale, B. (1987), *Postmodernist Fiction*, London: Routledge

McKinlay, A. and Starkey, K. (eds) (1998), *Foucault, Management and Organization Theory*, London: Sage

McLennan, G. (2006), *Sociological Cultural Studies*, Basingstoke: Palgrave Macmillan

McMillan, C. (1982), *Woman, Reason and Nature*, Oxford: Blackwell

Meehan, E. (2005), *Why TV is Not Our Fault: TV Programming, Viewers, and Who's Really in Control*, Lanham, MD: Rowman and Littlefield

Meek, R. (1976), *Social Science and the Ignoble Savage*, Cambridge: Cambridge University Press

Mendelberg, T. (2001), *The Race Card*, Princeton, NJ: Princeton University Press

Milchman, A. and Rosenberg, A. (eds) (1998), *Postmodernism and the Holocaust*, Amsterdam: Rodopi

Milgram, S. (1974), *Obedience to Authority: An Experimental View*, London: Tavistock

Miller, D. (1997), *Material Cultures: Why Some Things Matter*, London: Routledge

Miller, D. (1998), *A Theory of Shopping*, Cambridge: Polity Press

Miller, D. (2001), *The Dialectics of Shopping*, Chicago: University of Chicago Press

Miller, D. (2009), *Stuff*, Cambridge: Polity Press

Miller, D. (2012), *Consumption and its Consequences*, Cambridge: Polity Press

Miller, P. (1987), *Domination and Power*, London: Routledge

Minca, C. (ed.) (2001), *Postmodern Geography*, Oxford: Wiley-Blackwell

Minz, S. (1986, *Sweetness and Power: The Place of Sugar in Modern History*, new edn, London: Penguin

Mitchell, T. (1988), *Colonising Egypt*, Cambridge: Cambridge University Press

Mitchell, T. (2000), 'The Stage of Modernity', in Mitchell, T. (ed.), *Questions of Modernity*, Minneapolis: University of Minnesota Press

Miyoshi, M. and Harootunian, J. (eds) (1989), *Postmodernism and Japan*, Durham, NC: Duke University Press

Moeller, S. (1999), *Compassion Fatigue: How the Media Sell Disease, Famine, War and Death*, London: Routledge

Morgan, M. (2011), *The Cambridge Introduction to Levinas*, Cambridge: Cambridge University Press

Morozov, E. (2011), *The Net Delusion*, London: Penguin

Morris, L. (1994), *Dangerous Classes: The Underclass and Social Citizenship*, London: Routledge

Mouffe, C. (1989), 'Radical Democracy: Modern of Postmodern?', in Ross, A. (ed.), *Universal Abandon? The Politics of Postmodernism*, Edinburgh: Edinburgh University Press

Mouffe, C. (2013), 'Hegemony and Ideology in Gramsci' (first published 1979), in Martin, J. (ed.), *Chantal Mouffe: Hegemony, Radical Democracy and the Political*, London: Routledge

Munslow, A. (1997), *Deconstructing History*, London: Routledge

Muthu, S. (2003), *Enlightenment against Empire*, Princeton, NJ: Princeton University Press

Myerson, G. (1994), *Rhetoric, Reason and Society: Rationality as Dialogue*, London: Sage

Nandy, A. (1983), *The Intimate Enemy: Loss and Recovery of Self in India under Colonialism*, New Delhi: Oxford University Press

Nash, K. (2014), *The Political Sociology of Human Rights*, Cambridge: Cambridge University Press

Nava, M. (1996), 'Modernity's Disavowal: Women, the City and the Department Store', in Nava, M. and O'Shea, A. (eds), *Modern Times: Reflections on a Century of English Modernity*, London: Routledge

Nava, M. (2007), *Visceral Cosmopolitanism: Gender, Culture and the Normalisation of Difference*, London: Berg

Nava, M., Blake, A., MacRury, I. and Richards, B. (1997), *Buy this Book: Studies in Advertising and Consumption*, London: Routledge

Nencel, L. and Pels, P. (1991), *Constructing Knowledge: Authority and Inquiry*, London: Sage

Nesbitt, N. (2008), *Universal Emancipation: The Haitian Revolution and the Radical Enlightenment*, Charlottesville: University of Virginia Press

Newton-Smith, W. (1981), *The Rationality of Science*, London: Routledge

Newton-Smith, W. (1989), 'Rationality, Truth and the New Fuzzies', in Lawson, H. and Appignanesi, L. (eds), *Dismantling Truth: Reality in the Postmodern World*, London: Weidenfeld and Nicolson

Nicholson, L. (1995), 'Interpreting Gender', in Nicholson, L. and Seidman, S. (eds), *Social Postmodernism: Beyond Identity Politics*, New York: Cambridge University Press

Nijhoff, P. (1998), 'Bauman's Right to Inconsistency', *Theory, Culture and Society*, 15 (1): 87–112

Nisbet, R. (1962), 'Sociology as an Art Form', *Pacific Sociological Review*, 5 (2): 67–74 (published in book form by Transaction Publishers, 2001)

Nixon, S. (1996), *Hard Looks: Masculinities, the Visual and Practises of Consumption*, London: Routledge

Nixon, S. (2003), *Advertising Cultures: Gender, Commerce, Creativity*, London: Sage

Noakes, J. (2004), 'Hitler and the Third Reich', in Stone, D. (ed.), *The Historiography of the Holocaust*, Basingstoke: Palgrave Macmillan

Norris, C. (1990), 'Lost in the Funhouse: Baudrillard and the Politics of Postmodernism', in Boyne, R. and Rattansi, A. (eds), *Postmodernism and Society*, Basingstoke: Macmillan

Offe, C. (1996), *Modernity and the State: East, West*, Cambridge: Polity Press

O'Kane, R. (1997), 'Modernity, the Holocaust and Politics', *Economy and Society*, 26 (1): 43–61

Olusoga, D. and Erichsen, C. (2010), *The Kaiser's Holocaust: Germany's Forgotten Genocide*, London: Faber and Faber

Ortner, S. (1982), 'Is Female to Male as Nature is to Culture?', in Evans, M. (ed.), *The Woman Question*, London: Fontana

Outhwaite, W. (2010), 'Bauman's Europe, Europe's Bauman', in Davis, M. and Tester, K. (eds), *Bauman's Challenge: Sociological Issues for the 21st Century*, Basingstoke: Palgrave Macmillan

Outram, D. (2005), *The Enlightenment*, 2nd edn, Cambridge: Cambridge University Press

Owen, D. (ed.) (1997), *Sociology after Postmodernism*, London: Sage

Owens, C. (1983), 'The Discourse of Others: Feminists and Postmodernism', in Foster, H. (ed.), *Postmodern Culture*, London: Pluto Press

Oxaal, I. (1991), 'Sociology, History and the Holocaust', *Theory, Culture and Society*, 8 (1): 153–66

Pagel, M. (2012), *Wired for Culture: The Natural History of Human Cooperation*, London: Allen Lane

Pai, H.-H. (2008), *Chinese Whispers: The True Story behind Britain's Army of Labour*, London: Penguin

Pai, H.-H. (2016), *Angry White People: Coming Face-to-Face with the British Far Right*, London: Zed

Perpich, D. (2010), 'Levinas, Feminism and Identity Politics', in Atterton, P. and Calarco, M. (eds), *Radicalizing Levinas*, Albany: State University of New York Press

Pettinger, L. (2016), *Work, Consumption and Capitalism*, London: Palgrave

Picketty, T. (2014), *Capital in the Twenty-First Century*, Cambridge, MA: Harvard University Press

Pieterse, J. (1994), 'Unpacking the West: How European is Europe?', in Rattansi, A. and Westwood, S. (eds), *Racism, Modernity and Identity: On the Western Front*, Cambridge: Polity Press

Pieterse, J. (2009), *Globalization and Culture*, 2nd edn, Lanham, MD: Rowman and Littlefield

Pine, L. (2004), 'Gender and the Family', in Stone, D. (ed.), *The Historiography of the Holocaust*, Basingstoke: Palgrave Macmillan

Pomeranz, K. (2001), *The Great Divergence: China, Europe, and the Making of the Modern World Economy*, Princeton, NJ: Princeton University Press

Poole, R. (1990), 'Modernity, Rationality and the "Masculine"', in Threadgold, T. and Cranny-Francis, A. (eds), *Feminine, Masculine and Representation*, London: Allen and Unwin

Porter, R. (2000), *The Enlightenment*, 2nd edn, Basingstoke: Macmillan

Porter, R. (2001), *Enlightenment: Britain and the Creation of the Modern World*, London: Allen Lane

Poster, M. (1984), *Foucault, Marxism and History*, Cambridge: Polity Press

Power, M. (1999), *The Audit Society*, Oxford: Oxford University Press

Prakash, G. (1999), *Another Reason: Science and the Imagination of Modern India*, Princeton, NJ: Princeton University Press

Prakash, G. (2000), 'The Body Politic in Colonial India', in Mitchell, T. (ed.), *Questions of Modernity*, Minneapolis: University of Minnesota Press

Pulzer, P. (2010), 'National Socialism, Antisemitism and the Holocaust', in Wiese, C. and Betts, P. (eds), *Years of Persecution, Years of Extermination: Saul Friedlander and the Future of Holocaust Studies*, London: Continuum

Putnam, R. (2015), *Our Kids: The American Dream in Crisis*, New York: Simon and Schuster

Quayson, A. (2000), *Postcolonialism: Theory, Practice or Process?*, Cambridge: Polity Press

Quine, W. (1961), 'Two Dogmas of Empiricism', in Quine, W., *From a Logical Point of View*, New York: Harper

Rabinow, P. (1986), 'Representations are Social Facts: Modernity and Postmodernity in Anthropology', in Clifford, J. and Marcus, G. (eds), *Writing Culture: The Poetics and Politics of Ethnography*, Berkeley: University of California Press

Raddeker, H. (2007), *Sceptical History: Postmodern Approaches in Practice*, London: Routledge

Ramazonoglu, C. and Holland, J. (2002), *Feminist Methodologies*, London: Sage

Rasmussen, D. (2014), *The Pragmatic Enlightenment*, Cambridge: Cambridge University Press

Rattansi, A. (1994), 'Western Racisms, Ethnicities and Identities in a "Postmodern" Frame', in Rattansi, A. and Westwood, S. (eds), *Racism, Modernity and Identity: On the Western Front*, Cambridge: Polity Press

Rattansi, A. (1995), 'Just Framing: Racism, Ethnicity and Identity in a "Postmodern" Frame', in Nicholson, L. and Seidman, S. (eds), *Social Postmodernism: Beyond Identity Politics*, New York: Cambridge University Press

Rattansi, A. (1997), 'Postcolonialism and its Discontents', *Economy and Society*, 26 (4): 480–500

Rattansi, A. (2000), 'On Being and not Being Brown/Black British: Racism, Class, Sexuality and Ethnicity in Post-Imperial Britain', in Lee, J.-A. and Lutz, J. (eds), *Situating "Race" and Racisms in Space, Time and Social Theory*, Montreal: McGill-Queen's University Press

Rattansi, A. (2002), 'Racism, Sexuality and Political Economy: Marxism/Foucault/Postmodernism', in Bradley, H. and Fenton, S. (eds), *Ethnicity and Economy: 'Race and Class' Revisited*, Basingstoke: Palgrave Macmillan

Rattansi, A. (2005), 'The Uses of Racialization: The Time-Spaces and Subject-Objects of the Raced Body', in Murji, K. and Solomos, J. (eds), *Racialization: Studies in Theory and Practice*, Oxford: Oxford University Press

Rattansi, A. (2007), *Racism*, Oxford: Oxford University Press

Rattansi, A. (2011), *Multiculturalism*, Oxford: Oxford University Press

Rattansi, A. (2014), 'Zygmunt Bauman: An Adorno for "Liquid Modern" Times?', *Sociological Review*, 62 (4): 908–17

Rattansi, A. (2016), 'Race, Gender and Imperialism in Zygmunt Bauman's Sociology: Partial Presences, Serious Consequences', in Jacobsen, M. (ed.), *Beyond Bauman*, London: Routledge

Rattansi, A. and Westwood, S. (eds) (1994), *Racism, Modernity and Identity: On the Western Front*, Cambridge: Polity Press

Ray, L. (1999), *Theorising Classical Sociology*, London: Sage

Ray, L. (2007), 'From Postmodernity to Liquid Modernity: What's in a Metaphor?', in Elliott, A. (ed.), *The Contemporary Bauman*, London: Routledge

Ray, L. (2011), *Violence and Society*, London: Sage

Rifkin, J. (2009), *The Empathic Civilization: The Race to Global Consciousness in a World in Crisis*, New York: Penguin Group

Ringelheim, J. (1993), 'Women and the Holocaust: A Reconsideration of Research', in Rittner, C. and Roth, J. (eds), *Different Voices: Women and the Holocaust*, St Paul, MN: Paragon House

Ritzer, G. (1998), *McDonaldization*, London: Sage

Rodriguez, G., Boatcă, M. and Costa, S. (eds) (2010), *Decolonizing European Sociology*, Farnham: Ashgate

Rorty, R. (1979), *Philosophy and the Mirror of Nature*, Princeton, NJ: Princeton University Press

Rorty, R. (1989), 'Science as Solidarity', in Lawson, H. and Appignanesi (eds), *Dismantling Truth: Reality in the Postmodern World*, London: Weidenfeld and Nicolson

Rorty, R. (1991), *Philosophical Papers Volume 2: Essays on Heidegger and Others*, Cambridge: Cambridge University Press

Rorty, R. (1992), 'Cosmopolitanism without Emancipation: A Reply to Lyotard', in Lash, S. and Friedland, J. (eds), *Modernity and Identity*, Oxford: Blackwell

Rorty, R. (2000), *Philosophy and Social Hope*, New York: Penguin

Rosaldo, R. (1986), 'From the Door of his Tent: The Fieldworker and the Inquisitor', in Clifford, J. and Marcus, G. (eds), *Writing Culture: The Poetics and Politics of Ethnography*, Berkeley: University of California Press

Rosaldo, R. (1989), *Culture and Truth: The Remaking of Social Analysis*, London: Routledge

Rose, N. (1996), 'Governing "Advanced" Liberal Democracies', in Barry, A., Osborne, T. and Rose, N. (eds), *Foucault and Political Reason: Liberalism, Neo-Liberalism and Rationalities of Government*, Chicago: University of Chicago Press

Rosenau, P. (1991), *Postmodernism and the Social Sciences: Insights, Inroads and Intrusions*, Princeton, NJ: Princeton University Press

Ross, A. (ed.) (1996), *Science Wars*, Durham, NC: Duke University Press

Rothkopf, D. (2009), *The Superclass: How the Rich Ruined Our World*, London: Abacus

Rothschild, E. (2002), *Economic Sentiments: Adam Smith, Condorcet, and the Enlightenment*, Cambridge, MA: Harvard University Press

Rubenstein, R. (1978), *The Cunning of History*, New York: Harper and Row

Rutherford, J. (1997), *Masculinity and Empire*, London: Lawrence and Wishart

Sachsenmaier, D., Riedel, J. and Eisenstadt, S. (eds) (2002), *Reflections on Multiple Modernities*, Leiden: Brill

Said, E. (1979), *Orientalism*, London: Allen Lane

Said, E. (1988), 'Michel Foucault, 1926–1984', in Arac, J. (ed.), *After Foucault*, New Brunswick: Rutgers University Press

Saidel, R. (2006), *The Jewish Women of Ravensbrück Concentration Camp*, Madison: University of Wisconsin Press

Salecl, R. (2010), *The Tyranny of Choice*, London: Profile Books

Sassatelli, R. (2007), *Consumer Culture*, London: Sage

Satterwhite, J. (1992), *Varieties of Marxist Humanism: Philosophical Revision in Postwar Eastern Europe*, Pittsburgh: University of Pittsburgh Press

Savage, M. (2000), *Class Analysis and Social Transformation*, Buckingham: Open University Press

Savage, M. (2015), *Social Class in the 21st Century*, London: Pelican

Savage, M., Bagnall, G. and Longhurst, B. (2004), *Globalization and Belonging*, London: Sage

Savage, M. and Butler, T. (2013), *Social Change and the Middle Classes*, Basingstoke: Palgrave Macmillan

Scarman, Lord (1982), *The Scarman Report: The Brixton Disorders 1981*, Harmondsworth: Penguin

Scheurich, J. (1997), *Research Methods in the Postmodern*, London: Falmer

Schmidt, J. (ed.) (1996), *What is Enlightenment? Eighteenth Century Answers and Twentieth Century Questions*, Berkeley: University of California Press

Schmidt, J. (2000), 'What Enlightenment Project?', *Political Theory*, 28 (6): 734–57

Schmidt, J. (2001), 'Projects and Projections: A Response to Christian Delacampagne', *Political Theory*, 29 (1): 86–90

Scruton, R. (2012), *The Uses of Pessimism and the Danger of False Hope*, New York: Atlantic Books

Schwartz, B. (2005), *The Paradox of Choice*, New York: Harper Collins

Seidler, V. (1994), *Unreasonable Men: Masculinity and Social Theory*, London: Routledge

Seidman, S. (1992), 'Postmodern Social Theory as Narrative with a Moral Intent', in Seidman, S. and Wagner, D. (eds), *Postmodernism and Social Theory*, Oxford: Blackwell

Sharma, S. (2014), *In the Meantime: Temporality and Cultural Politics*, London and Durham, NC: Duke University Press

Shaw, M. (2007), *What is Genocide?*, Cambridge: Polity Press

Shaxson, N. (2011), *Treasure Islands: Tax Havens and the Men who Stole the World*, London: Bodley Head

Sim, S. (2015), *A Philosophy of Pessimism*, London: Reaktion Books

Simms, A. (2007), *Tescopoly: How One Shop Came Out on Top and Why it Matters*, London: Constable

Simms, K. (2015), *Hans-George Gadamer*, London: Routledge

Simons, H. (ed.) (1988), *Rhetoric in the Human Sciences*, London: Sage

Simons, H. and Billig, M. (eds) (1994), *After Postmodernism: Reconstructing Ideology Critique*, London: Sage

Sinha, M. (1995), *Colonial Masculinity: The 'Manly Englishman' and the 'Effeminate Bengali' in the Late Nineteenth Century*, Manchester: Manchester University Press

Sinnreich, H. (2010), 'The Rape of Jewish Women during the Holocaust', in Hedgepeth, S. and Saidel, R. (eds), *Sexual Violence against Jewish Women during the Holocaust*, Waltham, MA: Brandeis University Press and New England University Press

Skeggs, B. (1997), *Formations of Class and Gender*, London: Sage

Skeggs, B. (2004), *Class, Self, Culture*, London: Routledge

Skidelsky, R. and Skidelsky, E. (2012), *How Much is Enough? Money and the Good Life*, London: Allen Lane

Sklair, L. (2000), *The Transnational Capitalist Class*, Oxford: Wiley

Sklair, L. (2002), *Globalization: Capitalism and its Alternatives*, Oxford: Oxford University Press

Skocpol, T. and Williamson, V. (2016), *The Tea Party and the Remaking of Republican Conservatism*, New York: Oxford University Press

Slater, D. (1997), *Consumer Culture and Modernity*, Cambridge: Polity Press

Slote, M. (2007), *The Ethics of Care and Empathy*, London: Routledge

Smart, B. (1983), *Foucault, Marxism and Critique*, London: Routledge

Smart, B. (1990), 'Modernity, Postmodernity and the Present', in Turner, B. (ed.), *Theories of Modernity and Postmodernity*, London: Sage

Smart, B. (1992), *Modern Conditions, Postmodern Controversies*, London: Routledge

Smart, B. (2010), *Consumer Society*, London: Sage

Smart, C. (2007), *Personal Life*, Cambridge: Polity Press

Smith, D. (1999), *Zygmunt Bauman: Prophet of Postmodernity*, Cambridge: Polity Press

Social Mobility and Child Poverty Commission (2014), *State of the Nation 2014: Social Mobility and Child Poverty in Great Britain*, London: Social Mobility and Child Poverty Commission

Sofsky, W. (1999), *The Order of Terror: The Concentration Camp*, Princeton, NJ: Princeton University Press

Sokal, A. (1996), 'Transgressing Boundaries: Towards a Transformative Hermeneutics of Quantum Gravity', *Social Text*, 46/47: 217–52

Sokal, A. and Brickmont, J. (1998), *Intellectual Impostors: Postmodern Philosophers' Abuse of Science*, London: Profile Books

Sommer, R. (2010), 'Sexual Exploitation of Women in Nazi Concentration Camps', in Hedgepeth, S. and Saidel, R. (eds), *Sexual Violence against Jewish Women during the Holocaust*, Waltham, MA: Brandeis University Press and New England University Press

Southgate, B. (2003), *Postmodernism in History: Fear or Freedom?*, London: Routledge

Sparks, C. (2007), *Globalization, Development and the Mass Media*, London: Sage

Srnicek, N. and Williams, A. (2015), *Inventing the Future: Postcapitalism and a World without Work*, London: Verso

Stallabras, J. [1999] (2006), *High Art Lite: The Rise and Fall of Young British Art*, London: Verso

Standing, G. (2011), *The Precariat*, London: Bloomsbury

Standing, G. (2014), *A Precariat Charter: From Denizens to Citizens*, London: Bloomsbury

Stangneth, B. (2014), *Eichmann before Jerusalem: The Unexamined Life of a Mass Murderer*, New York: Knopf

Stanley, S. (2012), *The French Enlightenment and the Emergence of Cynicism*, Cambridge: Cambridge University Press

Steier, F. (ed.) (1991), *Research and Reflexivity*, London: Sage

Stepan, N. (1990), 'Race and Gender: The Role of Analogy in Science', in Goldberg, T. (ed.), *The Anatomy of Racism*, Minneapolis: University of Minnesota Press

Stephenson, J. (2001), *Women in Nazi Germany*, London: Pearson

Stibbe, M. (2003), *Women in the Third Reich*, London: Arnold

Stiglitz, J. (2012), *The Price of Inequality*, London: Allen Lane

Stillman, W. and Pfaff, E. (1964), *The Politics of Hysteria: The Sources of Twentieth Century Conflict*, New York: Harper and Row

Stoler, A. (1995), *Race and the Education of Desire: Foucault's 'History of Sexuality' and the Colonial Order of Things*, Durham, NC: Duke University Press

Stoler, A. (1997), 'Sexual Affronts and Racial Frontiers: European Identities and the Cultural Politics of Exclusion in Colonial South-East Asia', in

Cooper, F. and Stoler, A. (eds), *Tensions of Empire: Colonial Cultures in a Bourgeois World*, Berkeley: University of California Press

Stone, D. (ed.) (2004), *The Historiography of the Holocaust*, Basingstoke: Palgrave Macmillan

Stone, D. (2010), *Histories of the Holocaust*, Oxford: Oxford University Press

Stott, C. and Pearson, G. (2007), *Football Hooliganism: Policing and the War on the 'English Disease'*, London: Pennant Books

Street, J. (2011), *Mass Media, Politics and Democracy*, 2nd edn, Basingstoke: Palgrave Macmillan

Susskind, R. and Susskind, D. (2015), *The Future of the Professions: How Technology will Transform the Work of Human Experts*, Oxford: Oxford University Press

Sutton Trust (2006), *The Educational Backgrounds of Leading Journalists*, London: The Sutton Trust

Sutton Trust (2016), *Leading People*, London: The Sutton Trust

Taguieff, P.-A. (2001), *The Force of Prejudice: On Racism and its Doubles*, Minneapolis: University of Minnesota Press

Taylor, C. and Gutman, A. (1994), *Multiculturalism*, Princeton, NJ: Princeton University Press

Tester, K. (2001), *Compassion, Morality and the Media*, Buckingham: Open University Press

Tester, K. (2004), *The Social Thought of Zygmunt Bauman*, Basingstoke: Palgrave Macmillan

Tester, K. and Jacobsen, M. (2005), *Bauman before Postmodernity*, Aalborg: Aalborg University Press

Therborn, G. (ed.) (2006), *Inequalities of the World: New Theoretical Frameworks, Multiple Empirical Approaches*, London: Verso

Therborn, G. (2008), *Marxism and Post-Marxism?*, London. Verso

Thomas, N. (1994), *Colonialism's Culture: Anthropology, Travel and Government*, Cambridge: Polity Press

Thomas, M. (2009), *Belching Out the Devil: Global Adventures with Coca-Cola*, New York: Nation Books

Thompson, W. (2004), *Postmodernism and History*, Basingstoke: Palgrave Macmillan

Thorne, S. (1997), '"The Conversion of Englishmen and the Conversion of the World Inseparable": Missionary Imperialism and the Language of Class in Early Industrial Britain', in Cooper, F. and Stoler, A. (eds), *Tensions of Empire: Colonial Cultures in a Bourgeois World*, Berkeley: University of California Press

Thornham, S. (2000), *Feminist Theory and Cultural Studies*, London: Arnold

Todorov, T. (2000), *Facing the Extreme: Moral Life in the Concentration Camps*, London: Phoenix

Tomaselli, S. (1985), 'The Enlightenment Debate on Women', *History Workshop Journal*, 20: 101–24

Tomlinson, J. (1999), *Globalization and Culture*, Cambridge: Polity Press

Tonkiss, F. (2006), *Contemporary Economic Sociology: Globalization, Production and Inequality*, London: Routledge

Tormey, S. (2015), *The End of Representative Politics*, Cambridge: Polity Press

Trentmann, F. (2016), *The Empire of Things: How We Became a World of Consumers from the Fifteenth Century to the Twenty-First*, London: Penguin Random House

Tully, J. (2008), *Public Philosophy in a New Key: Imperialism and Civic Freedom*, Cambridge: Cambridge University Press

Turkle, S. (2011), *Alone Together*, New York: Basic Books

Turkle, S. (2015), *Reclaiming Conversation: The Power of Talk in a Digital Age*, New York: Penguin

UNDP (United Nations Development Programme) (2015), *United Nations Human Development Report*, New York: United Nations

UNWFP (United Nations World Food Programme) (2015), *World Food Programme*, New York: United Nations

Urry, J. (2000), *Sociology beyond Societies*, London: Routledge

Urry, J. (2001), *Mobilities*, Cambridge: Polity Press

Varcoe, I. (1998), 'Identity and the Limits of Comparison: Bauman's Reception in Germany', *Theory, Culture and Society*, 15 (1): 57–72

Varcoe, I. and Kilminster, R. (1996), 'Addendum: Culture and Power in the Writings of Zygmunt Bauman', in Kilminster, R. and Varcoe, I. (eds), *Culture, Modernity and Revolution: Essays in Honour of Zygmunt Bauman*, London: Routledge

Venturi, R. (2007), 'A bas Postmodernism, of Course', in Goulimari, P. (ed.), *Postmodernism: What Moment?*, Manchester: Manchester University Press

Vetlesen, A. (1994), *Perception, Empathy and Judgement: An Inquiry into the Preconditions for Moral Performance*, University Park: Pennsylvania University Press

Vetlesen, A. (2005), *Evil and Human Agency: Understanding Collective Evildoing*, Cambridge: Cambridge University Press

Virillio, P. (2001), *Virillio Live: Selected Interviews*, London: Sage

Virilio. P. (2002), *Ground Zero*, London: Verso

Viswanathan, G. (1989), *Masks of Conquest: Literary Study and British Rule in India*, New York: Columbia University Press

Vogel, U. (2000), 'The Sceptical Enlightenment: Philosopher Travellers

Look Back at Europe', in Geras, N. and Wokler, R. (eds), *The Enlightenment and Modernity*, Basingstoke: Macmillan

Wacjman, J. (2015), *Pressed for Time: The Acceleration of Life in Digital Capitalism*, Chicago: University of Chicago Press

Wallerstein, I. (1997), 'Eurocentrism and its Avatars: The Dilemmas of Social Science', *New Left Review*, 226, 93–108

Walsh, P. and Lehmann. D. (2015), *Problematic Elements in the Scholarship of Zygmunt Bauman*, www.academia.edu/15031047/Problematic_Elements_in_the Scholarship_of Zygmunt_Bauman (accessed 27 July 2016)

Walzer, M. (1986), 'The Politics of Michel Foucault', in Hoy, D. (ed.), *Foucault: A Critical Reader*, Oxford: Blackwell

Ward, S. (1996), *Reconfiguring Truth: Postmodernism, Science Studies and the Search for a New Model of Research*, London: Rowman and Littlefield

Warde, A. (1994a), 'Consumers, Identity and Belonging: Reflections on Some Theses of Zygmunt Bauman', in Keat, R., Whiteley, N. and Abercrombie, N. (eds), *The Authority of the Consumer*, London: Routledge

Warde, A. (1994b), 'Consumption, Identity-Formation and Uncertainty', *Sociology*, 28 (4): 877–98

Ware, V. (1992), *Beyond the Pale: White Women, Racism and History*, London: Verso

Waxman, Z. (2009), 'Thinking against Evil?', *History of European Ideas*, 35 (1): 93–104

Waxman, Z. (2010a), 'Rape and Sexual Abuse in Hiding', in Hedgepeth, S. and Saidel, G. (eds), *Sexual Violence against Jewish Women during the Holocaust*, Waltham, MA: Brandeis University Press and New England University Press

Waxman, Z. (2010b), 'Towards an Integrated History of the Holocaust: Masculinity, Femininity, and Genocide', in Wiese, C. and Betts, P. (eds), *Years of Persecution, Years of Extermination: Saul Friedlander and the Future of Holocaust Studies*, London: Continuum

Wedel, J. (2009), *Shadow Elite: How the World's New Power Brokers Undermine Democracy, Government and the Free Market*, New York: Basic Books

Wedel, J. (2014), *Unaccountable: How Elite Power Brokers Corrupt Our Finances, Freedom and Security*, New York: Pegasus Books

Weeks, J. (2014), *Economics of the 1%*, London: Anthem Press

Weiss, L. (1998), *The Myth of the Powerless State*, Cambridge: Polity Press

Wernick, A. (1991), *Promotional Culture: Advertising, Ideology and Symbolic Expression*, London: Sage

Wetherell, M. (ed.) (2009), *Identity in the 21st Century*, Basingstoke: Palgrave Macmillan

Whelan, F. (2009), *Enlightenment Political Thought and the Non-Western World*, London: Routledge

Wiggerhaus, R. (2010), *The Frankfurt School*, Cambridge: Polity Press

Wildt, M. (2010), 'Raul Hilberg and Saul Friedlander – Two Perspectives on the Holocaust', in Wiese, C. and Betts, P. (eds), *Years of Persecution, Years of Extermination: Saul Friedlander and the Future of Holocaust Studies*, London: Continuum

Wilkinson, I. (2005), *Suffering: A Sociological Introduction*, Cambridge: Polity Press

Wilkinson, I. (2007), 'On Bauman's Sociology of Suffering: Questions for Thinking', in Elliott, A. (ed), *The Contemporary Bauman*, London: Routledge

Wilkinson, R. and Pickett, K. (2009), *The Spirit Level: Why More Equal Societies Almost Always Do Better*, London: Allen Lane

Williams, H., Sullivan, D. and Matthews, G. (1997), *Francis Fukuyama and the End of History*, Cardiff: University of Wales Press

Williams, P. and Chrisman, L. (eds) (1993), *Colonial Discourse and Post-Colonial Theory: A Reader*, Hemel Hempstead: Harvester Wheatsheaf

Williams, S., Bradley, H., Devadason, R. and Erickson, M. (2013), *Globalization and Work*, Cambridge: Polity Press

Wilson, K. (2003), *The Island Race: Englishness, Empire and Gender in the Eighteenth Century*, London: Routledge

Wilson, K. (2004), *A New Imperial History: Culture, Identity and Modernity in Britain and the Empire 1660–1840*, Cambridge: Cambridge University Press

Wilson, W. (1987), *The Truly Disadvantaged: The Inner City, the Underclass, and Public Policy*, Chicago: University of Chicago Press

Wodak, R. (ed.) (2013), *Right-Wing Populism in Europe*, London: Bloomsbury

Wodak, R. (2015), *The Politics of Fear*, London: Sage

Wolff, J. (1990), 'Postmodern Theory and Feminist Art Practice', in Boyne, R. and Rattansi, A. (eds), *Postmodernism and Society*, Basingstoke: Macmillan

Wolff, J. (1993), 'On the Road Again: Metaphors of Travel in Cultural Criticism', *Cultural Studies*, 7: 224–39

Wolin, S. (2010), *Democracy Incorporated: Managed Democracy and the Specter of Inverted Totalitarianism*, Princeton, NJ: Princeton University Press

Wood, H. (2009), *Talking with Television: Women, Talk Shows, and Modern Self-Reflexivity*, Chicago: University of Illinois Press

Woodiwiss, A. (1993), *Postmodernity USA: The Crisis of Social Modernism in Postwar America*, London: Sage

Woodiwiss, A. (1997), 'Against Modernity: A Dissident Rant', *Economy and Society*, 1: 1–21

Wright, E. (2010), *Envisioning Real Utopias*, London: Verso

Zimbardo, P., Hanley, C. and Banks, C. (1973), 'Interpersonal Dynamics in a Simulated Prison', *International Journal of Criminology and Penology*, 1: 69–97

Index